Also by Michael Holzman

Lukács's Road to God

Writing as Social Action (with Marilyn Cooper)

James Jesus Angleton: The CIA, and the Craft of
Counterintelligence

Transgressions (novel)

The Black Poverty Cycle and How to End It

Guy Burgess

Revolutionary in an Old School Tie

Chelmsford Press   Briarcliff Manor, New York

"In his way he was a patriot." Nigel Burgess.

"The lines of loyalty in the 1930s ran not between but across countries . . . Never has there been a period when patriotism, in the sense of automatic loyalty to a citizen's national government, counted for less. When the second world war ended, the governments of at least ten old European countries were headed by men who at its beginning . . . had been rebels, political exiles or, at the very least, who had regarded their own governments as immoral and illegitimate." Eric Hobsbawm, The Age of Extremes, p. 144.

"None comes into the world with a saddle on his back, neither any booted and spurred to ride him." Richard Rumbold's speech from the scaffold.

Chelmsford Press
Briarcliff Manor, New York
ISBN-13: 978-0615895093
ISBN-10: 0615895093

For Jane

Acknowledgments

Archivists make the writing of history possible. The following did so for this book: Judith Curthoys, Archivist, Christ Church, Oxford; Ruth Frendo, Project archivist, Courtauld Institute; Shelly Glick, Briarcliff Manor Public Library; Colin Harris, Special Collections, Bodleian Libraries, University of Oxford; Mrs. P. Hatfield, College Archivist, Eton College; Trish Hayes, Archives Researcher, BBC Written Archives Centre; Caroline Herbert, Churchill Archives Centre, Churchill College; Nicholas Mays, Archivist, News International Limited; Don Skemer, Curator of Manuscripts, Department of Rare Books and Special Collections, Firestone Library, Princeton University; Pauline Testerman, Audiovisual Archivist, Harry S. Truman Library; Tracy Wilkinson, Assistant Archivist, Archive Centre, King's College, Cambridge.

The following also have patiently dealt with my inquiries and helped in other ways: Professor Richard Aldrich, Rupert Allason, Professor Michael Barrett, Michael Bloch, Katherine Bucknell, Miranda Carter, Lord Dobbs (Michael Dobbs), Sir Harold Evans, Peregrine Fellowes, Gavin Freeguard, Matthew Goodman, Professor Gabriel Gorodetsky, Professor John Haffenden, Henry Hardy, Paul Heardman, Professor Eric Hobsbawm, Cherry Hughes, Phillip Knightley, Lord Lexden (Alistair Cooke), Professor William Lubenow, Professor Wendy Moffat, Thomas Pakenham, Antony Percy, Robin Ramsay, Jeremy Reynolds, Elisa Segrave, Rachel Slama, Jonathan Smith, Professor Peter Stansky.

Errors are, of course, my own. I would be grateful to have them brought to my attention so that they might be corrected.

Table of Contents

Guy Burgess

Revolutionary in an Old School Tie

Introduction

Concerning Sources and Methods

Guy Burgess was a prominent figure in what we would now call the media in Britain from the mid-1930s to the mid-1940s, then a member of the Foreign Office. He was also a double agent, working for the British secret intelligence services and also passing enormous amounts of information to the Comintern and the secret intelligence services of the Soviet Union. Everyone knew him, according to Lord Astor, except Lord Astor himself, and as Mandy Rice Davies said of Lord Astor in another context, he would say that, wouldn't he? In the years after Burgess went to Russia in 1951 many people were quite concerned to say that they had not known him, or knew him only slightly, or never liked him anyway. There was a great weeding of files in those years, burning of letters, expurgating of diaries, not only because of fear of association with a Communist agent, but, perhaps as much, because of fear of association with a man who had never made any effort to conceal his homosexuality. As a consequence, research about Burgess has specific difficulties. Not only is the historical record incomplete: it has been falsified.

It is a foundational principle of research in the humanities no less than in the sciences and social sciences that research must be sufficiently well-documented as to be replicable and must clearly identify the sources used—books and articles by titles, authors, dates of publication; archival documents by archive, box, file number—so that other researchers can review them to determine if they actually contain the information presented and warrant the conclusions drawn from them.

Writing about secret intelligence matters can be scholarly, adhering to the rules mentioned above; or it can be operational, part of the overall secret intelligence effort of the agency or agencies involved; or it can be journalistic. The distinction is marked by the accessibility of the references and, to some extent, provenance. For example, that entertaining book *My Silent War,* published under the name of Kim Philby, is unsourced and has a Soviet secret intelligence agency provenance. It might be useful as pointing to (or away from) lines of research, but it is not in itself a valid reference for scholarship. Which is not to say that it might not be a valid *object* for scholarly research, as one in a genre of such products of secret intelligence agencies.

There is a rapidly expanding group of publications said to be based on the archives of secret intelligence organizations: Soviet, British, American, etc. These are usually selected either by the secret intelligence service in question, or by researchers specially commissioned by that service, or by researchers given (or who have taken) special access. The stories they tell are hardly ever generally available, in their archival context, for other scholars to confirm. As Miranda Carter has pointed out, "in all writing about espionage, historians are dependent on a series of fundamentally unreliable sources.

First there are the intelligence services – those, that is, who choose to provide information at all. They have their own agendas and their own idiosyncratic ideas of 'access'. The Russian Intelligence Archives, for example, have shed much light on what the spies actually did, but need to be treated with some skepticism. They are not open to the public. The several recent books on Soviet penetration of the West which claim to quote from these archives have all been written by either former KGB officers or their relatives . . . Despite promises to the contrary, even documents extensively quoted from in these books have not subsequently been made available to the public. The other major source for intelligence is the all-too-fallible memories of former intelligence agents, who usually have their own reasons for telling their stories . . . Then there are the secondary sources, books by espionage writers. Even conscientious writers have to make guesses about some things and to take others on trust; less conscientious ones – less sane ones even – have published all kinds of nonsense as fact.[1]

In such cases it is best to treat the documents in question and the arguments based on them, as one would the Philby book: as objects for, not as a basis for, analysis. Second best is simply to handle such material with great caution, segregating them from other sources and trying as best one can to cross-reference them with material available to the scholarly community. I have tried in this book to include only information from sources, mostly archival, to which any researcher can have access. As to assertions from the secondary literature, I have tried to follow the same rule, with rare exceptions accepting only those few that can be independently checked.

There is another factor in the rather extensive journalistic and secret intelligence literature quite specific to presentations of Guy Burgess's life and career(s). We might call this moral framing. Various activities are described and stigmatized and then those stigmatized activities are used to construct a moral framework for judging and presenting his actions. This is familiar in the cultural world, where a poet's, a painter's or a composer's political beliefs are taken as affecting the value of the poems of, say Ezra Pound, the paintings of Pablo Picasso, the music of Shostakovich. In regard to Burgess, we are repeatedly reminded in the journalistic accounts and those associated with the secret intelligence communities (not necessarily always different) that he was a homosexual, an alcoholic and untidy, with the implication that because of these he need not be taken seriously. It is, perhaps, unnecessary to point out that he lived in a social world where to be a homosexual was not in the least uncommon—one need only mention Harold Nicolson—where Prime Minister Churchill was known as an alcoholic when he took office (and when he left it) and where untidiness was as much a mark of public school background as anything else.

Many retrospective descriptions of Burgess invoke the observer's disgust at his sexual, culinary and clothing preferences. Martha Nussbaum has recently examined this "appeal to disgust" as a political strategy. "Often . . . the extension works . . . by imputing to people or groups properties similar to those that are found disgusting in the primary objects: bad smell, ooziness, rottenness, germiness, decay. Typically, these projections have no basis in reality. Jews are not really slimy, or similar to maggots, although German anti-Semites, and Hitler himself, said that they were."[2] Nussbaum also points out that "The appeal to disgust, sometimes covert and sometimes all too evident, has been a crucial part of the antigay strategy."[3] Lord Devlin, a British Law Lord wrote that "homosexuals are 'debauchees'; they are 'addicts,' whose immersion in sex is incompatible with being a reliable citizen."[4] Therefore homosexuals are declared to be incapable of patriotism; they are declared to be natural traitors. If Burgess is painted as the ideal type of homosexual traitor, no more questions need be asked. He was a traitor because he was a homosexual (and had dirty fingernails) and no inquiries into what he actually did, and even less why he did it, need be pursued.

If Burgess is not to be dismissed in this way, then we can begin to consider more interesting questions: Who was he? What, in fact, did he do, and why?

Notes to Introduction

---

[1] Carter, Miranda. Anthony Blunt: His Lives. London: Macmillan, 2001, p. 250.
[2] Nussbaum, Martha C. From Disgust to Humanity: Sexual Orientation & Constitutional Law. Oxford University Press, 2010, p. 16.
[3] Nussbaum, p. 8.
[4] Nussbaum, pp 8-9.

Chapter One

The Causeless Misery Of Parrots

My dear Harold,

. . . I am writing in the late morning. The early morning was spent lying in hot mineral water (natural hot) in a Georgian bath in what has been both a Christian & a Mohammedan place of worship, being scrubbed, washed in a way only Orientals wash (but I refused depilation) by a youth whose nationality I don't know, tho' not a Russian or Georgian, ?a Circassian? – with apparently waterproof Mascara round his eyes, an individual of great experience & technique & judging by the jealous grunts of a vast-Armenian, obviously a regular visitor, who had unfortunately for him arrived 5 minutes after me & missed that bus this morning, of great popularity. I went to the bath early because last night I was "with Georgians at a Party"! (See drawing by Sir Harry Luke in, I think, his "Cities & Men".)

My dear Harold, what a nice letter yours was, and so full of information. I was very touched and grateful. Gossip is, apart from the Reform Club & the streets of London & occasionally the English countryside, the only thing I really miss. The English Colony here, tho' dears, are apt to gossip about rather different things, and Russian gossip, even in English, though penetrating, indiscreet and amusing, is not about one's own parish and I moved rather late for it . . .

Thus Guy Burgess, writing from Tiflis to Sir Harold Nicolson, sometime (the letter is undated) between September 1958 and March 1959. Burgess had been living in the Soviet Union for seven years, but had just emerged from "purdah," as he put it, and begun to correspond with some of his old friends, allow himself to be seen at the theater and at concerts, attend embassy receptions and other social events. He would gradually become one of the sights of the Soviet capital, routinely interviewed by journalists, immortalized as "An Englishman Abroad."

Not all his thoughts were about nostalgic gossip. In the same letter he comments on Nicolson's recently published *Journey to Java:*

> I have read *Journey to Java.* Twice in fact – and with the greatest pleasure of the impossible to put down kind. I have so many corners of pages turned down with a view to possible comment that I shan't begin, or this letter, already vast, will never end. Only, one thing struck me as a possible cause of at least many of the cases of causeless misery you examine is that such misery is found in people who either don't seek or don't succeed in understanding the real world in which they live and in particular (as a Marxist I say this) the explanation, above all the historical explanation, of why it is what it is – and this includes, as a minor detail, why they are what they are. Without such knowledge, or at least the exercise of trying to attain such knowledge, individuals create a vacuum round themselves and angst replaces the air they should breathe. Marx wrote "Hitherto philosophers have tried to understand the world. The thing to do however is to change it." True, but the understanding comes first & surely distinguishes man from animals & savages – who also both have nameless terrors. All the dogs I've known have sometimes suffered from angst, particularly when their masters behave to them apparently irrationally – i.e. when the dog's ration of achieved understanding fails. Anything in that? The causeless misery of parrots. The historical complexity of our days & the desolate mud exposed by the retreating wash of the French Revolution, both terrains need careful examination if you're not to get lost or bogged down & plunge about in panic, lonely and screaming.

*   *   *

Who was this person, moving from one sentence to the next from humorous sybarite to Marxist philosopher, with barely a pause for a sympathetic observation about dogs and another about parrots? All too often we read history backward. Knowing the end of a particular set of circumstances we project that onto the beginning. The American Revolution succeeded, therefore the Founders were following a specific path to inevitable victory. China's great Ching dynasty ended in disaster, therefore it was fatally decadent. Burgess died, relatively young and, it is said, quite unhappy, in Moscow, therefore . . . This is especially the case when it is vital to the interests of the victors that the narrative is framed thus. It was vital to the secret intelligence services of the United States and Great Britain, and their governments, to minimize what Burgess and his friends had done, or might have done. They did so. And therefore Burgess is "remembered" as a traitor, exceptionally alcoholic,[1] a homosexual (negatively so designated), dirty and so forth. A person of no importance.

There is another way to tell the story. Let us begin, as he suggests, with attempting to understand the "historical complexity" of the world in which he lived.

Burgess was born in 1911. We might say that he would have begun to try to understand the world sometime in the late 1920s, or, at the latest, by the time he left Eton in 1929. How would he have viewed it? Politically, that world was dominated by the Empire ruled from Whitehall, which controlled a larger part of the area and a larger part of the population of the world than any state before or since. It exercised that control directly in the Empire proper— "British" India, much of Africa, parts of the Middle East, red bits and pieces scattered across the map from the Falkland Islands to Hong Kong— and indirectly, in varying degrees, by means of "advisors" and such, in Egypt, other parts of India, Iraq, etc. A schoolboy, particularly one from a military family like Burgess, might also have thought of the pink bits on the map—the Dominions: Canada, Newfoundland, the Irish Free State, Australia, New Zealand, South Africa—as in some way also parts of the Empire, and would have been right to do so.[2] And then there were places controlled in the later American style of "protection" and economic "cooperation": Argentina would come to mind as the type and much of China.

The areas under direct Imperial control, and some of those under indirect control, were all in fact actually controlled, in the first instance by Whitehall offices—their regulations and communications and financial arrangements—in the final analysis by military force, as demonstrated from time to time in Ireland until the establishment of the Free State (or until Bloody Sunday), in India at Amritsar (1919) and elsewhere, and, say, in the aerial bombardments of Iraqi villages and towns during the early 1920s. This violence practiced by those serving the Imperial government outside Britain corresponded to, and was participated in, by those in the Government within Britain, which had repeatedly used armed force against those they governed from the time of John Ball's Rebellion, through the early nineteenth-century "Peterloo" massacre and into the twentieth century. In some cases Imperial and Home Office violence had the same perpetrators, for example, Winston Churchill, who had sent troops into the Welsh mining villages before World War I and promoted the Iraqi air operations afterwards. The actions and words of the Government during the General Strike, which took place when Burgess was at the Royal Naval College, Dartmouth, indicated that from the point of view of the power of Whitehall, the miners and other manual laborers in Britain were in the same category as the inhabitants of the Asiatic and African parts of the Empire: they were the ruled, the Government, members of Parliament, and others in the so-called and very small middle and upper classes, were the rulers. The latter, whose families had in many cases for generations exercised the power of the state, believed, in short, what the Cromwellian Richard Rumbold in his final words from the scaffold had denied, "that Providence had sent a few men into the world, ready booted and spurred to ride, and millions ready saddled and bridled to be ridden."

Both British state and private violence were the instruments by which a delicate calculation was enforced. How much could be required of "those ridden" without extinguishing them? Occasionally, there were miscalculations; the most famous those in semi-colonial (or proto-colonial) Scotland and Ireland, largely depopulating those nations in the eighteenth and nineteenth centuries respectively. "Your sheep that were wont to be so meek and tame . . . be become so great devourers and so wild, that they eat up, and swallow down the very men themselves," as Thomas More, somewhat early, put it.[3] Or, perhaps, these were not miscalculations, but determinations that sheep were more valuable to the (partly indigenous) ruling class than their fellow countrymen. Eventually, as the Industrial Revolution took hold, the calculation stabilized with the equation resolved at a standard of living for the vast majority just sufficient in good times to avoid starvation. As a consequence the class divisions were visible on the bodies of the British people—the ruled had shorter, less healthy lives than the rulers. They were, on average, after generations of malnutrition, smaller. They seemed, to the tenth of the population that governed Great Britain and its Empire, nearly foreign in speech, hopelessly inferior in their presumed choices of housing, clothing, diet and education. Harold Nicolson illustrated the mental assimilation of the people of Great Britain to the subjects of the Empire by quoting the remark of Lord Curzon, seeing soldiers bathing behind the lines in Flanders: "Dear me! I had no conception that the lower classes had such white skins!" Having thought them to have black skins, no doubt, as proper for Imperial subjects.

After the First World War, when business demanded higher profits, the Government of the day helped drive down wages—precipitating the General Strike and, with its collapse, securing those profits from the pay envelopes of the miners and mill workers. In 1946, Ernest Bevin, who had been general secretary of the Transport and General Workers Union during the strike, and was then Foreign

11

Secretary of a Socialist Government, addressed the Conservative Party in a Parliamentary debate on a trade union bill. It was a speech, he said, he had wanted to give for twenty years.

> In 1924, let me remind the House, when the first Labour Government was in office, unemployment fell below the million mark. We struggled hard, patriotically—using that word in the right sense—to try to get our people back to work on the new basis. Then came the Election of 1924 in which my hon. Friends opposite were returned to power, not on a Trade Union Act, but on a "Red letter"* . . . Directly right hon. Gentlemen got into office they started to contemplate our return to the Gold Standard . . . We were brought back to prewar parity to gold
> . . . Suddenly, one day, the miners, who were the lowest-paid people in the country at that time—their position was, I believe, about 65th on the list of wage-earners—were faced with this enormous cut. What do you think of a Government and a City which, to adjust their finances, took a slice of bread off a miner, who was going down the pit to win the fuel with which to run industry? . . . The other industry which was attacked, was agriculture. The Conservative Party have always claimed to represent agriculture. What did they do? They wiped out the Wages Board, and cut agricultural wages from £3 a week to 28s. in order to meet the Bank of England and [Churchill] in the matter of restoring the Gold Standard . . . I asked Montagu Norman why he had done it and he said "Well, if a man is working, and is living on £3 or £4 a week, he causes so many imports and upsets the exchanges and the gold situation cannot operate." I asked him why he returned to it, and he did not answer.[4]

The General Strike was crushed, ironically enough, with the cooperation of the union leadership, including, crucially, if reluctantly, Bevin, who said "We look upon ourselves as the labour

---

* A reference to the forged Zinoviev Letter used by the Conservatives to discredit Labour.

side of management."[5] His problem in the 1920s and 1939s was that the owners did not recognize this view, only grudgingly recognized the existence of the unions and did what they could, when they could, to limit or eliminate them. The Government itself was still largely composed of members drawn from a few families, hereditary rulers, allied with such as the wealthy ironmonger Stanley Baldwin, who believed, and what is more remarkable, said, that the policy of their government was to enrich their friends and relatives by reducing the wages of the workers in their factories, mines and mills.[6] As a consequence, according to A. J. P. Taylor, after the victory of the owners over their workers in the General Strike, "to the general rejoicing of the educated, prosperous classes, the miners worked once more on terms which now seem to us, less than half a century afterwards, as remote and barbaric as serfdom."[7]

During Burgess's school years, three-quarters of British families had possessions worth less than £100; one-tenth of one percent of the population owned a third of the country and the richest one percent owned two-thirds of the national wealth.[8] That fortunate tenth of one percent was the world of Wellingtons and Rothschilds, Londonderrys and cabinet ministers, dukes and debutantes; the world of country house weekends and younger sons sent out to India to take their fortune; of the recreational mass killings of small animals; of golf; of the collecting of Old Master paintings; of a quasi-institutionalized heterosexual and marital promiscuity as described in the diaries of Duff Cooper, the novels of Anthony Powell, in motion picture costume dramas from that time to this. At the highest levels it was a world and a way of life that rivaled the extraneous luxury of the rulers of pre-Revolutionary Russia, or that of similar groups in twenty-first century America. At its lower levels it included the comfortable lives of all those able to afford pay a servant or two and reserve a room of their own for writing. It *could* include the odd Leonard Bast or D. H. Lawrence, but in general it *did* include only those men who had attended certain private schools—and their sisters, mothers and wives. The key to that strait gate was that crass thing, money. The annual fees Burgess's family would pay for him at Eton were over 240 pounds, about the annual wage of a woman certified as a teacher.[9] Those fees would consume the interest on 4,800 pounds: say, a quarter of a million pounds in today's money. Very few families could afford that tariff. It is no wonder that in the upper and upper middle class diaries and memoirs of the period everyone seemed to know everyone else: all the old boys had either fagged or been fagged by one another.

This is the world into which Guy Burgess was born: "The historical complexity of our days & the desolate mud exposed by the retreating wash of the French Revolution."

Notes to Chapter 1

[1] There is a book to be written about alcoholism in the British (not to mention American) ruling class, circa 1930 to 1970. Burgess's sometime friend Goronwy Rees went through a bottle of whiskey a day in the later part of that period and it was notorious that Winston Churchill's bloodstream was rarely, if ever, without a significant alcohol component, something that worried the French in 1940. For the former, see: Rees, Jenny. Looking for Mr Nobody: The Secret Life of Goronwy Rees. London: Phoenix, Orion, 1997, p. 10.

[2] "In the big naval towns people of all classes, including the working class, were very Empire-minded . . . Yet outside these centres with a direct connection, there were many working people for whom the Empire meant little." Branson, Noreen and Margot Heinemann. Britain in the 1930's. New York, Praeger Publishers, 1971, p. 298.

[3] More, Thomas. Utopia. Book I "Pasturage Destroying Husbandry," in Craik, Henry, ed. English Prose. Vol I. New York: The Macmillan Company, 1916. 162.

[4] Hansard, February 13, 1946.

[5] Branson, Noreen and Margot Heinemann. Britain in the 1930's. New York, Praeger Publishers, 1971, p. 86.

[6] "Baldwin . . . said on 30 July 1925: 'All the workers of this country have got to take reductions in wages to help put industry on its feet.'" Taylor, A. J. P. English History: 1914-1945. Oxford University Press, New York, 1965, p. 239.

[7] Taylor, p. 146.

[8] Taylor, p. 171.

[9] Branson and Heinemann, p. 168.

Chapter Two

Plymouth to Cambridge

Facts about the life of Guy Burgess can be peculiarly difficult to come by, but we can, at least, begin with the satisfying matter-of-factness of Census returns and Service records. Guy Burgess's paternal grandfather was a Colonel Henry Mills Burgess, who had "served with the expedition from Aden against the Foodlee Arab Tribe in 1866, including the destruction of Shugra" and later "with the Burmese Expedition in 1887 in command of the Royal Artillery, Upper Burmah Field Force," building the Empire.[1] His son, Guy Burgess's father, Malcolm Burgess, was born in Aden in 1881, joining the Navy as a mid-shipman in 1898 at the age of 17. After a rather shaky start—a collision, neglect of duties, "inclined to be lazy but improving"—by 1910 his service record noted that he was "ingenious & resourceful," tactful and zealous, and, finally, by 1912 a "very good officer of high zeal & ability." The year his eldest son was born, then-Lieutenant Malcolm Kingsford de Moncy Burgess was assigned to *HMS Isis,* an Eclipse class masted cruiser. Ships of this type were used by the Royal Navy to keep the sea-lanes open for British trade, or, alternatively, to blockade the trade of others. The *HMS Isis* could be found from time to time in Canadian waters, or just as likely in the Far East. It was, in a way, a floating embodiment of Empire. Malcolm Burgess reached the rank of Commander in 1916, moved his family for a year to Ismailia,[2] where he was on the staff of the Rear Admiral, Egypt, and then, in poor health, retired at his own request in 1922, dying of a heart attack (failure of the aortic valve) September 15, 1924 at his wife's family's country house, West Lodge, West Meon, Hampshire, age 41, leaving his widow

17

with two boys. The heart trouble was to be passed on to his elder son.

Guy Francis de Moncy Burgess—usually "Guy," sometimes "Burgess," only officially, at the B.B.C. and in the Foreign Office, "Mr Burgess," and hardly ever Guy F. deM. Burgess, was born at 2 Albemarle Villas, Devonport, Plymouth (a now Grade II listed building) on April 16, 1911.[3] Two weeks earlier, on the night of Sunday, April 2, when the 1911 Census was counted, the Albemarle Villa household consisted of the very pregnant Evelyn Mary, then 26, having been married for three years; her mother, Maud Gillman, then 51, of Southsea, having one other living child; a visitor, Edith May Gordon-Smith, aged 24 and single, also of Southsea, and four servants: a sick nurse, a housemaid, a cook and a maid, ages 22 to 30. A typical household of the lower part of the upper tenth.

Guy Burgess's mother's family, the Gillmans, had long been resident in Southsea, now part of Portsmouth, where they had been bankers and occasional Justices of the Peace at least since the mid-eighteenth century.[4] In 1911 William and Maude Gillman, Burgess's maternal grandparents, were living at 47 Clarence Parade, a large house overlooking the seafront, with their widowed son-in-law Major (later Lt. Colonel) Bertie Dwyer, 38, and his son, Denys (later Major) Angus Lambert Dwyer, and five servants: parlour maid, cook, housemaid, kitchen maid and nurse. William Gillman was a relative of the distinguished naval family of Grant, partners in the family bank of Grant, Gillman & Sons. "The Gillmans had a yacht, a car when to have one was more impressive than to have a yacht; and they looked out across the Solent from Rutland House as if they owned the sea and the Navy."[5] Not in Southsea that Census day, Evelyn Burgess's brother, Angus George Gillman, M.C., was then 28 years old. He would become a Major in the Royal Field Artillery and would die in France, at Vimy, in the Spring of 1917. His parents dedicated a memorial window to him in the local Cathedral in 1920.[6] His mother, Guy Burgess's grandmother Maud Gillman, died in 1927; Guy Burgess's grandfather William Gillman, J.P., lived for 82

18

years, dying in November, 1935, leaving Evelyn Burgess as the last of that line and, apparently, very well-provided for.[7]

Good, solid, bourgeois facts.

We have, then, a family typical of one aspect of the late-Imperial lower upper class: large Regency houses overlooking the sea; a large, but not historic, country house; domestic servants in their half dozens; the officers' Mess and the Sessions of the Justice of the Peace.[8] Commoners (despite the hopeful "de Moncy"), bankers and officers on the Gillman side, deeply rooted in Portsmouth; hereditary military on the Burgess side. Of course "Burgess" means bourgeois, which makes it fitting enough.

A couple of years before his father retired from the Navy, Guy Burgess was sent, at age 9, as was the custom among people such as the Burgesses and Gillmans, to a boarding school: Lockers Park School, Hemel Hempstead, Hertfordshire, about halfway between London and Milton Keynes. Lockers Park, founded in 1874, was one of the earliest purpose-built preparatory schools in England. In the following years it established itself as one of a handful of schools sending boys to Eton, Harrow and Winchester as well as Rugby and Stowe and Haileybury. The school in Burgess's time published advertisements such as this: "T. W. Holme, M.A., formerly of Winchester, and New College, Oxford: for 14 years Assistant-Master at Harrow School and N. B. Woodd Smith, M.A., formerly of Winchester and New College, Oxford, prepare boys between the ages of 8 and 14 for the Public Schools and Dartmouth . . .

> The House, healthily situated on a gravel and chalk soil, was built expressly for a Preparatory School . . . The Buildings include a School Chapel, Library, Swimming Bath, Gymnasium, Squash Racquet Court and Rifle Range and Laundry . . . Terms: 50 guineas a term . . . There is a medical fee of one guinea a term, a fee of two guineas a term for laundry and one guinea a term to cover all games, Library Books and School Lectures.

There were also eight to ten pounds in fees for optional items, such as violin or shooting lessons. Families with boys at Lockers Park would not have much left over from a couple hundred pounds a year. In Burgess's case, that most likely would have been a charge to his Gillman grandfather.

The "Sets" (houses) at Lockers Park, were named for famous army and navy captains, which would have suited Burgess's background and his family's ambitions for him. His set was Kitchener, named for Lord Kitchener of Khartoum, overseer of Boer concentration camps, ruler of Egypt, image and synecdoche of Empire. At Lockers Park there was (and is) a system of "effort grades, emphasizing attitude and application as the most important elements of education." The marks ranged from "G. for really good work throughout," to "B. for really bad work." "These reports refer exclusively to industry and attentiveness in class, and care in written work, not to ability nor necessarily to place in class." According to the school's historian, Burgess played for the First XI football, but he did not make the cricket team. "He was very intelligent and tried hard and in the [grades] for effort he was never given anything other than S – meaning satisfactory and was often given VG – very good." He left the school in September, 1923, ranked second in his class, habituated to industriousness, promptness, attentiveness.[9] Burgess's classmates at Lockers Park included Peter Watson (art collector and co-founder of *Horizon*), Thomas Mitford (brother of his famous sisters and later famously a Nazi-sympathizer) and James Lees-Milne (architectural expert and diarist): all from families a few or many notches higher in the social order than the Burgesses.

In January, 1924, Burgess, under-age for his father's school, the Royal Naval College, Dartmouth, went, unusually, to Eton for a year. Listed in the Third Remove of E, his House Tutor was Francis Wellesley Dobbs and his Classical or Modern Tutor was Charles Routh. The following year, when he was old enough to transfer to Dartmouth, he did well there at drill, sports and his classes, earning compliments from his instructors as "excellent officer material." In 1926, at age fifteen, he won prizes for essays on naval operations, science, geography and other subjects. In the summer term of 1927 he won yet more prizes "for general history, for an analysis of Napoleon's military career . . . for scripture and 'Notes on Picture

Making'." A natural, or at least, hereditary, member of the Imperial officer class, when he had to withdraw from Dartmouth after not quite three years (because of eyesight not up to the exacting standards of the Navy), he did so "with an honourable discharge and glowing references to the headmaster of Eton."[*]

Accordingly, in Michaelmas Term (Fall), 1927 Burgess joined his younger brother Nigel, Burgess minor, at Eton.[10] He was placed in the Upper Fifth (B), Third Remove—again with Routh and Dobbs—listed at the bottom of group IX as was the custom for a new student. Burgess was an "Oppidan," not a "Scholar;" his mother paid fees. He did not reside in College, but around the corner, in a "House" nominally in town, but virtually contiguous with the school's own set of buildings. The small group of scholars "tended to produce clergymen, scholars and schoolmasters; [the much more populous] Oppidan Eton soldiers, statesmen, bankers" (two out of three for the Burgess/Gillmans).[11] Oppidans lived in a cluster of private houses across the high street from the College, of a size and style reminiscent of American fraternity houses. In those days each House Master owned his house (which was called by his name) and ran it as a business, collecting fees from the parents of the boys. If a House Master moved to a bigger house (thus increasing his revenue), the house name went with him. A boy could live in two or three buildings during his time at Eton, each successively referred to by the same name. The average House Master; his deputy and assistants; a dame, her assistant and domestic servants, cared for some four dozen boys aged between 13 and 18. Meals were taken in the house's dining-room, although toast and other snacks could be had in a boy's own room. The houses had drama and arts groups as well, figuring largely or not in the memoirs of old Etonians, as to their taste and experience. Each house was dominated, and, in a sense, managed, by a group of older boys, led by the house captain

---

[*] Sometime during his childhood Burgess had a severe case of mumps. This left one of his testicles atrophied, without apparent consequences for his later sexual activity.

and the captain of games. Younger boys served the older boys, tending their fires and seeing to their comfort. It could be a violent environment, where sheer physical size and strength were encouraged to subject the smaller, weaker and, especially, the younger, with beatings, canings and, perhaps, the occasional rape.

That said, Burgess's Eton was as much an ideal as a place. With its ancient buildings and playing fields overlooked by Windsor Castle across the Thames, it was strongly associated with monarchy and aristocracy. The older boys wore "tails": black morning suit, black silk top hat, white bow tie (sold by the gross, to be worn once and discarded). Class lists carefully distinguished Smith from Mr. Smith from Lord Smith. It was a place of rituals, costumes, language and manners studiedly different from those used elsewhere, each such careful distinction a reminder of the status of its inhabitants, their destined role in the very small British ruling class of the time. (The careers of Burgess and Fitzroy Maclean, for example, were pursued within hailing distance of one another until nearly the end.) In the memoirs and biographies of men of Burgess's generation and class, many of whom seem never actually to have ever applied for a job, there is a recurring motif of opportunities thrown in their path. They seemed, somehow, always to land the plum assignment. (Stefan Collini has written, *à propos* of Graham Greene, of those "who grew up on the lower slopes of those peaks of privilege and gentility that dominated English society . . . 'we still lived in a world of influential friends' . . . of . . . gilded youths who expected the world to pay attention to them . . ."[12]) Burgess's contemporaries at Eton included his Lockers Park classmates, Watson, Mitford and Lees-Milne; Alfred "Freddie" Ayer, the philosopher; Fitzroy Maclean and Wilfred Thesiger, writers and explorers; Michael Berry and Rupert Hart-Davis, newspaper publishers; Alan Pryce-Jones, later editor of the *Times Literary Supplement*, the American sportsman Robert Grant III and Randolph Churchill. Ayer and Berry were good friends of Burgess's for a quarter century and more. Burgess would play racquets with Grant in New York just weeks before traveling to Moscow.

Eton in those years was for many of its boys an introduction to homosexual relationships. Anthony Powell in his autobiography describes this tight little world of adolescent friendship, the coming into consciousness of the first stirrings of talent and taste and preferences, whether for games or command, submission or study. Lees-Milne and Pryce-Jones, for example, were famously sought after by older (and not just older) boys. Tom Mitford was the great love of the former, who recalled how:

> On Sunday eves before Chapel at five, when the toll of the bell betokened that all boys must be in their pews, [Mitford] and I would, standing on the last landing of the entrance steps, out of sight of the masters in the ante-chapel and all the boys inside, passionately embrace, lips to lips, body pressed to body, each feeling the opposite fibre of the other."[13]

One can hardly imagine Burgess, at Eton or later, referring to his sex organ as a "fibre," which may be why he and Lees-Milne, although frequenting the same circles, and some of the same beds, for a quarter century, did not get on.

Boys at Eton had their own study-bedrooms that offered a certain measure of privacy, but not one that could be guaranteed. To turn once more to Lees-Milne, that chronicler of Etonian passion, in his diary under June 3, 1991, he commented on the recent death of a Lieutenant-Colonel Berkeley Villiers, "who was the first boy to seduce me . . ."

> I remember the incident extremely well, I aged fifteen at most. In the middle of the performance Michael Rosse, then his great friend, came into Berkeley's room and like the perfect gentleman he was fetched something he had left on the mantelpiece without turning his head in our direction."[14]

Burgess thrived at Eton. He enjoyed the common and special school ball games and such. He was, however, a participant in, rather than a champion of, the obsessive Etonian sports activities, although he was on the Eton soccer Eleven and got his House colors for the Eton field game and in 1930 he was listed in the crew of the

10-oar boat Monarch,[15] becoming, if he was not already, a good swimmer. His academic career at Eton was quite another thing altogether. The Eton school day in Burgess's time began at 7:30 in the morning, Monday through Saturday. The last class was at five. The two-hour classes rotated through the week, so that on Monday, say, they were Latin Prose, Divinity, History, French and Math, while on Thursday they were Science, Latin Grammar, Latin "Construe," with the afternoon free. The rota also included Drawing, English and Geography. In addition to the curriculum, its lectures and examinations, each boy was assigned to a tutor, often a new graduate of Cambridge or Oxford, who gave him extra instruction and extra books, religious and general counseling.

At Eton Burgess read the novels that one might expect him to have read: Trollope and Bennett, on the one hand, Proust and Firbank on the other. He read poetry by Browning, T. S. Eliot and Wilfrid Scawen Blunt. He heard Harold Nicolson lecture to the school on the situation in Germany. He went down to London to the French Exhibition at Burlington House. Each year his work in Essay and History earned the peculiar Eton distinction "Sent Up for Good," that is, his papers were shown to the Headmaster.[16] He learned his Latin and his French, perhaps also his science and math. He won a number of prizes for his drawings, which early attained a distinctive style with a strong caricatural line. In Michaelmas Term, 1928 he earned Distinction in Trials (good marks on the examination), twice. By July, 1928, he was ranked 20th of the First Hundred[*] and he finished his Eton career ranked seventh in the First Hundred, winning the Gladstone Memorial Scholarship in 1930 (£100 for one year, a considerable sum), first in his class on an examination ("trial") in "C" (lower Sixth Form),[17] having taken second place for the Rosebery History Prize in 1929, and obtained distinction in Trials three times in his last year at Eton. He graduated second among the Oppidans.[18] It was a notable school career.

---

[*] Fitzroy Maclean, the future Foreign Office Mandarin, ranked first, with no one near him.

In December, 1928, when Burgess was 17 years old, (Sir) Robert Birley, who taught him history at Eton (and was later Headmaster), wrote to his tutor F. W. Dobbs that Burgess "had a gift for plunging to the root of any question and his essays were on occasion full of insights. His career in the upper school passed wholly without blemish . . ."[19]

> At the moment his ideas are running away with him, and he is finding in verbal quibbles and Chestertonian comparisons a rather unhealthy delight, but he is such a sane person, and so modest essentially that I do not feel that this very much matters. The great thing is that he really thinks for himself . . . It is refreshing to find one who is really well-read and who can become enthusiastic or have something to say about most things from Vermeer to Meredith. He is also a lively and amusing person, generous, I think, and very good natured. He should do very well.[20]

(Harold Nicolson's son Nigel, at Eton a few years later, memorialized Birley in his autobiography as a great teacher, gentle but for an enthusiasm for flogging boys.[21])

Eton gave Burgess a classical education, a passion for the study of history (he would have been thought of as one of the most promising historians of his year), a sense of belonging to an elite and, no doubt, a certain amount of homosexual experience. He left Eton in July, 1930, but returned throughout his life, in fact, in conversation, and in imagination. He nearly always wore his old school tie. Eton was crucial, perhaps obsessively crucial, to Burgess's sense of himself. This was—is—not uncommon.

While Guy Burgess was still at Eton, almost exactly five years after Commander Burgess's death, his mother married another member of the professional officer class, Lieutenant-Colonel Bassett (retired), who had served as British Resident in Jeddah during the period when T. E. Lawrence and St. John Philby were fostering Arab nationalism as a counterforce to Ottoman, and a prelude to British Imperial, power.[22] Burgess's mother had been an officer's wife, then his widow, now she was again the wife of an officer [Retd.], "Mrs.

Bassett" for the rest of her life. Perhaps her first husband's connections to Arabia had brought her together with Colonel Bassett.

The triangular correspondence among the Imperial agents in Arabia, the Arab Bureau in Cairo and the Viceroy in New Delhi (or Simla) that had passed through Bassett's hands presents a vivid picture of the Empire attempting to bring order to the unsettled conditions in Arabia as various tribal leaders, emirs and would-be kings contended, as they thought, for sovereignty; sovereignty, in fact, being doled out, as ever, from Whitehall, Cairo, and Simla, through regular functionaries, like Colonel Bassett, or less regular, like St. John Philby (whose son bore the imperial nickname of "Kim"). Here, from a bound volume of copies of official correspondence typed on the Empire's heavy paper, is a typical message from the Arab Bureau in Cairo to Bassett in Jeddah:

> Tell [Hussein bin Ali, King of Hejaz] that I regret to see that he is under a misapprehension regarding object of mission to IBN SAUD. The necessity for coordination of military plans was never more urgent than at present and mission will impress this on IBN SAUD and report what assistance he requires in order to cooperate effectively in Arab movement. London's suggestion was that STORR'S knowledge of Arabian affairs would be very helpful to members of the military mission, more particularly if he was accompanied by a capable and accredited Agent. This does not permit of STORRS proceeding via KOWEIT and BASRA . . . As STORRS is due to leave London at once, an urgent reply is required as to whether King is definitely unable to guarantee his safe passage to IBN SAUD.[23]

To which Bassett replied, in part:

> I do not think any misunderstanding possible of the King's various communications which have been carefully translated. Although he has held throughout that the BASRA or KOWEIT route is preferable he gave way on this point in his telegram and subsequent message of Nov.10th. I sent copies of these to you with my secret letter No.11/7/1 of 11th. He is, in my opinion, backing out and rather clumsily. Is it the wish of the High

Commissioner that I should push the matter further? King still expects Storrs to come to Jeddah and it is his intention in order to meet him to stay here until the end of the month.[24]

The Hashemite king was being difficult; Ibn Saud was ambitious. This is summed up by a typical comment from Philby (who was himself viewed as "unsound" by the regular Army officers in the field): "Ibn Saud displays consuming jealousy of Sherif whose assumption in correspondence of title of "King of Arab Countries" galls him to distraction, while at the back of his mind is the suspicion that Sherif's attitude in this connection is based on some secret understanding with us."[25] It was a long way from Southsea.

Despite the fact that all of Guy Burgess's close male relatives, living and dead, were or had been military officers, except his maternal grandfather, the banker, and every other male Burgess or Gillman had gone from school into uniform or business, Guy Burgess, age 19, went to Trinity College, and Cambridge, the Florence of the Fens, set him on quite a different path from those followed by the various colonels, commanders and Justices of the Peace crowding his family tree.

Cambridge in those days could hardly have been more cloistered, more distant from Jeddah or, say, the Black Country. According to Burgess's friend Julian Bell: "In the Cambridge that I first knew, in 1929 and 1930, the central subject of ordinary intelligent conversation was poetry. As far as I can remember we hardly ever talked or thought about politics . . ."[26] For an undergraduate Cambridge was, as it were, like some outsized stony, crenellated set of ducal castles, with its attendant town, apparently untouched by Empire or industry. The part, the large part, of Cambridge, where the colleges line up between the river and the curving street that changes its name as it passes, is a landscape of dry grey and yellowish-grey stone, cousin to the ancient centers of the great medieval cities of Europe. Within the stone carapaces of the ancient colleges there were soft green quadrangles, hall, chapel, library and finally, in the innermost chambers of the Nautilus, the fellows and undergraduates, cocooned in rooms not unlike—very much like, as a matter of fact—

the rooms Burgess had known at Eton. The colleges were, for eyes trained in the European tradition, beautiful. (One undergraduate felt that living there was like being told that whenever one went to a dance one's companion would be Botticelli's *Primavera*.) [27] Trinity College, with fewer students than Eton, was a place where it was easy to know and be known, to come to the attention of those dons who made it their business to notice undergraduates who might well make their way in the world, attracting notice.

Burgess was easy for the talent spotters to spot—handsome, athletic, already the brilliant conversationalist he would remain all his life; carrying those prizes from Eton; looking forward to the prospect of additions to the collection, he was soon immersed in the study and social routines of a Cambridge undergraduate. Eric Hobsbawm, also a historian, a Communist and a near contemporary, described "the essential elements in a Cambridge education outside the natural sciences" as:

> [T]he weekly essay written for a private session with a 'supervisor', and the Tripos, the degree examination in two parts, at the end of a one-year and a two-year course. Lectures were less important . . . Good students soon discovered that they could get more out of an hour's reading in the magnificent libraries of college, faculty and university than an hour's listening to undemanding public speech.[28]

(Unless the lecturer in question was the Regius Professor of History, George Macaulay Trevelyan, in which case it was worth one's while to attend and listen.)

> Everything was designed to make us into pillars of a tradition reaching back to the thirteenth century . . . Undergraduates wore their short black gowns to go to lectures and supervisions, into the obligatory collective dinner in college halls and (with caps) whenever out in the streets after dark, policed by more amply gowned and capped Proctors, assisted by their 'bulldogs'. Dons entered lecture rooms with their long gowns billowing and the squares planted with precision on their heads. Scholars read the

Latin grace to the standing multitude before dinner and lessons in ancient chapels.[29]

Cambridge (like Oxford and London itself) is famously a place of clubs and societies. Guy Burgess, upon arriving at Trinity College, joined the University Pitt Club, as any Burgess or Gillman would, a club catering then to men from public schools, where, he said, he "drank a bottle of Liebfraumilch '21 (at 3s. 6d.)* every day at luncheon."[30] It still occupies space in a building at 7a Jesus Lane (a block and a half from Trinity College), which was originally designed as the "Victorian Roman Baths," in the form of a small classical temple, in 1863 by Sir Matthew Digby Wyatt. Kings Edward VII and George V had been members, as had John Maynard Keynes. It was a place for Burgess to drink with other young men who would not mind drinking with royalty; to misbehave in an approved, traditional, fashion.

Not all Cambridge's clubs were devoted to drinking. Undergraduates interested in the stage could indulge that interest in the Amateur Dramatic Club, around the corner from the Pitt Club's premises. Cambridge drama then was dominated by George "Dadie" Rylands, who had been at Eton with Cyril Connolly and Steven Runciman, later the historian of Byzantium (and who as a young don fancied Burgess[31]). Rylands had gone on to King's College (as was the custom for many Eton graduates) where he read English and won a fellowship, joining the English faculty and remaining there for the rest of his very long life, teaching poetry and fostering in the Cambridge Marlowe Society "a nursery where those who were to become famous in the theatre learnt to speak Shakespeare's verse."[32] Noel Annan notes that Rylands "often caused havoc," presumably because of his good looks, and that "In each generation a new set of undergraduates streamed through his rooms," presumably for *their* good looks. He was closely connected to Bloomsbury; he was an

---

* As compared with "the 30s a week on which a man, wife and two children had to manage."

Apostle and possibly an alcoholic. For many undergraduates, including Burgess, he was the center of a certain Cambridge world.

In his second term, Burgess got a First in Mays,[33] the examination given that month, and worked with Rylands at the A. D. C. Theatre, where, in June, 1931, he designed the scenery for a production of Shaw's *Captain Brassbound's Conversion,* produced by Rylands, starring Ryland's favorite, Arthur Marshall,[34] as Lady Cicely Waynflete, with Michael Redgrave as Captain Brassbound.* According to Redgrave's biographer, Alan Strachan,

> Dadie set this 1890s play in modern dress, the better no doubt to give Arthur, to whom he had taken an instant shine, a last chance to dazzle Cambridge with his legs. They, and Arthur, predictably stole the show, although Michael was widely admired and certainly looked suitably exotic. As did the sets, also much admired, the work of an old Etonian undergraduate at Trinity, Guy Burgess . . . he took his work on *Brassbound* extremely seriously and all involved were impressed by his attention to detail. The production was such a success that extra shows had to be added, with cars and trains bringing social London to see it . . .[35]

Geoffrey Rossetti (a rather emotional Leavisite undergraduate) reviewed the production in the *Cambridge Review,* noticing that Burgess's "scenery was in every way adequate, not exaggeratedly realistic nor exaggeratedly stylized, but a pleasantly supportive setting for the play." This was significant recognition: most other A.D.C. sets of the time were designed by Vanessa Bell or Duncan Grant.[36] In this way Burgess would have become known to Bloomsbury, to Rylands; to Keynes, who backed A.D.C., to his wife Lydia Lopokova; to Vanessa Bell, her husband and son; probably to Virginia and Leonard Woolf.

---

* Redgrave was already recognized as an actor in the first rank in his generation. He and Burgess remained on friendly terms up to and beyond their last meeting a quarter century later in Moscow.

The stage doors of the A.D.C. led to a whole world of interlocking personal relationships, in the Bloomsbury fashion, but not limited to Bloomsbury. At the time of Rylands' *Captain Brassbound's Conversion* production, Redgrave was broadcasting on the B.B.C. programs produced by Hilda Matheson, who was a lover of Vita Sackville-West, and therefore known to Harold Nicolson.[37] Redgrave was also a friend of a young don, Anthony Blunt, with whom he had put out an undergraduate magazine called *The Venture*.[38] And Redgrave was one of a group including Blunt and Julian Bell, to whom about this time Keynes gave one of the lunches he enjoyed giving to undergraduates.[39] Bell seems to have pioneered a certain informality in attire common to some in this set. He "had never got away from the almost compulsive untidiness of his childhood: his clothes were always in need of repair, he could rarely be bothered to comb his hair, or button his collar or shirt buttons."[40] Habits similar to those for which Burgess was later to be known. It may have been during the summer after *Captain Brassbound* that Rylands, Arthur Marshall and Victor Rothschild encountered Somerset Maugham in Monte Carlo and went with him to his Villa Mauresque to enjoy Maugham's comprehensive hospitality.[41]

Perhaps it was through Redgrave, or perhaps through Bell, Blunt's sometime lover, that Burgess met Anthony Blunt, just embarking on his brilliant career as an art historian.[42] Or, perhaps, it was not possible for anyone at that time at Trinity not to meet Burgess. Blunt, writing when all was over, recalled: "It was, I think, in the summer of 1931 that I first met Guy Burgess, who had come up to Trinity from Eton in 1930.

> On that occasion I did not take to him, because he began immediately to talk very indiscreetly about the private lives of people who were quite unknown to me; but as I got to know him better I became fascinated by the liveliness and quality of his mind and the range of his interests. There was no subject in which he did not have something stimulating to say and although his ideas were not always supported with full evidence or carefully thought out reasons there was always something in

31

them to provoke thought and set one's own mind working along new lines. He could be perverse in argument and in behavior, but in the former he would wiggle back to [reality] and in the latter he would apologise in such an engaging manner that it was difficult to be angry for long.[43]

In July, 1931, three of Burgess's sketches were published at Eton in "Motley: An Ephemeral Magazine Edited by a Present Etonian," which included verse by Aldous Huxley and others of the "best of Etonian talent." One, entitled "Soul portrait of a very clever boy," looks much like Anthony Blunt.

Blunt, bowled over by Burgess, brought him into the Apostles in 1932.[44] The Society of the Apostles is now one of the better known, more publicized, secret societies, similar to the various secret intelligence agencies and Skull and Bones in that regard. Founded in 1820 as the Cambridge Conversazione Society, a discussion group of Evangelical Tories, it gradually became a central institution in the life of the University, attracting such as Tennyson, George Trevelyan and James Clerk Maxwell. By the end of the century its intellectual standards had become higher and its religious standards looser. Friendship among Apostles, rather than Evangelicalism, became the Society's over-riding value, with an emphasis on frank disclosure of feelings and faults. Around 1900 it was the intellectual standards of Apostles that were emphasized when the philosophers G. E. Moore and Bertrand Russell, and the mathematician G. H. Hardy, were central members of the Society. Then, the "homosexual phase in Apostolic life," according to the Society's historian, Richard Deacon, "bloomed" when it came to be dominated by Lytton Strachey and John Maynard Keynes,[45] the phase fading slightly in the next generation. Deacon insists that it "should be stressed that the portrait of the Apostles of the 1930s as 'a centre of homosexuality' is inaccurate.

There was nothing remotely like the flamboyant homosexuality of the Strachey-Keynes era. What ever there was of this nature was relatively discreet in Apostolic circles. Indeed, discretion on all counts was an essential dictum of the Apostles at that time.

32

Indiscretion was frowned upon as a lack of internal discipline. [Even] Guy Burgess, who occasionally bragged of his homosexual conquests . . . could be astonishingly discreet on occasions . . ."[46]

The Apostles held the loyalty of its elect after their graduation, when they became known as "Angels," some of whom all their lives attended, when in Cambridge, Saturday night meetings, its annual meetings in London. In the early 1930s, the Angels included the Regius Professor of History, G. M. Trevelyan; E. M. Forster; Desmond MacCarthy, literary critic; Edward Marsh (Churchill's private secretary until retirement in 1937); James Strachey (the psychoanalyst); Keynes, of course; Bertrand Russell; Leonard Woof; Dadie Rylands. Typically, "Julian [Bell] loved the Society; he continued to regard it as the pinnacle of Cambridge intellectualism and he came in from Elsworth for its . . . gatherings,"[47] during which one or another of the Apostles would stand before the fire and read out a paper to his fellows and elders, after which it would be discussed. If an undergraduate could survive that experience, which would not be gentle, he would be prepared for most other intellectual gladiatorial arenas. Of men of Burgess's own time, in addition to Blunt, there were or would soon be, Julian Bell, Eric Hobsbawm, Leo Long, Victor Rothschild and Michael Straight. In the next few years Hobsbawm, Long and Straight were known as more or less open members of the Communist Party.

This was a certain Cambridge elite, tending toward the humanities (although Rothschild was a scientist, as well as, of course, a Rothschild, with all that implies[48]), mutually admiring and supportive, helpful, in general, to one another when help was required.

*   *   *

We have, to this point, concentrated on a very small part of the world in which Burgess lived. That small world—Lockers Park and Eton, Cambridge and the Apostles—was a glasshouse in a wasteland.

After the failure of the General Strike—and, in particular, after the way that it failed—had reduced organized labor in Britain to the junior partner in Bevin's industrial management team, a sort of stupor had fallen over the unions, rejecting the class struggle, accepting their "place" in society, hoping for a few more pence per hour (or a few less of a reduction) in the next contract, a few more votes for Labour in the next election. The unemployed, in their euphemistic "special areas," were in a different kind of stupor: that induced by chronic malnutrition. In this way the country was kept safe for the bright young things, whose doings and faces filled the newspapers and fill the novels of and about the time. The Empire continued to expand. If at its heart, India, the Congress Party was already set on independence, in Whitehall, and in the pages of *The Times,* Gandhi and the Nehrus, father and son, and their associates, were merely colonial politicians, when not Churchillian "niggers": nothing to worry about there. Closer at hand, the League of Nations, although crippled without the United States exercising full membership, did appear to provide a basis for the peaceful resolution of international conflicts and the beginnings of international cooperation. Germany had something like a democratic government, seeming, for the moment, prostrate, inward looking and marginalized. The Soviet Union, where Stalin had just achieved supreme power, was embarking on the task of building socialism in one country. Mussolini was much admired, much condescended to. During those years E. M. Forster went to India in search of exoticism and love; Auden and Isherwood, Spender and Lehmann to Germany and Austria for a slightly different kind of sexual tourism; Oxbridge dons and young women went to Moscow, notebooks in hand, and everyone went to Italy (although hardly anyone did so for the politics). But in Britain itself, by the end of Burgess's first term at Trinity, unemployment had reached two and a half million and the second Labour government was doomed by a financial crisis it could neither understand nor solve.[49] Undergraduates, particularly first year undergraduates, cannot be expected to pay much attention to the condition of society. They have their own preoccupations. But if we are to think about Guy Burgess, how he saw the world, it is useful to consider "the historical complexity" of his days, and appropriate to do so with reference to accounts of that time by historians whose views he would later share.

According, then, to the Communist historians Noreen Branson and Margot Heinemann (the latter of whom, John Cornford's Krupskaya, was at Cambridge with Burgess), in the mid-1930s the "lower classes" included more than three-quarters of the families of Great Britain. About 70% of British families lived on four pounds per week or less and a good many of the British families living on between four and ten pounds per week—say, $26,000 per year in current dollars for a family of five—would also have been counted among the lower classes by contemporaries. (A school teacher, if a man, paid, on average, six and a half pounds a week, might stand for the lowest reaches of a middle class including, say, 15% of the population.) As the poverty line in Great Britain today is about $20,000 per year for a family of four, nearly ninety per cent of the British people were living in poverty during the Thirties, and half were living in extreme poverty: half of those living on a less than adequate diet and nearly a third on a diet that was seriously deficient.[50] If we survey the world at the beginning of the twenty-first century for countries with similar income distributions, we must look to equatorial Africa and Andean South America. Branson and Heinemann cite Seebohm Rowntree's survey of poverty in York: "Unskilled men in most industries, and skilled men as well in the most depressed industries, generally earned too little throughout the thirties to keep a family at a standard that would maintain full health . . . it is estimated that some 47 per cent of adult male workers earned less than 55s a week, and 23 per cent less than 45s. Very large numbers indeed therefore must have failed to reach the standard 'below which no worker should be force to live'".[51]

Matters were worse, of course, for the unemployed, of whom there were, by 1931, nearly three million—perhaps a quarter of the potential working population. The unemployment benefit for a family of four was thirty shillings per week (seventy-eight pounds or

$117 in today's values), about half what was then considered a subsistence income. During the early 1930s, "Means Testing" was instituted by the National Government, which limited benefits in much of the country to the least amount paid to those employed by local business and this only after all assets and savings, down to the family piano, had been sold or exhausted and the pensions of the elderly and the earnings of the children deducted.

> Unemployment benefit was enough to keep the family from outright starvation, but not very much else. It meant an unbalanced diet dominated by bread and margarine and tea with condensed milk, so that health began to deteriorate. It meant that when clothes wore out they could not be replaced, and breaking a cup or plate could be a minor disaster . . . the 30s a week on which a man, wife and two children had to manage was in real terms about half the amount considered necessary for minimum subsistence . . .[52]

Unemployment was concentrated in the "special" or "distressed" districts—the mining areas of Wales and the North, the old industrial Midlands, where up to a quarter of the British population lived. As the historian A. J. P. Taylor told the story: "The members of the National government may be seen in a newsreel, assembling for discussion: stern features, teeth clenched, as they face the crisis. They would hesitate at nothing to save the country, to save the pound. The result of their courage was that the children of the unemployed had less margarine on their bread. After this resolute decision, ministers dispersed to their warm comfortable homes and ate substantial meals. Such was 'equality of sacrifice'."[53]

Education for most children was a mere gesture, with a quarter of all school rooms filled with more than sixty pupils.[54] "In 1931 only one adolescent in five received any secondary education . . . and the proportion declined slightly during the thirties . . . Out of every thousand children at an elementary school only four managed to reach a university; less than one in a thousand reached Oxford and Cambridge."[55] Lockers Park, Eton, Trinity College were exotic preserves, invisible from the streets of Manchester or the pit villages of Wales.   There the school leaving age was fourteen and most children went directly into the factories, down into the mines or into domestic service.   Boys remained employable in the pits and factories after their fathers were put out of work, as they could be paid less. Therefore, "it was common in mining areas to see fourteen-year-old boys, with black faces, plodding wearily home from the pit while their fathers stood unemployed on the street corner."[56] Goronwy Rees visited Merthyr Tydfil in 1931:

> It was once a very prosperous colliery town of perhaps 70,000 people. Now every one of them is out of work and have been for a year. In the mornings all the streets are absolutely crammed with the colliers talking and smoking cigarettes, as if it were a Saturday afternoon or the evening after a Cup Tie. But most of the colliers stay in bed till tea time because they have nothing to do and they needn't eat in bed. Most of them have five or six children. If there is ever a local election, the only candidates are Labour or Communist, anyone else would be unthinkable.[57]

The girls from the distressed districts would leave home at fourteen, so that their earnings, no matter how insignificant, would not be deducted from the family's unemployment benefit.[58] Some became nurses; most became servants in the homes of the "middle" class, some, no doubt, took other employment. For those middle class intellectuals looking into the "Condition of England" at the time, it was as if those whose work supported them had come from some forgotten outpost of Empire: "What we have found in some of the more remote mining villages is this: Girls of 17-20 who have never slept alone in a room, who have never known what it is to have ordinary bedclothes, and some who are unfamiliar with knives and forks . . ."[59] These were revelations of class difference and destitution that would be repeated during the evacuation of children from the East End of London early in the war. Such were conditions over much of London, Wales, the formerly industrialized North, the Scottish cities, in the 1930s.

Even Cambridge was beginning to notice that personal relations, although absorbing, were not the whole extent of the world. The sense of crisis that had been growing since the Wall Street stock market crash was beginning to cause anxiety beyond the Special Areas. As one of its last gestures in support of the working class, the Labour Government had been able to raise pay for coal miners and the unemployed in 1930. But then, all through 1930, there was the paradoxical situation of a Labour government, led by its Prime Minister, Ramsay MacDonald, increasingly obsessed with balancing the budget and maintaining the gold standard at the expense of rising unemployment and renewed reductions in living standards for most people in Britain.[60] The crucial moment for the Labour government came when a group including Oswald Mosley, David Lloyd George and Keynes urged deficit spending and further governmental intervention in the economy. "Mosley wanted planned foreign trade; public direction of industry; and a systematic use of credit to promote expansion."[61] These were refused. Mosley resigned from the government in February 1931 and formed the New Party with a handful of adherents. The economic and unemployment situation continued to worsen and the government's policy continued to be to lower taxes and cut unemployment benefits.

When there was a run on the banks and panic in the government, MacDonald sided with the bankers against the unions and the Labour Party representatives of the latter in the Cabinet could not go on. At the end of August, using a trick that became popular among anti-Communist politicians on the Left, MacDonald submitted his resignation and formed a coalition Government, in effect a Conservative Government with MacDonald, who had then been expelled from the Labour Party, as a figure-head Prime Minister. It was something of a coup d'état. For people like Harold Nicolson, on the periphery of power, "Everything seems heading towards violence & civil war."[62] The new government cut the wages of everyone from teachers to sailors. On September 15, 1931 the sailors, more to be feared than teachers, went on strike and the government backed down a bit on their pay cuts. On September 21 the gold standard was suspended and the pound fell more than a quarter of its value against the dollar, but then stabilized. The world had not ended. The government's policy of wage cuts to maintain the gold standard had been unnecessary: the result of economic ignorance and class hatred.

Unemployment worsened; wages were forced down; people in the North and in Wales grew increasingly desperate. It was a peculiar feature of the suffering of the unemployed and those living on starvation wages in their Special Areas that they were physically distant from the country's small middle class in the Home Counties. Responding to this, Wal Hannington, a militant of the rapidly growing Communist Party of Great Britain, invented the Hunger March: that nearly unique method of propaganda and recruitment.[63] In the autumn of 1932 the National Unemployed Workers' Movement (NUWM) organized a national hunger march from the North to London to present a "monster petition" against the means test. Margot Heinemann described it as follows:

> These hunger marches in which contingents of unemployed spent many arduous weeks on the road, holding meetings to explain their case and to appeal for support in the towns through which they passed, were a special form of demonstration intended to have a national impact. They required many weeks of careful preparation, collecting funds to supply boots for the marchers, enforcing a rigorous medical check to ensure that only those who were fit to stay the course took part . . . On this occasion, from the end of September onwards, contingents from Scotland, Lancashire, Yorkshire, the North-East Coast and elsewhere had been moving down the main roads toward London . . . On 27 October when the marchers reached Hyde Park and a crowd numbering some hundred thousand was there to welcome them, the mounted police made repeated baton charges, there was bitter fighting and many were hurt. In the days that followed the same thing was repeated in many London streets. The leaders of the NUWM were arrested and the great bundles of petition, which its sponsors claimed held a million signatures, were seized by the police and never reached their destination.[64]

In his diary, under 24 September, 1931 Nicolson remarked, after lunch with Stephen Spender: "Stephen is going bolshy like most of my young friends." Surveying the options available: democracy, fascism, "the Nazi experiment," Nicolson himself was at a loss to choose. Although convinced that democracy in Britain was nearly finished, he thought the English character unsuitable for the "discipline" of fascism. His leader, Oswald Mosley, disagreed and made his pilgrimage to Rome. In the October general election the National Government—effectively the Tories—won five times as many seats as the Labour opposition (incidentally wiping out Mosley's New Party). John Strachey, son of the editor of *The Spectator*, cousin of Lytton and James, situated firmly on the border between Bloomsbury and the aristocracy, later a friend of Guy Burgess and a Government Minister, had worked with Oswald Mosley first within the Labour Party and then, with Nicolson as well, in the New Party. But as Mosley moved right and Nicolson clung to the center, Strachey moved left. In 1931, according to Strachey's biographer, Strachey "chose communism because he felt nothing else would, or could, save what was best in western civilization . . . In 1931, he saw the situation in Manichaean colours: communism was the only chance of saving the world from fascism."[65]

By the end of the year, Strachey was one of the editors of the *Daily Worker*. When asked why he had gone in with the Communists, Strachey and many others might have replied with Thoreau: "What are you doing outside?" Strachey had become a Communist in all but the matter of carrying a Party card, but the Party was, and remained, unsure of him. As his Party mentor, Palme Dutt, commented to him:

> It is one thing to reach a certain intellectual agreement with the correctness of the communist analysis, as demonstrated by events. It is another thing to reach real revolutionary consciousness, so that the question of entering the revolutionary movement no longer appears as a question of making sacrifices, losing valuable opportunities of work etc., but, on the contrary, as the only possible basis of work and realization.[66]

Strachey did not take that final step. Most of his *The Coming Struggle for Power** is a replication of the historical narrative of *Capital* in the form of a series in *Spectator:* Marx for North Oxford, Bloomsbury and Belgravia.

Unemployment in Depression Britain peaked in January, 1933. Clement Attlee spoke at Cambridge "about child poverty in England, and his speech shocked many in his audience," including Burgess. When in March 1933 the Cambridge Union debated the abolition of the Means Test, "which we felt bore heavily on the unemployed," one young Union official remembered. "It was a grim debate. The suffering and semi-starvation in the outside world was beginning to be realized in the Union. The vote was carried."[67] The nearly continuous crisis of the previous half decade in Germany had culminated in Hitler's appointment as Chancellor at the end of January, the Reichstag fire a month later and Hitler's acquisition of dictatorial powers a month after that, nearly simultaneously with Franklin Roosevelt's inauguration and his famous "Fear itself" speech, which Nicolson, for one, took to be an assertion of Roosevelt's own intention to assume dictatorial powers if he thought it necessary. That Spring, Sir Stafford Cripps was calling for a socialist dictatorship in Britain if the Labour Party regained power.[68]

In the middle decades of the twentieth century both the Soviet Union and its dependent Communist parties (with the possible exception of that of Italy) and the United States and *its* dependent governments promulgated a monolithic view of Communism useful to both. But putting to one side the Fourth International, P.O.U.M. and such, Britain had two quite separate Communist traditions: an older, indigenous tradition stemming from William Morris's adaptation of the intellectual currents set in motion in England by the residence there of the Engels and the Marx family and the more familiar Leninist mode, introduced after the October Revolution and closely linked to Moscow. Sir Stafford Cripps, a wealthy intellectual

---

* Published in November, 1932, by Victor Gollancz, with whom Strachey would run The Left Book Club.

41

property rights lawyer, who was eventually Attlee's "Iron Chancellor" in the post-war Labour government, was perhaps the last important representative of the indigenous, democratic Communist tradition. Although Cripps' Socialist League was never politically significant—at best a sort of mirror image of Mosley's New Party— the English Communist tradition, which Morris had traced to John Ball's Rebellion, was and remains, a quite distinct coloring of thought on the Left in England. In the 1930s it made it possible to think of oneself as a Marxist and then, perhaps, as a Communist, without automatically adhering to Stalinism or thinking that Marxism was intrinsically Russian. After all, *Capital* had been written in London by a German. Like Strachey and, at some moments, Cripps, many British people were communists, but not members of the Communist Party—and no less revolutionarily inclined for that.

According to Sheila Grant Duff: "1932 was the year when it first became fashionable for the idealistic British Left to look with favour at Russia, a country which claimed to have solved the problems of slumps and unemployment.

> It was the year when David Low, the cartoonist, and Kingsley Martin, the Editor of the *New Statesman,* produced their *Russian Notebook,* when a delegation from the Fabian Society helped to inspire the Webbs' massive tome *Soviet Communism: A New Civilisation . . .*

Sheila Grant Duff went to Russia that summer with Goronwy Rees, visiting Moscow and Leningrad, factories and museums. "I left the Soviet Union little wiser than when I arrived, and still as prepared as before to defend its 'new civilization.'

> Russia was our hope of peace and our protection from poverty, for were not wars and unemployment the consequence of an economic system whose motive was private gain rather than public good? . . . I count myself fortunate to have had in my youth an ideal to believe in which still seemed realizable.[69]

Goronwy Rees had come out of a clergyman's home in Wales to dazzle Oxford, winning a place at All Souls and cutting a swathe through the available women there and those on the fringes of Bloomsbury. He left Sheila Grant Duff for Rosamond Lehmann and Lehmann for another. He, and Philip Toynbee were the Oxford, heterosexual, equivalents of Burgess: brilliant talkers, alcoholics in the making, destined for great things or, at least, destined to be leader writers for the more respectable newspaper. They, with Anthony Blunt and Donald Maclean, were Burgess's friends and drinking companions, off and on, from the early-1930s until 1951.

Cambridge itself had a quietly growing Communist presence that began in the sciences with dons like J. D. Bernal, who had visited Soviet Russia in 1931 and had collegial relations with Soviet scientists. It gradually became noticed by other dons that some of their outstanding undergraduates had become Communists. It is said of David Haden-Guest, a philosopher who would die in Spain, that his tutor, writing "to congratulate him on his brilliant first-class honours degree," commented: "I suppose you will celebrate your success in the usual way by attacking the 'lackeys of the Bourgeoisie', and being locked up for it."[70] Bernal added to the number of Communist undergraduates at Cambridge by recruiting his extraordinarily numerous (female) lovers and through his influence on other students, not all scientists, with whom he was less intimately, if, perhaps, more intensely, involved.

That summer, Burgess's room in New Court, close to the river and the beautiful Wren library, already held a collection of Marxist classics.[71] "Burgess's interest in socialism developed during his second year, prompted, he said, by his study of nineteenth-century European history . . . Burgess was elected to the Historical Society committee in November 1931—at the same meeting where Maurice Dobb addressed the members on communism, a talk followed by what the minute book recorded as an 'animated discussion.'"[72] Maurice Dobb was another recruiter for the Party, or, at least, for Communism. At the end of his second year, Burgess was awarded a

First in Part I of the History Tripos and was elected a Senior Scholar of Trinity.[73]

At about this time the as yet very small group of Cambridge Communists had decided to move from their isolation in the laboratories and their limited work with their comrades in the town to make "a more concentrated effort in the University itself."[74] To this end Haden-Guest founded the Marxist study group within the (non-Communist) Cambridge University Socialist Society.[75] The group had twenty-five members in 1932 and had affiliated with the Communist Party of Great Britain.* It was in this context that Burgess met James Klugmann, an undergraduate who was already a Party member, and began to read the standard fare of Marxist study groups: Lenin's *The State and Revolution* (given him by Haden-Guest), Marx's *The XVIIIth Brumaire of Louis Bonaparte, Class Struggles in France* and *The Civil War in France.*[76]

When, after a sabbatical year spent in Continental art galleries, Anthony Blunt, then already a Fellow of his college, returned to Cambridge in the autumn of 1933, he found "that Cambridge had been hit by Marxism and that most of my friends . . . including Guy Burgess . . . had either joined the Communist Party or were at least very close to it politically."[77] Half a dozen years later 1,000 students out of an undergraduate community of 7,000 would be members of the Cambridge Socialist Society.[78] Eric Hobsbawm, a bemused Kings undergraduate whose intellectual formation had taken place not at Eton but in the far tougher environments of Vienna and Berlin, recalled that a few years later, "As soon as I arrived, my politics had been discovered and I was immediately invited to join the Cambridge Student Branch of the Communist Party . . . We felt that what we wanted *personally* was not of interest to the Party, so long as it did not conflict with the Party line. But it was our duty not only to get good degrees but to bring Marxism into our work . . ."[79] That was one path that a would-be revolutionary could take, the pedagogical: Marcusianism before the Sixties.

---

* The treasurer was H. A. R. "Kim" Philby, then a Trinity undergraduate.

By then although politics was inescapable for Burgess and many other Cambridge undergraduates, it was as yet not all-consuming. Burgess and Blunt, already inseparable, frequently went down to London to the museums and galleries, discussing the pictures about which Blunt would write in *The Spectator*. On one of these expeditions Blunt fell in love with a badly damaged seventeenth-century painting of uncertain provenance, a *Rebecca and Eliezer at the Well*. He thought it was, as doubtfully advertised, by Poussin. It was priced at one hundred pounds. Blunt did not have a hundred pounds to spare and asked Victor Rothschild, who, of course, did, for a loan. Rothschild bought the painting and, in a characteristic gesture, perhaps thoughtful, asked Burgess to pick it up from Duit's gallery in Jermyn Street and deliver it to Blunt.[80] Burgess remained close to Rothschild for another decade, perhaps two, but is not otherwise recorded as delivering gifts on his behalf.

We have a description of Burgess, at age 22 already recognizably deploying one of the personae he would deploy for the rest of his life, picking up the young journalist Michael Burn at an undergraduate cocktail party in Trinity in the summer of 1933. "I was just finishing my book on Brooklands [motor raceway]," wrote Burn, "and wore a Brooklands tie clip."

> One of the guests [Burgess] came across the room and asked me how I had come by it. It turned out that racing cars were one of his passions. He invited me back to his rooms in College and I stayed the night . . . I saw him quite often during the ensuing years . . . He made no secret of being homosexual and a Marxist . . . He had blue eyes and tight wavy hair, was a good swimmer and looked menacingly healthy. I have seen his looks described as "boyish"; he did convey a dash of pertness and sham-innocence, as if he had just run away after ringing some important person's doorbell. Something still clung to him of his term as a 13-year-old at Dartmouth. His rolling, lurching walk gave the impression that he was about to charge into somebody or something, and go overboard . . . he was the most stimulating talker I had so far met . . . he was in love [w]ith Marxism; more

45

precisely with the Marxist interpretation of history . . . Gossip came next to Marxism and sex among his *plats du jour* . . . social gossip, political gossip, literary, especially homosexual, gossip; of which last there had been a high tide that very spring of 1933 in Cambridge . . .[81]

Burgess seemed set to receive good marks for Part Two of the History Tripos, but collapsed during finals, unable to finish, and was given an aegrotat (an ungraded degree awarded to those too ill to take finals but deemed to have deserved honors).[82] Burgess's tutors nonetheless awarded him the Earl of Derby's Studentship in Trinity College[83] and agreed that he could "return in the following autumn term to begin work on a thesis on the 'intellectual background of the Puritan Revolution.'"[84]

In part as the first leg of Blunt's journey to Rome for a sabbatical, Victor Rothschild drove Blunt, Burgess, Dadie Rylands and Anne Barnes[85] (who, although married to George Barnes, was in love with Rylands) to Monte Carlo in his Bugatti.[86] It was perhaps on this visit that Rylands formed his tutorial relationship with Somerset Maugham, who adopted him as an arbiter of prose style.[87] Later in the summer, Burgess joined Blunt in Rome, where Blunt was pursuing his studies at the British School. Ellis Waterhouse, the Librarian of the British School (and an old school friend of Blunt's), recalled: "We had a jolly interesting time. The trouble was that Burgess liked going to noisy places and I didn't. He was very funny and Anthony was devoted to him. He used to tell us stories about his adventures with politicians and young boys and Anthony and I used to decide they were probably untrue. He was the biggest liar in the western hemisphere [sic], you know. But they were very funny . . . [Politics] was all Guy wanted to discuss. He was exceedingly intelligent about politics and Anthony followed what he did . . ."[88]

Burgess returned to Cambridge in the autumn of 1933 as a research student, teaching and doing research as research students do. The career of that monumental Cambridge figure, George M. Trevelyan, Burgess's might-have-been *Doktorvater,* had begun with research into the Peasants' Rising and he would have found

Burgess's research interests sympathetic. Trevelyan had taught at the London Working Men's College and at this time he was still drifting slowly leftward from his Northumberland gentry and Macaulay/Trevelyan Liberal origins, with an abiding interest in the condition of the people and revolution—in regard to the latter, however, only in Italy.[89] If the German Revolution, because of poor weather, occurred indoors, as poetry, the orientation of much of the English intelligentsia leftward, in equally poor weather conditions, occurred first at least in Wren's library.

*   *   *

Finally, as the class struggle nears its decisive stage, disintegration of the ruling class and the old order of society becomes so active, so acute, that a small part of the ruling class breaks away to make common cause with the revolutionary class . . . Especially does this happen in the case of some of the bourgeois ideologists, who have achieved theoretical understanding of the historical movement as a whole.[90]

*   *   *

At the beginning of the 1933/4 academic year Cambridge was propelled into a new stage of left-wing activism by the arrival at Trinity of the seventeen-year-old John Cornford, as if some undergraduate Lenin had arrived at an academic Finland Station.[91] Cornford, the undergraduate orator, and the postgraduate James Klugmann, the Party organizer, transformed collegiate musings about the Marxist interpretation of history into *action,* that most typical Thirties ideal of political life. In what seemed to many to be a pre-revolutionary context—mass unemployment, enormous inequities in income and opportunities, a political structure closed to the vast majority of the population—some of the residents of the colleges had become uneasy, believing that they should do something, take some action, but not knowing what acton they should take. Cornford and Klugmann pointed the way forward: "to build a mass anti-Fascist movement among students; to form a big revolutionary Socialist organisation."[92]

Cornford was a handsome, magnetic, overwhelmingly focused scion of Cambridge intellectual aristocracy. When, a year earlier, at sixteen, "in his thinking if not in actual fact . . . [he] had become a Communist . . ." his mother, a poet and translator, wrote to ask if the term 'Hunger Marchers' was not sentimental and unjustified, he had answered:

> I think the Hunger Marchers were really hungry . . . B. Seebohm Rowntree calculates that the price of living for a family of 5—*without* considering *rates or rents*—is 31s. 8d. . . . once rents and rates have been deducted, it might be possible to buy enough food for the week: but there is still the cost of lighting and fuel, as well as occasionally doctors, unemployment insurance, etc. In Stoke some families that had been evicted erected huts out of their furniture, and stretched sheets on top. There were *fined 10s.* and told that it wasn't allowed. And the iniquity of the Means Test is that, while formerly the dole was fixed, so that wages had to be a few shillings above, or else no one would work, the new provision is that benefit shd. be below the rate of wages—so that where one employer is able to enforce a wage-cut, the benefit level in the whole district must come down.[93]

The adolescent Cornford, as much a Darwin as a Cornford classicist, having moved toward the Party during his final years in school at Stowe, had gone on to study at the London School of Economics, where he was a protégé of Frank Strauss Meyer, the American "founder of the student Communist Party movement in the UK."[94] An undisclosed informant told Richard Thistlethwaite of M.I.5 that Meyer taught Cornford "all he knew about Party discipline and organization. CORNFORD co-operated with MEYER on the Student Vanguard and then went to Cambridge where he set up a similar periodical called Cambridge Left."[95] It was in London that Cornford had become a Party militant, on the lines of Sartre's friend Nizan: the street corner and meeting hall orator as infant prodigy.

Cornford arrived at Cambridge with Ray Peters, a working class woman, with whom he had a child, separated from her and then began a liaison with Margot Heinemann, later a historian of the Communist Party, whose father was a banker.[96] Cambridge was soon to be in love with Rupert John Cornford, as it had been in love with his parents' friend Rupert Brooke. According to Peter Stansky and William Abrahams, the biographers of Cornford and Julian Bell: "The difficulty is that John was many-faceted, but preferred to behave as though he were not . . . Friends who knew him in one context took away a totally different impression from those who knew him in another."[97] But most knew him as, with Klugmann, the leader of Cambridge Communism, the orator of the famous photograph, the organizer of demonstrations. Cornford "was a zealous Communist; he was a dedicated Communist; he was also a Communist who enjoyed being a Communist . . . he had no interest in 'social life' as a diversion: he did not want to meet people, or go to parties . . . Personal relations, which are, after all, the important requisite for gossip . . . counted for very little with John . . ."[98] Cornford had no small talk. "When he determined to spend an evening 'working on the masses,' as he called it, he would come into someone's rooms with a muttered apology, and stand or shuffle in a painfully awkward way for a minute or two; then he plunged without preface into an argument on politics or Marxist theory, and quickly lost his uneasiness, talking well, even aggressively."[99] Cornford wrote for Cambridge publications, chalked slogans on pavements, argued, gave speeches, organized demonstrations and marches, helped break up Fascist demonstrations. "Of a whole generation of pioneer Communists in the Universities . . . [Cornford was] the most brilliant, the most sectarian, the most conspiratorial, the most devoted and full of animal energy, the most in need, at times, of a haircut and a shave."[100]

By all accounts Cornford's brief life was completely devoted to the Communist Party (with just enough left over for his studies and the two successive objects of his romantic affections). "Once," Victor Kiernan recalled, "When he was in a philosophical frame of mind I asked him what single thing in the universe gave him most satisfaction, and he answered, after thinking for a minute, 'the existence of the Communist International,'"[101] the Comintern. If Hobsbawm, Dobb, Bernal, followed the pedagogical revolutionary path, helping generations of students find their road to Marx, Cornford and Klugmann followed the Leninist path, *organizing* for the revolution.

An early victory for Cornford and Cambridge Communism came toward the end of 1933. Again according to Stansky and Abrahams, if "one were in search of a date to establish when many of the younger people turned Left, a good choice would be Saturday, November 11, 1933," Armistice Day.

> On that day, under the leadership of John Cornford and his friends, a variety of organizations, from pacifists to communists, joined forces in a manner that suggest the later Popular Front, and staged a massive anti-war demonstration in Cambridge . . . The Socialist Society and the Student Christian Movement joined forces to make the day more meaningful. There was to be a three-mile march through the town to the Cambridge war memorial, where a wreath would be placed, bearing the inscription, 'To the victims of the Great War, from those who are determined to prevent similar crimes of imperialism'. The words 'of imperialism' were removed by order of the police, who felt they were not conducive to maintaining the public peace. Even so, the day was tumultuous.

The demonstration brought together committed members of the Communist Party of Great Britain with others of the emerging student Left, including Julian Bell and Guy Burgess.

> Bell and Burgess were in Bell's Morris car. "I tried to use the Morris as an armoured car (stript of everything breakable)," he wrote to his brother, Quentin. The armour of the car was mattresses. Burgess navigated into the line of march, where "the hearties" pelted them with tomatoes. "But they made a couple of good charges at the enemy—'hearties' again, attempting to break up the parade—before they were ordered out by the police.

Julian merely changed his tactics, drove round through a circuitous route and rejoined the march towards its head."[102]

All good fun, and participation in such demonstrations, as would happen again in the Sixties, was an efficient entryway to other forms of political activity.

By December, Marxism was a discussion topic even at a meeting of the Apostles.[103] A couple of years later Julian Bell, recalled in an article in the *New Statesman & Nation*:

> By the end of 1933, we have arrived at a situation in which almost the only subject of discussion is contemporary politics, and in which a very large majority of the more intelligent undergraduates are Communists, or almost Communists. As far as an interest in literature continues it has very largely changed its character, and become an ally of Communism under the influence of Mr Auden's Oxford Group . . . It is not so much that we are all Socialists now as that we are all Marxists now. The burning questions for us are questions of tactics and method, and of our own place in a Socialist State and a Socialist revolution.[104]

It was around this time that the Cambridge Communists joined their work in "the town" with their work in "the colleges," by organizing the Trinity waiters to protest against a system in which they were hired at the beginning of each term and fired at the end, to live on the Dole until needed. Guy Burgess had some role in what turned out to be a successful "industrial action" as a result of which the waiters were given regular employment.[105] He worked with Cornford in other activities, including a protest against high rents for council house tenants and discussions with Indian nationalist students.[106] (Burgess at this time believed that the path to Socialism in Britain ran through the Indian independence movement. Or, as Sheila Grant Duff wrote: "All that I hated in Nazi Germany was at this very moment going on in British India: censorship, imprisonment, dictatorship, military rule for military purposes."[107]) Margot Heinemann recalled that at this time she had "joined the party because this was the organization that was trying to do

51

something about unemployment and fascism."

> We thought that everyone was winnable for the cause because capitalism was so obviously such a rotten system. Even Guy Burgess was on our side. I remember going on a march with him. He was wearing a Pitt Club yellow scarf singing, "One, two, Three, Four, Who are we for?, We are for the Working Class."[108]

As in the previous year, "At the time of the Hunger March of February 1934 . . .

> From all over the country groups of the unemployed were to march to London to protest against the inadequacies of the dole and other relief measures resorted to by the Government. The aim of the [Socialist] Society was to arouse a maximum of student support for the north-east coast contingent of marchers, who would be coming through Cambridge on their way to London . . . Several days before the advent of the marchers, meetings were held to explain their grievances, explaining again and again 'why students should be concerned with the militant working-class movement' . . . On the day, an advance party from the Society went out to Huntingdon to meet the marchers, and led them to Girton—the college farthest out from town—where a demonstration had been organized, and girl students handed out refreshments . . . Then the students and the unemployed formed up together and marched back down the long hill into Cambridge.[109]

Heineman wrote: "The hunger marchers were older men and very fragile. Their faces had fallen in and they had ill-fitting boots. After seeing them it was only a matter of time before I joined the party."[110]

Heinemann joined an organization that included, as we have seen, Haden-Guest, Klugmann, Cornford and Philby. Donald Maclean, at Trinity Hall, the son of a Liberal Cabinet Minister, became part of the central group of Cambridge Communists as soon as, if not slightly before, he arrived from Gresham's School, where he and Klugmann had been friends. At nearly six feet four inches in height, he was a highly visible presence in the marches and demonstrations of the period.[111] Alan Nunn May, a physicist, and a fellow Trinity Hall student, was also a member of the Party. By this time "even Guy Burgess" had joined the Party.

Of course for Burgess, in addition to politics there was research to attend to, not to mention affairs of the heart. Under the second heading, Burgess had been elected a Research Scholar by Trinity. Under the third, writing to Dadie Rylands ("Dadie dear") from Ascot Hill, Ascot, Berkshire,* during the 1934 Easter vacation, Burgess regretfully declined an invitation to accompany Rylands on another visit to the South of France ("I've been counting up my pennies . . . I have I find no money at all").

> I am very depressed indeed with no news of any kind and reading Blake about the man in the moon. Did you read Desmond [MacCarthy] on William Morris in the S-Times –I may cut article as [Basil] Willey – which book I am reading again and which seems so much a better thing than I could ever have attempted that I am in one way glad but in another sorry because if I do try and do anything on the subject his work is so good that it will be impossible not to think in his terms (having come near his matter) – So Dadie please write to me – it would be lovely if you said you wished I was coming and lovely if you told me the <u>news</u> –because I would <u>give anything</u> to come.
> Much love . . . Guy[112]

Two announcements then: a youthful love for Rylands (something routine for Rylands) and the end of Burgess's plans for a career of historical scholarship (also routine news for a don, paralleling a similar situation at the time for Julian Bell, who was failing to make progress with his postgraduate research on Alexander Pope).

---

* Apparently a country residence of his family at that time.

Burgess's article on Willey's book (*The Seventeenth Century Background: Studies in the Thought of the Age in Relation to Poetry and Religion*) had in fact appeared the previous week in *The Spectator*. "The Seventeenth Century Synthesis," begins: "English historians have not as a rule been attracted to the writing of histories of English Thought, but for no period has this neglect been so marked as for the seventeenth century."[113] This period was important for Burgess as when "the proper study of mankind became for the first time Man, and not God." Burgess then turns to his review: "Mr. Willey, in a brilliant book, has examined the nature of this change in attitude, has isolated the general restatement that the seventeenth century put forward, and has considered the relation between this change and the literature of the period." Burgess touches on Kant, Chillingworth, saints Thomas Aquinas and Augustine, Francis Bacon and Duns Scotus, Thomas Browne, David Hume and the Cambridge Platonists: a fairly comprehensive reading list. He concludes, as he had begun, with compliments:

It rests to be said that the style and attitude of Mr. Willey's book are extremely pleasant: there is the sense of excitement and of conquest which is so often the unique gift of an untouched subject. There is also something finer and more rare, a sense of intellectual responsibility as well to the present as to the past, an integrity which justifies one in placing Mr. Willey's book on the thought of the seventeenth century in the same rank as Leslie Stephen's classic for that of the eighteenth.

Burgess's farewell to early modern scholarship established his qualifications to have pursued that endeavor. Its publication in *Spectator* placed him in the intellectual journalistic world of Bloomsbury as "in many ways an original and serious historian."[114] He was not quite 23 years old.

That spring, Julian Bell's dissertation had finally been rejected by King's College (despite the fact that one of the two readers was a family friend, Roger Fry) and John Cornford had published a kind of revolutionists creed in the journal *Cambridge Left:* "The Struggle for Power in Western Europe." Austrian Social Democracy had been destroyed by Dollfuss; Hitler had come to power, but had not yet completely done away with either the Weimar Constitution or the Communist Party of Germany; the Spanish Civil War was in its earliest phases. Cornford summarized that extremely unstable—and unpromising—situation and laid down the doctrine of the Popular Front, the armed struggle, the correctness of the "line" of the Communist International. "The absolute necessity of revolutionary leadership for a successful armed struggle is made clearer than ever before to the European working class. And as the decisive struggles rapidly approach, so by the example of the Austrian movement will the working class gather strength in its own power to overthrow capitalism by direct struggle, and throw aside the gentlemen who prefer the 'democratic' road to Fascism to the revolutionary road to Soviet Power."[115] This rhetorical manner, steeped in that of Marx, might be called the analytical predictive, casting an analysis of the conditions of the present into pictures of the future, and seeking to buttress the authority of the analysis with the picture so painted. The times were such that Cornford was not much more radical than Stafford Cripps, M.P., who, in a pamphlet called *Forward to Socialism* was callng for "the radical reform of the machinery of government, a five-year plan of socialization, and an alliance with Soviet Russia."[116]

Kim Philby, who had graduated with a good degree in economics, told his tutor Maurice Dobb that he would like to contribute to the anti-fascist struggle. Dobb gave him introductions to acquaintances in Paris—members of the Willi Münzenberg—Otto Katz circle of the Comintern. They sent him on to Vienna, where he stayed until the following Spring, observing, if not participating in, the failed working-class revolt there and marrying Litzi Friedmann, a Communist activist, whom he helped emigrate to Britain. Litzi Philby's friend, the photographer and Comintern talent spotter, Edith Tudor-Hart, was already there. (Tudor-Hart was sufficiently important in the Austrian Communist Party-in-exile in London to be under continuous surveillance by M.I.5.[117])

Burgess became friends with Isaiah Berlin and Goronwy Rees at the beginning of the 1934 Summer term. There was then a dinner, often mentioned in memoirs of the time, at the Oxford home of Felix Frankfurter, who was spending a year as the Eastman Professor. Burgess was staying with Maurice Bowra, the famous Oxford talent-spotter. According to A. J. Ayer's biographer, Ben Rogers, the dinner party included "Freddie" and Renée Ayer, Goronwy Rees, Isaiah Berlin and Bowra. "Talking twenty-five years later, Frankfurter remembered these Oxford friends as an 'extremely clever, almost excessively clever young crowd'."[118]

> [T]here was a dispute between Isaiah, Freddie Ayer, Guy Burgess . . . and the lawyer Sylvester Gates as to whether Wittgenstein's dictum 'Whereof one cannot speak, thereof one must be silent' occurred once or twice in the *Tractatus*. Ayer and Berlin said it was once; Gates said it was twice. Bets were taken, and a taxi was dispatched to Freddie's rooms to procure a copy of the sacred text. It revealed that Wittgenstein had in fact pronounced the sentence twice: once in the preface, once in the conclusion. Both Ayer and Berlin paid up.[119]

Rees took to Burgess at once:

> After dinner they walked back to All Souls together and drank whisky in the deserted smoking room late into the night – the first of many such evenings over a bottle of Jameson's . . . They talked, according to Rees, about the relation of painting to the Marxist interpretation of history and about the busmen's strike Burgess was helping to organize in Cambridge and [Rees] found that there was "something which was, as it were, his very own, in everything he had to say."[120]

It was to be a long-lasting, fatal, friendship.

There are three letters from Burgess to Isaiah Berlin at Oxford from September, 1934. Two describe arrangements for a visit by

Burgess to Berlin at All Souls,* the third, what appears to be the beginning of a regular correspondence in Burgess's usual style, mixing gossip and more serious considerations.

Dear Shaya –

I have tried to write before – but thought perhaps if I waited I might think of something to say. This has not occurred. I did enjoy myself – as always – very much indeed – tho' having not lived in society – only because there now is none – in Cambridge I fear I was exhausted & dull – I wish there had been more discussion of your book – I do feel so very strongly that to isolate the development of thought from history – even in the service of making a set[?] of dual process of it – is so difficult & in the case of social thought impossible – You cannot I think talk about either the Revisionists or the Fabians without talking about the change in the incomes of England & Germany home[?] industry to foreign investment – which I know you know – however this can't be gone into now – I hope your week end was not ruined – as of course A's & mine couldn't have been – by Victor's absence – Thank you very much – Love Guy

[p.s.:] I have been reading Bernal too – it seems to me of course that a non-technical book can be written on a technical subject – I personally would prefer to read Tawney on the history of England to Trevelyan – but I think B's essay is irritating –[121]

"Victor," in these circles, was always Rothschild.

Anthony Blunt recalled that political activity in Cambridge was ever-increasing that year, whipped forward by James Klugmann and John Cornford evangelizing the undergraduates for the Communist Party: Cornford making speeches, Klugmann organizing.[122] V. G. Kiernan remembered that Burgess was also a well-known member of the group, busy converting the undergraduate "masses."

---

* One of these includes the information that "Kim Philby is here (tell Maurice [Bowra]) staying with me – having been fighting in Austria," which seems to imply that Berlin knew Philby.

Guy Burgess was one of those – James Klugmann and John Cornford were the chief – who helped to induct me into the Party. We belonged to the same college, and hence to the same 'cell'. I remember Burgess as a rather plump, fresh-faced youth, of guileless, almost cherubic expression. I heard him spoken of as the most popular man in the college, but he must have suffered from tensions; he smoked cigarettes all day, and had somehow imbibed a notion that the body expels nicotine very easily. He told me once a story that had evidently made a deep impression on him – of a Hungarian refugee who had been given shelter at his home, a formerly ardent political worker reduced to a wreck by beatings on the soles of the feet. I came on Burgess one day in his room sitting at a small table, a glass of spirits in front of him, glumly trying to put together a talk for a cell meeting that evening; he confessed that when he had to give any sort of formal talk he felt foolish.[123]

During the long vacation of 1934 Burgess went to Russia with an Oxford Communist, Derek Blaikie, on a trip organized—but not participated in—by Goronwy Rees, who already had made the trip in 1932.[124] On the way out they stopped in Hamburg and in "the night, from their comfortable berths on board ship, they heard distant shooting. It was the night of June 30th, 1934—Hitler's 'night of the long knives.'"[125] In his conversations with Tom Driberg in Moscow many years later, Burgess, speaking, perhaps, from his experience in mid-century Russia rather than during that student visit twenty years earlier, claimed that he had arrived at a clear-eyed, realistic view of life in Stalin's Russia, its limitations and potential, and that when he got back to England he had reported on his visit from that point of view to the Cambridge Communists.

That August of 1934, Burgess again wrote to Rylands from Ascot Hill, this a very long, broken-hearted amendment to his earlier letter. Burgess now told Rylands that the reason he did not wish to travel with his party to the South of France was not a lack of funds. He said that he had a first understood that it would be a small group, and himself: "For as far as I can remember we originally arranged to go this summer to the S. of France almost a year ago. The party as it then stood was I think you and Artie[126] and myself and we were to have the type of holiday we did not have last year and I looked forward to it enormously." Then the party had gradually expanded, to include, among others, Anne Barnes, whose behavior (and even more that of Victor Rothschild) the previous summer had apparently been anti-social. (Anne Barnes's husband George, like Burgess had attended Dartmouth and Cambridge, then taught at the former and during Burgess's time at Trinity was Assistant Secretary to the Cambridge University Press.[127]) "And this situation was of course made hardly bearable by the fact that it existed in the S. of France in relation to the sort of life we were living there, and not only because of the evenings . . . all I mean of course is that on a holiday, which must exist so largely purely within personal relations, I thought I would be miserable." As the group became larger Burgess's feeling that he would be unhappy deepened. He then decided to go to Rylands and make his feelings clear.

> And so I wrote to you - - but when I wrote I said I had been very worried and asked you to write back if you did not understand. You did not do so. I continued to worry and came anxiously to Cambridge to try to see and talk to you. I think it was both unfriendly and unkind of you to do what you did which was more or less to refuse to see me. I had thought you would know how fond I was of you and would realize how anxious I would be or at least have been prepared to talk [and?] not to have hurt me with so little knowledge of what had happened.

Burgess was clearly in love with Rylands and now crushed by his indifference. As young people do in such situations, Burgess apologized: "I know that I can behave in a way that appears inconsiderate to my friends . . . but I thought you knew . . . that I do try to live up to my affections for people." Finally, having written himself out of sorrow and apologies for Ryland's lack of consideration, he turns to practical arrangements:

> When I wrote to you refusing to go to France I had no other plans at all. When I came up to Cambridge I had none, but I met

Victor [Rothschild] he asked me when I was going to France as
he was going . . . with Gerald. I said I wasn't and he said would
I come . . . There then seemed no reason why I shouldn't go with
him, since the choice [then] was simply between doing so and
staying at home with my family, with whom I do not get on.
This means that if I go – which is probable – we shall be in
France at the same time. Whether we meet and do things in the
evening depends on you. We need not even probably meet
unless you choose. But I do hope, after this letter, you will and
that something of the holiday I originally looked forward to will
happen. Love Guy.

[Postscript at top:] A bad letter – but if you're in London before
the 4th I'd love to see you—could you let Douglas[128] know I may
be staying near him?

Burgess's family, with whom that summer he did not at this time
get on, was limited to his mother, his younger brother Nigel and their
stepfather, Lieutenant Colonel Bassett, Burgess's maternal
grandfather, the de facto head of the family, having died about this
time. The step-father was the problem.

One day in the summer of 1934 Kim Philby had a talk with a
man, whom, at the recommendation of Edith Tudor-Hart, he had met
in London's Regent's Park. Arnold Deutsch was a middle class
Viennese, about thirty years old, who held a doctorate in Chemistry
from the University of Vienna. He spoke German, English, French,
Italian, Dutch and Russian. He was the *beau ideal* of the Comintern
intellectual revolutionary: highly educated, middle class, charming
and not Russian. During their park bench talk Deutsch invited
Philby to become a "deep penetration agent." Philby was to publicly
terminate his association with the Communist Party, Communists
and Communist sympathizers and pursue a career that would put him
in a position of influence in Britain. Philby, then Maclean, then
Burgess, then Blunt, agreed to do so. (According to Modin,
Burgess's meeting with Deutsch, characteristically, was in a pub, not

a park.) Later Burgess, or perhaps Blunt, brought in John Cairncross, a brilliant, unclubbable Scott. And then, perhaps, Goronwy Rees. They were among at least twenty people in Britain Deutsch recruited for the Comintern.[129] This was another way to be a revolutionary.

In the autumn of 1934 Michael Whitney Straight, a wealthy American who had been studying at the London School of Economics, arrived at Trinity College.

> On my first evening there . . . I wandered into a candlelight service in Kings College Chapel. I sat, staring at the stone columns that arched upward into the darkness and listening to the thin voices of the boys choir. It was a new world for me; I was alone in it and in awe of it; I was content.[130]

One evening that November, "Two students in black gowns stood in my doorway. One had a birdlike head and manner; his name was James Klugman [sic]. The other had black, curly hair, high check bones, and dark, deep-set eyes. His entire body was taut; his whole being seemed to be concentrated upon his immediate purpose. His name was John Cornford."[131] Klugmann and Cornford were there to recruit Straight ostensibly for the Cambridge Socialist Society, but actually for the Communist Party. He immediately joined the one, then the other. Straight also became a significant financial contributor to the Party. He told his mother:

> I'd lived in fear that I was incapable of loving. Now I've learned that I'm able to love the Communist students . . . I'm filled with a violent, uncontrollable love for [Cornford, Klugmann and Dobb]; an extraordinary sense of comradeship . . . James in particular is so delightful. I've been with him and Whitney's friend Guy Burgess and an art historian named Anthony Blunt all evening. Now at half past eleven I sit here and try to describe the terrible significance of it all."[132]

Michael Whitney Straight, as viewed from Moscow, was part of the network.

We can assume that Deutsch and his colleagues and successors maintained contact with their British recruits. As how this was done, and by whom, is explained at great length by many experts, few of whom agree about either how it was done or by whom, we can at least assume it *was* done. It is possible, indeed, that the network was maintained by Burgess. The website of the Foreign Intelligence Service of the Russian Federation includes a few dozen short biographies of historical figures of interest to the Russian Foreign Intelligence Service and, presumably, to its predecessors. That concerning Guy Burgess includes the statement that he, "having extensive connections in government, parliamentary and military circles, actively contributed to the career development of other agents in London residency, and also *served to connect them to the intelligence network*."[133] (Emphasis added.) There seems no reason to doubt this.

Burgess lingered in Cambridge through Michaelmas Term, 1934. According to V. G. Kiernan, he was still active in the Trinity College Communist group in October "and was giving talks on Marxist interpretations of history at the Trinity History Society,"[134] but shortly thereafter he resigned his Party membership.[135]

Notes to Chapter Two

[1] Hart, Lieutenant General H. G. (edited by his son). The New Annual Army List, Militia List and Yeomanry Cavalry List, for 1896. London: John Murray, Albemarle Street, 1896, p. 661.

[2] Lean, E. Tangye. The Napoleonists: A Study in Political Disaffection 1760/1960. London: Oxford University Press, 1970, p. 346.

[3] Albemarle Villas is a group of detached stucco houses described in Pevsner's Buildings of England. "The first scattered group of villas and terraces occupying choice positions on elevated sites overlooking Stonehouse Creek and the Docks appeared circa 1825. They display the same neo-classical spirit as the new urban centres of Plymouth and Devonport. The best group is near the junction of Paradise Road and Devonport Road. Albemarle Villas by Foulston, a string of eight neat detached stucco houses set en echelon, two or three bays wide with side entrances and a pretty variety of Grecian ironwork full verandas, garden gates and railings." The Burgess house has two reception rooms, five bedrooms, and views of the sea.

[4] www.geocities.com/layedwyer/gillman.htm accessed 24 July 2010. (The Portsmouth bank, Grant, Gillman & Long did business from 1846 to 1887. It successor was taken over by Lloyds Bank Ltd. in 1903. See: www.banknotes4u.co.uk/private_bank_chq.htm accessed 24 July 2010)

[5] Lean, p. 345.

[6] Gillman family information: "Angus George Gillman was a Major in the Royal Field Artillery who died on 29/04/1917 at the age of 34. He is buried at Ecoivres Military Cemetery, Mont-St Eloi. He was the son of William and Maud Gillman, of Portsmouth. In Kelly's 1912 Directory William Gillman is shown as a JP living at 47 Clarence Parade, Southsea. William and Maud Gillman paid for this memorial to their son in the form of a reredos and lancet window in the Cathedral which in 1920 was still St Thomas's Parish Church. The memorial was dedicated on 29th February 1920. The installation of the various aspects of the memorial took place at the same time as some structural work was being carried out by the architect. During this operation original parts of the early church were uncovered including the lancet window which was incorporated into the memorial. The stained glass image in the window depicts Major Gillman as St George kneeling before Christ. In the late 1920s William and Maud Gillman were asked to fund further modifications to the east

end of the church which they appeared pleased to do.   It is not known when the reredos was removed and placed in store.   Major Gillman is one of 81 names to appear on the World War 1 Memorial outside the Cathedral and he is listed on the Guildhall Square Cenotaph.   The Gillman Family Grave   The Gillman family grave is in Highland Road Cemetery. There is a memorial to Major Gillman on the headstone, part of which reads as follows: "Maud Gillman, died 27th January 1927, aged 67. Also of William Gillman J.P., husband of the above, died 11th November 1935, Aged 82 years. Also Angus George Gillman M.C., Major Royal Field Artillery, Their only son, Served in France 1914 - 1917, Killed at Vimy 29th April 1917, Aged 34."
www.memorials.inportsmouth.co.uk/churches/cathedral/gillman.htm
7 William Gillman's funeral was attended by a cousin of Evelyn Burgess, Rear-Admiral Grant, five Justices of the Peace and other gentry. He left his granddaughter a sufficient fortune that nearly 150,000 pounds remained at her death in 1964. Lean, E. Tangye. The Napoleonists: A Study in Political Disaffection 1760/1960. London: Oxford University Press, 1970, p. 347.
8 At current valuations the Plymouth and West Meon houses together would bring well over two million pounds.
9 Barden, Ruth J.D. A History of Lockers Park: Lockers Park School, Hemel Hempstead, 1874 – 1999. Sacombe Press, Ltd., n.d.
10 Eton college Chronicle, Thursday, October 6, 1927, No. 2026.
11 The quotation and much of what follows about Eton is from Robert Skidelsky's description of John Maynard Keynes's Eton in Skidelsky, Robert. John Maynard Keynes: Hopes Betrayed 1883-1920, New York: Penguin Books, 1983, pp. 74ff. Although they belonged to different generations, Eton was not given to rapid change and Burgess, like Keynes, left it "very recognizably the adult he was to be for the rest of his life."
12 Collini, Stefan. "On the Lower Slopes," review of Shades of Greene: One Generation of an English Family by Jeremy Lewis. London Review of Books, 5 August 2010, p. 8.
13 Bloch, Michael. James Lees-Milne: The Life. London: John Murray, 2009, p. 20.
14 Bloch, p. 20.
15 Eton Vikings Club, The Eaton Boating Book, Third Edition, Eton: Spottiswoode, Ballantyne & Co. Ltd., 1933, p. 598.
16 "'Sending Up For Good': No boy is to be sent up for good who has been

other than punctual and well conducted during the School-time."
Meritorious exercises showing industry, accuracy and ability in a. Any
literary subject. B. Mathematics or Science. C. Drawing or Music." The
Eton Calendar for the Lent School-Time, 1927, p. 135.

[17] "In 1929 HN Gladstone offered to found a prize in memory of his father,
the prime minister, William Gladstone. He suggested it be for political
economy and finance, but the Provost wrote to say that it would be best if
the exhibition be awarded to "some deserving boy" on the results of the July
Examination and unrestricted as to subject as it would be difficult to include
Political Economy and Finance in the examinations as they were not school
subjects. This was agreed and it was further agreed that it be for £100 for a
year and held at the University (i.e., Oxford or Cambridge). There would be
no fund invested as the payment would be made to Eton annually from the
Gladstone Memorial Fund. The final terms were that the boy also had to
have a good Eton record, regard being had both to his performance in the
July Exam. And to his need of assistance at the university." Personal
communication from Mr. John Browne-Swinburne through the kindness of
Mr. Peter Steel.

[18] Personal communication from Mrs. P. Hatfield, Eton College Archivist,
August 5, 2010 and Driberg, Tom. Guy Burgess: A Portrait with
Background. London: Weidenfeld and Nicolson, 1956, p. 10.

[19] Boyle, Andrew. The Fourth Man: The Fourth Man: The Definitive
Account of Kim Philby, Guy Burgess, and Donald Maclean and Who
Recruited Them to Spy for Russia. The Dial Press/James Wade, 1979, p.
79.

[20] Quoted in Driberg, p. 11.

[21] Nicolson, Nigel. Long Life: Memoirs, London: Phoenix, 1997, p. 58.

[22] As late as 1930 he listed his mother as his closest relative: Address of
Parent or Guardian Mrs. Bassett, West Lodge, West Meon, Hants. Eton
College Chronicle, No. 2123, p. 783.

[23] National Archive, UK, 9 November 1917, letter from Wingate (Arbur,
Cairo) FO 882/8, IS/17/21.

[24] National Archive, UK, 19 November 1917, letter from Bassett FO 882/8,
IS/17/23.

[25] National Archive, UK, 15 December 1917, telegram from Cox, Baghdad
to High Commissioner, Cairo, FO 882/8, IS/17/26.

26 Bell, Julian. New Statesman & Nation, February 16, 1935, p. 224. Quoted in Stansky, Peter and William Abrahams. Journey to the Frontier: Two Roads to the Spanish Civil War. Little, Brown and Company. An Atlantic Monthly Press Book. Boston, 1966, p. 109. Bell had returned to Cambridge as a research student the term Burgess first went up to Trinity. He submitted a dissertation on Pope at the end of 1931, another in autumn 1933, but failed to obtain a fellowship. Stansky, Peter and William Abrahams. Journey to the Frontier: Two Roads to the Spanish Civil War. Little, Brown and Company. An Atlantic Monthly Press Book. Boston, 1966, pp. 85; 89; 97.

27 Hobsbawm, Eric. Interesting Times: A Twentieth Century Life. London: Allen Lane/Penguin, 2002, p. 110.

28 Hobsbawm, p. 110.

29 Hobsbawm, pp. 102-3.

30 Driberg, p. 17.

31 Carter, Miranda. Anthony Blunt: His Lives. London: Macmillan, 2001, p. 99. Runciman told Cherie Hughes: "I have no doubt that Cornford made an impact on Burgess first and then through Burgess on Blunt. I always had a soft spot for Guy. He was provocative but it was all done with a certain light-heartedness. Communism sat very strangely on him. But one didn't take it very seriously. But he was the only person who managed to explain Marxism to me in a way that made sense." In Penrose, Barrie and Freeman, Simon. Conspiracy of Silence: The Secret Life of Anthony Blunt. New York, Farrar Straus Giroux, 1987, p. 108.

32 Annan, Noel. The Dons: Mentors, Eccentrics and Geniuses. London: HarperCollins, 2000, pp.170ff.

33 Driberg, p. 15.

34 Then well known for his female roles on the Cambridge stage, later a well-known television actor.

35 Strachan, Alan. Secrets Dreams: A Biography of Michael Redgrave. London, Orion, 2004, p. 109.

36 Scrapbook relating to Michael Redgrave's performances at Clifton College (1923-25), ADC Theatre (1926-32), and Cranleigh School (1932-33). Victoria and Albert Theatre Collections Centre, Michael Redgrave Archive, THM/31/1/1/1. Rossetti's review of a work by Queenie Leavis, signed G.R., was taken by the Leavis's to be by George Rylands, ending their friendship.

[37] Strachan, Alan. Secrets Dreams: A Biography of Michael Redgrave. London, Orion, 2004, p. 109.

[38] British Library, ADD Ms. 88902/1.

[39] Skidelsky, Robert. John Maynard Keynes: Hopes Betrayed 1883-1920, New York: Penguin Books, 1983, p. 293.

[40] Stansky and Abrahams, p. 85.

[41] Hastings, Selina. The Secret Lives of Somerset Maugham: A Biography. New York: Random House, 2010, pp. 373-4. It could have been the next summer, no date is given.

[42] Blunt had been awarded a First at Trinity the previous year and would be elected to a fellowship the next for a dissertation on Italian artistic theory.

[43] British Library, ADD Ms. 88902/1, handwritten addition, page 14.

[44] From 1932 onwards Blunt wrote regular articles for The Spectator "As far as the speculation part of these articles were concerned, I relied a great deal on discussion with Guy. I often visited the exhibitions concerned with him and I have known few people with whom I have more enjoyed looking at pictures or buildings . . ." British Library, ADD Ms. 88902/1, handwritten addition, page 15.

[45] Deacon, Richard. The Cambridge Apostles: A history of Cambridge University's elite intellectual secret society. New York: Farrar, Straus & Giroux, 1985, p. 56.

[46] Deacon, pp. 66-7.

[47] Stansky and Abrahams, p. 91.

[48] "In October 1933, [Keynes met] Victor Rothschild . . . a scientist, more interested in driving fast cars and collecting books and pictures than in politics. Maynard was soon dining with victor and his wife Barbara, daughter of St John and Mary Hutchinson, at their family residence, Palace House, in Newmarket, full of pictures of horses . . ." Skidelsky, p. 495.

[49] Taylor, p. 284.

[50] Branson, Noreen and Margot Heinemann. Britain in the 1930's. New York, Praeger Publishers, 1971, pp. 154; 209.

[51] Branson and Heinemann, pp. 146-7.

[52] Branson and Heinemann, pp. 20-1.

[53] Taylor, A. J. P. English History: 1914-1945. Oxford University Press, New York, 1965, p. 317. This sort of statement returned as farce in the autumn of 2010.

[54] Taylor, p. 184.

[55] Taylor, p. 308.

[56] Branson and Heinemann, p. 52.

[57] Rees, Jenny. Looking for Mr Nobody: The Secret Life of Goronwy Rees. London: Phoenix, Orion, 1997, p. 55.

[58] My late mother-in-law was one of these. Her great-grandmother had worn a brass collar, proclaiming that she was the property of the mine in which she worked.

[59] Tom Jones quoted in Branson and Heinemann, p. 159.

[60] A set of policies embraced by the British coalition government, with more ideological consistency, in 2010.

[61] Taylor, p. 285.

[62] Nicolson, Harold. Diaries in The Vita Sackville-West and Harold Nicolson manuscripts, letters and diaries [microform]: from Sissinghurst Castle, Kent, the Huntington Library, California, and other libraries, reel 13, p. 142. Omitted from published editions of Nicolson's diaries.

[63] Taylor, p. 349.

[64] Branson and Heinemann, pp. 28-9.

[65] Thomas, Hugh. John Strachey. New York: Harper & Row, 1973, pp. 111-2.

[66] Thomas, p. 123.

[67] Carter, p. 107.

[68] Burgess, Simon. Stafford Cripps: A Political Life. London: Victor Gollancz, 1999, pp. 80-1.

[69] Grant Duff, Sheila. The Parting of the Ways: A Personal Account of the Thirties. Peter Owen: London, 1982, pp. 43-5.

[70] The tutor was not Bernal. Brown, Andrew. J. D. Bernal: The Sage of Science. Oxford: Oxford University Press, 2005, p. 108.

[71] Blunt, in his unpublished memoir, claims that Burgess's history tutor regarded Burgess as the most brilliant man of his year.

[72] Costello, John. Mask of Treachery. New York, William Morrow and Company, 1988, p. 203. There is no reason to suspect that Costello invented this detail.

[73] Driberg, p. 15.

[74] Stansky and Abrahams, p. 104.

[75] Stansky and Abrahams, p. 205.

[76] Driberg, p. 19.

[77] British Library, ADD Ms. 88902/1, handwritten addition, page 17.

[78] Cecil, Robert. A Divided Life: A Biography of Donald Maclean. London: The Bodley Head, 1988, p. 24.

[79] Hobsbawm, p. 111-113.

[80] This version of a famous story is from Carter, p. 87.

[81] Burn, Michael. Guy Burgess: The spy who loved me and the traitor I almost unmasked

The Times (London) May 9, 2003
www.timesonline.co.uk/tol/life_and_style/article882580.ece?token=null&of fset=12&page=2, accessed 20 August 2010.

[82] It is not unlikely that Burgess's papers were marked by Trevelyan himself, who was "an assiduous examiner" in these years: Cannadine, David. G. M. Trevelyan: A Life in History. London: Penguin Books, 1992, p. 216.

[83] Personal communication, Jonathan Smith, Archivist, Trinity College.

[84] Carter, pp. 102-3.

[85] See Annan, p. 191.

[86] Carter, p. 102.

[87] Hastings, pp. 373-4.

[88] Penrose, Barrie and Freeman, Simon. Conspiracy of Silence: The Secret Life of Anthony Blunt. New York, Farrar Straus Giroux, 1987, pp. 106-7.

[89] Cannadine, p. 14

[90] From the Communist Manifesto, quoted in Cornford, John. "Left?", in Sloan, Pat. editor. John Cornford: A Memoir. Fife: Borderline Press, 1978 reprint of 1938 Jonathan Cape, p. 123.

[91] "While external events played their role in creating an appetite for left-wing politics at Cambridge, the reason why 'Marxism hit Cambridge' in the autumn of 1933 was largely because the small Communist group at the university was taken over by two determined and persuasive young men from Trinity: James Klugmann, a postgraduate, and John Cornford, a first-year undergraduate." Carter, p. 109.

[92] Sloan, p. 100 quoted in Stansky and Abrahams, p. 210.

[93] Stansky and Abrahams, p. 185.

[94] National Archives, UK, Frank Strauss Meyer file, KV2/3501) 28/01/1931-03/08/1955.

[95] National Archives, UK, Christopher Cornford File, KV 2/1997. John Cornford's responsibility for the Left Review is also noted on his own file card in KV 5/119.

96 Heinemann later lived and had a daughter with J. D. Bernal. Cornford's son was raised by Cornford's parents and had a distinguished career in progressive organizations. (Personal communication from Peter Stansky.)

97 Stansky and Abrahams, p. 208.

98 Stansky and Abrahams, p. 217.

99 Kiernan, Victor. "Recollections," in Sloan, p. 116.

100 A Group of Contemporaries. "Cambridge Socialism, 1933-1936" in Sloan, p. 95.

101 Kiernan, p. 120.

102 Stansky and Abrahams, pp. 106-8.

103 Carter, p. 112.

104 Bell, Julian. New Statesman & Nation, February 16, 1935, p. 224. Quoted in Stansky and Abrahams, p. 109.

105 Driberg, p. 20.

106 Driberg, p. 22.

107 Grant Duff, p. 104,

108 In Penrose and Freeman, p. 98.

109 Stansky and Abrahams, pp. 214-5.

110 In Penrose and Freeman, p. 98.

111 Robert Cecil's biography of Maclean is useful: Cecil, Robert. A Divided Life: A Biography of Donald Maclean. London: The Bodley Head, 1988. However, his belief that Maclean had been seduced at Cambridge by Burgess was violently denied by the latter, who was not in the habit of denying his conquests.

112 The Papers of George Humphrey Wolferstan Rylands, GBR/0272/PP/GHWR/3/73, King's College Archive Centre, Cambridge.

113 The Spectator, March 23, 1934, p. 466.

114 Deacon, p. 116. From 1932 onwards Anthony Blunt wrote regular articles for The Spectator "As far as the speculation part of these articles were concerned, I relied a great deal on discussion with Guy. I often visited the exhibitions concerned with him and I have known few people with whom I have more enjoyed looking at pictures or buildings; but basically my ideas [then] conformed to the art for art's sake doctrine advanced by Bloomsbury." British Library, ADD Ms. 88902/1, handwritten insert, p. 15.

[115] Cornford, John. "The Struggle for Power in Western Europe," in Sloan, pp.147-8.

[116] Burgess, Simon. Stafford Cripps: A Political Life. London: Victor Gollancz, 1999, p. 91.

[117] National Archive, Kew, KV 2/1012-14. In the summer of 1951 the British secret intelligence services seem to have realized that Litzi Philby, with her Comintern connections, on the one hand, and Edith Tudor-Hart's photography enterprise, on the other, may have had some role in the conveyance of documents from London to Moscow.

[118] Rogers, Ben. A. J. Ayer: A Life. New York: Grove Press, 1999, p. 111.

[119] Ignatieff, Michael. Isaiah Berlin: A Life. London: Chatto & Windus, 1998, p. 82.

[120] Rees, Jenny. Looking for Mr Nobody: The Secret Life of Goronwy Rees. London: Phoenix, Orion, 1997, p. 71.

[121] MS. Berlin 103, Bodleian, Oxford. Colin Harris, the Superintendent of the Special Collections Reading Rooms, Department of Special Collections, far exceeded any reasonable expectations in sifting the Berlin correspondence for traces of Burgess.

[122] Blunt's memoir. British Library, ADD Ms. 88902/1.

[123] Kiernan, V. G. V.G. Kiernan on Treason, London Review of Books, vol. 9 No.12, 25 June 1987, pp. 3-5.

[124] Rees, Jenny, p. 62.

[125] Driberg, p. 29. Blaikie, born Derek Kahn, was a friend of Isaiah Berlin and the previous year had been included in the latter's Portofino vacation plans.

[126] Arthur Marshall, actor, school teacher and writer who had a long affair with Rylands. See Annan, p. 190.

[127] West, W. J. Truth Betrayed. London: Duckworth, 1987, p. 45.

[128] Perhaps the actor Douglas Seale.

[129] Deutsch had been a member of the Communist Party of Austria since 1924; working for the Comintern from 1928 as a courier and "agent-svyaznika," helping maintain the network, he had traveled to Romania, Greece, Syria, and Palestine. In 1932 he had joined the Foreign Section of the NKVD as an "illegal," a secret intelligence agent working without diplomatic protection. He moved to London in February, 1934, where he became a member of the psychological faculty of the University of London.

Also in 1934, Deutsch helped recruit a cypher clerk in the British Foreign Office. Deutsch was recalled to Moscow in September, 1937. In 1942 he was sent to do illegal work in the Western Hemisphere. The ship that was carrying him was torpedoed by a German submarine and all aboard died. See: http://svr.gov.ru/history/dejch.htm for Deutsch and for Philby http://svr.gov.ru/smi/2004/bratishka20040125.htm. These are publications of the Foreign Intelligence Service of the Russian Federation accessed on May 21, 2011.

130 Straight, Michael. After Long Silence. W. W. Norton & Company, Inc.: New York, 1983, p. 57.

131Straight, p. 59.

132 Straight, pp. 70-1. Straight dates this to the fall of 1935, but it is more probably the fall of 1934. Whitney Straight, Michael Straight's brother, was a race car driver and later an RAF fighter pilot and war hero. It is interesting that Michael Straight connected Burgess with his brother. Perhaps they met at Broadlands or the RAC.

133 http://svr.gov.ru/history/ber.htm

134 Kiernan, V. G., letter quoted in Carter, p. 113.

135 Driberg, p. 22.

Chapter Three

London Talks

> He was very much at loose ends . . . he had no
> definite place in life, in society; and he was not at all
> sure, now that he had not been made a Fellow of
> King's, of what he wanted to do. He thought of
> finding some sort of temporary job in London . . .[1]

Thus his biographers on Julian Bell in the summer of 1934.
Change "King's" to "Trinity" and it would fit Guy Burgess's
situation when he went down to London at the beginning of 1935.
He was not sure which way to turn. He seems to have put his name
in as a tutor at Eton, but was not offered a position.[2] He was too old
to take the Foreign Office examination; it was too late to follow
Philby, Spender and John Lehmann to Vienna, too early to go to
Spain. One weekend while Burgess was thinking about possible
careers, he went to stay at a Rothschild country house, Tring Park, a
home of the widowed Mrs. Charles Rothschild and her children,
much frequented by her son Victor's friends. Burgess remembered
that

> At the dinner-table there was much talk of world politics: the
> house of Rothschild had been deeply disturbed by Hitler's
> accession to power . . . Mrs. Rothschild complained that [the
> British Rothschild bank staff] were out of touch with the realities
> of the modern world, and that she had lost a good deal of money
> since 1931 . . .

Mrs. Rothschild, born Rozsika Edie von Wertheimstein, was
Hungarian: beautiful, athletic, interested in politics; said to read each
morning the principal European and English newspapers with that

familiar Hungarian linguistic facility. She had been impressed, no doubt, by Burgess's knowledge of current events and his way of fitting those events into a historical framework. Recalling his correct prediction of the direction of arms shares (up) a couple years before, which had led to a successful speculation by Victor Rothschild (who had paid Burgess a hundred pounds for the tip), "She now, therefore, invited him to become, on a quite informal basis, her personal financial adviser; gave him a list of all her investments . . . and asked him to write her a monthly report, for which she paid him an allowance of £100 a month."[3] Isaiah Berlin told Michael Ignatieff that he thought during this period Burgess and a partner, probably Rudolph Katz, published a City Letter, with many subscribers.[4] (Christopher Isherwood said something similar to the FBI in 1951.[5]) Mrs. Rothschild had many advisors, read many newsletters, as such wealthy and intelligent people do. She had formed a favorable opinion of Burgess's advice and being a Rothschild, she was willing to pay for it. Mrs. Rothschild's favorable opinion of Burgess at this point was not uncommon. According to Noel Annan, "many serious people thought Guy Burgess the youth one of the most brilliant, compelling, promising human beings they had ever met."[6] With an income for his financial advice from Mrs. Rothschild, and possibly, through Katz, others, Burgess moved into a flat at 38 Chester Square, Belgravia, near Victoria station (and not far from the Park Lane Rothschild colony), then and now a good address, where flats today exchange hands for a million pounds or more.[7]

Burgess was a very sociable man, already at Cambridge frequenting contiguous British ruling class social groups: that of the old boys of his school, Eton; that of graduates of Trinity College, Cambridge and the wider Oxbridge network; and that of the Apostles. In London he soon added to these membership in two of the great clubs occupying Italianate palaces along Pall Mall: the Reform and the Royal Automobile Club , of which John Strachey was also a member). The Reform, originally identified with the Liberal Party, with its well-furnished library and at least equally well-furnished bars, was the natural London home for any English gentleman not actually a Tory. Burgess told Harold Nicolson, in a letter from Moscow, that the Reform Club was one of the few things he missed. Newspapers could be read, or slept under, there; meals taken; bedrooms found; friends met, governments made and unmade; information gathered. The RAC is of a different character. Designed by the architect of the Ritz, and showing it with its marble staircases, its library is only useful, naturally enough, if one were, like Burgess, interested in automobiles. But like the Reform, the RAC offers food, drink and sleeping quarters. It also benefits from a gymnasium, an Ottoman swimming pool and Turkish baths (offering interesting alternative overnight accommodation). Burgess was a frequenter of both the latter facilities. It is not unlikely that he from time to time also visited pubs in the Soho and Mayfair areas of London during this period, as later. He probably also attended private parties, not all of which were conducted at the level of the dinner parties Felix Frankfurter gave in Oxford, but at some of which, at least, as at high table at All Souls, people felt free to talk.

The summer of 1934 was a time when, at least for a segment of the British intelligentsia, Communism was becoming almost respectable. France and the Soviet Union had signed treaties of mutual assistance with Czechoslovakia, bringing the Soviet Union into a sort of ancillary status in the Concert of Europe. At the International Congress of Writers for the Defense of Culture, E. M. Forster said that "English freedom was race-bound and class-bound; it meant freedom for Englishmen, not for Indians and Africans, and freedom for the well-off, not for the down-and-out for whom it 'did not signify a plate of fish and chips' . . . 'I am not a communist, 'though perhaps I might be one if I was a younger and a braver man, for in communism I see hope. It does many things which I think evil but I know that it intends good . . . Fascism does evil that evil may come.'"[8] In August Michael Straight and Anthony Blunt went on one of the group tours to Moscow (the former for the factories, it was said, the latter for the paintings). The following term in Cambridge Straight devoted himself to Communist political work, attending only the occasional lecture by Keynes or John Hilton. One day in

November he was visited by his mother's (and Aldous Huxley's) friend Gerald Heard. Straight invited John Cornford to join them for lunch. Heard challenged Cornford on the subject of dictatorship: "'Do you really believe,' asked Gerald, 'that any individual is wise enough or good enough to hold unchallenged authority, even for an hour?' John paused at that. He said at last, 'We have to put the fear of God into the bourgeoisie.'"[9] Around this time Goronwy Rees, not necessarily on orders from the Comintern, succeeded in getting a job at *The Times* for a few months, then tried, but failed, to be taken on by the B.B.C.[10] Donald Maclean, more likely under instructions, joined the Foreign Office towards the end of October, 1935 (wittily having assured his examiners that he had nearly recovered from his undergraduate Communism) and was assigned to the League of Nations and Western Department. He would be assigned to the British Embassy in Paris in September, 1938.[11]

The League of Nations Union had organized a "Peace Ballot" at the end of June, 1935, on which nearly half the British electorate voted for the League of Nations and disarmament. Mussolini began the Second Italo-Abyssinian War that same month. The historian Peter Stansky has observed that "Pacifism, or anti-war-ism, in the winter of 1935 was the chief, really the only serious political concern of most Cambridge undergraduates."[12] Communists and such—undergraduates like Cornford and professional politicians like Stafford Cripps—saw these anti-war organizations as an opportunity to build the United Front. At the Labour party conference at the beginning of October, reaching out to the wider anti-war movement, Cripps said that "every war entered upon by a capitalist government is and must be an imperialist and capitalist war."[13] With all parties running on peace platforms, the voter turn-out in the election the next month was unusually low. The Labour Party increased the number of its seats in Parliament; the Liberals continued their decline; the National Government remained essentially Tory.

Hannah Arendt, reading Aristotle through Marx, wrote that an individual's choice of a path for their life is always constrained by the historical circumstances in which they find themselves. The *vita contemplativa* is the least subject to those circumstances. There is nearly always the possibility of turning inward. But otherwise individuals are faced with a crossroad where three ways meet: the intimate life of body and family, the social and the political lives. Sometimes the last of these expands, leaving little room for the others. Sometimes it contracts, leaving no possibility for what Aristotle thought essential to a truly human existence. In the mid-1930s, in Britain, the political life offered an unusually wide and intense range of choices. There was the conventional political life of the Parliamentary parties. There was Mosley's path, soon to lead to Fascism (or, for people like Tom and Unity Mitford, National Socialism). And there was the Marxist road, which, in itself, offered a variety of possibilities: Hobsbawm's choice, that of what might be called an ideologist; Cornford's choice, the Party organizer at that moment, with the possibility of revolutionary action in the right circumstances; the underground path that was pointed out by Arnold Deutsch—work, silence, biding one's time until one was in a position to influence events. Kim Philby and Donald Maclean were exemplars of this aim, achieving, as each nearly did, the command of one of the more strategic offices of the government. This seems at first to have been Burgess's aim as well.

Hobsbawm recalled that, after Burgess's resignation from the Party, his contemporaries in the Cambridge branch of the Communist Party "regarded [Burgess] as a traitor, because he took care to advertise his alleged conversion to right-wing views as soon as he had gone down."[14] Burgess was soon working for the new Conservative Member of Parliament for Chelmsford, Captain John Macnamara, as a secretary and personal assistant.[*] (Macnamara was a professional Army officer, like Burgess's step-father and paternal grandfather.) Michael Straight gave a vivid description of Burgess at

---

[*] Chelmsford, the county town of Essex, was at that time a center of high technology, home to Marconi's electrical and Hoffman's ball-bearing factories, although set in an essentially agricultural landscape. Macnamara's papers are not publicly accessible.

meetings of the Apostles at this time: While in "his guise as Captain Macnamara's secretary, Guy pointed to fascism as the wave of the future.

> He voiced no such opinions in the meetings of the Apostles. In any discussion of ideas he was always ready with an apt quotation, an amusing anecdote, a suggestive analogy, a mocking riposte. If the question before the society was political, he spoke in metaphors that were distant and obscure. If he was challenged to state his own convictions, his bright blue eyes would widen. He would look at the challenger with a beguiling smile, and then speak of other things.[15]

Macnamara and Burgess soon joined the Anglo-German Fellowship, which had been formed in October, 1935, following the dissolution of the Anglo-German Association the preceding April. (The Association had displeased the Nazis by admitting Jews as members.) The Fellowship had as its objectives: "to promote good understanding between England and Germany and thus contribute to the maintenance of peace and the development of prosperity." It claimed that "'membership does not imply approval of National Socialism.' In reality, however," according to Ian Kershaw, "the organization served largely as an indirect tool of Nazi propaganda in high places, a vehicle for exerting German influence in Britain."[16] Its membership comprised representatives of many large businesses, such as Unilever and ICI, and a good swathe of the aristocracy, including lords Mount Temple, Londonderry, Lothian, Redesdale and the Duke of Wellington. It also included Kim Philby.[17] Anthony Blunt wrote in his unpublished memoir:

> The intellectual somersault that Guy had then to perform, his pretence of sympathy with Nazism and his joining the Anglo-German Fellowship, have been described, but it has not, I think, been brought out how much agony he went through in performing them. He would much rather have remained an open party member . . . But his belief in the cause of Communism was so complete that he accepted without question that he must obey the order . . .[18]

Macnamara was often on his feet in the House in 1936, speaking on various military matters, as might be expected, and also on a scattering of other issues, some about pigs, perhaps in response to inquiries from his more rural constituents. Then on July 10th, rather surprisingly, he gave a speech protesting against "Jew-baiting" by the police: "It is ungentlemanly and very un-English, and I very much hope that we shall all be able to use our influence, and, if necessary, our force, to stop a very horrid evil that seems to be creeping in."[19] This probably did not go down well with his colleagues in the Anglo-German Fellowship. Toward the end of 1936 he traveled to Spain as one of a six-member Parliamentary inquiry group, including the Liberal M.P. Wilfrid Roberts. In a Parliamentary speech on December 18, Macnamara gave a highly nuanced appraisal of the situation in Spain, describing the various Loyalist parties and their lack of appreciation for one another, describing the domination of Franco by Germany and Italy, and warning of the growing military strength of Germany and the threat perceived by France from German forces in Spain. He ended by calling for an *effective* non-intervention policy, one which would force the withdrawal of the Germans, the Italians and the Russians from Spain. In the course of his analysis of the Spanish situation, Macnamara informed the House that

> Most of us know that nowadays there are two Russias; there is Russia the State, and there is Russia the Third International. Most of us know that these two do not necessarily always see eye to eye, and that there has been a certain attempt on the part of Russia as a State to settle down into a petite bourgeoisie [sic] and to liquidate the Third International as far as it is concerned with the State. That may be so, but at the same time I do not think we can altogether excuse the Russian State for not having jumped a bit more firmly on the Third International for interfering in Spain before the revolt started.[20]

It is not unlikely that this distinction between the Soviet Union and the Third International was one that Macnamara was accustomed to hear made by Burgess (who, as a matter of fact, told Driberg that he had helped draft Macnamara's report on his Spanish visit). The following speakers, including Wilfrid Roberts, praised Macnamara's work on the Spanish inquiry group and endorsed his observations and most of his conclusions.

Macnamara was clearly well-respected, particularly, as would be expected, in military matters, and ideologically increasingly close to the boundary between the Conservative and Liberal parties. Harold Nicolson, for example, drifting leftward himself, was comfortable recommending Macnamara as an unofficial Foreign Office inspector of the situation in the Balkans in October, 1936.[21] The Conservative diarist "Chips" Channon would place Macnamara in the group of Conservative "insurgents" against Chamberlain in March, 1938,[22] when Macnamara was joint secretary with Wilfrid Roberts of the Basque Children's Committee, which ran a refugee camp for these young Loyalists at Stoneham in Hampshire.[23] We must assume, as Burgess was Macnamara's secretary, and by the Angletonian rules, that from this time Burgess had access to all such information that was available to a back-bencher like Macnamara and that he passed that which he found of interest to his Comintern contacts.*

Macnamara and Burgess visited Germany in 1936 as part of another fact-finding group, including the Venerable J. H. Sharp, Church of England Archdeacon in South-Eastern Europe (whom Nicolson referred to as Macnamara's "queer Archdeacon friend") and Tom Wylie, Private Secretary to the Permanent Under-Secretary at the War Office.[24] It was at this time Burgess also developed "an acquaintanceship" with Edouard Pfeiffer an assistant to the sometime French premier, Daladier.[25] There are some colorful stories about Burgess's time in Germany and Paris with these men, most of the stories, if not all, originating with Burgess himself. Just as secret intelligence officials sometimes cultivate hobbies—James

---

* Angletonian rules: After James Jesus Angleton, long-serving chief of the counterintelligence staff of the Central Intelligence Agency, who held that it must be assumed for counterintelligence purposes that anything a person *could* have known *was* known by that person.

Angleton's fishing and orchids, for example—at least in part to provide a reservoir of stories to distract the curious, so Burgess would entertain his listeners with accounts of the amusements found by himself, Macnamara, Sharp, Wylie and Pfeiffer in Germany and Paris. Those stories, whether or not true, served—continue to serve—their distracting purpose.[26]   In this case, we are meant to listen to the stories and not think about what Pfeiffer might have known of the actions and intentions of the French government and what of that he might have told Burgess. And what of that Burgess might have passed along to the NKVD residence in Paris (that in London being in hiatus).[27]

Others simply saw Burgess's charm, charm that even extended to the resolutely heterosexual Louis MacNeice, who wrote Anthony Blunt in 1936 that Burgess was "quite the nicest of your pals by a long way."[28] MacNeice, who had been to school with Anthony Blunt and was then teaching at Birmingham, visited Blunt in Cambridge early in 1936, to make arrangements for a trip to Spain during the Easter vacation.   In *The Strings are False,* MacNeice provides a glimpse of John Cornford:

> In the afternoon I drove back to Birmingham, giving a lift in my little car to . . . John Cornford, also a Cambridge undergraduate, clever and communist and bristling with statistics . . . for him the conception of career was completely drowned in the Cause; he was going to Birmingham to stand trial for causing an obstruction while distributing communist pamphlets in the Bull Ring [where the Chartist Movement had been launched in 1838]. John Cornford was the first inspiring communist I had met; he was the first who combined an unselfish devotion to his faith with a really first-class intelligence.[29]

The political ferment of the time and this increasing attraction of the far left for wealthy Americans like Michael Straight and poets like MacNeice (as well as Auden and Spender) were also symbolized and accelerated by the formation of the Left Book Club by John Strachey, Victor Gollancz and Stafford Cripps in the Spring of 1936. The Club, with its monthly selections, newsletter and discussion groups, was soon a typical presence in the homes of those in England who had lost faith in the traditional political parties. *The Struggle for Peace,* by Cripps himself, was one of the 1936 selections.

The Struggle for Peace, despite its title, was not a pacifist tract. Cripps argued that international peace is impossible among capitalist, imperialist, countries, which require the economic stimulus of the armaments industry to produce high levels of profits for the shareholding class and the armaments themselves to maintain their empires.[30] He was especially biting about conditions in India:

> The condition of starvation and poverty in India, the Fascist methods that are adopted to keep down every expression of popular opinion and feeling, and the enslavement of the economic life of that great continent in the interests of the British, are such intolerable incidents of imperialism that no one who has taken the trouble to study these things could tolerate the system which imposes them upon their fellow-workers in India.

He then writes, prophetically: "India to-day is ruled by the force of British arms, and, however benevolent that rule may consider itself, its continuance will not be tolerated indefinitely by the Indian people."[31] His prescription for world peace, and better conditions for the colonized peoples, is revolution in Britain: "a workers' Government must come by democratic methods or revolution before we in this country can start to build up a true world peace . . . a workers' Government in Great Britain will immediately free India from British imperialism."[32] Cripps had no illusions about the methods used by the Russian Revolution, which, he writes, had "been marked by excesses which no normal human being could do other than loathe . . . the privileged classes who resisted the change were destroyed or escaped into exile . . . If the irresistible force of change meets the immovable rock of entrenched class privilege, there will indubitably be an explosion in this country . . . I ask the younger generation to face these facts, and to save themselves and their elders by their determined action at this most critical period of our history."[33] Sir Stafford Cripps, M.P., was condoning, if not calling for, revolutionary violence.

Having been "sheep-dipped" (to use a C.I.A. term of art) by his time as Captain Macnamara's right-wing secretary, Burgess, following Deutsch's instructions, went looking for a position with one of the great institutions of the time. The B.B.C., the British Broadcasting Corporation, was then at one of its peaks of prestige and influence. Less than ten years old, with a monopoly on broadcasting, it was viewed, like *The Times,* as an authoritative source of news. It presented itself as a sort of alternative Church, or, given the background of its Director General, John Reith, a sort of alternative Scottish Kirk, with a mission to educate, inform and entertain, with the emphasis on the first two of these. The "Ullswater report" on the B.B.C., just then completed, had found that "As to staff . . . there was a fair field and no favour in recruitment; posts were filled with sole regard to the capacity and promise of the candidates."[34] As it happened, in the winter 1935/36 the B.B.C. was looking for additional staff for its Talks Department. In the way that these things are done the staffing officers at the B.B.C. asked the Cambridge University Appointments Board for suitable candidates. C. V. Guy, Secretary of the Board, wrote in response on November 15th to B. E. Nicolls Controller (Administration) at the B.B.C., mentioning three candidates, specifying that "G. F. de M. Burgess would appear to be much the likeliest of these three candidates."

The College describe him as a man of quite first-rate ability, who might have been expected to be a strong candidate for a Trinity Fellowship but he decided against an academic career, being really more interested in current affairs than in learning. Burgess went through the communist phase, I think; I do not think he has any particular politics now but I expect they are rather towards the left. He is a somewhat highly-strung fellow, too, but gets on uncommonly well with people, including being notably successful with a number of stupid pupils [sic] when he supervised for his College during his last year here. He really seems a most versatile fellow. He seems to have a real gift for friendship in quite a wide circle, including a close friendship with an ex-miner here.* He has done a good deal of journalistic work. Burgess is a man of considerable self-assurance and a fellow for whom it is easy to feel both admiration and liking.[35]

Therefore, on the 26th, D. H. Clarke, General Establishment Officer, B.B.C., sent Burgess a letter asking if he wished to be considered for a position with the Corporation. Burgess responded in the affirmative on the 5th of December and solicited letters of reference from his elders among the Cambridge Apostles. Regius Professor of Modern History George Trevelyan duly wrote that same day to Cecil Graves, Deputy Director-General (a personal friend):

I believe a young friend of mine, Guy Burgess, late a scholar of Trinity, is applying for a post in the B.B.C. He was in the running for a Fellowship in History, but decided (correctly I think) that his bent was for the great world – politics, journalism, etc. etc. – and not academic. He is a first rate man and I advise you if you can to try him. He has passed through the communist measles that so many of our clever young men go through, and is well out of it. There is nothing second rate about him and I think he would prove a great addition to your staff. [36]

Given such recommendations, Burgess was interviewed for a Talks position on December 30, but, for unspecified reasons, was not selected.[37] A January 2, 1936, memorandum concerning that interview described, however, arrangements for an interview in Manchester for an opening there: "It transpires that he is working on the Times at the moment as a sub-editor and cannot be free until the beginning of February . . . The D[irector] G[eneral] saw Burgess today, as he likes to see all Talks Assistants, and liked him." This was remarkable. The Director General at that time was Sir John Reith, in effect the founder of the B.B.C. It was not the usual thing for any human being to be liked by Sir John.

---

* Perhaps James Lees-Milne.

Oliver Woods, who had begun working for *The Times* in 1934 and spent his entire career there, eventually writing the newspaper's history, recalled that at "the beginning of 1936 Burgess . . .

succeeded in getting himself a trial as a sub-editor on *The Times*—the standard method of entry in those days—and for a month he conscientiously traveled by tube from Victoria to Blackfriars station every afternoon to take his place at the very bottom of the subs' table. Burgess behaved impeccably for once, wearing a suit and staying sober, but . . . after four weeks in the frigid gloom of Printing House Square he was told that *The Times* considered him unsuitable.[38]

The B.B.C., on the other hand, did think Burgess "suitable." It simply was not sure what to do with him. Burgess was tentatively offered a position as North Regional Talks Assistant in Manchester. He was interviewed in Manchester on January 17, 1936 (somehow securing leave from *The Times* to do so), but "he appeared anxious not to leave London" and therefore was told on 20 January 1936 that he had not been selected. This episode ended with a letter from Burgess (who was again at Ascot Hall), to Nicolls, at B.B.C.: "I think the Manchester business probably turned out rightly – I think I would have gone – but [they are] quite right about my Metropolitan leanings. And now I should like to ask you whether you would still consider me – whether you are prepared to – for a job in London, should one become vacant – I am not committed to the Times and should like to work for you in London if anything turns up and you will have me." Burgess always preferred London.

In March, 1936, Goronwy Rees, having passed through the *Times* and failed to be taken on by the B.B.C., became Assistant Editor of the *Spectator* at £500 a year and took a flat around the corner from Burgess, in Ebury Street.[39] Harold Nicolson's unpublished diaries for the next ten years furnish a sort of handbook of sightings of Burgess in that central part of British life triangulated by the B.B.C., the Pall Mall clubs and Whitehall. Given the great and largely successful efforts to erase Burgess from that social context, they significantly add to our understanding of the way in which he was situated within it. That Spring, Nicolson's diary records a flurry of meals with Burgess. On March 3ʳᵈ, Nicolson noted, as a routine occurrence, that after he had dined at the House of Parliament with Megan Lloyd George, Kenneth Lindsay and Cynthia [Mrs. Gladwyn] Jebb, they were joined toward the end of the meal by Burgess. (The next evening Nicolson dined with King Edward and Mrs. Simpson, making considerably less of it than would Chips Channon.) On March 17ᵗʰ Nicolson had a Bloomsbury dinner with Mary Hutchinson, the mother of the first wife of Victor Rothschild; Maynard Keynes and Burgess. On April 30ᵗʰ Nicolson and Burgess lunched at the Travellers, the Foreign Office club. On May 14ᵗʰ, Nicolson hosted another dinner at the House, this time including Burgess and Burgess's former employer, Macnamara. (On the 28ᵗʰ Nicolson took Macnamara back to his rooms in King's Bench Walk [K.B.W.]* from the House and they sat up talking until 1:30 in the morning. "He seems the best of the new members.") On June 17ᵗʰ, Nicolson dined alone with Burgess at the Café Royal, commenting in his diary: "He is very entertaining." And on June 24ᵗʰ, there is lunch with Burgess, "who is full of gossip, and [I] bring him back to K.B.W., as I have a masseur coming."[40]

Europe was emerging from Depression into preparations for war. Britain had begun re-arming on a large scale late in 1935.[41] Germany, of course, had been doing so from the moment of Hitler's accession to power. On March 7, 1936, Hitler had a token force of the German Army re-occupy the Rhineland. The French Army, formidable on paper, watched. The British government informed Hitler that it would like to talk about his plans. He said he wanted peace. John Strachey, the Communist propagandist, and Robert Boothby, the Conservative M.P. were "Walking down St James's

---

* Nicolson's rooms, 4, King's Bench Walk, barristers' residential chambers of the Inner Temple, were registered in the name of his eldest brother, Lord Carnock, who, although a member of the Bar, no longer practiced. It included Nicolson's study, an oak-panelled sitting room, two bedrooms, and a small kitchen and bathroom.

Street . . . when the startling news [of the occupation of the Rhineland] appears . . . we both agreed that it was the opening move of World War Number Two; and ought, as such to be challenged—if necessary by force of arms."[42]   Driberg wrote that when Hitler occupied the Rhineland, Burgess had flown to Paris,

> From Pfeiffer [sometime Secretary-General of the Radical Party] and his other friends there he learned that the French cabinet had decided by a majority of only one not to resist Hitler unilaterally, but that the vote would have been very different if it had been possible to get any assurances of support from the British Government . . . When he got back to London, he described what he had been told to a friend of his, a distinguished novelist, who happened to work for the Secret Service: a few days later he was astonished to receive from the same friend a sum of money sufficient to cover his Paris expenses.[43]

Something like, or not quite like, that. This could have been a way for someone (perhaps David Footman) to open a subscription, as it were, to Burgess's information: Burgess, then, was obliged to M.I.6 for the funds; M.I.6 to Burgess for the information.[44] In any case, in lieu of information about Burgess's contacts with others, it dates Burgess's first association with British Secret Intelligence to March, 1936, two years after Philby's park bench talk with Deutsch. From the point of view of Deutsch and his friends, Burgess had penetrated M.I.6. He was to function as a double agent for the next eight years.

In mid-May, having conquered Abyssinia, Mussolini declared a new Roman Empire, playing the part of Disraeli to Victor Emmanuel's Queen Victoria. In June, Jawaharlal Nehru wrote:

> A Liberal democratic Spain is attacked by Fascists and reactionaries and even in England there is a great deal of sympathy for the rebels. I think that if England had the kind of Government that France has today and the two joined hands with Russia, war would be unlikely. But the tragedy is that England flirts with Germany and thus encourages fascism.[45]

The Spanish Civil War began on July 18th. John Cornford was the first British volunteer on the Loyalist side. Burgess's friend Whitney Straight (brother of Michael Straight) sold an airplane to one of Franco's purchase agents (which may have been merely Straight profiteering rather than an ideological declaration).[46] More than forty years later Anthony Blunt told *The Times* that it was just before the outbreak of the Spanish Civil War that Burgess recruited him for underground work. "'I was persuaded by Guy Burgess that I could best serve the cause of anti-fascism by joining in his work for the Russians', because 'the Communist Parry and Russia constituted the only firm bulwark against fascism, since the Western democracies were taking an uncertain and compromising attitude towards Germany'." [47] That summer, much of literary London went to Paris for another meeting of the International Association of Writers for the Defence of Culture. John and Rosamond Lehmann were there, as were Day Lewis, Stephen Spender, Rees and Burgess. Rees, who was on the executive committee of the British Section, was much taken with Louis Aragon. Burgess preferred Theodore Dreiser.[48]

The B.B.C., having decided to set up a "training reserve," so as to have a pool of candidates for openings, Nicolls sent a letter to Burgess on July 17, 1936, offering an interview on the 24th for a place in it. This was accepted by Burgess, giving as his references Trevelyan, P. D. (later Sir Dennis) Proctor[49] (as "Principal at the Treasury") and Captain John Macnamara, M.P.[50] On August 10th, Burgess's old tutor sent the B.B.C. a recommendation (with the usual reference to former Communist enthusiasms): "Guy Burgess is an exceptionally able young man, with perhaps the liveliest mind I have known in any of my pupils for five years.

> After a period of enthusiastic communism during his last years here, he has now I believe arrived at some form of left wing conservatism, but how long that will last I should be sorry to predict. Since he went down he has been doing a good deal of free lance journalism, and had a temporary post with The Times. I think journalism is his first love, and that what he really likes is

the varied and exciting life of knocking up and down behind the scenes of politics. He is very good company, and I like him personally. But there is no doubt that he has the faults of a nervy and 'mercurial' temperament, and if by 'taking him without any qualms' you mean taking him with complete confidence in his reliability—well, he is not that sort of man. I do not mean that he is untrustworthy in the sense that you could not be sure of his doing what he was told. But if you take him, you will be getting quite first class and extremely fertile brains, and a most vigorous personality; and you will be taking risks. On the whole I think that if I were in your place I should think it worth while to take them.[51]

A week later, Nicolls received a recommendation from Proctor: "I have known Mr. Burgess for about six years, beginning when he was an undergraduate at Cambridge, and latterly I have known him well in London.

I should say that he is a very suitable person for employment on your staff. I do not know what particular side of the work at the B.B.C. he would be employed on, but for anything in the news or programmes side I think he would be admirable. He has a very fresh, keen mind and is always full of ideas, while at the same time he has a very holistic sense of what is and is not practical. In fact, I should say you would get in him someone with the good qualities of the enthusiast, without the usual attendant difficulties in fitting him into a working organization. Also, he has an unusually wide range of interests and sympathies. He is, I believe, a very good historian – and is certainly an interesting and very fertile one in conversation – he has a deep interest in literature and painting – and has studied both with a good deal of originality – and he is a close and penetrating observer of current politics. In fact he is one of those people whose opinion one likes to know, and attaches some value to, on any subject of current interest. And it is an opinion backed up by a pretty varied range of experience, as you no doubt know from the facts of his career. Altogether I think he will be a very real asset to your staff.[52]

Having been so vetted and celebrated, Burgess joined the B.B.C. Training Reserve on October 1, 1936.

From then until nearly the end of the year the country was pre-occupied with the over-lapping Spanish Civil War and Abdication crisises. Harold Nicolson's diary, typically, bounced back and forth between them. He noted on December 7th: "Jack Macnamara arrives back from Spain. His general view is that the Government would certainly win were it not for the invasion of Spain by German and Italian 'volunteers.'" On December 9th, returning to his rooms in King's Bench Walk at the decisive moment in the Abdication crisis, his then-roommate, James Pope-Hennessy, who was of the King's party, hissed at Nicolson from his bed: "'Goodnight Regicide' and turns away in rage."[53]

Arnold Deutsch decided, late in 1936, that Kim Philby had sufficiently established his pro-fascist bona fides over the previous year, which had included monthly visits to Berlin, to send him to Spain to report on the war from the Fascist side, supposedly as a free lance journalist, but actually on a stipend from Soviet intelligence.[54] John Cornford, fighting for the Republic, was killed in Spain on December 28, 1936. He had written his own epitaph:

> *Freedom is an easily spoken word*
> *But facts are stubborn things. Here, too, in Spain*
> *Our fight's not won till the workers of all the world*
> *Stand by our guard on Huesca's plain*
> *Swear that our dead fought not in vain,*
> *Raise the red flag triumphantly*
> *For Communism and for liberty.*[55]

Two years later Burgess asked Margot Heinemann to let John Lehmann have another of Cornford's poems, now the most famous, "Huesca," for *New Writing*.

> *Heart of the heartless world,*
> *Dear heart, the thought of you*

Is the pain at my side,
The shadow that chills my view.

The wind rises in the evening,
Reminds that autumn is near.
I am afraid to lose you,
I am afraid of my fear.

On the last mile to Huesca,
The last fence for our pride,
Think so kindly, dear, that I
Sense you at my side.

And if bad luck should lay my strength
Into the shallow grave,
Remember all the good you can;
Don't forget my love.

Cornford was the British Communist Party's only charismatic middle class leader. His shallow grave held what had been one set of possibilities for the future of his country. That path to revolution was closing.

*   *   *

According to the "Special Confidential Report" on Burgess for the B.B.C. Training Reserve course, Burgess had "Probably the best brains of any other member of the present course.

He is extremely well informed on all historical and political subjects. Can write a very good broadcast talk, topical talk or eye-witness account. His editorial ability has shown itself to be of a high order in the News Bulletins which he has framed for the school programmes. He seems to be well qualified for a talks assistant or news editor or sub-editor . . . Unfortunately, his diction is bad and it is this defect alone which prevents us recommending him as an O.B. assistant . . . he could probably fill a good many positions in Public Relations and some in Programme Administration but he would be more valuable to us in the long run if he were started as a programme assistant doing practical work on the floor of the studios.[56]

Consequently, on the first of April, 1937, Guy Burgess, bad diction and all, was appointed to the Talks department of the B.B.C. at a salary of £300 per annum. His direct supervisor was George Barnes, husband of Dadie Rylands' admirer, Ann.

The B.B.C. that Burgess had just joined was an intensely bureaucratic, hierarchical organization, operating as if it were part of the Imperial civil service. According to W. J. West, "Few of the B.B.C.'s programmes had any political content.

> Politics was confined almost exclusively to news broadcasts and to talks, and the department of the Corporation responsible for the arrangement of who was to speak, and one what subject, was the appropriately named Talks Department . . . a retired diplomat, Sir Richard Maconachie, had been put in to head the department, but most of the day-to-day running devolved to his deputy, George Barnes. The real power, however, rested largely with the producers who assembled the programmes. Radio producers . . . could insist on who they wanted round them to do the necessary work . . . in practice it was [the] Talks Producer who actually chose the speakers and monitored their texts.[57]

The Talks department provided programming for the most part in fifteen or twenty minute segments. Producers, like Burgess, either on their own initiative of or in consultation with the Director and/or the Assistant Director of Talks, would commission or accept a concept from an outside expert and at that stage or after seeing the first draft of a script and arranging for a voice test, would send out a contract at anything from six to ten guineas (21 shillings, when a pound was 20, just to show this was a gentleman's enterprise). Successive draft scripts would go back and forth, occasionally higher authority would be consulted, then, if satisfactory, the talk would be broadcast, live, from Broadcasting House, near the top of Regent Street. At first, Burgess was apprenticed to another producer (Miss Quigley), with whom he worked on miscellaneous talks and readings and then a series of talks on Food and Exercise.

Burgess's domestic arrangements had become regularized, if that is the word, when a few weeks before he joined the Talks Department, Jack Hewit, a young man trying to survive in London as a supernumerary in the musical theater, was taken to a party at the War Office apartment of the resident clerk, Tom Wylie (who was, as it happened, one of Kim Philby's contacts). Hewit recalled: "I met everyone there, Anthony Blunt, Guy Burgess. It was a very B.B.C., art-intellectual party . . .

> The conversation was fascinating but there was no food and that was the only reason I was there. Then I was attacked by someone called Otto [sic] Katz, a great fat slob of a man.* Harold Nicolson said, c'mon for God's sake. Then Guy rescued me . . . I was pissed, stoned and weak from hunger. I told Guy I had to go. He said, hang on and I will give you a lift. He was utterly charming, wildly good-looking and totally untidy. We went to his flat in Chester Square. I spent the night with him . . . But that night we sort of started a relationship. Oh yes, he was a good lover. I just didn't leave. I became Guy's keeper. He was someone who needed looking after. You dressed Guy in a clean shirt, brushed his suit and he would look immaculate. By the time he got to the door he looked as if he had been through a bush. Cigarette ash would fall like snowflakes from him. His nails were filthy. He got them just by scrabbling . . . always scrabbling around for everything. I used to scrub them and make

---

* This was almost certainly Rudolph, not Otto, Katz. The former was homosexual; the latter was not. Nor could Otto Katz be described as fat. Hewit's confusion of the names of the two may point to his later familiarity with Otto Katz, the Comintern agent. See photograph and descriptions in KV 2/2179, Kew.

him take a bath twice a week . . . I wasn't a manservant. That's wrong. I kept on my own place. I did his washing and looked after him and slept with him . . . He was the most promiscuous person who ever lived. He slept with anything that was going and he used to say anyone will do, from seventeen to seventy-five . . . If anyone invented homosexuality it was Guy Burgess.[58]

Hewit remained with Burgess as long as Burgess remained in London.

There is a story in Kim Philby's *My Silent War,* set in March, 1937, that Philby, having been arrested in Seville under suspicion of being more curious about Franco's airfields and troop movements than was fitting for a pro-Fascist journalist, had been detained and in the process had swallowed a piece of paper containing the codes with which he was communicating with his Comintern contact in Paris. Released, he sent a letter to Paris explaining the situation. He was told to go to Gibraltar to meet a courier who would give him his new codes and more money. The courier, according to Philby, was Guy Burgess. If the story is true, it must have been a quick trip for Burgess, as there is no indication in the B.B.C. records of his taking time off from work that month.[59] (Of course, laying false trails was one of Philby's amusements, or, perhaps one should say, one of his accomplishments.) Philby was then taken on by *The Times,* accredited at the headquarters of the Nationalists in Seville with a recommendation from the German Embassy in England, which described him as "an ardent supporter of fascist ideas." That recommendation gave Philby access to Franco himself and others in the Nationalist leadership. Philby passed the information he gathered to Major Alexander Orlov, the representative of the NKVD and the Security Adviser to the Republican government of Spain, who met with him in Narbonne, near the Spanish border. Philby also sent information to the Paris residency, with notes in invisible ink between the lines of innocuous postcards.[60]

By this time Deutsch had been replaced as the London resident for the NKVD, as, most probably, Burgess's contact, by Major Theodore Maly.

94

We can follow the development of one of Burgess's first independently developed and produced B.B.C. programs in the files for (Sir) Roger Fulford, then with *The Times*.[61] The series begins in February, 1937, when Burgess suggested that Fulford do a talk on the Coronation of King George IV. (Fulford had written a biography of the King.) Burgess and Fulford were already on terms of friendship—"My dear Guy . . . Yrs ever, Roger". On March 14th, Fulford sent a note giving some idea of the way that professional and personal relationships overlapped: "How would 12:30 on Friday April 2 do for another rehearsal? We might 'lunch' afterwards?" And a letter from Fulford a few weeks later concludes: "I much enjoyed myself at your party the other night." The Coronation talk was broadcast on April 3rd. The correspondence then turns to another of Burgess's ideas: "I am still looking for someone to do the series of about five talks called "They came to England" describing the experience of travelers such as Erasmus and Julius Caesar on first setting foot on this wretched island and I still think you might do it, or know someone who would."[62] Fulford jumped at the idea of the series and in a letter of the 28th of April, Burgess confirmed that Fulford would give the talks on alternate Thursdays from July 15th. Fulford was paid eight guineas for each of six talks. The notes from Fulford are hand-written, those from Burgess typed—Burgess very professional, very much in charge.

At the same time as the Fulford project was developing, another project came to an abortive conclusion. A Dr. Harry Barron had been besieging the B.B.C. with ideas for talks on industrial development. At first Burgess was encouraging, writing on February 2nd that the ideas were good and suggesting a meeting. Barron quickly wrote a script on "raw materials," which Burgess rejected on the 22nd, finding it "dull," but offering to read a revision. Barron took a few weeks to submit the revision, which met with Burgess's approval. In mid-March Burgess scheduled him for a voice test. At the end of the month Burgess sent Barnes a memorandum enclosing four further scripts. "I am convinced that this type of subject and talk appeals to a class of listener for whom we do not ordinarily cater sufficiently; that is, the class that can only be called the 'technician' class, the large number of people who read Darwin, attend night classes and are interested in popular science and industry." On the other hand, both Barnes (who agreed about the "technicians") and Burgess did not think Barron's work very good. The initially proffered talk was broadcast on May 3, the others rejected.[63]

In an undated letter on B.B.C. paper, but marked "answer please 38 Chester Square," Burgess wrote to quite a different correspondent: Christopher Isherwood: "Dear Christopher—

Here I am in this place. One thing is – at the moment a drive for short stories. Have you anything that you would like to be/let be read – Preference is of course for unpublished stuff – but this is not final – I, for instance, would so much like 8000000 families to hear the Nowaks – though I haven't gone into censorship xxx (difficult) – You get a little money (7 guineas upwards – what you can ask for & get away with – for 15 minutes) – Do let me know – (Fee is confidential me to you, & proposal unofficial).

There's nothing much to say – Rolf K. is in Switzerland getting on Hell's nerves and/or having Hell on his – It is – & will be for you, too, if you will – I think the act of a friend to both to keep them together – this depends on propaganda on R. rather than on H. – tho' the situation will presumably change in the Argentine. At the moment R. is tiresome & exacting, H. tiresome & smug. But both as nice as could be & I think suited. Sincerity & affection in a young boy could never stand [?] R's difficulties so I think his will off with & lucky to get xartish intrigue & great affection, which is genuine.*

I did like meeting you so much that time & have never thanked you for your letter – so let us keep in touch – at least to extent of meeting when you come to England if you will let me know. Letters are, for me, more difficult. I have seen a certain

---

* Kate Bucknell suggest that "Hell" is, perhaps, Hellmuth Roder, who was later in Isherwood's Hollywood life, with Fritz Mosel.

amount of Wyston, Wiston, Wistin H. A. since I saw you & I must say became devoted at once – I imagine usual & originally unintended effect.

Let me know if B.B.C. story idea interest you – also, if not a bore, any ideas of others who B.B.C. wld tolerate-- & do let's meet.

Guy Burgess64

"Rolf" was Rudolph Katz, who was at this time based in Argentina. "Wyston, Wiston, Wistin" was, of course, W. H. Auden. The semi-humorous triple attempts at spelling an unfamiliar name was typical of Burgess.

On May 25th Burgess (for the Director of Talks) wrote to David Footman that he had just read Footman's book *Balkan Holiday,* enjoyed it, and thought that Footman "might not be just the person to give some travel talks of a rather personal nature."[65]   Footman forwarded Burgess's letter to his (literary) agent, who wrote Burgess about terms. On June 3rd the Programme Contracts Executive of the B.B.C. named the terms as seven guineas for a 2,000-word talk. Footman agreed and submitted a script, "Albania, Fish and a Motor Car." (The accompanying note from Footman to Burgess was on Royal Automobile Club letterhead.)   The acceptance of the script was followed by a voice test and that by a fifteen minute broadcast on August 2nd at 12:30 p.m.   On the 5th, the head of the Talks Department, Sir Richard Maconachie, wrote a note to Burgess, telling him that he had found the script "really amusing," and suggesting that Footman be asked to do more talks "on the same lines."[66] Burgess replied "I am glad you liked this . . . Trouble is— we only got him after three approaches as he wants money for his work (He is a busy civil servant with literature a side line)." In the following month Burgess and Footman exchanged more notes (and contracts) about other scripts, one accepted by Burgess, one not, the one accepted sufficiently successful to be broadcast first in November and then again in January, 1938. Footman's civil service responsibilities had to do with secret intelligence. He served as the Belgrade resident of M.I.6, then as head of the political section in

London.[67]   Which was to prove useful to Burgess, or may have already, if it was indeed Footman with whom Burgess had dealt in 1936.

Harold Nicolson had been a frequent broadcaster on the B.B.C. for quite some time before Burgess joined the Talks Department. Once Burgess was in place, an increasing amount of Nicolson's broadcasting was produced by him.   For example, on April 20th Nicolson went "to see Guy Burgess for a moment about my Paste and Paper series" and then Nicolson went, coincidentally, "on to luncheon at the Russian Embassy."   On June 18th he gave another "Paste and Paper" talk. "I go to Studio 3.B and sit there all good and quiet. Guy Burgess comes in to see whether I am all right, and then goes out again . . ." After the broadcast Nicolson and Burgess went out to dinner. Of course, Nicolson dined out nearly every night, with dukes and M.P.s, society hostesses and foreign ambassadors. Occasionally also with amusing young men like Burgess. Dinners or drinks with Burgess after Nicolson's broadcasts—and later, after meetings of the Governors of the B.B.C.—would be routine occasions for gossip (or the collection of information) for nearly a decade.

For the young men who had turned to the left at Cambridge the magnetic pull of the war against Fascism was steadily increasing. "There was another evening in the spring of 1937 that is still vivid for me," Michael Straight wrote nearly fifty years later. "Julian Bell . . . had returned to England from China. He was determined to join the International Brigade in Spain. He wrote to his mother, "It's too late for democracy and reason and persuasion and writing to the *New Statesman* saying it's all a pity. The only real choices are to submit or to fight."[68] Bell spoke along the same lines at a meeting of the Apostles in Cambridge, saying "that in a world in which no cause was above reproach, one had still to choose, and at the same time, to maintain one's own integrity."[69] In the third week of June, 1937, Burgess attended the annual Apostles dinner, that year at the Ivy restaurant. After dinner some of the group went on to a party at the home of a senior Apostle, Edward Marsh, in Gray's Inn.[70] (Marsh,

Churchill's secretary, was a connection with that then out-of-favor politician.) Perhaps it was at this party that, in a story told by Quentin Bell, Burgess tried to dissuade Julian Bell from going to Spain. He was unsuccessful.[71] Six weeks later Bell was in Spain, where he died.

At about the time of the Apostles dinner at the Ivy, the B.B.C. recommended increasing Burgess's salary to £400 per annum, with the notation "that he be given an undertaking that, provided his work continues to justify it, annual increments will bring it up to £600 by the time he is thirty. Thereafter, they should be on the scale rates."[72] B.B.C. salaries at this time were based on age (as opposed, say, to merit or length of service). Burgess was 26, which was young for his responsibilities, and therefore he was paid less than his colleagues, which he, and Barnes, felt was unfair.

Anthony Blunt rather uncharacteristically, hosted a series of parties that summer. He had been taken on by the Warburg Institute, with its singular library of art historical and related materials, and moved into a flat at 30 Palace Court, on the north side of Hyde Park.[73] Burgess would usually be at the parties Blunt gave there, as would Wylie, Marsh, Straight, Nicolson and, on at least one occasion, Isaiah Berlin.[74] Burgess also attended more specialized parties, not all of which were in England. He took annual leave from the B.B.C. between August 10th and 25th, traveling to Germany, where there remained some opportunities for entertainment, for those who were not known to be Communists and did not appear to be Jewish. "Ivan Moffat remembered 'when Guy Burgess, Brian [Howard] and several other friends were in some Salzburg night-club in 1937, the whole party dressed up in lederhosen, with Brian lashing Guy all the way down the table with purple-paragraph whips.

> Brian used Guy by alternately laughing with him and then lashing out to smash him. Sitting there at the head of the table, he was like the driver of a ten-mule team, his great cracking whip lashing out all down the table, encouraging some, crushing others. To Guy, above all, Brian was unsparing, but Guy loved it[75]
> . . .

Brian Howard was Jewish, and, according to the stereotypes of the time, looked it, which makes the story, at that date, curious. Be that as it may, the story might be connected with Isaiah Berlin's recollection that Burgess had joined an organization called Britannia Youth, which took English schoolboys to the Nuremberg rallies.[76] That would have been convincing cover for his Comintern activities.

Toward the end of 1937 Burgess helped produce a series of programs by Lydia Lopokova (Mrs. Maynard Keynes). Lopokova had written to Charles Brewer, B.B.C. Director of Varieties, in mid-November offering "a series of, say, four or five studies of childhood and adolescence by the Russian classics . . . and I would translate them myself or get them translated for me."[77] After some intermediate correspondence, Burgess wrote to her with production details on December 21st:

Dear Madame Lopokova,

I am sorry I have not written before about the Russian short stories, but the question is only just cleared up. I have got a date for you on Saturday, January 29th, from 10.45 – 11.0 p.m. This, as you see, is a quarter of an hour period. I cannot quite remember how long the story you read to me lasted, but I think it was round about six minutes. We did speak of another story about a bad boy which you thought would go well (and I agree) with the story that you read about the good boy and which you also thought was a bit longer. The whole talk should come to about 13 minutes, but of course if the two stories together do not quite fill this time it does not matter, as you may wish to make one or two nice remarks between the two. These of course would have to be written down.

I wonder if you will let me know if you can manage this date and will be able to let me have a manuscript about ten days before and be good enough to give my best wishes to yourself and Maynard . . .

It was agreed to broadcast "Studies of Childhood and Adolescence from the Russian Masters, Selected and Presented by Lydia Lopokova" at ten guineas each (rather more than the going rate for fifteen minutes). Burgess's final letter to Lopokova on the subject, just before Christmas, suggested Saturday, January 29th, 10.45 – 11.0 p.m., Saturday, February 19th, 10.40 – 10.55 p.m. and Friday, February 25th, 10.45 – 11.0 p.m. "Can you manage these dates? If you can, I think it would be better if you did the talks with Salmon as I am over-working just now and in any case he has more experience of this kind of work that I . . . My renewed and apologetic regards to you both . . . Yours sincerely, Guy Burgess". The apologies being for routine bureaucratic confusion and from a young Apostle's awe of Keynes.

Burgess spent the holiday in Cannes with his mother and Blunt, where he met the seventeen-year old Peter Pollock, an heir to the Accles & Pollock light engineering firm, who returned with Burgess to Chester Square. Pollock later said that he "adored all the people [Burgess] could pour into my lap—all the people I'd read about: Ros[amond] Lehmann and E. M. Forster. And I was fascinated by his brain. He was the best conversationalist I ever knew apart from Francis Bacon."[78] After the war Pollock would indeed move on from Burgess to Bacon and then on to Tangier, where, and later again in London, he lived with the actor Paul Danquah. Pollock was the great love of Burgess's life.

1938 began with a typical event of the period, a rally of the Left Book Club on January 16th, at the Albert Hall and repeated at the Queen's Hall. John Strachey, Harry Pollitt (head of the Communist Party of Great Britain), the left-wing publisher Victor Gollancz, and Sir Charles Trevelyan spoke; Paul Robeson sang. Money was collected for Spanish Relief. That month Burgess was in correspondence with Nicolson ("My dear Nicolson") about a panel discussion with Leo Amery, former Secretary of State for the Colonies, on "Colonial Concessions to Germany"[79] and with Blunt for a series "At Home To-Day" to include a talk on the Winter Exhibition at the Academy (for six guineas).[80] On February 11th, Burgess wrote Nicolson (now "Dear Harold") about a series he would be running called "Forgotten Anniversaries." The letter opens with an apology: "I did mean to talk more about this broadcasting possibility to you on Wednesday evening, but I was enjoying what we did talk about so much that I never got down to it" and ends with "I do hope that you will be able to manage this and also that we shall meet again fairly soon. Yours sincerely, Guy." They apparently met that evening, Burgess bringing with him Michael Burn, Nicolson writing on the 12th: "My dear Guy . . . I like your friend Bowen [sic] very much indeed. I must try to get hold of him again" and Burgess responding on the 14th "Dear Harold . . . I am so glad you like Mickey—his surname, by the way is Burn." A contract for one of the Forgotten Anniversaries followed a couple of weeks later (at fifteen guineas). In the meantime Burgess had also spoken to Blunt about the Forgotten Anniversaries series for a talk on Michelangelo and the Sistine Chapel, which was the first of several Blunt presented in the series. These talks commissioned by Burgess were important steps in Blunt's career, making him known to B.B.C. listeners as an art historian and connoisseur.

On the 12th of January, Sir Richard Maconachie, the Director of Talks, included Burgess in his confidential reports on the staff:

> Brilliantly able, widely read and with a keen sense of humour he is delightful company. Has produced some admirable programmes, and is always likely to do so when really interested. Seems to be rather lacking in self-confidence when faced with an awkward situation, and owing to a natural impatience with routine is inclined to make slips in matters of detail. He realizes this and has improved a great deal in this direction recently. Is keen on his work, and with more experience will be of even more value than he is now.

On the 1st of April the salary increase to £400 was confirmed.

In early 1938, there was a bright line in Whitehall between those, led by Churchill, who believed that Hitler and Mussolini wished a second European war, making it inevitable, and those, led by Prime Minister Chamberlain, who believed that war could be avoided (and armaments expenditures minimized) by cultivating friendly relations at least with Mussolini. Mussolini's price for this was British recognition of his conquest of Ethiopia; the British Government, to some extent, wished for less Italian involvement in the Spanish Civil War. Daladier was now the French Prime Minister; Pfeiffer his Chef de Cabinet. Fitzroy Maclean, Burgess's classmate at Eton, who at one time or another was in a position to know, confirms that: "By this time [Burgess] had another part-time activity: when the occasion offered he did odd jobs for the British Secret Intelligence Service . . .

> Guy was used by Monsieur Pfeiffer as a courier for confidential letters from Monsieur Daladier to Mr Neville Chamberlain, the then Prime Minister, who preferred whenever possible to conduct his foreign policy himself, thus by-passing the Foreign Office and eventually provoking the resignation of the Foreign Secretary, Mr. Anthony Eden . . .The letters in question did not, however, remain confidential as they were intended to for the simple reason that Guy was apparently having them photographed for a branch of the Intelligence or Counter-Intelligence Service (and possibly for other customers too) on the way. It seems possible that he was also the bearer of the notorious secret correspondence conducted at this time by Mr. Chamberlain with Signor Mussolini.[81]

Burgess told Trevor-Roper that he had carried messages from Chamberlain, through Sir Joseph Ball and then Count Grandi, Italian Ambassador in London, to Mussolini in January-February 1938, with assurances that Chamberlain had determined to get rid of Anthony Eden.[82] When, at the end of February, provoked by all this passing of notes behind his back, Eden resigned, both Burgess's patrons, Harold Nicolson and Jack Macnamara, spoke in the Commons in favor of Eden during the subsequent debate.

In mid-March Burgess appears to have had a breakdown. His doctor wrote a Medical Certificate to the B.B. C.: "Mr. Guy Burgess has been to see me this afternoon and I suggest that he . . . have a holiday considering the state of his nerves." Burgess went on sick leave on March 15 and his mother took him off to the South of France. She was back in London by April 8th, but Burgess remained in France for another few weeks.[83] On April 8, 1938 a Dr. Lousel wrote to Maconachie, "Mr. Guy Burgess's mother, Mrs. Bassett, came to see me to-day on her return from the south of France where she has been looking after her son. She informs me that he is better, but that she did not think him well enough to return just yet. He is still in a very nervous state and suffering from insomnia. Mrs. Bassett tells me that he is very sensible and does not go out or touch any alcohol. From what she tells me I feel it would be wiser to allow him to stay away another week or so." [84] (Burgess must have been very distressed indeed. One can only speculate as to why, as there are no indications what it might have been.[85]) Burgess sent a telegram to Barnes from Paris on the 25th saying that he hoped to return shortly. He must have meant that as a matter of days (or hours), as toward the end of April he began to produce a series of eleven talks on Eastern Europe. Another series, this on the Spanish Civil War, "Both Sides of the Line," was broadcast in the National Service of the B.B.C. during March, April, June and August of 1938, using several different speakers. At least one of the talks, by Cecil Gerahty, broadcast on 25th March 1938, was produced by Burgess.[86] (Gerahty was co-author of the pro-Franco "The Spanish Arena," published by the now little-known Right Book Club in 1939.) In May, when Konrad Henlein, the Sudetenland leader, visited London "privately," Burgess arranged for Hewit to take a temporary job as a telephone operator at Heinlein's hotel so as to obtain, presumably for M.I.5, a list of telephone numbers Heinlein called.[87]

Burgess spent some weekends that summer with Rosamond Lehmann, the sister of the writer and editor John and the actress Beatrix, who had a large house in Ipsden, Oxfordshire, where she entertained the interlocking Bloomsbury and Oxbridge sets. Rosamond Lehmann had married Wogan Philipps, an artist and Communist who had gone to Spain. While he was in Spain, she conducted an affair with Goronwy Rees (which would be followed by a longer affair with C. Day Lewis). According to her biographer, Lehmann found "Burgess, handsome, warm-hearted, permanently disheveled . . . immensely engaging . . . Burgess would arrive at Ipsden, bathe . . . in the river, then sit smoking and drinking, avidly talking politics until far into the night, arguing for a form of intellectual Marxism, pro-Communist and violently opposed to any form of appeasement with Hitler . . . Burgess regarded Goronwy [Rees] as one of his three closest non-homosexual men friends. "I think he is generous, appreciative, sympathetic, loyal, trustworthy,' Guy wrote to Rosamond, adding teasingly, "With him as you know charm & looks are left out." Many years later, Rosamond wrote that she had loved Guy and found him a most stimulating friend. "We discussed Victorian novels – he urged me to read Mrs Gaskell and *Middlemarch*."[88]

Rees, John and Rosamond Lehmann, Day Lewis were active in the international Popular Front literary set of the time, providing protective coloration for Burgess less questionable than his right-wing acquaintances. In any case, he liked them, and, for a time, they him.

Maconachie wrote Nicolson on the 19th of April proposing that he do a series entitled "The Past Week," "In which the speaker would deal discursively and not too seriously with the happenings of the previous week." On the first of June Burgess sent Nicolson a contract for these talks, to be presented each Monday through the summer, at twelve guineas a talk, about £200 in all. The first program was broadcast the evening of Monday, July 18th. The series went well, with much "fan mail," as the B.B.C. bureaucracy put it.

A letter from Burgess to Blunt ("Dear Anthony . . . Yours, GB") on July 22nd gives some idea of the work-a-day details of Talks production at the B.B.C. "Here is your script," wrote Burgess.

Your final summing-up hasn't yet come in but I have arranged, both from the point of view of dealing with this and to quiet Bill, for you to have a final run through Monday before the broadcast at 3.15.
Christopher Salmon will be looking after you, so ask for him.
I think the talk in its existing form gives you plenty of time for any summing-up you like to do. Between you and me, the talk

was definitely on the short side at rehearsal, but this doesn't matter. I think you should sit facing the clock so that you can keep an eye on it and gag a bit at the end if you think the talk is too short or cut if you have taken too long. Christopher Salmon will give you a timing run through.
Paris is going to be alright, I think. See you Tuesday.[89]

Burgess and Blunt were going to Paris for another meeting of the International Association of Writers for the Defence of Culture, this entitled: "For Peace and Against the Bombardment of Open Cities" along with Rosamond and John Lehmann, Rees, C. Day Lewis and Stephen Spender.[90] The two-day convention was attended by 1,100 delegates from thirty countries, Viscount Cecil and Pierre Cot, former French Air Minister, presiding. It was an occasion when Burgess would have been able to meet people in Paris whom he did not, or did not often, see in London. In this context, Robert Cecil, writing about Donald Maclean, pointed out that "In 1938 [Comintern agents] Willi Muenzenberg and Otto Katz launched in Paris a polemical magazine for the intelligentisa, *Die Zukunft* (The Future), which attracted such English contributors as Harold Nicolson, Norman Angell and E. M. Forster; its editorial office would have been for [Donald] Maclean both a congenial and a convenient meeting place . . ."[91] Burgess also may have found his way there for its congeniality and convenience for his purposes. Although some people, including Muenzenberg and Katz, were becoming uneasy about events in the Soviet Union, John Strachey assured the readers of *Left News* that the Soviet show trials of old Bolsheviks were justified: "No one, who had not . . . fixed his mind in the contrary opinion, could read the verbatim account of the trials without being wholly convinced of the authenticity of the confessions . . . no man can advance his political education more than by studying this supreme historical document . . . the terrible story of the terrorist plots against the Soviet leaders."[92] In fact, those present at the trials, such as Fitzroy Maclean, could only marvel at the dramaturgy.

Other matters were rapidly coming to a crisis as Germany threatened Czechoslovakia and Nicolson's private information pointed toward an imminent invasion of Britain by Germany. Burgess was back in London by August 1st, he and Nicolson discussing scripts and dining at the Reform Club. (Nicolson noted in his diary that "Guy . . . is equally depressed" over Czechoslovakia as was Walter Lippmann, whom Nicolson had seen earlier.[93]) On the 11th Burgess wrote to Nicolson, humorously cautioning that the series was called "The Past Week," and not "My Past Week," and then passing on some political gossip. Nicolson replied on the 14th "My dear Guy . . . I agree that the great British public do not want to hear about how much I enjoyed staying with Willy Maugham. (What a talk I could have given them about the Duke of Windsor !!!!!)."[94] Not to mention encounters with Maugham's young friend Lulu "now a pure nancy boy beautifully dressed and very soigné" of whom more below.

Much of Burgess's time at the B.B.C. in late 1938 was taken up with a series of talks, running half an hour each, on the historical importance of the Mediterranean: a subject seen as timely in view of the Spanish situation. (Series of this sort were both popular and influential, followed as they were by hundreds of "Discussion Groups" around the country.) Sir Richard Maconachie sent a letter on August 2nd to the historian E. H. Carr, then a professor at the University of Wales, asking Carr to serve as an interlocutor on the series, after the initial talk by "some well known figure—perhaps Mr. Winston Churchill."[95] Maconachie's letter stated that if Carr were interested "my colleague, Mr. G. Burgess (who, with Mr. W. Newton, will be in charge of the series) will arrange to call upon you when convenient and discuss further details." Carr replied the next day, expressing interest, but asking that the series might be delayed until the first quarter of 1939. In the meantime he proposed meeting Burgess in London on August 8th. They met and Carr agreed to begin the series, as proposed, in October, with a fee of 110 guineas for the whole set of talks. By August 10th Churchill had agreed to be the lead speaker. Burgess wrote that day to Carr, laying out the agreed topics and speakers (most of whom were academics) for the series. According to W. J. West, "Although each interview appeared to the unsophisticated listener to be a spontaneous discussion, it was in fact fully scripted. The method used to get this result was as follows. The contributor first wrote a brief essay on the subject to be dealt with. This was sent to the interviewer, who wrote out a trial dialogue in question-and-answer or 'discussion' form. The programme's producer then edited this and returned it to the writer for comment and final alterations . . . Burgess always had the last word, and this for the severely practical reason that the series was one of those which only went out after being vetted by the Foreign Office."[96]

On the twelfth of August, Burgess, continuing to put in place Blunt's series on art, wrote to the latter:

> I have been trying to get hold of you about various things – nothing of any importance – as I am going away in a week. Elizabeth [Bowen?] tells me that you will be at Palace Court on your way to Cambridge this (Saturday) morning. Perhaps you would ring me up when you get there; I shall be working at the B.B.C.
>
> I want to discuss among other things the possibility of broadcasts this autumn (not the big series, but just one or two isolated talks, possibly under the title "Round the Galleries").[97]

Burgess was on leave for much of the last week or two of August.

By the end of the month the Munich Crisis was overwhelming all other matters at the B.B.C. On Sunday, August 28th, Nicolson wrote to Burgess ("My dear Guy"), enclosing his script for that evening and commenting that "I feel strongly that the public, at this juncture, has got to be alarmed." Indeed. On September 4th, President Benes of Czechoslovakia agreed to the autonomy demands that the country's German minority with the support (or at the instigation) of Hitler had been making. Nicolson was scheduled that evening to deliver one of his talks on the B.B.C. series produced by Burgess. The Assistant Director of Talks, George Barnes, believed that the political situation required consultation with the Foreign Office, despite the B.B.C.'s statutory independence from

Government supervision. Barnes thought the situation sufficiently important, and unusual, to record an hour-by-hour account of his negotiations with the Foreign Office, on the one hand, and Nicolson, on the other, beginning at noon when he first saw Nicolson's script. According to Barnes' memorandum, he took the script to (Sir) Reginald Leeper at the Foreign Office's News Department,[*] who approved of it, but told Barnes that he wanted it passed by Sir Alexander Cadogan, Permanent Undersecretary for Foreign Affairs. The latter stated that "in view of the gravity of the situation" the Foreign Office recommended that no talk touching on the Munich Crisis be given that night, but that although this was a strong recommendation, it could not command the B.B.C., which statement itself was, in fact, tantamount to a command. Barnes consulted up the B.B.C. hierarchy to the Controller of Programmes (to whom Maconachie was responsible) and was directed to avoid political comments in the talks that evening. The remainder of the afternoon and evening was spent in negotiations between Barnes and Nicolson over exactly what the latter would be able to talk about, Nicolson offering to cancel the talk, an action which was viewed by the Foreign Office as nearly as bad as giving a talk about the Czech crisis. Eventually a line was identified, which Nicolson agreed not to cross, and the talk was presented with Barnes standing by to cut it off if Nicolson strayed across the agreed line.

As expected, Benes's proposals did not satisfy the Sudeten Germans and on September 13 they revolted against the Prague government, which suppressed the revolt without difficulty. (As it, it is thought, it would have repelled a German invasion, if given the opportunity to do so.) Two days later Chamberlain flew to Berchtesgaden and offered to partition Czechoslovakia. Nicolson recorded in his diary for Monday, the 19th, that when he arrived at the B.B.C. "I am met by Maconachie and Guy Burgess and deliver

---

[*] Leeper became head of the Political Intelligence Department, responsible for the Political Warfare Executive, in 1938.

my talk in a voice of ironic gloom. I then go to the Café Royal with Guy where we meet James Pope-Hennessy who is almost in tears over England's shame . . . Not a very bright day in our rough island story."[98] Burgess wrote a letter to Nicolson a few days afterwards "from now onwards, since Parliament has stopped sitting the only talks we are having on world affairs are, in fact, yours and I am thus able to encourage you to do (what I know you would like to do)—to discuss rather seriously and for most of the talk the various political events of the past week – i.e. to do exactly what you did in your talk about Czechoslovakia ten days ago."

> I hope we may meet on Monday . . . Incidentally, you remember what you said to me about Hitler making a great peace speech? From one or two comments that I have heard, this does seem portentously likely, even going to the extent of coupling with it a demand for a conference of the allied powers (? excluding Russia) to make a new settlement to take the place of Versailles for the whole of Southern and Eastern Europe as well as the Colonies. What do you think? I only mention this as I heard it on quite good (semi-confidential authority, but it is only a guess (inspired).[99]

This would be typical of the sort of tid-bit that Burgess might have then passed along to his contacts in various secret services.

Benes, brow-beaten and sleep-deprived, acquiesced on the 21st. The following day Chamberlain met with Hitler at Godesberg. Hitler demanded an immediate occupation by Germany of the German areas of Czechoslovakia. Chamberlain persuaded him to wait until October 1st. Back in London trenches were dug in the parks and gas masks were distributed. Czechoslovakia mobilized on September 23rd. The Soviet Union reiterated its adherence to its mutual assistance treaty with Czechoslovakia. France ordered a partial mobilization on the 24th. On the 26th of September the British Foreign Office warned that if Germany invaded Czechoslovakia, Britain and France would go to her assistance. Duff Cooper (First Lord of the Admiralty) mobilized the British fleet on the 27th. On the 28th, in a dramatic, perhaps stage-managed, scene in Parliament,

Chamberlain announced that Hitler had agreed to a four-power conference at Munich. The following day Chamberlain flew to Munich and on the 30th received his scrap of paper from Hitler.

Just at this moment, Donald Maclean left London to become Third Secretary in the Paris Embassy.[100] He would remain there until the German occupation of the city. While Maclean was a Third Secretary in Paris he "saw virtually everything – not only the telegrams and formal dispatches, but even the Ambassador's personal letters to Sir Alexander Cadogan . . . and Sir Orme Sargent (at the Foreign Office)."[101] There were few career members of the Foreign Office in those days. A Third Secretary was not as inconsequential a personage, nor as lacking in opportunities, as might be assumed. On the other hand, the people with whom he met outside of office hours would not be noted, even if their names were Münzenberg or Katz. Kim Philby, to complete the picture, was in Spain as a stringer for *The Times,* reporting to various audiences from the Nationalist side of the lines.

In view of the crisis, Churchill asked to cancel his program that was to have opened the series on the Mediterranean. There are two accounts of the subsequent meeting between Churchill and Burgess. The first was recorded by Burgess in May, 1950, as he was leaving the United States. The second he told to Driberg a few years later. The second is the version accepted (and printed) by Martin Gilbert, Churchill's biographer. They do not greatly differ: the following narrative combines the two. In 1950, Burgess recalled: "I had met Mr. Churchill before dining with Venetia Montague and he had been most friendly.

I was extremely upset by the events of Munich Week and in fact I ultimately resigned from B.B.C. in order to try to join up as a result of them and as a result of his conversation . . . I rang Mr. Churchill up and said, "Could I come down?" He said, "Yes, by all means", and I had a Ford V-8 which I was very fond of at the time and I drove down to [Chartwell, near] Westerham to see Mr. Churchill, and arrived, I think, at about 11 o'clock in the morning. The door was opened by the butler and I saw Mr.

Churchill sitting in his study by himself immediately afterwards, and I said to Mr. Churchill: "It was very kind of you to see me. I simply do not know what I ought to do and before doing anything I would like to have your views."

In other words, Burgess's reason for visiting Churchill was for advice on his personal situation: what was a person in his situation to do in this crisis? The canonical version[102] has the picturesque detail that Churchill "was carrying a trowel when Guy arrived," which would have been rather odd if Churchill had been in his study. In any case, that version continues: "Guy said he was sorry Churchill felt he could not do the broadcast.

Churchill said he couldn't think about such things at such a time. Guy said how strongly he agreed with all the Churchill had been saying in public. Churchill said: "Well, I'm pleased to find that I have the youth of the country"—with a quizzical glance—"or some of it, with me . . ." And so they proceeded inevitably, like millions of other Britons that day, to talk of the great affairs that pre-occupied them . . .

Churchill showed Burgess a letter from Benes asking for his advice and assistance, asking Burgess, rhetorically, "What advice can I return?

What assistance can I offer? Here am I"—Churchill added, rising from his seat and thumping his chest—"here am I," said Mr. Churchill, thumping himself on the blue boiler suit that he was wearing, "here am I," said Mr. Churchill, "an old man, without power and without party. What help shall I give? What assistance can I offer? What answer can I return?"

Burgess said: "Don't be downhearted. Offer him your eloquence. Stump the country. Make speeches. Awaken people to the issues at stake."

"Ah-h-h, yes, yes, my eloquence; that indeed Herr Benes can count on in full and some would say in overbounding measure.

"But, Mr. Burgess, what other help have I to offer? What else is there? What can I give?

"You are silent, Mr. Burgess. You are rightly silent. What else? What else? What else have I to offer? One thing. One thing. My son Randolph, Randolph, who is already, I trust, a gentleman, is training to be an officer.

More silence.   "We had a bit of mutual hatred about Chamberlain and about Simon . . ." The Driberg version continues:

They went on to discuss wider aspects of the crisis. Guy found that, as he had expected, Churchill took the view that if Hitler had been resisted by Chamberlain, either the Czechs and therefore France, Britain and Russia would have fought or, quite possibly, there would have been no need to contemplate war at all. Guy may have told Churchill of the rumour then current in Prague and Paris that the Gestapo were planning to assassinate the German Ambassador in Prague, so that what would be presented to the world as a Czech crime could be used as a *casus belli*. Guy's analysis of this rumour (which he had submitted to the Secret Service) was that it was a deliberate Nazi propaganda leak, designed to give the impression that Germany wanted and was ready to fight; and that, if this was so, it tended to support the view that Hitler was bluffing both the world and his own general staff, who were less ready to fight than he . . .

After some further exchanges, Churchill ended the conversation by saying: "Well, Mr. Burgess, in this war that you and I—but not, apparently, His Majesty's Government—know is coming, I think they will give me a job of some kind. I hope to be employed again; and I shall be. Now I want to give you a book of mine to celebrate this conversation, which has sustained me. It is a volume of my speeches edited by my son Randolph.

He went off to another room, and came back with a copy of the book. It was *Arms and the Covenant*. "I must write in it," he said. He wrote: "To Guy Burgess, from Winston S. Churchill, to confirm his admirable sentiments. September, 1938."

He added that, if he got a job in the coming war, and if Guy brought him the book, he would remember their conversation and would find something worth doing in the war.

This conversation was one of the high points of Burgess's life.[*] He felt that in some way it validated him: as a young man he had been taken seriously by one of history's demigods—no matter how much he loathed most of what Churchill represented. Burgess kept the book, taking it out to show others on ceremonial occasions. Half a century later it somehow emerged from the archives of the FBI and came into the possession of Malcolm Forbes. It was sold at auction by his son in 2010.

Burgess and Churchill "had talked together for some hours. During that whole time, Burgess recalled, Churchill sat alone in a blue boiler suit, 'with no other callers, no messengers bringing urgent despatches [sic], no important secretaries with papers for him to read or sign; during the hours that this conversation lasted, the telephone did not ring once.'"[103] Burgess went back to London and that evening wrote two letters to Churchill (on Ascot Hill letterhead, crossed out and "British Broadcasting Corporation, Portland Place" substituted). The first was official: "I have now spoken to my chief, Sir Richard Maconachie, about the discussion we had to-day on your broadcast. He asks me to say how very sorry we are that, owing to the political situation, you find yourself unable to undertake your talk next Thursday."[104] The second letter, again on Ascot Hill letterhead, crossed out, this time with Burgess's home address of 38 Chester Square substituted, and dated "Saturday," was personal. It began: "Dear Mr. Churchill,

I've put the broadcast position officially on another sheet. I cannot help writing more personally to thank you for the way you received me to-day and for your book & the inscription.

---

[*] Sheila Grant Duff tells a similar story of a visit to Churchill, in her case in October, 1938. She, too, was given an autographed copy of *Arms and the Covenant* (Duff, Sheila Grant. The Parting of the Ways: A Personal Account of the Thirties. Peter Owen: London, 1982, pp. 157ff.).

The one unfortunately is already historic for the world, the other will be for me.

I feel I must in the situation we now find ourselves, and since I myself try to feel as a historian (I was a scholar at Cambridge, where I taught for a while) put what I feel on paper to you who listened so sympathetically this morning & on whom, as I see it, so much now depends. You will excuse the exaggerations (tho' I feel we are in a situation whose dangers cannot be exaggerated).*

The letter continued with the type of analysis that Churchill himself would have performed, sketching the historical context and a plan to defend the Empire (to which, rather than "Britain," Burgess repeatedly refers). A few days later, on October 4th, in the middle of the Munich debate, Burgess wrote a memorandum to the Director of Talks at the B.B.C., officially reporting "Part of Conversation with Mr. Churchill on Saturday, October 1st."

Mr. Churchill complained that he had been very badly treated in the matter of political broadcasts and that he was always muzzled by the B .B.C. I said I was not myself in possession of the facts and, in any case, had nothing to do with such matters, since I believed that the allotment of space was settled by arrangement and discussion between the B.B.C. and the political parties. I imagine that he was referring to a past controversy that I believe (though I didn't say so) there was over India and election time.

He went on to say that he imagined that he would be even more muzzled in the future, since the work at the B.B.C. seemed to have passed under the control of the Government. I said that this was not, in fact, the case, though just at the moment we were, as a matter of courtesy, allowing the Foreign Office to see scripts on political subjects. The point is W.S.C. seems very anxious to talk. [Last sentence handwritten.]

---

* See the Appendix for the complete letter.

While Burgess had been writing his lengthy letter to Churchill, Duff Cooper had resigned as First Lord of the Admiralty. Cooper's resignation speech opened the Munich debate on the afternoon of Monday, October 3ʳᵈ. The Labour Party leader, Attlee, was, for once, eloquent: "We have been unable to go in for care-free rejoicing. We have felt that we are in the midst of a tragedy. We have felt humiliation. This has not been a victory for reason and humanity. It has been a victory for brute force."[105] Then, on October 5ᵗʰ, Churchill gave his great speech (not impossibly slightly influenced by his conversation with Burgess and the latter's letter) ending with: "And do not suppose that this is the end. This is only the beginning of the reckoning. This is only the first sip, the first foretaste of a bitter cup which will be proffered to us year by year unless by a supreme recovery of moral health and martial vigour, we arise again and take our stand for freedom as in the olden time."[106] There was humiliation but, for the moment, not war. Writing to his friend, Robert Boothby, the anti-appeasement Conservative M.P., on the day of the Munich debate in the Commons, John Strachey stated:

> The issue during the coming months, and years, if we have so long, is that of the independence of this country. It is not a question now of whether this country is to become socialist or remain capitalist—or any issue intermediate between these two. It is a question of whether or not we are to be free to choose what we are to become. If a mixture of liking for the German and Italian *regimes*, and terror of war, is to govern our rulers' world policy, we shall very soon cease to be a free and interdependent sovereign state in the full meaning of the word.[107]

Nonetheless, business at the B.B.C., more or less as usual, continued. On October 10ᵗʰ Burgess wrote to Carr in regard to a typical bureaucratic trivia nightmare: Carr's name had been omitted from the description of the program in the Radio Times. Burgess expresses himself as "horrified" and apologizes three or four times before going on to discuss scripts. Each week thereafter there are letters from Burgess with details about the program production process and letters from Carr complaining about it. This from

Burgess on October 28 is typical:

> Now as to Monday, I hope to be back in the office by 12 o'clock but am not absolutely certain of my ability to do so. I hope you will be able to get ahead with the development of the talk. Please, if it suits you, use Miss Hosford (my Secretary) for dictation to help with the preparation of the script. I should certainly arrive before you leave but, if not, would you both please leave a message as to where I can speak to you by telephone. I don't want to be confronted on Thursday with an incomplete manuscript, as we shall only have bare time for rehearsal, so I shall try to rehearse Miss Monroe before our meeting together.

On December 14th (after many intervening) there is another such: "Here is the script typed out now . . . You will see that I have made two minute alterations, one on page 3 and one on page 12. There first one is to remove the impression that we have talked about nothing else but Anglo-Italian rivalry, in order to placate the F.O. . . . May I repeat what I said on the 'phone, that I do think this is a most admirable talk?"

When, on October 11, Burgess and Nicolson had one of their periodic dinners, the latter, even though he was an M.P., appeared to believe that Burgess had the better sources of inside information.

> Guy tells me what happened about the famous *Times* leader suggesting the cession of the Sudetenland was as follows. They took it first to the Czechs who said "We could consider that if only add in guarantee of our later integrity". They then took it to the Germans who said "that's all right provided there is no guarantee". They then left out the guarantee.[108]

But on November 24th it is Burgess who is looking for advice from Nicolson. The latter goes to the Reform Club "to have a talk with Guy Burgess who is in a state about the B.B.C."

> He tells me that a technical talk by Admiral Richmond about our strategic position in the Mediterranean (which had been definitely announced) was cancelled as a result of a telephone

message from Horace Wilson to the Director General. This has incensed him, and he wants to resign and publish why. I urge him to do nothing of the sort.[109]

Burgess was to take part of Nicolson's advice.

In the midst of international and B.B.C. tempests, Burgess found time in the first week of November to produce a talk by Christopher Isherwood entitled "China in War-Time," based on Isherwood's journey through China with W. H. Auden. In addition to his literary reputation, Isherwood was a person of interest to the British (and later, American) secret intelligence services. There is a nearly sixty-page-long Secret Service file on Isherwood at the British National Archives, beginning with an intercepted letter (December 1, 1932) from John Strachey introducing Isherwood to Gerald Hamilton, whom Isherwood would make famous in his *Berlin Stories* as "Mr. Norris".[110] In September, 1933, Olive Mangeot wrote to Hamilton, then in Shanghai, that she "believes that Christopher is staying in Paris with Dr. Katz." The extract is annotated, referring to the Comintern agent Otto, not the businessman Rudolf, Katz. Otto Katz, in turn, was the subject of extensive surveillance by the British authorities, with some attention paid, inter alia, to his relationship with the actor Peter Lorre, rather more to that with the politician Ellen Wilkinson. (Wilkinson was at the center of a network of relationships on the Left, from the Comintern operative Otto Katz to M.P.s Stafford Cripps, Nye Bevan and, especially, Herbert Morrison.) Isherwood, Auden and Spender were occasional B.B.C. broadcasters, working with Burgess and his colleagues in Talks and with producers in other departments. In 1951, Isherwood tried to place Burgess, for the FBI, in the London of the late 1930s:

> He advised that he met Burgess in the late 1930's when Burgess was employed by the British Broadcasting Company in London. He saw Burgess frequently in 1938 at the Café Royal and at parties . . . Isherwood furnished the names of the following persons whom he believes know Burgess: E. M. Forster, a novelist . . . Ralph Katz, now known as Rudolfo Katz, who publishes a financial guide and report in Buenos Aires . . . Jack

Hewitt, of London, who was described as an advertising man . . . W. H. Auden . . . Stephen Spender knew Burgess well. Lord Inverchapel, the former British Ambassador to the United States was also friendly with Burgess. He also mentioned Joseph Ackerley, who as the literary editor of the B.B.C., knew Burgess as a fellow employee and as a part of the literary crowd at the Café Royal.[111]

Isherwood (and Auden) had stayed with Inverchapel (Archibald Clark Kerr), then Ambassador to China, in Shanghai, where Clark Kerr had apparently been amused by the amusements they found there.

The relationship between Isherwood and Hewit—which was highly emotional at least for the latter—indicates that the relationship between Isherwood and Burgess in the late-1930s was fairly close. Burgess, then, produced radio programs for Isherwood and facilitated his acquisition of Hewit as a lover, when Isherwood was temporarily in want of one. In return Isherwood seemed to have been in the habit of snickering with his mentor, E. M. Forster, about Burgess. Forster wrote to Isherwood on November 14th (the Auden-Isherwood play, *On the Frontier* opened that night at Maynard Keynes's Arts Theatre in Cambridge, with Lydia Lopokova as leading lady, music by Benjamin Britten): "I can't feel that Guy Burgess matters. I used to take him seriously, but he used "a priori" where it made no sense, which I found disconcerting. The situation, the taking away someone from someone, is more serious I agree, but if J. is a strong character this won't matter either."[112] "J." was Jack Hewit, whom Isherwood was about to take with him to Belgium for a few weeks.

Anthony Blunt's art historian friend and colleague Ellis Waterhouse believed that "The curtain lines of this period were spoken, if my memory is correct, [on January 19, 1939] on platform 3 at Waterloo Station. Messrs Auden and Isherwood were being seen off to the United States, and a voice I never identified said, 'I suppose everyone in England worth saving is here'" Jack Hewit gave Isherwood, as a keepsake, his [Hewit's] first champagne cork, then

119

"left the platform in tears and was taken home by Benjamin Britten and Peter Pears" (the latter of whom made a pass at the disconsolate young man).[113] Isherwood had told Hewit that he would be taken along, or sent for later. Neither would take place. "One morning on deck," mid-Atlantic, Isherwood "turned to Auden and said: 'You know, I just don't believe in any of it any more—the united front, the party line, the anti-fascist struggle. I suppose they're okay, but something's wrong with me. I simply can't swallow another mouthful." And Auden answered: "No, neither can I."[114] The anti-fascist struggle, to which Isherwood here referred, was something in which John Cornford and Julian Bell had believed sufficiently to die for it. As had—and would—many more.

Six months after the passing-of-an-era scene on Platform number 3 of Waterloo Station, on June 17, 1939, Forster wrote to Isherwood:

> At a Cambridge commemoration dinner this week, Guy Burgess, supported by Anthony Blunt, came fussing me because you had behaved so badly to Jackie. As I daresay you have, and they then wanted me to read a letter from you to him which they had brought to the banquet. This I declined to do, to their umbrage. I could not see why I had to, when neither you nor J. had requested me to do so. G.B. [Guy Burgess] was insistent I should write to you, which I should have done in any case. He is [a] most cerebral gangster.[115]

Forster was one of the few people who did not find Burgess charming. Nor did he think it necessary for a man of his class, such as Isherwood, to behave well toward the likes of Jack Hewit and thought it tiresome that Burgess disagreed.

On December 12, 1938, Guy Burgess had sent a handwritten memorandum to the B.B.C. personnel department through the Director of Talks: "I should like to hand in my resignation, as from to-day. I should like to make it clear that my reasons for taking this step do not arise out of any failure to enjoy working under the existing Director of Talks."[116] Burgess told Driberg that he had resigned to take a "regular job" with Section Nine of the Secret Intelligence Service after the B.B.C., where he had "an established position," refused to second him to the Secret Service. As having an established position, that is, a permanent, not temporary, job was always important to Burgess, moving from one to what was described as a six-month temporary assignment was a decision he was not likely to have taken lightly.[117] It did make him the first of his Comintern group to find employment in the British secret intelligence services. His employment there, and what he learned about it, mattered. Secret intelligence organizations are, among other things, defence mechanisms of the state (or "realm"). The way in which they function, their officers and the personalities of those officers, what is known by them and what they do not know, are of vital interest to the secret intelligence organizations of other states. They are among a state's most closely guarded secrets.

To use the term common in discussing these matters, at least from the beginning of 1939 Burgess was a mole.

A Note on Burgess and the Conservative Office

According to Isaiah Berlin, the first job Burgess got after leaving Trinity, much to the surprise of friends not as close as Blunt, was at the Conservative Central Office, "working with a man called Stannard, whose real name was Steinhardt, and Lord Longford, then Frank Pakenham."[118] Stannard and Frank Pakenham worked in the Conservative Research Department, "Neville Chamberlain's private army," at 24 Old Queen Street, under the direction of (Sir) Joseph Ball.

The Director of the Department throughout the Chamberlain years, Joseph Ball, who was knighted for his services in 1936, was a man who played many roles, most of them carefully hidden from view. He was one of M.I.5's most successful and least scrupulous officers . . . Lacking any kind of moral compass, there was quite literally no misdeed to which he himself was not prepared to stoop."[119]

The Conservative Research Department was founded, effectively by Chamberlain, to provide policy and related research for the Conservative Party, its office holders and candidates. Burgess might have found the Conservative Research Department ideologically less uncomfortable than might be supposed, as, during those years, Chamberlain was following a domestic policy of Tory populism: identifying issues in education, housing and health care that could be dealt with to the benefit of the working class, albeit within a Conservative policy structure. [120] It would have been useful to Burgess in two ways: as a setting where his research skills, still fresh from Cambridge, could be put to use and appreciated, and as a résumé item underlying his move from Left to Right. It might also have brought him into contact with Joseph Ball, a relationship which they might have found mutually beneficial. Be that as it may, it is not possible to verify Berlin's account: the Conservative Research Department has no records showing Burgess's employment in any capacity and Joseph Ball denied, in court, any contact with Burgess.[121] Perhaps Isaiah Berlin had confused two of Burgess's stories; perhaps Ball was not telling the truth and the records of the Conservative Research Department have been edited. Be that as it may, there are strong indications that Burgess knew Ball, if not in 1934, most probably a few years later.

Notes to Chapter Three

1 Stansky, Peter and William Abrahams. Journey to the Frontier: Two
Roads to the Spanish Civil War. Little, Brown and Company. An Atlantic
Monthly Press Book. Boston, 1966, p. 112.

2 Card, Tim. Eton Renewed: A History from 1860 to the Present Day.
London: John Murray, 1994, p. 187. Dennis Robertson, at Cambridge,
when asked, would not give him a reference.

3 Driberg, Tom. Guy Burgess: A Portrait with Background. London:
Weidenfeld and Nicolson, 1956, pp. 30-1. The story has been confirmed by
Miriam Rothschild, Victor Rothschild's sister. The hundred pound a month
figure is surprising—that would be something over $8,000 in today's
money. It would be interesting to know for how many months this stipend
ran and to see the advice given in return, but the Rothschild Arcives are not
forthcoming.

4 Interview with Michael Ignatieff, 8 February 1974 (Tape MI 7); transcript
in the possession of Henry Hardy, Wolfson College, Oxford; © The Isaiah
Berlin Literary Trust, courtesy of Henry Hardy. Rudolph, or Rudolfo, Katz
is not to be confused with Otto Katz, the associate of Willi Munzenberg.
The earliest notation in the M.I.5 file on Katz in the National Archives,
Kew, is for September, 1936, but it is possible that he visited England
earlier without coming to the attention of the authorities. He was a German
Jew, primarily resident in Argentina, traveling frequently to London on
behalf of Argentine weapons manufacturers. By 1939, at the latest, he was
receiving a quarterly retainer from James de Rothschild, presumably for
financial advice. His secret police file at Kew contains, among much else,
photo copies of checks from James de Rothschild. See KV 2/2178, Kew.

5 KV 2/2587, Kew.

6 Annan, Noel. New York Review of Books, 22 October 1987, quoted in
Carter, Miranda. Anthony Blunt: His Lives. London: Macmillan, 2001, p.
78.

7 The address in the journalistic sources is given as 28. For 38 see B.B.C.
Staff Record Form, B.B.C. Written Archives Center, Caversham; London
Gardens Trust: www.londongardenstrust.org/guides/chelsea.htm. Burgess
lived there 1935-1940.

8 Grant Duff, Sheila. The Parting of Ways: A Personal Account of the
Thirities. Peter Owen: London, 1982, p. 91; Furbank, P. N. E. M. Forster,
A Life. New York and London: Harcourt Brace Jovanovich, 1977, p. 193.

[9] Straight, Michael. After Long Silence. W. W. Norton & Company, Inc.: New York, 1983, p. 67.

[10] "In fact Goronwy's collaboration with Guy did not last very long, but for a period he supplied him with fairly high grade political gossip from the High Table of All Souls, of which he was a Fellow and where many former fellows, some of whom occupied high positions in government or the civil service, often spent the week end to relax from their official duties." Blunt, Anthony. British Library, Add. Ms. 88902/1, p. 38.

[11] Cecil, Robert. A Divided Life: A Biography of Donald Maclean. The Bodley Head, London, 1988, p. 51.

[12] Stansky and Abrahams, p. 228; 231.

[13] Taylor, A. J. P. English History: 1914-1945. Oxford University Press, New York, 1965, p. 381.

[14] Hobsbawm, Eric. Interesting Times: A Twentieth Century Life. London: Allen Lane/Penguin, 2002, p. 101.

[15] Straight, p. 95.

[16] Kershaw, Ian. Making Friends with Hitler: Lord Londonderry, the Nazis and the Road to War. New York: Penguin Press, 2004, p. 143.

[17] http://svr.gov.ru/smi/2004/bratishka20040125.htm.

[18] Blunt, Anthony. British Library, ADD Ms. 88902/1, pp. 24-25. Philby, as he would, tells a more colorful story about Burgess's decision to resign from the Communist Party of Great Britain and begin underground activities in *My Secret War*. He also described the action in a different order, with Blunt's adherence to the Comintern preceeding Burgess's.

[19] Hansard, HC Deb 10 July 1936 vol 314 cc1583.

[20] Hansard, HC Deb 18 December 1936 vol 318 cc2832.

[21] [21] Nicolson, Harold. Diaries in The Vita Sackville-West and Harold Nicolson manuscripts, letters and diaries [microform]: from Sissinghurst Castle, Kent, the Huntington Library, California, and other libraries, reel 13.

[22] Channon, Sir Henry. "Chips": The Diaries of Sir Henry Channon. Edited by Robert Rhodes James. London: A Phoenix Giant Paperback, 1993, p. 153.

[23] "Politics pervaded all aspects of camp life. Though children, their political commitment was forged by the civil war and the passion that the Spanish bring to their politics. "Their smoking and interest in politics were the most noticeable things about them," said Mr Albert Arthur remembering his days as a young volunteer at the camp. On one occasion a group of

---

children went without supper rather than wear the yellow armband - to differentiate them from those who had already eaten - because it was the colours of Franco's Moroccan troops.

"The main purpose of the camp was to give time for the Basque Children's Committee to find homes for the children's stay in England; have them medically checked and record all details for their eventual return to Spain." www.spanishrefugees-basquechildren.org/C5-Stoneham_Camp.htm

24 Driberg, p. 32. Burgess had met Wylie a year or two earlier, through Philby, who had been assigned to cultivate Wylie, but disliked him. Philby tells one of his characteristically amusing stories about how he passed Wylie on to Burgess:

"I arranged a (small) cocktail party, inviting both Wyllie and Burgess. I introduced them and left them to it, drifting from guest to guest as a good host should. Soon loud voices were raised in the Burgess-Wyllie corner; all was clearly not well. I caught Burgess's eye and he bounced aggressively across the room. 'Who', he asked loudly, 'is that pretentious young idiot who thinks he knows all about Proust?' I replied that I did not know anything about pretensions or Proust, but Wyllie was not an idiot. He had a very important job in the War Office. 'Ho,' said Burgess and wheeled back to Wyllie . . . Before they left the party, they had made a date." Philby, H. A. R. Jr. "Autobiographical Reminiscences," in Philby, Rufina, Lyubimov, Mikhail and Hayden Peake. The Private Life of Kim Philby: The Moscow Years. New York: Fromm International, 2000, p. 235.

It is not impossible that Wylie mentioned War Department matters to Burgess, and, therefore, it would be assumed, for counterintelligence purposes, that he did.

25 Driberg, p. 32.

26 Among the stories is the classic tale of the naked athlete as ping pong table net.

27 Modin, Yuri. With Jean-Chalrles Deniau and Aguieszka Ziarek. Translated by Anthony Roberts. My Five Cambridge Friends: Burges, Maclean, Philby, Blunt, and Cairncross by their KGB Controller. New York: Farrar Straus Gioux, 1994, p. 79.

[28] MacNiece, Louis to Anthony Blunt, 7 May 1936, King's College Library, MacNeice Letters, quoted in Carter, Miranda. Anthony Blunt: His Lives. London: Macmillan, 2001, p. 96.

[29] MacNeice, Louis. The Strings are False. An Unfinished Autobiography. London: Faber and Faber, 1965, p. 157.

[30] "The reason for getting rid of capitalist control . . . is because war is inherent in a system which is based upon economic competition." Cripps, Stafford. The Struggle for Peace. London: Victor Gollancz Ltd, 1936, p. 104.

[31] Cripps, Stafford. The Struggle for Peace. London: Victor Gollancz Ltd, 1936, p. 89.

[32] Cripps, p. 116; p. 127.

[33] Cripps, pp. 154-5.

[34] Reith, J. C. W. Into the Wind. London: Hodder & Stoughton, 1949, p. 245.

[35] Extract from letter from Mr. Guy of Cambridge Appointments Board, B.B.C. Written Archives Center, Caversham.

[36] B.B.C. Written Archives Center, Caversham.

[37] Regrets letter 13 December 1935. B.B.C. Written Archives Center, Caversham.

[38] Page, Bruce. Leitch, David. Knightley, Phillip. Philby: The Spy Who Betrayed a Generation. Andre Deutsch, Limited, London, 1968, p. 72. The Times had given Burgess a one-month trial as a home sub-editor from December 29, 1935 to January 24, 1936. He was one of a number of young men who passed through the department on trial during that period.

[39] Grant Duff, p. 111.

[40] Nicolson, Harold. Diaries in The Vita Sackville-West and Harold Nicolson manuscripts, letters and diaries [microform]: from Sissinghurst Castle, Kent, the Huntington Library, California, and other libraries, reel 13. Nicolson was rather better placed in Westminster than Macnamara and Mayfair, enhancing Burgess's access to information from Parliament, Government, and Society. The last of these was of interest during the Abdication Crisis.

[41] Taylor, A. J. P. English History: 1914-1945. Oxford University Press, New York, 1965, p. 409.

[42] Thomas, Hugh. John Strachey. New York: Harper & Row, 1973, pp. 150-1.

43 Driberg, p. 37.

44 During World War II, Footman, as head of a German unit of Section V of M.I.6, supervised John Cairncross. Cairncross, p. 114.

45 Grant Duff, p. 118.

46 After Long Silence, p. 86.

47 Carter, Miranda. Anthony Blunt: His Lives. London: Macmillan, 2001, p. 163; 165.

48 Hastings, Selina, Rosamond Lehmann. London: Vintage, 2003, p. 195 and Rees, Jenny. Looking for Mr. Nobody: The Secret Life of Goronwy Rees. London: Phoenix, Orion, 1997, p. 93.

49 Sir Dennis Proctor, an Apostle, classicist and senior civil servant. Later chairman of the Board of Trustees of the Tate.

50 B.B.C. Staff Record Form, B.B.C. Written Archives Center, Caversham.

51 Letter from J. Burnaby, Tutor, Trinity College, August 10, 1936, B.B.C. Written Archives Center, Caversham.

52 Letter to Nicolls from P. D. Pollock, 5 Peel Street, Campden Hill; W.8 Park 7921, August 18, 1936, B.B.C. Written Archives Center, Caversham.

53 Nicolson, Harold. Diaries in The Vita Sackville-West and Harold Nicolson manuscripts, letters and diaries [microform]: from Sissinghurst Castle, Kent, the Huntington Library, California, and other libraries, reel 13. "In August 1936 a new young man burst into Harold [Nicolson]'s life in the form of James ("Jamesey") Pope-Hennessy, then at Balliol with Harold's son Nigel. Jamesy was the younger son of Richard Pope-Hennessy, a retired general and something of a dullard, and his wife Dame Una, a formidable literary bluestocking who brought up her two boys to have wide intellectual and artistic interests . . . He was part Malay, is grandfather, a colonial governor, having married a lady of mixed blood . . . He quickly seduced Harold, who would remain infatuated with him for the rest of his life . . . James Lees-Milne also capitulated to the advances of this enchanting twenty-year-old, and they began an intermittent affair which would last for a decade." Bloch, Michael. James Lees-Milne: The Life. London: John Murray, 2009, p. 110. Nigel Nicolson called James Pope-Hennessy his "closest male friend." The geometries of these relationships are sometimes complex. Nicolson, Nigel. Long Life: Memoirs. London: Phoenix, 1997, p. 64.

54 Foreign Intelligence Service, Russian Federation, Newsletter, September 8, 2006, http://svr.gov.ru/smi/2006/krzv20060809-11.htm

[55] Cornford, Rubert John. "Full Moon at Tierz: Before the Storming of Hesca" in Sloan, Pat (editor). John Cornford: A Memoir. Dunfermline, Fife: Borderline Press, 1978. p. 244.

[56] Staff Training School, Course: October 1 to December 31, 1936, B.B.C. Written Archives Center, Caversham.

[57] West, W.J. Truth Betrayed. London: Gerald Duckworth & Co., Ltd, 1987, p. 45.

[58] In Penrose, Barrie and Freeman, Simon. Conspiracy of Silence: The Secret Life of Anthony Blunt. New York, Farrar Straus Giroux, 1987, pp. 202-3.

[59] Foreign Intelligence Service, Russian Federation, Newsletter, September 8, 2006, http://svr.gov.ru/smi/2006/krzv20060809-11.htm. It is puzzling how Burgess would have traveled, under the conditions then pertaining, from London to Gibraltar and back over, say, a long weekend.

[60] Foreign Intelligence Service of the Russian Federation, Newsletter, January 25, 2004, http://svr.gov.ru/smi/2004/bratishka20040125.htm

[61] Contributors, Roger Fulford, Talks file 1, 1937-1962, B.B.C. Written Archives Center, Caversham. During World War II Fulford was in the War Office (M.I.5) and then assistant private secretary to Sir Archibald Sinclair, the Secretary of State for Air.

[62] West, pp. 52-3.

[63] Talks, Barron, Harry Dr., Talks file 1, 1937-1949, B.B.C. Written Archives Center, Caversham.

[64] KV 2/2587.

[65] Contributors, Footman, David, Talks file 1, 1937-1962, PP/GB 27th May, 1937, B.B.C. Written Archives Center, Caversham.

[66] Contributors, Footman, David, Talks file 1, 1937-1962, B.B.C. Written Archives Center, Caversham.

[67] Jeffery, Keith. The Secret History of MI6. New York: The Penguin Press, 2010, pp. 285-6.

[68] Straight, p. 108.

[69] Straight, Michael, letter to Stansky and Abrahams, quoted in Stansky and Abrahams, p. 393.

[70] Marsh had retired from the Civil Service, in which he had been Private Secretary to the Secretary of State for the Colonies, in 1937. Most of his career had been spent as Churchill's private secretary in whatever position Churchill happened to occupy at a given moment. Deacon, Richard. The

Cambridge Apostles: A History of Cambridge University's Elite
Intellectual Secret Society. Farrar, Straus & Giroux, New York, 1985, p.
67. Dates of Apostles annual dinners courtesy Professor William Lubenow,
personal communication.

71 Burgess told Driberg that Julian Bell's parents, Clive and Vanessa, had
asked him to, but he had felt that he "could not conscientiously do so"
(Driberg, p. 35), something he still regretted twenty years later.

72 Burgess Personnel File, Memorandum of 22 June 1937, B.B.C. Written
Archives Center, Caversham.

73 Carter, Miranda. Anthony Blunt: His Lives. London: Macmillan, 2001,
p. 209.

74 Carter, p. 201.

75 Lancaster, Marie-Jaqueline. Brian Howard: Portrait of a Failure. San
Francisco, Greencandy Press, 2007, p. 232.

76 Ignatieff, Michael. Isaiah Berlin: A Life. London: Chatto & Windus,
1998, p. 95. Date given as 1937 in Ignatieff's 1994 interview with Berlin.

77 Kings College Archive, Box 149/ 8.

78 Carter, pp. 229-230. Pollock told Carter that he had not enjoyed sex with
Burgess. As he did have a strong sexual relationship later with Francis
Bacon, who was renowned for his masochism, it may have been the case
that Pollock and Burgess both favored the reciprocal, "active," role. Carter,
p. 209.

79 Contributors. Nicolson, Harold. Talks. B.B.C. Written Archives Center,
Caversham.

80 Contributors. Blunt, Anthony. Talks. B.B.C. Written Archives Center,
Caversham.

81 Maclean, Fitzroy. Take Nine Spies. Atheneum: New York, 1978, p.
228. This is close to, and may be based on the account Burgess gave
Driberg, during the Munich period: "As the crisis drew near, Guy [sic] paid
a number of visits to Paris to see [Edouard] Pfeiffer and others, including
some of the French Rothschilds . . . On behalf of Pfeiffer he carried letters
to a man of title closely associated with the Prime Minister and also with an
unofficial intelligence organization which supplied information not only to
Chamberlain but to Sir Horace Wilson, head of the Civil Service . . . These
letters were, in effect, private communications from Chamberlain and
Daladier; presumably to ensure greater secrecy, the exchanges were signed
by subordinates on both sides of the Channel and entrusted neither to the

post nor to the diplomatic bags. Neither the principals nor Pfeiffer and his opposite number knew that, on the way, Guy would call at a flat in the St. Ermins Hotel in Westminster and meet there a man who took photostatic pictures of the letters while he waited." Driberg, Tp. 40.

[82] Page, Bruce. Leitch, David. Knightley, Phillip. Philby: The Spy Who Betrayed a Generation. Andre Deutsch, Limited, London, 1968, p. 77. The Burgess/Trevor-Roper communication has been impossible to track down. Cherry Hughes, working with Page, Leitch and Knightley, interviewed Trevor-Roper, who despised Ball. See Trevor-Roper, Letters from Oxford: Hugh Trevor-Roper to Berdard Berenson, Davenport-Hines, Richard, ed. London: Weidenfeld & Nicholson, 2006, pp. 27-8.

[83] Mrs. Basset had an apartment in Arlington House, Piccadilly, built in 1934-36 as a private residential block backing onto Green Park and adjoining the rear of the famous Ritz Hotel, Piccadilly.

[84] Burgess Personnel File, B.B.C. Written Archives Center, Caversham.

[85] It is not impossible that it was in March, 1938, not March of the previous year, that Burgess delivered the codes to Philby at Gibraltar.

[86] Talks Index Cards, B.B.C. Written Archives Center, Caversham, information courtesy of Ms. Trish Hayes.

[87] Driberg, p. 40. Hewit told this story to many interviewers after 1951.

[88] Hastings, p. 190.

[89] B.B.C. Written Archives Center, Caversham. Reference PP/GB 22nd July, 1938.

[90] Hastings, p. 195.

[91] Cecil, Robert. A Divided Life: A Biography of Donald Maclean. The Bodley Head, London, 1988, p. 56.

[92] Thomas, Hugh. John Strachey. New York: Harper & Row, 1973, p. 170.

[93] Nicolson, Harold. Diaries in The Vita Sackville-West and Harold Nicolson manuscripts, letters and diaries [microform]: from Sissinghurst Castle, Kent, the Huntington Library, California, and other libraries, reel 13.

[94] Aside from Lulu, perhaps, Nicolson had enjoyed a dinner party attended by the Duke and Duchess of Windsor. The Duke "scandalized" the company by referring to the Duchess as "Her Royal Highness." Nicolson, Harold. Diaries and Letters, 1930-1939. Edited by Nigel Nicolson. New York: Atheneum, 1966, pp. 351-2.

[95] Contributors. Carr, E.H. Talks. B.B.C. Written Archives Center, Caversham.

[96] West, p. 55;6.

[97] Burgess Personnel File, B.B.C. Written Archives Center, Caversham, 12th August, 1938.

[98] Nicolson, Harold. Diaries in The Vita Sackville-West and Harold Nicolson manuscripts, letters and diaries [microform]: from Sissinghurst Castle, Kent, the Huntington Library, California, and other libraries, reel 13.

[99] West, p. 54.

[100] Cecil, p. 51.

[101] Cecil, p. 57.

[102] The account of the meeting given to Driberg by Burgess was accepted by Churchill's biographer Martin Gilbert. Gilbert, Martin. Winston S. Churchill. Volume V: 1922-1939. London: Heinemann, 1976. pp. 990-1. Burgess's introduction to Churchill came through his fellow Apostle, Edward Marsh, Churchill's longtime secretary. Deacon, Richard. The Cambridge Apostles: A History of Cambridge University's Elite Intellectual Secret Society. Farrar, Straus & Giroux, New York, 1985, p. 133.

[103] Gilbert, p. 991.

[104] The Sir Winston Churchill Archive, CHAR 2/350/23.

[105] Gilbert, p. 993.

[106] Gilbert, p. 1001.

[107] Thomas, p. 177-8.

[108] Nicolson, Harold. Diaries in The Vita Sackville-West and Harold Nicolson manuscripts, letters and diaries [microform]: from Sissinghurst Castle, Kent, the Huntington Library, California, and other libraries, reel 13.

[109] Nicolson, Harold. Diaries and Letters, 1930-1939. Edited by Nigel Nicolson. New York: Atheneum, 1966, p. 380.

[110] KV 2/2587.

[111] KV 2/2587.

[112] Forster to Isherwood, 14-11-38 in Zeikowitz. Letters between Forster and Isherwood on Homosexuality and Literature. Palgrave Macmillan; annotated edition (August 5, 2008), p. 77.

[113] Carter, pp. 236-7.

[114] Isherwood, Christopher. Diaries, Volume One: 1939-1960. Edited and Introduced by Katherine Bucknell. London: Methuen, 1996, p.6.

[115] Forster to Isherwood, 17-6-39 in Zeikowitz. Letters between Forster and Isherwood on Homosexuality and Literature. Palgrave Macmillan; annotated edition (August 5, 2008), p. 81.

[116] Burgess Personnel File, B.B.C. Written Archives Center, Caversham.

[117] Driberg, p. 49.

[118] Interview with Michael Ignatieff, 8 February 1974 (Tape MI 7); transcript in the possession of Henry Hardy, Wolfson College, Oxford; © The Isaiah Berlin Literary Trust, courtesy of Henry Hardy.

[119] Cooke, Alistair. "'Neville Chambrlain's Private Army'," in Cooke, Alistair, ed., Tory Policy-Making: The Conservative Research Department, 1929-2009. London: Manor Creative, n.d., p. 10.

[120] Cooke, pp. 5-26

[121] I am grateful to Alistair Cooke, Lord Lexden, for information (or the lack of it) concerning Burgess in the Conservative Research Departments records. Sir Joseph Ball's papers are in the Bodleian archives, MS. Eng.c.6656.

Chapter Four

Secret Intelligence Service Section D

> "It is well in all cases to go on the old
> [Counter Espionage] axiom: "Once an
> agent, always an agent—for someone.'"
> *Norman Holmes Pearson*[1]

In late March, 1938, "Admiral 'Quex' Sinclair, then current C, as
the head of SIS [M.I.6] was known in Whitehall, borrowed an officer
from the army, Major L. D. Grand, and told him to start a new
section in the secret service.

It was to be called Section D. Grand's task was to look into the
theory of secret offensives: how could enemies be attacked,
otherwise than by the usual military means? While peace lasted,
he was to *do* nothing; but he was to think over sabotage, labour
unrest, inflation, anything else that could be done to weaken an
enemy, and if he could he was to make outline plans for them.
He was to consider who could do the work on the spot –
communists, perhaps, or Jews? And he was to consider means
of propaganda, to shift enemy opinion.[2]

Major Lawrence Grand "had some of the gifts needed for a
successful secret service leader, including a striking personality.

He was tall, handsome, well tailored, with a heavy dark
moustache; wore a red carnation; smoked cigarettes, almost
without cease, through an elegant black holder; had an equally
elegant wit. He was brimful of ideas and energy, and he had a
rare gift: he gave full trust to those under him, and backed them
up without question against outsiders.[3]

This was the organization Burgess, perhaps at the suggestion of David Footman, had resigned from the B.B.C. to join.[4] W. J. West, the historian of Second World War radio propaganda, speculated that Burgess (whom he says was at this point "well known as a brilliant radio producer") was brought into association with Section D through his activities as a courier for Horace Wilson, Chamberlain's back-channel advisor, who, West speculated, could have introduced him to Major Grand.[5] The connection could just as well have been made by Sir Joseph Ball (if there was a connection between Ball and Burgess). In the absence of documentation, three possible sponsors from the secret world will suffice. Burgess plunged into the work of Section D. As early as January, 1939 he was already deep into "wireless schemes."[6] He was to spend most of 1939 helping to set up the propaganda apparatus for Section D, sometimes as the liaison officer between that organization and the Ministry of Information. He also acted as liaison between Section D, Electra House (forerunner of the Political Warfare Executive) and the Joint Broadcasting Committee (J.B.C.).[*] The Joint Broadcasting Committee was run by Hilda Matheson, who, when Burgess was an undergraduate had been Michael Redgrave's producer for his programs on the B.B.C. The J.B.C. was housed at 71 Chester Square, fifty feet from Burgess's flat at 38 Chester Square.

In March, 1939, after the Germans had taken what had been left of Czechoslovakia after Munich, Major Grand submitted a plan to Lord Gort, the chief of the Imperial General Staff, to put Section D on a war footing. This was agreed to by Gort and Foreign Minister Lord Halifax a few days later. Grand "was authorized . . . to embark on sabotage and leaflet work in the Czech borderlands and Austria, and to put out leaflets and to prepare sabotage in any areas now obviously threatened by Germany in eastern and south-eastern

---

[*] A memorandum of December 20, 1939 in the B.B.C. archives concerning a meeting between Matheson and representatives of the Ministry of Information refers to Burgess as a representative of the Joint Broadcasting Board to the Ministry.

Europe."[7] At the end of the month, Matheson asked Harold Nicolson (her lover Vita Sackville-West's husband), to help her with "a very secret bureau which is to broadcast to Germany." Nicolson said that he would and joined the Committee, the J.B.C.'s governing body, which seemed to have no other active members.[8] Burgess, West tells us, assisted for a time by Paul Frischauer and his wife, a refugee couple, worked with the J.B.C. to produce covert recordings "at first only in German, which could be played on . . . equipment in Germany itself, or from neighbouring countries . . . The records contained not merely propaganda but variety programmes with the latest German hit songs."[9] (These did not yet include "Lili Marleen.") Much of this material, including translations of speeches by Chamberlain and other high officials, were transmitted either by Radio Luxemburg or by clandestine equipment. Burgess, then, knew the dimensions and contents of this aspect of the British propaganda effort and was in a position to freely, if secretly, communicate that knowledge to his contacts, all the more so in view of his status as an official in Section D of M.I.6.

The comparatively overt side of the J.B.C. was organized in April of 1939 as a "'Goodwill' organization, not associated with the B.B.C., to promote the broadcasting of material addressed to friendly or potential neutral countries (including the self-governing Dominions) willing or anxious to receive them. It aimed at the issue of broadcast programmes in countries which might not wish to accept propaganda from British official sources."[10] The J.B.C. prepared these overt programs, viewed as propaganda by the organization itself, as distinguished from the "objective" self-image of the programming of the B.B.C., although they were similar to many on the B.B.C., such as talks by politicians and academics, as well as musical programs (for example, a recording of the Kings College Choir) "sound pictures, and "sound documentaries," which were sent to radio stations around the world. This activity of the J.B.C. was divided into geographical sections: Latin America, Southern Europe, Arabic Speaking Countries, etc.

A letter from Matheson to Mary Fisher, daughter of H. A. L. Fisher, Warden of New College, Oxford, tells us something about the mission, activities and atmosphere of this side of the organization.

Dear Mary,

Are you still feeling that you would like to do a job? If so, this work is growing fast and we are about to burst forth into regular programmes for France, Italy, Spain and Portugal, and possibly Switzerland. I shall have to get somebody to take on these countries as a bunch and be responsible for thinking out and discussing with their representatives what programmes reflecting English life, ideas, and literature they would be willing to take. I need some one who knows at least France and Italy and who has a pretty wide range of interests. Do you think you would like to consider it? It is a stimulating and amusing company in which you would work, and you could get home for most weekends, anyway. I could give you about £350 to start with. Do let me know what you feel and when you could start.[11]

The overt programs produced by the J.B.C. were sent (free) to the countries for which they were intended (in the languages of those countries) by telephone or on discs, or occasionally the scripts were sent for local production. Propaganda aimed at German audiences was a special case. It "was envisaged by Matheson that the JBC would have greater freedom than the B.B.C. to develop propaganda for the German audience in the critical months of August and September [1939] . . .

There were meetings in July 1939 to discuss "close liaison" [between the JBC and the B.B.C.], yet liaison was never easy even after war broke out and after officials instructions were issued that the main functions of the JBC—an independent organization—were to prepare programmes first for clandestine distribution in enemy countries in conjunction with Electra House and second for use in neutral and friendly countries in conjunction with the Foreign Publicity Division of the Ministry of Information.[12]

We have, then, three broadcasting organizations: Electra House, primarily responsible for "Black Propaganda" content, that is, more or less, lies; the Joint Broadcasting Committee, responsible for both content and media, the former consisting of both the sort of thing produced by Electra House and other materials, including concerts, the latter both recordings and transmissions, and the B.B.C. itself, which, it is said, told no lies on its radio waves. Burgess, on the payroll of Section D of M.I.6, appears to have dipped in and out of all three organizations, broadening his knowledge of the British propaganda effort. He kept in touch with Nicolson, in the latter's role as a member of the J.B.C.'s board, for instance, discussing broadcast propaganda with him over lunch at the Reform Club late in April, 1939. When on Friday, May 5th, Burgess called on Nicolson, the latter noted in his diary that "He wants us [J.B.C.] to get Geneva to broadcast foreign news from the L[eague] of N[ations] station regularly each hour."[13] Early in June Burgess had a conversation with Nicolson, during which "He tells me dreadful stories about his childhood and in the intervals we discuss foreign broadcasts."[14] The "dreadful stories" might be about his father's death.[*] Or might not. Six weeks later, when Burgess and Nicolson talked again, the latter noted that Burgess "is organizing his wireless very well."[15]

As Burgess was organizing his wireless, Europe was preparing for war. All that summer a low-level British delegation in the Soviet Union talked about an alliance. Burgess told Driberg that on August 5th, the day the British delegation sailed for Leningrad, he had dinner with the head of his Section (Grand). "Guy remarked that he hoped they [the delegation] would reach agreement quickly. His chief, shocked by his naivety, said that that was, of course out of the question: they had no power to reach agreement, and indeed their instructions were to prolong the negotiations without reaching agreement."[16] Which might well have been the case. The talks ended on August 21. They failed (or succeeded, depending on one's point

---

[*] While having sex with his wife, who could not shift him and had called in her young son to help.

139

of view) for many reasons, one of which might have been the Soviet assessment that as the British had not stood up to the Japanese in China, which was of significant economic interest to the Empire, they could not be counted on to stand by their old enemy, the Soviet Union. And, in a mirror image of contempt, the British Government, and the British military, in particular, thought that an alliance with the Red Army, decimated by the Purges, would be of little use.[17] The distrust between London and Moscow, characteristic of these negotiations, lingered.

On August 23 the German Foreign Minister, Ribbentrop, who had traveled to Moscow by airplane, rather than slow freighter, and his Soviet counterpart, Molotov, signed the Nazi-Soviet pact. In his unpublished memoir, Anthony Blunt tells the story of Burgess's reaction to the news. "Guy and I were in France, on our way to Italy when Guy got a telegram ordering him back to London from "D," the organization within M.I.6 for which he was working. On the way back we bought a newspaper in which the Russo-German non-aggression pact was announced . . . " They left the car at Boulogne with the Automobile Association representative to ship back to London (a benefit of Burgess's membership in the Royal Automobile Club).

> During the day [Burgess] produced half-a-dozen justifications for [the Russo-German pact], of which the principal argument was the one which eventually turned out to be correct, namely that it was only a tactical maneuver to allow the Russians time to rearm before the eventual and inevitable German attack. He also used an argument which he had frequently brought up during the previous months, that the British negotiations which had been going on for an Anglo-Russian pact were a bluff . . . Whether this was true or not I had and have no means of knowing, but Guy certainly believed it at the time—and no doubt passed on his opinion to his Russian contact.[18]

That last phrase is of interest, given Blunt's—and Burgess's—reticence in these matters. Of course it was not merely Burgess's opinion: it was information he had received from the head of

140

Section D. It would be reasonable for an intelligence analyst to take it as authoritative.

Germany, having secured its Eastern flank, duly invaded Poland on September 1st. After some hesitation, Britain and France declared war on Germany two days later. The Soviet Union invaded Poland from the east two weeks after that and shortly thereafter all Polish territory was occupied by either Germany or the Soviet Union (except those small parts which were taken by Slovakia and Lithuania). In November the Soviet Union invaded Finland, beginning a complicated war with that country that lasted until March, 1940, Britain and France continually on the verge of intervention, planning to seize the mines in northern Scandinavia and to bomb the Baku oil fields, but never quite intervening, seizing the mines or bombing the oil fields.

Burgess and Nicolson had a conversation on September 15th about the proper approach to domestic propaganda in war-time. Nicolson's notes in the unpublished pages of his diary are as follows:

> Guy Burgess . . . has an idea that we cannot get this country to win only by saying "Away with Hitler," nor can we get the Germans to capitulate by saying "Hitler must go." We must provide some other alternative. He thinks we should create a German Committee [in London] similar to those which we created for Czechoslovakia and Poland during the last war. These people would be an alternative government. I do not think that will work. In the first place the exiled Germans will not cooperate with each other. In the second place we want a larger idea to give people ideas. Something like the Federal Europe. You can not expect young men to give their lives just to down Hitler. You must give them some more positive and constructive aim.[19]

But five days later Nicolson met with Duff Cooper (then between offices after resigning over Munich), who "Thinks it frightfully important that we should organize a representative group among the German exiles in this country and he proposes to create a small Committee consisting of himself, [Nicolson], Wickham Steed and Horace Rumbold to organize such an Association." After meeting with Duff Cooper, Nicolson dined with Rob Bernays, Sibyl Colefax, Ronald Cartland, and Burgess at the Savoy Grill, where they probably discussed the German Committee project and the war in general.[*] Concerning the latter: "Cartland is extremely pessimistic about our prospects."[20] For the next few months there are, from time to time, comments in Nicolson's diaries about the German exile group that had been created after, if not consequent to, Burgess's suggestion.

Discussions about B.B.C. propaganda became intense with the success of the broadcasts from Hamburg of William Joyce, "Lord Haw-Haw." According to Asa Briggs' definitive history of the B.B.C., various aspects of how to counter the Hamburg broadcasts "had been examined at length inside the B.B.C.'s own Talks Department. There, Guy Burgess, among others, had joined with Maconachie, Barnes and John Green in protracted discussion."[21] Given Burgess's variety of roles and organizations in the propaganda effort, he also may well have taken a part "when in January 1940 there were representations from the TUC that German trade unionists in exile should broadcast to Germany, Electra House, while supporting the idea, insisted that each case should be considered on its own merits.

> Speakers, it insisted, would not be "out of touch with thought in their country". The general policy of not employing German refugees to give talks or to take part in features, was to shape the pattern of broadcasting to Germany for the rest of the war. At this time, however, Electra House was also opposed to including insulting, brutal, or facetious attacks on Hitler, and held that there was plenty of evidence to suggest that the Germans were not enthusiastic about the consequences of the launching of a great offensive in the West . . .The less controversial idea of

---

[*] Sibyl Colefax was a prominent interior designer and society hostess; Bernays an M.P., possibly one of Nicolson's lovers. Cartland, also an M.P., was to die at Dunkirk. His sister was a novelist.

regular commentators, which was initiated by Electra House, was settled in February 1940, when Lindley Fraser, Professor of Political Economy at Aberdeen University, was appointed.[22]

As a representative of the J.B.C., Burgess met with Nicolson at the beginning of November, 1939, while tending to the arrangements for Rosamond Lehmann to broadcast in French from Paris for the J.B.C. Nicolson gave him a letter of introduction to the playwright Jean Giraudoux, then serving in the French Foreign Ministry.[23] (Burgess did a favor in return for Nicolson the next month, advising him on possible jobs for Victor Cunard, cousin of the more famous Nancy Cunard, who had been fired from his position at Chatham House.[24]) In March, 1940, Burgess took Rosamond Lehmann to Paris in order for her to do the broadcasts. Lehmann's biographer describes a non-event:

> The flight over was hazardous owing to fog, Paris cold and semi-deserted, the staff at the radio station had no idea who she was or why she was there, and Burgess turned up only briefly, muttered a quick apology and disappeared. Most of the day Rosamond spent awaiting a threatened air-raid in the cellars of the Hôtel Crillon before catching her plane back to London.[25]

Burgess, meanwhile, had used the trip to Paris to look up "some of his old contacts."[26] These could have included Philby, who was working for *The Times* as a correspondent at the headquarters of the British Expeditionary Force in France, and Maclean, who was at the Paris embassy.[27] Perhaps Pfeiffer as well, and one or two others whom he may have been particularly eager to see as Beria had closed the London secret intelligence residency in January, as untrustworthy, and was not to reopen it until the end of the year.[28]

Burgess's time in England was not completely taken up by propaganda work. There was, for example, the small world of literary life centered on "the Horizon crowd" the writers who contributed to the famous literary monthly, funded by Peter Watson (who had been at school with Burgess), which Cyril Connolly edited with Stephen Spender.* A. J. Ayer brought Burgess to a party at the South Kensington studio maisonette Connolly shared with Peter Quennell and Arthur Koestler. The occasion was Spender's marriage (his second) to Natasha Litvin. There is a photograph by Cecil Beaton showing Ayer, Connolly, Sonia Brownell (later Sonia Orwell), Louis MacNeice, Burgess and the architect Erno Goldfinger among others.[29] Goldfinger, in addition to lending his name to a famous thriller villain, designed, among many other projects, the post-war headquarters of the *Daily Worker*. MacNeice, who was close to Spender (and Auden, for that matter), on the one side and Blunt, on the other, as we have seen, also had long been friendly with Burgess. Burgess's presence at the wedding party was later felt to have been embarrassing, particularly when, six years later, Connolly wrote one of the first newspaper attacks on Burgess's character. Spender, for his part, spent much time after Burgess's move to Moscow removing references to him from his private papers and, in as far as he could, from the papers and recollections of others. Nonetheless, Burgess had been a member of his wedding; we have Beaton's photograph to attest to it.

The first crisis of the war in the West came with the German invasions and occupations of Denmark and Norway, the latter, in part, due to the negligence or incompetence of the First Lord of the Admiralty, Churchill. There were dramatic scenes in Parliament, the Chamberlain Government fell and a coalition was formed with Churchill (nonetheless) as Prime Minister. At the beginning of May Churchill asked Nicolson to join the Government as Parliamentary Secretary for the new Minister of Information, Duff Cooper. In order to help Nicolson prepare for this, his first Government post, Nicolson turned to Burgess: "Guy Burgess comes round to see me and explains more or less the functioning of the Ministry."[30] At this time Burgess, in addition to being knowledgeable about the Ministry of Information, appeared to have become "more or less the guiding

---

* Watson's lover, Denham Fouts, was Isherwood's model for Paul in *Down There on a Visit*.

spirit at the JBC." According to Bickham Sweet-Escott, at inter-departmental meetings on propaganda during June and July 1940, "There were no minutes, there was no agenda, and no chairman . . . there never seemed to be less than twenty-five people in the room.

> Besides the heads of 'D', innumerable other departments were represented—Terry Harman from Electra House, Hilda Matheson from the B.B.C., and a floating population from the Ministry of Information, and occasionally the Foreign Office and the Ministry of Economic Warfare. What generally happened was that somebody would throw a bright idea into the arena and let the others tear it into pieces, a process which was often amusing, but generally unprofitable . . . On the few occasions when it was agreed that action should be taken, it usually seemed to be obscure who was expected to do the job, and I never discovered that any of the ideas really led to action. There was one boiling July afternoon when, with dog-fights between the RAF and the Luftwaffe going on over our heads, Guy Burgess . . . nearly convinced the meeting that the way to end the war was to wait for a westerly wind and then send off large numbers of balloons in the direction of central Europe, hoping that incendiary bombs attached to them would set the cornfields of the Hungarian *puszta* on fire and starve the Germans out.[31]

At about the same time, a whole group in Section D had devoted itself to attempts to attack the Danube gorge, the Iron Gates, without success.

During this period, probably through Section D, Burgess was involved with the Local Defence Volunteers training school at the Osterley Park estate in Hertfordshire, near London. Burgess lectured at Osterley Park on politics and how to work with Continental trade unionists and underground radicals.[32] The founder of the school, Thomas Wintringham, who had been prominent in the British contingent of the International Brigade, and Eric Blair/George Orwell, who trained at Osterley Park, seem to have thought of it as a training ground for an armed English revolutionary force, as well as a school for last-ditch defenders in case of a German invasion.

According to W. J. West, Orwell and others felt that "Not since Cromwell and the days of the Levellers had social revolution been so real a prospect in England." [33] Again, according this time to Paul Anderson, in 1940 "Orwell became convinced that Britain was growing ripe for a socialist revolution and that the Home Guard . . . could play the role of a workers' militia in that revolution."[34] It was as if, for people like Orwell, the revolutionary dreams of Julian Bell and John Cornford were about to be realized.

The late Spring and early Summer of 1940 were an unending series of disasters for the British Empire. The Dutch, then the Belgian, then the French armies collapsed; the withdrawal of the British Expeditionary Force from Dunkirk was completed on June 3; Paris was occupied by the Germans on June 13th; the Red Army occupied Lithuania, Latvia and Estonia and the French signed an armistice with Germany on the 22nd, with Italy on the 24th. Anthony Blunt had joined the Army in September, 1939 and by mid-December he was a captain in charge of port security in Boulogne. In June, 1940, there being no longer any need for British port security in Boulogne, Blunt was evacuated to England and joined M.I.5, housed, after September, at 58 St James's Street (across the street from the Ritz and Arlington House, where Burgess's mother had an apartment). Maclean, newly married, made a dramatic escape from Paris and settled down to work at the Foreign Office. Philby went into Section D of M.I.6, with some help from Burgess, as part of the latter's contribution "to the career development of other agents in London." Later, perhaps as early as the Summer of 1951, this would have been noted in Washington and Whitehall, perhaps also in Moscow when it came time to make decisions about where Burgess would live out his life.

The Foreign Office decided that the assistance that the nominally neutral Soviet Union was giving to Germany might be minimized if an Anglo-Soviet trade agreement was reached. Sir Stafford Cripps, the intellectual property lawyer who was leader of the extreme Left in British politics, volunteered for the job and by May 24 was on his way to Moscow, officially appointed Ambassador to the Soviet

Union on June 2, arriving in Moscow, via Romania, on June 12. Burgess's Eton classmate, Fitzroy Maclean, by then a Russian expert at the Northern Department of the Foreign Office, was busy all month arranging the particulars of Cripps's status, which was complicated by his political standing and his seat in Parliament. Various rules were examined, loopholes discovered, work-arounds taken. There was also a problem concerning a visa for Cripps's Russian-born economic advisor, Professor Michael Postan, for whom, when those probles turned out to be insurmountable, a substitute was needed and there were other, routine, difficulties with the Moscow posting: the embassy was understaffed; the household cooks, drivers and maids worked for the Soviet Government; the fact that the Soviet Union was more or less allied with Germany, which was at war with Britain, and what, exactly, Cripps was supposed to do.[35] After an initial period of idleness, perhaps due to Soviet reluctance to offend Germany, Cripps and his small embassy staff were soon, then overwhelmingly, busy with trade negotiations.[36] Fitzroy Maclean, for his part, was desperately trying to get permission to leave the Foreign Office and enlist in the Army.

With regular warfare coming to an end in Western Europe, M.I.6's Section D and MI R(esearch) began planning for British support of Partisan groups that might appear. The historian of the Special Operations Executive states that "As early as 25 May the chiefs of staff had foreseen that France might collapse, and that if she did 'the creation of widespread revolt in Germany's conquered territories would become a major strategic objective.'"[37] Burgess told Driberg that he was then given the assignment of going to Moscow to explore whether the Comintern or other organizations headquartered there might wish to cooperate with M.I.6 in support of anti-German activities in the occupied countries. (According to Yuri Modin, David Footman had introduced Burgess to Valentine Vivian, head of Section V of M.I.6, who decided that it would be a good idea for Burgess to go to Moscow under diplomatic cover.[38]) Which brings us to the curious episode of the expedition to Washington, D.C. by Burgess and Isaiah Berlin.

In 1994, Berlin told Michael Ignatieff that during those dramatic weeks, like Fitroy Maclean, he had been trying to find a role in the war effort, but unlike Maclean, he was not fit for duty in the Army. Harold Nicolson, at the Ministry of Information, was receiving a steady stream of people seeking his approval for one thing or another (often to leave Britain for America). He noted in his diary for June 17, 1940: "The Reynaud Cabinet has resigned and Pétain has formed a new Ministry including Darlan. The Germans have broken through as far as Dijon, and the French are apparently evacuating the Maginot Line and destroying the works . . . Isiah [sic] Berlin came and wants to go to Russia."[39] (It will be recalled that at this point the Soviet Union was still allied with Germany.) Nothing coming of that meeting, Berlin then wrote to the Foreign Secretary, Lord Halifax, on June 21st, saying that he wanted to go to Moscow because he thought he could be of some help there in the war effort, which he could not contribute to in the normal way because of his disability and origins.[40] A few days after that, Guy Burgess, whom Berlin had not seen for a couple of years, paid a visit to Berlin in his rooms at Oxford. Berlin, and his friends the Rothschilds, were, as had been Hobsbawm and his friends, suspicious of Burgess, believing that he had turned fascist. Burgess assured Berlin that he had not, in fact, done so. He told Berlin that he was working for M.I.6, that he was going to Moscow, and suggested that if Berlin did indeed wish to go to Moscow in an official capacity he should go at once to see Nicolson again at the Ministry of Information.[41] Berlin therefore again traveled down to London and in his account of this meeting he has Nicolson sending him on to the Foreign Office to see Gladwyn Jebb, who was at that moment the Private Secretary of the Permanent Under Secretary, Sir Alexander Cadogan.

Half a century on, Berlin remembered Jebb saying: "Harold talked to me about this, it's a jolly good idea. Now look, we can't send you by Norwegian tramp to Russia because they're all sunk these days. There are two ways of going, one is via South Africa and

Persia, the other is via America and Japan.* Which do you prefer?"
Berlin preferred the route via America and Japan. "OK, we'll fix
that up. Right, now look, only one thing here, I forgot to add that
Guy's going with you if you don't mind, he's got his own stuff to do,
nothing to do with you . . . you needn't know anything about it at all.
But you'll both be carrying bags, diplomatic bags, that's the best way
of doing it." When the question of a visa came up, Berlin told Jebb
that as he was born in Riga "I'm not sure that I'd be really safe in the
Soviet Union because there is a clause about being Naturalised, that
your country of Naturalisation can't protect you in your country of
origin unconditionally." Jebb then remembered that a few days
earlier Stafford Cripps's economic advisor, Michael Postan, had
been refused a visa by the Soviets because of his birth in Czarist
Russia. Nonetheless, Jebb told Berlin that, for some reason, he
believed that although a visa from the Soviet Embassy in London
had not been honored, one from the Soviet Embassy in Washington
would be.

Evidently, there had been a conversation between Nicolson and
Jebb before this visit of Berlin's to London ("Harold talked to me
about this, it's a jolly good idea"). Berlin's duties as a press attaché
would fall within Nicolson's purview at the Ministry of Information.
Nicolson and Jebb had decided that Berlin's travel to Moscow would
serve as cover for Burgess's mission ("Guy's going with you if you
don't mind, he's got his own stuff to do, nothing to do with you . .
."). The diplomatic bags meant, of course, that this was a Foreign
Office activity. (The familiar "Guy" as Jebb's reference to Burgess
is notable in light of Lord Gladwyn's memoirs, in which he claims to
have barely known Burgess, and intensely disliked and mistrusted
what little of him he did know. But of course, as Duff Cooper
observed, old men forget.) The Foreign Office had oversight of the
various propaganda organizations and M.I.6 and therefore in some

---

* This was the route followed in August when Stafford Cripps's family
traveled out to join him in Moscow.

fashion Burgess, and indeed Grand, were under Jebb's supervision and were about to become even more closely under his control.

Some light on subsequent events is shed by documents concerning conversations in May-June 1940, when Cadogan had asked for opinions of Major Grand and his work. "Gladwyn Jebb was the most damning of all. Grand's judgment, he wrote with evident relish, 'is almost always wrong, his knowledge wide but alarmingly superficial, his organsation in many respects a laughing stock, and his is a consistent and fluent liar'." At a meeting with the Foreign Secretary at the end of June, about the time when Berlin was meeting with Jebb, "Menzies [head of M.I.6] effectively washed his hands of Grand."[42] Grand, apparently, did not know that he was about to be released for other duties, because after Berlin met with Jebb, Berlin had lunch with Burgess and they then went off to see Grand, whom Berlin remembered saying: "Ah well you're going off to Russia with Guy here, you know there's a lot of business to be done there. The Achilles heel of these people is of course the Caucasus, that's where the oil comes from. If we can hit them there, that will be much more useful to us than anything else."[43]

That was a bit of a red herring, but it brings us to one of the nearly forgotten stories of the early days of the war. As we have seen, in February, 1940, as the Russo-Finnish War was entering its final phase, Britain and France planned a two-pronged attack on the Soviet Union: across northern Sweden and Finland in the north, while seizing the oil fields at Baku in the south. In March the British moved light bombers to Syrian, Iraqi and Indian air bases in preparation for bombing the oil fields and laying mines at the mouth of the Volga. There were also plans to send submarines into the Black Sea to attack the oil tankers that were delivering Soviet oil to the Germans. At this point Stalin decided to end the war with Finland, in part because of these threats to the oil regions of Batum and Baku.[44] Bradley Smith has traced how, "Even after British popular enthusiasm for challenging Stalin for the sake of "gallant Finland" had evaporated due to [Finnish] Field Marshal Mannerheim's acceptance of Russian armistice terms in March 1940, the Royal Air Force (RAF) continued to make detailed plans for raids on the Soviet oil center at Baku . . . ,"[45] plans that were completed perhaps six weeks before Burgess's visit to Isaiah Berlin at All Souls College. [46] The rationale for these plans gradually shifted from destroying oil facilities as part of an attack on the Soviet Union to doing so to prevent them from falling into the hands of the Germans after the June 22, 1941 invasion. "On 22 July 1941, Ambassador Cripps explicitly mentioned the idea of the British destroying valuable Soviet installations in the Caucasus in a conversation with Stalin, but the Soviet leader, rather unsurprisingly, did not agree, and replied the Soviets would destroy the oilfields and refineries themselves if necessary."[47] In the end, the Red Army did not collapse; and, even though the Special Operations Executive (SOE) continued to worry this bone, the whole matter became moot after Stalingrad.[48] It was perhaps something like this that Major Grand had in mind when he made his cryptic statement to Berlin. On the other hand, he may have been "a consistent and fluent liar."

After the Franco-German Armistice had been signed on June 22nd rumors of an imminent German invasion of England became increasingly pressing and detailed. On June 28th, Alexander Cadogan complained in his diary that his office was "A regular bear-garden. Everyone wanting everything at once. Dalton ringing up hourly to try to get a large finger in the Sabotage pie. I wrote a minute on it last night, which S[ecretary] of S[tate] must see first."[49] On June 29th, Nicolson recorded in his diary: "Stafford Cripps refuses to have Shia Berlin as his Press Attaché . . . Guy Burgess comes to see me and I tell him there is no chance now of his being sent to Moscow."[50] It is not clear whether Nicolson was referring to Burgess or to Berlin with that "his," although it was probably Berlin. Nevertheless, on the first of July Burgess and Berlin received their Courier's Passports, presumably courtesy of M.I.6. The next day, Berlin again visited Nicolson at the Ministry of Information: "Isiah [sic] Berlin comes, having been refused the post of Press Attaché in Moscow by Stafford Cripps. He has a wild idea of going to Washington and working his way to Moscow from there."[51] Nicolson seems not to have known, or to have forgotten, that the route via Washington had been Jebb's idea.

On the first of July, at higher levels in the Government, a meeting chaired by Halifax, the Foreign Minister, and including Hugh Dalton, Minister of Economic Warfare, Gladwyn Jebb, "C" and others agreed that "We have got to organize movements in enemy-occupied territory comparable to the Sinn Fein movement in Ireland . . .

> This "democratic international" must use many different methods, including industrial and military sabotage, labour agitation and strikes, continuous propaganda, terrorist acts against traitors and German leaders, boycotts and riots . . . What is needed is a new organization to co-ordinate, inspire, control and assist the nationals of the oppressed countries who must themselves be the direct participants.[52]

This organization was to be named the Special Operations Executive, with Labour M.P. Hugh Dalton as its first chief. The War Cabinet approved the creation of the SOE at a meeting on July 22nd. Reginald Leeper was put in charge of the foreign broadcasts of Electra House as Director of Enemy Propaganda and a division of labor in regard to types of propaganda broadcast to enemy countries between the B.B.C and Electra House was agreed.[53]

In the meantime, Berlin and Burgess received visas for the United States on July 8th and on the 9th they are on-board the *SS Antonia* en route to Quebec.[54] The Battle of Britain began the next day. Some people, such as William Empson, would have thought it an odd moment to be leaving England.[55] But, of course, Burgess and Berlin were doing so in support of the war effort. During this, his first journey to America, Berlin wrote to his parents almost daily. His first letter, July 9th (SS Antonia, Cunard White Star), began with typical assurances of well-being: "I could not be more comfortable, confident or happy . . .

> My travelling companion is completely under my thumb (not a very oppressive one you will complain) I have conveyed to him the suspicions of the House of R. which will keep him in order.

The telephone number of his office is Whitehall 8066 for renseignements [information]. They are, I must say, marvelous at arranging exits for their officials, the whole proceeds with streamlined smoothness.

Burgess and Berlin were traveling in (different) first class cabins, by permission of and on orders of His Majesty's Government, that is, the Foreign Office, and at its expense. It is not clear what suspicions of the House of R[othschild] Berlin had discussed with his parents: perhaps the supposed pro-Fascist leanings mentioned by Burgess in his meeting with Berlin; perhaps something about his way of life. The next day, as a result, presumably, of the operations of Berlin's thumb: "Mr Burgess promises to drink [only] ½ bottle of wine a day and no spirits."[56] The following Tuesday, the 16th, as they were approaching Newfoundland, Berlin wrote to his parents that his "plans are to let my companion proceed further if he feels he is in a hurry. And stay myself until the path is clear. Anyhow & do whatever they think best at the Embassy." The ship docked in Quebec on the 20th and Berlin and Burgess took a train to Montreal, then flew to New York, where they stayed for two days. Berlin remembered that while they were in New York Burgess said "I'm going to see Michael, Michael Straight." (Straight, in his book about the period, says that the meeting with Burgess took place, not in New York, but in the Washington suburb of Alexandria, Virginia. He describes it as an effort by Burgess to activate him as an agent, an effort he describes as unsuccessful.[57]) Berlin went off by himself to see Felix Frankfurter, in Massachusetts, who offered to write a recommendation to Cripps. Re-united, Berlin and Burgess stayed in Washington with John Foster, legal advisor at the British Embassy, meeting Joseph Alsop, who liked Berlin but disliked Burgess "because he wasn't wearing socks," in July, in Washington.

Monday, the 22nd of July (the day that the War Cabinet approved the creation of the SOE), Burgess and Berlin called at the British Embassy. On Wednesday, the 24th, Berlin cabled to Jebb:

Russians here unexpectedly helpful. Frankfurter and other prominent persons very friendly and prepared to intercede in the manner contemplated. Russian visa granted but do not in any event propose to proceed until and unless His Majesty's Ambassador [Cripps] formally request appointment of Press Attaché and Moscow and London agree. Hope this meets with your approval.

The next sequential telegram (marked as corrupt), from the British embassy is from Burgess for "D" through "C": "Do instructions to return apply equally to Berlin who is communicating with Mr. Jebb? Also should [grp. undec.] educational project here with possible [?examination] in official collaboration be investigated. Returning immediately on reply. Regret any mistakes in original scheme imagine disarmament measure implied in cancellation irrevocable."[58] There are evidently more garbled words in this cable than indicated. Berlin apparently had told Jebb about Frankfurter's offer to intercede with Cripps. It appears that Berlin had told Burgess about plans for "an educational project" in which Berlin would be involved in Washington. This may have had something to do with the British Information Services. Burgess had evidently heard from "D", (now) Colonel Grand, that "the original scheme" had been cancelled (including the perhaps garbled "disarmament measure") and he was to return, having only been in Washington for a couple of days.

Burgess's apology ("Regret any mistakes") was probably beside the point. In the first place, Cripps thought he was having enough trouble getting the Soviets to trust him without having M.I.6 operatives foisted on him. In the second, Dalton was bringing into SOE the scattered irregular warfare and propaganda agencies, of which Section D was one. Jebb was moving over from the Foreign Office to assist him as Chief Executive Officer and Jebb, not approving of Grand, the latter was soon resuming his career in military engineering.[59] It is common in transitions of this type to at least suspend projects of the former regime. On the 27th Fitzroy Maclean (still) at the Foreign Office cabled to Ambassador Lothian: "It is not desired that either Berlin or Burgess should proceed to Moscow. Burgess should return to the United Kingdom immediately. Berlin, who is not in the employ of His Majesty's Government, must do what he thinks best."[60] This last sentence seems to imply a change in Berlin's status, as he was, apparently, in some sense "in the employ of His Majesty's Government" when he traveled to the U.S., as his travel was paid for by that Government.

Burgess left by air for the UK on the 30th. On the 31st Berlin wrote his parents: "Guy B. has been recalled and will by now have telephoned to you: The Clipper – Lisbon, and Lisbon-England services are now regular if expensive. If I have to return that way I'll try to pay in £, so you may get wire requiring you to pay someone something in London . . . " Not being "in the employ of His Majesty's Government," he would have to pay his own way home. Even though he was staying with John Foster, an official at the British Embassy, Berlin appears not to have been informed, or to have ignored the fact, that the British Government had decided not to have him continue on to Moscow. Berlin remained in the United States, continuing to lobby the Foreign Office to let him go on to Moscow, to no effect but to make himself quite unpopular with both Cripps and the Foreign Office.[61] On the other hand, he saw the Felix Frankfurters whose "view is that I either go on or go back, but all agree that much negotiation still remains to be done."

The ambassador, Lord Lothian, cabled the Foreign Office on the first of August that the British Embassy in Washington had been told by the Soviet embassy that they had received instructions to grant diplomatic visas not only to Burgess but also to Berlin on receipt of passports from the British embassy. Burgess having returned, Lothian stated that he "should be glad to learn if I may forward [Berlin's] passport to Soviet Embassy to enable him to obtain a diplomatic visa." The reply to Lord Lothian from Fitzroy Maclean at the Foreign Office of August 3 was blunt: "Mr. Berlin is intolerable . . . You should do nothing to assist Mr. Berlin in obtaining Soviet visa. As he has already been informed, it is not desired to employ him at Moscow.[62] On August 18th Fitzroy Maclean cabled to Cripps in Moscow: "I understand that Mr. Berlin has suggested in a telegram to you from Washington that in principle we agree to his being attached to your staff. This is not the case. Indeed we have repeatedly informed Mr. Berlin that it is not desired to employ him in Moscow." And that was the end of the matter, insofar as it pertained to Isaiah Berlin going to Moscow in 1940.

There were a flurry of enquiries in London about the episode in January 1941, when Berlin's special passport somehow reached the Foreign Office. Fitzroy Maclean declared that "If we had been consulted, we should certainly have had something to say about [Mr Berlin] being sent to Moscow." It emerged that the passport was issued "at the request of a Colonel J. N. Tomlinson of the Passport Control Department, together with one for Mr. G. de Moncy Burgess, also to Moscow." And there is a note in the file that "The courier passport is of course only a cover for the documents he carried -- & bears no relation to the reasons for or the arrangements for the actual journey of which of course we know nothing." Followed by: "Col Tomlinson was formerly employed by the D organization and no doubt in that capacity asked that Mr. Berlin should be given a Courier's Pass. S.O.2.,* as now constituted, know nothing of the matter." Maclean minuted: "It seems odd that Colonel Tomlinson should have taken it upon himself to send Mr Berlin to Moscow at a time when we were doing what we could to prevent him from going there. I really think that Northern Department might have been consulted. It would be interesting to know what D's organization intended that Mr Berlin and Mr Burgess should do in Moscow." The reply to this (from J. M. Addis) is that "Colonel Tomlinson did no more than give a telephone message on behalf of a superior (now happily liquidated, I understand). He remembers no more of the incident." At this point the matter is allowed to drop "It would be very difficult to push the enquiry further. I think Mr. [Fitroy] Maclean agrees that we need not proceed."[63]

On Sunday, August 18, 1940, as the Battle of Britain continued

---

* Special Operations Executive, Operations (as opposed to S.O.1, propaganda.

in the skies over Southeastern England, Burgess dined at the Wyndham club with Nicolson, who noted in his diary: "He is just back from America. He is still determined to get in touch with the Comintern and use them to create disorders in occupied territory."[64] The first half of that sentence is sufficiently ironic. A decade and a half later Burgess told Driberg that he had indeed persuaded Grand to send him to Moscow to propose to the Russians that they enter into an agreement with Great Britain for support of the various national Resistance organizations, the British to assist the Communist-led units in Western Europe if the Soviets would support the non-Communist anti-Nazi forces in the East. Burgess's "scheme" was premature. In July, 1940, there were no Western European resistance organizations, the Franco-German armistice having been signed only a few days before Burgess contacted Isaiah Berlin, and the Soviet Union was not only allied with Germany, the Red Army was not for the last time the occupying force in much of Eastern Europe.

On the other hand, in June, 1940, there had been a vague Foreign Office attempt to re-open discussions with the Soviet government through Cripps' Mission to Moscow. Then, in October, 1940, there were Cabinet level discussions of an exchange of air force staff between Great Britain and the Soviet Union.[65] In May, 1941, Cripps, in order to unfreeze his negotiations with them, warned the Soviets that the British government might seek a separate peace with Germany.[66] "When war broke out, 'all believed', recalled Litvinov later, 'that the British fleet was steaming up the North Sea for a joint attack with Hitler on Leningrad and Kronstadt'."[67] On June 22, 1941, the day after the German invasion of the Soviet Union, the Foreign Office directed Cripps to warn the Soviets that their codes were insecure. And, a few days later, "Dalton recorded in his diary that he wanted to attach someone to the embassy staff in Moscow who could cooperate with the NKVD." Before the end of the month, a Colonel Robert Guiness actually flew to Moscow to serve as the temporary SOE representative there, as Burgess had planned to do a year earlier. On June 28th, the chief officers of a British combined services military mission arrived in Moscow. On August 6th, Dalton dined with Sir Stewart Menzies, head of M.I.6, and they agreed that Communists from other countries might be highly valuable agents, especially in France and Germany. According to Bradley Smith, the expert on these matters, "This may well have been the genesis of a program adopted during the later stages of the war, through which the NKVD provided agents that the SOE trained and equipped at bases in the United Kingdom and the RAF subsequently airlifted to drop points on the Continent."[68] In September Colonel Guiness was replaced by Brigadier General George Hill as chief of what had become the SOE mission in Moscow.

Within weeks of the German invasion of the Soviet Union, the infrastructure for exchange of intelligence information was in place in Moscow and then, reciprocally, in London. In Moscow, the liaison arrangement was between A. P. Osipov, in the Foreign Department of Beria's NKVD and General Hill.

> Osipov and Hill prepared a handbook for partisan operations which laid down their functions and purpose and established regulations for coordination with the Red Army. In addition to writing the handbook, they tackled the problem of conditioning the Red Army Command to make full use of partisans . . . In early 1942 Hill had a personal meeting with Beria . . . [who] wanted to know whether the SOE would agree to its promise to drop NKVD agents behind enemy lines, to which Hill replied that SOE would do so to the limits of possibility."[69]

During the course of the war there was a steady, if not altogether smooth, exchange of all war-relevant information between London (and later, Washington) and Moscow, excepting only the details of ULTRA (but not its products), and the atomic bomb project. The exchange included order of battle information, weapons characteristics and performance and appraisals of enemy intentions, both tactical and strategic.

In sum, in June, 1940, Burgess had the idea of establishing a liaison relationship between the British Empire's secret intelligence services and those of the Soviet Union, an idea that was implemented, on a greater scale, a year later. For reasons that are not at all clear, he involved Isaiah Berlin in the project. When the project itself was temporarily derailed by the bureaucratic turmoil attendant on the establishment of SOE, Burgess immediately went back to London.[*] By September the Special Operations Executive, with Jebb as chief executive officer, had taken over all propaganda activities.[70] After his return from Washington, Burgess occupied himself with his school for saboteurs at Brickendonbury Hall as Section D was absorbed into SOE. We have a glimpse of him, perhaps around this time, in the memoirs of Hugh Skillen. Skillen was visiting RAF Chicksands, a listening station for the Bletchley enterprise, located in Chicksands Priory, which, he wrote, was "'a delightful old house' with a dining room from which an old carp pond could be seen. 'The legend was that carp had been there for centuries since the time of the monks.'

> There was a fine table at which a dozen could have been seated very comfortably but we were usually four in number at lunch or dinner. At the head of the table was a Rear-Admiral or some very senior naval rank . . . opposite me was a young, very attractive Wren officer, who as [the Rear-Admiral's] secretary or aide-de-camp . . . On my right was a handsome debonair lieutenant in the Intelligence Corps: Guy burgess. After dinner, we sometimes played darts in the mess, Burgess and I with the Wren, and Burgess and I would go to a pub in the evening for a quiet drink.[71]

Berlin lingered in the United States, establishing, on the one hand, relationships in the American government and the British Embassy, and, on the other hand, relationships with the American principals of the Zionist organizations, both of which would prove

---

[*] It is possible that, as usual with Burgess, he had more than one reason for his actions. Perhaps he was having difficulty maintaining contact with the Comintern and wished to clarify matters by meeting with the authorities in Moscow.

useful to him (and he to them) later in the war. One might note in passing that Berlin's relationship with the Zionist organizations, from the point of view of the Foreign Office, was highly suspect, as those were anti-Imperial organizations, parallel to, say, the Indian National Congress in India, the leadership of which was imprisoned for most of the war.

If one wished to indulge in the necessarily arbitrary exercise of selecting a specific day as marking the beginning of the end of the British Empire, Saturday, September 7th, 1940 would have a strong claim. The synecdoche of Empire is its capital city. London, as much as any imperial capital since Rome, was the embodiment of Empire, drawing in the active and frozen labour of the British isles, then of an entire world of peasants and laborers, from Shanghai to Lagos. Even in 1940 it seemed untouchably solid, the great Imperial buildings of Whitehall facing one another across streets narrowed by their colonnaded mass; the Embankment and the bridges; the docks and the City. It was unique, irreplaceable. The weather on September 7th was hot and clear, the temperature in the nineties, more like Los Angeles at that time of year than London. At 4:43 p.m. the air-raid sirens went off, warning of the approach of a first wave of what turned out to be 348 German bombers and 617 fighter escorts, the aircraft forming a composite object in the sky 20 miles wide. The second raid, beginning at 8:10, included another 318 bombers. This raid continued until 4:30 the next morning. The first raid destroyed the docks and those parts of the East End nearby. The flames rising from the docks could be seen for 30 miles. The second raid spread the destruction widely across London. The bombers returned nearly every night for two months, then less regularly. It seemed to be the end of London. Charles Ritchie, then a young Canadian diplomat, observed:

> Our ears have grown sharp for the sounds of danger – the humming menace that sweeps from the sky, the long whistle like an indrawn breath as the bomb falls . . . The paint is beginning to peel off the great cream-coloured houses in Carlton House Terrace and the grand London squares . . . Every now and then

one comes upon a gap in a row of houses or a façade of shops. In the gap is a pile of rubble where the bomb has hit. I suppose gradually there will be more and more such gaps until the face of London is pitted and furrowed with them . . . I walked home down St. James's Street under a brilliant moon to the usual orchestra of guns. There were autumn leaves thick on the street, leaves on the pavements on St. James's Street! It is like the Fall of Rome![72]

The Blitz did not end until May 10, 1941.[73]

In October, Victor Rothschild leased the flat at 5 Bentinck Street (near Oxford Street), where he had lived when married to one of the second-generation "Bloomsberries," Barbara Hutchinson, to Teresa Mayor, who would become his second wife, and Patricia Rawdon-Smith, Anthony Blunt's only recorded female lover.[74] They asked Blunt to share the flat, furnished and decorated in the Rothschild style, and the rent. Burgess moved in shortly thereafter. The future Lady Rothschild and the future Baroness Llewelyn-Davies of Hastoe had bedrooms on the top floor; Blunt, and later Burgess, in separate rooms on the floor below, where Jack Hewit was also to be found: with Burgess when Peter Pollock was not, with Blunt then, and when fighting with Burgess. Baroness Llewellyn-Davies recalled:

> The flat was a maisonette on three floors of a purpose-built office block, the ground floor of which was occupied by a medical magazine, the Practitioner. On the first level were the kitchen and sitting room. On the second floor were Blunt's bedroom and a dressingroom-cum-bathroom. Guy's rooms—a bedroom and a bathroom – were on the same floor, down the corridor from Blunt's accommodation . . .There was a housekeeper, an Irish girl called Bridie, who came in every day to clean and cook for whoever happened to be in the flat.[75]

John Strachey, becoming steadily rather more eminent and rather less Communist, lived at Bentinck Street for a time, endlessly talking politics, receiving from Burgess, according to Strachey's biographer, "one lasting benefit: a concern for music, of which previously he had been ignorant: Burgess lived in a perpetual atmosphere of Mozart and late Beethoven quartets."[76] Strachey, chief intellectual propagandist for the Communist Party of Great Britain in the Thirties, had joined the R.A.F. at the beginning of the War, serving well in a series of staff positions. With Burgess as his producer, he broadcast as "Squadron Leader Strachey," becoming a popular B.B.C. figure, primarily valuable to the R.A.F. as an apologist for the terror bombing of German cities.[77] At the end of 1942, Strachey became Public Relations Officer to the Assistant chief of Air Staff, Air Marshal Sir Richard Peck at the Air Ministry.[78] In this position he had information concerning R.A.F. deployments, plans and capacities aspects of which may have been communicated to Burgess and thence onward.

Life at Bentinck Street was not all politics and Mozart. Miranda Carter noted that while at Bentinck Street Strachey "was thought to be conducting an affair, though with whom nobody could remember, and [there was] also the architect Richard Llewellyn Davies, who was after Patricia Rawdon-Smith." Not to mention at "least two M.I.5 officers—Desmond Vesey and Patrick Day—[who] stayed there for a while.

> Among other regulars were Dennis Proctor,[79] Brian Howard, Eric Kessler – a . . . Swiss diplomat – and Andrew Revai – a . . . Hungarian journalist friend of Blunt's . . . Kim Philby came occasionally to see Burgess, and Hewit remembered once meeting John Cairncross . . . Ellis Waterhouse, Dadie Rylands, Peter Montgomery and occasionally [Louis] MacNeice . . . came to visit.[80]

As did J. D. Bernal, Malcolm Muggeridge, James Pope-Hennessy, Guy Liddell and, of course, Victor Rothschild. "Burgess wrote to Peter Pollock in the autumn of 1941: 'My dearest dear . . . there seem to be even more people to breakfast than usual . . . 8 the other day (not counting someone who left at 5 am)'."[81] It sometimes must have seemed like the Blitz equivalent of summers at Gatsby's. However, we should balance this image with the fact that all four of the tenants were employed in the capital's bureaucracies and, among the other reasons visitors would spend the night in the cellar (sitting room, bedrooms) of 5 Bentinck Street was to avoid walking to their homes through streets the darkness of which was only relieved by the flames of bombed out buildings. (Strachey twice narrowly escaped being killed during the Blitz.) Jack Hewit remembered "no orgies while I lived there – more's the pity. I wish there had been. There was only one big party while was there and that was on my birthday in May, 1944. Everyone worked very hard."[82]   And Baroness Llewellyn-Davies told her interviewers: "Everyone who was there was working eighteen hours a day and we scarcely saw each other . . . One came home and went to sleep. I know what people have said about the orgies but I never saw anything like that."[83] Compare to, say, this from Elias Canetti's description of Roland Penrose and Lee Miller's house, where "the women especially, had something lascivious about them, and they relished their own movements, as well as those of their partners. The atmosphere was thick and . . . in the basement, there were the most astounding goings-on . . ."[84] Photographed, no doubt, by Lee Miller.

We have another glimpse of life at Bentinck Street from Nicolson's diary of April 22, 1941:

Lunch at the United Services with Guy and James [Pope-Hennessy] . . . Dine early . . . I go round with Guy Burgess to his rooms on Bentinck Street. Two ladies are there. One of them [Patricia Rawdon-Smith] is Phil Noel Baker's secretary. I say that Phil is so passionate that he makes wisdom sound like hysteria. She is impressed by that remark which in fact was an improvisation.

Noel-Baker was at this time having an affair with Megan Lloyd George, M.P., who would often broadcast for Burgess on The Week in Westminster.* From this point forward, at the latest, it would be

---

* Noel-Baker was to be Joint Parliamentary Secretary to the Minister of War Transport from 1942 to 1945, Chairman of the Labour Party from 1946 to 1947, Secretary of State for Air, 1946-47 and Secretary of State

easier to speculate about what Burgess did not know about the activities and secrets of the British Government, its Parliament, Ministries and intelligence agencies, than what he knew. And what he knew, it is most likely, he passed along to his Russian connections.

Miranda Carter harvested some letters of the period, from Burgess to Pollock, which give some sense of the place and the relationship between the two, its progress, or lack thereof:

1941: James Pope-Hennessy has "totally and violently and very sweetly but also embarrassingly fallen for me." ("James wrote to me asking me if I would give Guy up," Pollock recalled, "and he would love him for ever. He was besotted. Guy was rather pleased."85)

N.D.: "Would you like to meet Freddy Ashton? . . . I rather struck up with him – he is most civilized and sweet I think."86

c. 1945: "Nor does it, as things are [he wrote after a tiff {MC}] look likely that you will meet [Laurence] Olivier who I am at last getting to know – at least not, I think through me. Miaow. . ."87

Given the scattered sour comments about Burgess in the diaries of James Lees-Milne, it is probably pertinent that by 1943 James Pope-Hennessy was James Lees-Milne's closest friend: "They . . . spent exhilarating nights strolling among the ruins of London discussing life and literature, sometimes pub-crawling in disreputable districts in search of adventure."88 Retrospective dislike of the beloved's former lovers is not uncommon.*

---

for Commonwealth Relations, 1947-1950. He won the Nobel Peace Prize in 1959 for his work with the United Nations.

* Burgess told Driberg that in Moscow he sometimes used the name Jim Andreyvitch Eliot, the Jim after Lees-Milne. This can be taken as a joke, but on whom it is difficult to say. Perhaps the "Jim" was really for James Pope-Hennessy. "Eliot" was, of course, George Eliot.

In November, 1940, Burgess was again called upon to play the role of relationship counselor in a love affair, as he had, unsuccessfully, for Hewit and Isherwood. This time it was that between Goronwy Rees and Rosamond Lehmann and he was equally unsuccessful. Lehmann had learned of her lover's engagement to another woman by reading the announcement in *The Times.* "Desperately she tried to make contact with Goronwy . . . Guy Burgess, summoned to a council of war, was [one of those] made to write [to Rees] . . . Burgess was the first to receive a reply, the gist of which he conveyed, as promised, to [Lehmann at] Ipsden: Goronwy, stung by Rosamond's conviction that in marrying he could only fail, had immediately made up his mind that it was his one possible course of action."[89] According to his daughter, Rees, alcoholic, unreliable, secretive and promiscuous, was not to be persuaded by appeals to decency.

After Burgess's return from Washington the propaganda agencies had been brought closer together, then merged. "A new series of liaison meetings between the representatives of the B.B.C. and Electra House started in October 1940, with a daily news and news talks meeting, a weekly meeting to discuss general directives, and a fortnightly meeting to discuss general programme questions."[90] In November, 1940, Brigadier General Gubbins was brought into SOE. (Like Julian Bell, an admirer of Michael Collins, he wrote a handbook on "The Art of Guerilla Warfare.") Sir Frank Nelson, a businessman, came in as head of Special Operations, at first with Grand as′ his deputy, then without Grand's services. There was a general shakeup of what had been Section D. Boxes on the organization chart were moved from place to place. New office space was acquired. Partitions went up and down. Many new people came in; most old people went out. Gubbins did not care for Burgess, perhaps because of his association with Colonel Grand's unorthodox regime, perhaps for personal reasons, and he and Jebb agreed that Burgess should serve the war effort in some other capacity.[91] Various other officials retrospectively claimed credit for moving Burgess out of SOE. None claimed credit for leaving Kim

Philby to continue his work in M.I.6.

According to Donal O'Sullivan, because of the penetration of SOE by Burgess and Philby, "From November 1940, the Soviet leadership regularly received details of communications between London and British embassies in the USSR, the USA, Canada, Turkey, Iran, Japan and other countries, the weekly digest of the SIS, protocols of the War Cabinet as well as counter-intelligence material on the Soviet embassy. A large part of Ambassador Cripps' correspondence with the Foreign Office was read simultaneously by the Soviet Leadership."[92] The Foreign Office material, at this point, would most probably have been a contribution from Donald Maclean.

In mid-December Burgess was medically examined, preparatory to being called up for military service. He was deemed fit and declared that he was ready to serve.

Notes to Chapter Four

[1] Norman Holmes Pearson's revised version of the History of Office of Strategic Services, p. 524. Beinecke Rare Book and Manuscript Library, Za Pearson, Section 4, Wooden File Box 1, Row 1, OSS, Yale University. Quoted in Holzman, Michael. "The Ideological Origins of American Studies at Yale." American Studies, Summer 1999.

[2] Foot, M.R.D. SOE: An outline history of the Special Operations Executive 1940-46. University Publications of America, 1986, p.11.

[3] Foot, p.11.

[4] ". . . in the course of his regular visits to Broadcasting House, Footman seems to have decided that Burgess was worth introducing to M.I.6." West, W. J. Truth Betrayed. London: Duckworth, 1987, p. 63.

[5] West, p. 116.

[6] On Wednesday, January 25, 1939, Burgess visited Harold Nicolson to discuss broadcasting propaganda (his "wireless scheme"). Nicolson, Harold. Diaries in The Vita Sackville-West and Harold Nicolson manuscripts, letters and diaries [microform]: from Sissinghurst Castle, Kent, the Huntington Library, California, and other libraries, reel 13.

[7] Foot, p.13.

[8] Nicolson, Harold. Diaries in The Vita Sackville-West and Harold Nicolson manuscripts, letters and diaries [microform], reel 13, entry for Wednesday, March 29, 1939.

[9] West, p. 118.

[10] Joint Broadcasting Committee File 2, January 1940 – March 1941, B.B.C. Written Archives Center, Caversham.

[11] Joint Broadcasting Committee File, January 29, 1940, B.B.C. Written Archives Center, Caversham.

[12] Briggs, Asa. The History of Broadcasting in the United Kingdom, Volume III: The War of Words. New York: Oxford University Press, 1995, p. 168.

[13] Nicolson, Harold. Diaries in The Vita Sackville-West and Harold Nicolson manuscripts, letters and diaries [microform], reel 14, Thursday, April 27, and Friday, May 5, 1939.

[14] Nicolson, Harold. Diaries in The Vita Sackville-West and Harold Nicolson manuscripts, letters and diaries [microform], reel 14, entry for Tuesday, June 13, 1939.

15 Nicolson, Harold. Diaries in The Vita Sackville-West and Harold Nicolson manuscripts, letters and diaries [microform], reel 14, entry for Wednesday, July 26, 1939.
16 Driberg, Tom. Guy Burgess: A Portrait with Background. London: Weidenfeld and Nicolson, 1956, p. 52.
17 Gillies, Donald. Radical Diplomat: The Life of Archibald Clark Kerr, Lord Inverchapel, 1882-1951. I. B. Tauris: London, 1999, p. 107.
18 British Library, ADD Ms. 88902/1, pp. 37;40.
19 Nicolson, Harold. Diaries in The Vita Sackville-West and Harold Nicolson manuscripts, letters and diaries [microform], reel 14.
20 Nicolson, Harold. Diaries in The Vita Sackville-West and Harold Nicolson manuscripts, letters and diaries [microform], reel 14, entry for September 20, 1939, continued in published version.
21 Briggs, p. 139.
22 Briggs, p. 165.
23 Nicolson, Harold. Diaries in The Vita Sackville-West and Harold Nicolson manuscripts, letters and diaries [microform], reel 14, entry for November 2, 1939.
24 Nicolson, Harold. Diaries in The Vita Sackville-West and Harold Nicolson manuscripts, letters and diaries [microform]: from Sissinghurst Castle, Kent, the Huntington Library, California, and other libraries, reel 14, entry for December 8, 1939.
25 Hastings, Selina. Rosamond Lehman. Vantage: New York, 2003, p. 207.
26 Driberg, p. 56.
27 Newsletter, Foreign Intelligence Service, Russian Federation, January 25, 2004, http://svr.gov.ru/smi/2004/bratishka20040125.htm
28 "Returning to the Cambridge Five: Triumph or Failure?" Newsletter, Foreign Intelligence Service, Russian Federation, April 3, 2008, http://svr.gov.ru/smi/2004/bratishka20040125.htm
29 Rogers, Ben. A. J. Ayer: A Life. New York: Grove Press, 1999, p. 170. Koestler was probably in prison as an illegal immigrant at this time.
30 Nicolson, Harold. Diaries in The Vita Sackville-West and Harold Nicolson manuscripts, letters and diaries [microform], reel 14, entry for May 18, 1940.
31 Bickham Sweet-Escott. Baker Street Irregular. London, Methuen, 1965, p. 36. Quoted in Page, Bruce. Leitch, David. Knightley, Phillip. Philby:

The Spy Who Betrayed a Generation. Andre Deutsch, Limited, London, 1968, p. 129-130.

[32] Driberg, p. 58. The plans for the school can be viewed at Kew.

[33] West, W. J., ed. George Orwell: The Lost Writings. New York: Arbor House, 1985, p. 17; 25.

[34] Anderson, Paul. Introduction. Orwell in Tribune: 'As I Please' and Other Writings, 1943-7. London: Politico, 2006, p. 21.

[35] The political background is to be found in Clarke, Peter. The Cripps Version: The Life of Sir Stafford Cripps. London: Allen Lane, Penguin Press, 2002, pp. 183 ff. See also FO 371/24845; 29464 ff.

[36] Clarke, pp. 183-93.

[37] Foot, p.18.

[38] Modin, Yuri. With Jean-Chalrles Deniau and Aguieszka Ziarek. Translated by Anthony Roberts. My Five Cambridge Friends: Burges, Maclean, Philby, Blunt, and Cairncross by their KGB Controller. New York: Farrar Straus Gioux, 1994, p. 83.

[39] Nicholson, Harold. Diaries and Letters, v. 2, The War Years 1939 – 1945 (New York, 1967), p. 96; Nicolson, Harold. Diaries in The Vita Sackville-West and Harold Nicolson manuscripts, letters and diaries [microform], reel 14.

[40] Berlin, Isaiah. Hardy, Henry, ed. Flourishing: Letters 1928-1946. Chatto & Windus: London, 2004, p. 302.

[41] Interview with Michael Ignatieff, 8 February 1974 (Tape MI 7); transcript in the possession of Henry Hardy, Wolfson College, Oxford; © The Isaiah Berlin Literary Trust, courtesy of Henry Hardy.

[42] Jeffery, Keith. The Secret History of M.I.6: 1909-1949. The Penguin Press: New York, 2010, p. 352-3.

[43] Interview with Michael Ignatieff, 8 February 1974 (Tape MI 7); transcript in the possession of Henry Hardy, Wolfson College, Oxford; © The Isaiah Berlin Literary Trust, courtesy of Henry Hardy. On the other hand, Berlin told Verne Newton in a letter fifteen years after the Ignatieff interview that his "assignment was conceived wholly separate from any of Burgess's machinations." Newton, Verne W. The Cambridge Spies: The Untold Story of Maclean, Philby, and Burgess in America. Madison Books, Lanham, Maryland, 1991, p. 365.

[44] This story can be followed in the diplomatic traffic preserved in the Foreign Relations of the United States (FRUS) for 1940.

45 Smith, Bradley F. Sharing Secrets with Stalin: How the Allies Traded Intelligence, 1941-1945. Lawrence, Kansas: University of Kansas Press, 1996: pp. 9-10.

46 National Archives, UK, FO 371/24847. "Even after the Air Ministry bowed to the force of unpleasant reality following the fall of France and gave up its dreams of long-range bombing operations against Russia, Britain's covert warfare activities in the Special Operations Executive (SOE) continue to float up proposals for . . . sabotage operations against the USSR." A year later, in June, 1941, as Germany began its attack on Russia, SOE, which believed that the Red Army would be quickly destroyed, decided to send oil demolition experts from the Middle East into southern Russia. The SOE quickly established a two-part organization, one portion of which was to be centered in the Middle East, where the demolition teams were preparing for action. The other portion was in Moscow, where a pair of British SOE officers were to coordinate with the Russians. In the end, the Soviets did not agree to the plan; the Red Army did not collapse; and, even though SOE continued to worry this bone, the whole matter became moot after Stalingrad.

47 O'Sullivan, Donal. Dealing with the Devil, New York, Peter Lang, 2010, p. 32.

48 National Archives, UK, FO 371/24847.

49 Dilks, David (ed.). The Diaries of Sir Alexander Cadogan, O.M.: 1938-1945. G. P. Putnam's Sons: New York,1972, p. 308.

50 Nicolson, Harold. Diaries in The Vita Sackville-West and Harold Nicolson manuscripts, letters and diaries [microform], reel 14. Nicholson, Harold. Diaries and Letters, v. 2, The War Years 1939 – 1945 (New York, 1967), p. 98. One reason that Cripps may have refused to accept Berlin as press attaché is that there were no British reporters in Moscow: "The restrictions imposed on journalists were so severe that Cripps advised the British government that it would be fruitless to send reporters to Moscow." Gorodetsky, Gabriel. Stafford Cripps in Moscow, 1940-1942: Diaries and Papers. Edgware, Middlesex, Great Britain: Vallentine Mitchell, 2007, p. 17.

51 Nicolson, Harold. Diaries in The Vita Sackville-West and Harold Nicolson manuscripts, letters and diaries [microform], reel 14. Omitted from the published text.

52 Foot, p.19.

[53] Briggs, p. 250.

[54] NA\701.4111, Burgess, Guy 7-840. See Newton, p. 365.

[55] James Angleton tried to get Empson a job in America about this time. Empson responded:

> It is very kind of you to be still thinking about getting me a job in America, and I hope to work there some time after the war, but I don't think I could, or would want to, go till then . . . this is the proper place for an Englishman to be at present. . . .

"This is the proper place for an Englishman to be at present," "this" being in the middle of the Battle of Britain. Holzman, Michael. James Jesus Angleton, The CIA, & the Craft of Counterintelligence. Amherst: The University of Massachusetts Press, 2008, p. 24.

[56] Berlin, Isaiah. Letters: 1928-1946. Edited by Henry Hardy. Cambridge University Press, 2004, pp. 314. Bodleian Library, Oxford, MS. Berlin 293, Parents' letters, 1938-41.

[57] Straight, Michael. After Long Silence. W. W. Norton & Company: New York, 1983, pp. 142-3.

[58] National Archives, Kew, FO 371/24847, accessed April 30, 2010.

[59] Foot, Mp.22.

[60] Berlin, Isaiah. Letters, pp. 318-9.

[61] In addition to the matter of the absence of reporters in Moscow, Cripps was uneasy about the efforts of British intelligence to plant agents (covertly, rather than overtly) in Moscow. He wrote on October 9, 1941: "The other thing that has made us all very cross is that we cannot persuade the intelligence services not to look upon the present conditions as an opportunity to get all sort of secret information asa to Russia which they haven't been able to get for the last 20 ears. They are always tring to send disguised spies of some sort out here . . . Of course the Russians find out and it makes them quite properly and naturally suspicious of everyone else. Nothing could be better calculated to destroy all chance of cooperation, and yet, the departments at home will go on tring to deceive them and us too sometimes. I and the others have protested again and again, but apparently the authorities are not strong enough to control their own intelligence departments." In Gorodetsky, p. 180.

[62] Berlin, Isaiah. Letters, pp. 324-5.

[63] Berlin, Isaiah. Letters, pp. 334-5.

64 Nicolson, Harold. Diaries in The Vita Sackville-West and Harold Nicolson manuscripts, letters and diaries [microform], reel 14.

65 National Archives, UK, CAB 79/7.

66 Gorodetsky, p. 12.

67 Gorodetsky, p. 114.

68 Smith, Bradley F. Sharing Secrets with Stalin: How the Allies Traded Intelligence, 1941-1945. Lawrence, Kansas: The University of Kansas Press, 1996, p. 20. This is an excellent and little-cited source in regard to Second World War Anglo-American intelligence exchanges with the Soviet Union.

69 Knight, Amy. Beria: Stalin's First Lieutenant. Princeton: Princeton University Press, 1993, pp. 122-3.

70 Jeffery, Keith. The Secret History of M.I.6: 1909-1949. The Penguin Press: New York, 2010, p. 352-3.

71 McKay, Sinclair. The Secret Listeners: How the Y Service Intercepted German Codes for Bletchley Park. London: Aurum Press Ltd., 2012, pp. 89-90.

72 Ritchie, Charles. The Siren Years: A Canadian Dipolmat Abroad, 1937-1945. Toronto: McClelland & Stewart Ltd, 1974, pp. 65-8.

73 Stansky, Peter. The First Day of the Blitz. New Haven and London: Yale University Press, 2007.

74 "Tess Rothschild was as much a Cambridge figure as her husband . . . Three of her ancestors were Fellows of St John's and her father was a great-nephew of the philosopher John Grote. . . she was sent to Bedales, where she became head girl (a distinction which delighted her devoted friend Arthur Marshall, the connoisseur of schoolgirl novels). At Newnham she was the most celebrated actress of her day . . . During the Second World War she worked for M.I.5 and became assistant to Victor Rothschild, in anti-sabotage operations. His first marriage had ended, and in 1946 they married." Obituary: Teresa, Lady Rothschild. Noel Annan and James Ferguson, The Independent, Friday, 31 May 1996.

75 Interview with Parry (Baroness Llewelyn-Davies of Hastoe in Penrose, Barrie and Freeman, Simon. Conspiracy of Silence: The Secret Life of Anthony Blunt. New York, Farrar Straus Giroux, 1987, pp. 255.

76 Thomas, Hugh. John Strachey. New York: Harper & Row, 1973, p. 202.

77 Thomas, p. 219.

[78] Thomas, pp. 214-5.

[79] "SIR: About six months ago you published a remarkable article by Michael Mason about the debate in London University on whether Anthony Blunt should keep his emeritus chair (*LRB*, 20 March). It was a reasoned appeal to consider Anthony Blunt 'as a human being in the round' instead of treating his very name as 'a kind of mantra of hatred'; and the author concluded that the University of London had won a good opinion of itself in history by its vote on that occasion . . . The charge of treason in the technical sense has been very fairly put on one side by a legal authority who himself shares the view of the minority that Blunt should nevertheless have been expelled from the Academy. A 'traitor' engaged in 'treason' is someone who aids and abets an enemy with whom his country is at war, and what Anthony Blunt did for most of the war was to give help to an ally enthusiastically acclaimed as such by the whole country. Even the Soviet-German non-aggression pact, while it lasted, did not make Russia an *enemy* country. What Anthony Blunt did then (and afterwards) was determined by what he had done before war broke out; and it is to his actions in the Thirties, and what his motives were then, that anyone with a true sense of history should direct his attention. We do not know in detail what those actions were; but we should be able to understand why he took them . . . For my own part, I will only say that I am still proud to count him as one of my dearest friends." Dennis Proctor Lewes. London Review of Books, Letters, Vol. 2 No. 18 · 18 September 1980.

[80] Carter, Miranda. Anthony Blunt: His Lives. Macmillan: London, 2001, p. 265.

[81] Carter, p. 265.

[82] Penrose, Barrie and Freeman, Simon. Conspiracy of Silence: The Secret Life of Anthony Blunt. New York, Farrar Straus Giroux, 1987, p. 258.

[83] Interview with Parry (Baroness Llewelyn-Davies of Hastoe in Penrose, Barrie and Freeman, Simon. Conspiracy of Silence: The Secret Life of Anthony Blunt. New York, Farrar Straus Giroux, 1987, pp. 255-6.

[84] Canetti, Elias. Party in the Blitz. New York: New Directions, 2005, pp. 147-8.

85 Carter, p. 266.

[86] Carter, p. 265.

87 Carter, p. 265.

---

[88] Bloch, Michael. James Lees-Milne: The Life. London: John Murray, 2009, p. 151. After the war Lees-Milne was close to Anthony Blunt, pp.180; 219.

[89] Hastings, Selina. Rosamond Lehman. Vantage: New York, 2003, p. 209.

[90] Briggs, p. 252.

[91] Foot, p.145.

[92] O'Sullivan, p. 32.

Chapter Five

The Week in Westminster

Burgess did not go into the Army; he went back to the B.B.C. The Talks Department, seizing the chance to regain Burgess's services, had the B.B.C.'s General Establishment (Personnel) Officer request a military deferment for him, noting that "He did extremely good work in our Talks Department until 11th January, 1939, when, to our regret, he decided to resign from the Corporation's service.

> Shortly afterwards he was employed in M.I. activities by the War Office and has continued in that work until the present date . . . Burgess had considerable and successful experience with us previously on the preparation and production of Talks, and it will be a very great advantage indeed to us to retain his services indefinitely on the same type of work . . . I understand that there has been some reorganization in the M.I. branch where he was employed, and that by agreement with his chief, Burgess can be – in fact has been – released from his duties and is free to start with the Corporation . . . The work of our Home Talks Department has become very much more important owing to the propaganda aspect of their output, and the importance of helping to maintain morale by suitably prepared and balanced programmes. In addition to general Talks, Burgess will be concerned in supervising a series of Talks in our Army Educational Series . . . I am sure that you will appreciate that there are many pitfalls and difficulties to be met in producing talks under wartime conditions, and we are extremely fortunate in finding that Burgess is available to resume his previous occupation with us, subject to our being able to secure his reservation from military service.[1]

On the 20th, George Barnes, Assistant Director of Talks, supplemented this with the comment: "Mr. Burgess has to an extent not perhaps possessed by other members of the Department 'the propaganda mind.' The phrase was used of him to me in conversation with Mr. Harold Nicolson. D[irector of] T[alks] concurs". It is interesting that in the tight little world of Whitehall, no disparaging word about Burgess had passed from Jebb in SOE to the B.B.C. Perhaps Jebb's doubts about Burgess arose a decade later than he indicated in his memoirs.

Burgess went back to work at the B.B.C. the same day Barnes wrote his letter, at a salary of £540 per annum, as "Assistant in the Talks Department. The duties include[d] the preparation and production of talks both single and in series, the editing of manuscripts and the rehearsal of speakers at the microphone, and any other duties . . ." The salary matter, once again, rankled. On the 17th of February Burgess sent a memorandum to the personnel department on that topic:

> You will remember that when we originally discussed my re-appointment to the B.B.C. you told me that this was the scale figure for someone of my age and grade joining the talks department without previous experience of broadcasting . . . I made the point then that I had had two years of experience in the job I am now doing . . . [which] would in fact bring the salary offered more in line with what I was receiving from other government departments, including the Ministry of Information, before rejoining the corporation . . . I should also like to make the point that my two years' absence from the corporation has been largely connected with propaganda, broadcasting and otherwise . . . instead of my salary being based on the scale of <u>no</u> experience, it should be based on that of <u>four</u> years.[2]

Ten days later the request was rejected. Burgess was told that there was a policy against individual negotiations. In March, Barnes wrote that he had seen Burgess about his salary: "He was under the impression that he is now getting less than he would have got had he not left the Corporation. When I explained that this was not so in accordance with your memo. of 7th March, he agreed to drop the matter and gladly accept the decision. " Salaries at the B.B.C. were still set entirely on the basis of the age of staff, not their talents or experience. Burgess filed a handwritten memorandum, apologizing for raising the matter of the salary, stating that he had misunderstood the regulations.

George Orwell would be appointed as an Empire Talks Assistant in the Indian Section of the B.B.C. in mid-August, 1941 (at a salary of £680 p.a., being eight years older than Burgess). He produced cultural and news talks, duties parallel to those of Burgess at the Home Service and those of William Empson, who had joined the Far Eastern section. Eric Blair (as Orwell usually called himself in bureaucratic matters), Empson and Burgess came from similar slices of the British upper middle class and occupied neighboring positions on the far left of the British political spectrum, running, say, from Orwell's Fourth International affiliations through Empson's connections with the Communist Party to Burgess's affiliations. Blair and Burgess collaborated on programming at least once and it is not impossible that Empson and Burgess did so as well: the three producers having similar duties for differing audiences. On the other hand they were in some sense competitors for broadcasting and writing talent.

Burgess spent much of 1941 producing miscellaneous Talks programs, including the "Signpost" series, "The World Goes By," "Five Minutes for Fire Guards," a series for the "Home Guard," another called "Can I Help You?" and the enormously popular "John Hilton Talking," which was directed to a heterogeneous audience of "those affected by the war," which meant, by that time, nearly everyone in England.³ These were much like the programs that he had produced in the late-Thirties. For example, "Can I Help You?," broadcast twice a month, aimed "at helping ordinary listeners to solve some of their wartime problems. In particular, we try in this series to interpret official regulations to people who have difficulty with what must be an intimidating mass of official instructions to the ordinary man. These talks take the form of a dialogue between an enquiring listener and an expert . . ."[4]   In the ordinary course of B.B.C. matters, Burgess would have had a hand in writing, or at least editing, these playlets.   A senior member of the B.B.C. staff wrote in June to a colleague, "head-hunting," as it were: "With reference to the discussion at yesterday's European Board, I wonder whether you have considered the possibilities of using Mr. Guy Burgess for the Liaison Officer post, which was tentatively mentioned.

> I understood that he had left the Corporation, but I met him the other day at Broadcasting House and discovered that he was back temporarily, with either Home News or Home News Talks. What his future plans are I do not know but he certainly has a first class mind and an unrivalled political knowledge.[5]

*   *   *

British diaries and letters in early 1941 are filled with anxiety about the expected German invasion of Britain and generally bad news on the active fronts of the war: "We have got our backs against the wall" (Nicolson).   During the first months of 1941 Churchill moved the war to North Africa, where what was referred to as the British Army was very much an all-Empire and Commonwealth affair: Australians, New Zealanders, Nigerians, South Africans, Canadians and especially Indians.   These Imperial forces were at first successful, pushing the Italian section of the Axis back from Egypt, but then Rommel was sent to Tripoli to save Mussolini's legions.   He did so and began his drive toward Cairo and the Suez Canal.   The Greeks had defeated an Italian invasion in November, 1940, but despite British intervention, Greece and Yugoslavia were occupied by the Germans in April, 1941.   On May 10, Rudolf Hess, the Deputy Führer, parachuted into Scotland, intending to meet with the Duke of Hamilton.   Philby informed the London NKVD residence that during his talks with British military intelligence officers Hess claimed that he had arrived in Britain, with Hitler's knowledge, to conclude a compromise peace.   Moscow received this information on the 18th and came to the conclusion that the British might accept

Hess's proposals, sign a peace treaty with Germany, followed by a military alliance directed against the USSR, a conclusion reinforced, as we have seen, by Cripps.[6] Toward the end of the second week in June London was awash in rumors about a forthcoming German move East, rumors that reached Stalin from many sources—from Richard Sorge in Tokyo, from a source in the Gestapo, from agents throughout Europe. The Soviets interpreted the (ambiguous) British warnings as a disinformation campaign to cover an anti-Soviet Anglo-German reversal of alliances (see Molotov quotation above). Quite possible, but, as it happened, not true. Germany did in fact invade the Soviet Union on the 22nd. On June 30th, with the Germans victorious all along the enormous Eastern Front, Nicolson heard that Molotov had told Cripps that the Soviets had been taken by surprise by the German invasion as "they had been expected to be asked for their money [that is Ukraine and Baku] before their life,"[7] which had been the German pattern from Czechoslovakia forward.

Burgess and Nicolson appear to have been particularly close at this time, with the latter sharing not only B.B.C. and political gossip with the former, but also details of his personal life. Nicolson had a very intense, nearly amorous, relationship with his elder son, Nigel (whom he called Niggs), who was in the Army. On Friday, June 27th, Nicolson dined "at the Greek restaurant with Niggs, James [Pope-Hennessy], and Guy.

> Augustus John is there and comes to talk to us. Niggs goes off in a taxi at 9.0. We say goodbye. He is so gay and fine. I rather stagger back and then drink hard all night. Guy who is tactful and really understands takes me to the Boeuf where I meet Daniel Sykes and Paddy Brody and many other memoirs of my past life. But my heart aches for Niggs. "What a lucky man you are" says Guy—and how right he is.[8]

Le Boeuf sur le Toit, in Orange Street, was a nightclub that had opened, according to the historian of "Queer London" "in response to increased demand during the Second World War."[9] This was the period when apparently both Nicolson and Burgess were intimate with Pope-Hennessy. The two, however, do not appear to have

180

monopolized Pope-Hennessy's favors. (Nicolson's diary that summer and fall repeatedly refers to James Pope-Hennessy's unhappiness about a failed love affair, which does not seem to have involved Burgess.)

The Soviet Union entered a de facto alliance with the British Empire on July 12th. Harry Pollitt, who had been removed as Communist Party of Great Britain Secretary for supporting the war, was restored to his position. It was no longer an "imperialist" war. For the next few months most observers, particularly those in the British Foreign and War offices, were convinced that the Soviet Union, like Poland, would soon cease to exist. The B.B.C. thought that, be that as it may, there would probably be an increase in interest in Russian matters and asked staff to suggest programming ideas. According to Asa Briggs, Director of Talks "Maconachie argued against talks or features on Russian political history but in favour of talks on Russian 'cultural achievements'. Guy Burgess, also in the Talks Department, supported this view."[10] Burgess prefaced his list of possible talks with an indication of the range of his contacts: "The suggestions which follow are put down hastily, as the problem is urgent . . . I have had several informal conversations with John Strachey and Professor Bernal and one or two people at the M[inistry] of I[nformation] and the Foreign Office, but what follows is not intended to be in any sense a worked-out scheme." Under the heading of Literature he suggested selections from *War and Peace,* for its parallels to the German invasion of Russia and "the famous hunting scene which is probably the most beautiful description of old Russia and which was Lenin's favourite passage in Tolstoy, and one which he is said to have been reading, and to have referred to . . . on the day of his death." As to modern literature he mentioned Zoshchenko, whom he called a popular satirist, the poet and travel writer Nicholai Tikhonov and Ilya Ehrenburg. Under the heading of Science, Burgess stated that Bernal had agreed to advise the B.B.C. on such matters and had suggested J. G. Crowther and Haldane (if the ban on his broadcasting were lifted and Haldane would cooperate) in the event that Bernal were to be too busy with government work.* "Culture: There is possibly something to be done both in history and the arts. Dr. [Francis] Klingender [art historian], Dr. Blunt are possible speakers on Art – neither are Communists [sic]. Christopher Hill (a Fellow of All Souls) is a Communist but is also probably the best authority in England on Russian historical studies. Ballet and Music are probably easily covered." Burgess went on to suggest three "wider topics" with possible speakers: economic planning, "the Soviet Union as a Federation of states," that is, ethnic nationalism: "John Lehmann has written a certain amount of interesting stuff on Trans-Caucasia for the Geographical Magazine and should be safe on this topic" and Soviet foreign policy. W. J. West annotates the remarks about who is and who is not a Communist by pointing out that during the War all speakers on B.B.C. had to be cleared by M.I.5, which meant that, given Burgess's connections with both organizations, he knew that M.I.5 knew that Hill was a Communist and that it did not know that Blunt, in some sense, was.[11] The reference to Lehmann is of interest, possibly another indication of a relationship of some kind between them.

Nicolson was sacked from his Government office in the Ministry of Information on the 18th of July in a Cabinet reshuffle. Six months after his dismissal from the Government, his wounds had not yet healed. Dining at "Brooks' with James Lees-Milne, James P.H., Guy Burgess.

> We discuss everything and mainly the question of success. James [P.H.] says "It is ridiculous of you, Harold, not to realize that it does not matter your having been a failure at the M. of I., since you have written such good books." This annoys me, since I was not a failure at the M. of I., but merely politically inconvenient. I say that I should rather be able to send 100 tons of grain to Greece then write an immortal work. That impresses them since they agree.[12]

---

* Haldane (the famous geneticist), had broadcast for the Republic during the Spanish Civil War, hence the ban at the B.B.C.

Nicolson had been given the somewhat hollow consolation prize of being made a Governor of the B.B.C. This put him and Burgess in a potentially awkward position bureaucratically, as their social relationship could seem to short-circuit the chain of command. Nevertheless, it gradually became Nicolson's habit after meetings of the B.B.C. Board of Governors to stop by Burgess's office to talk or to go off with him for a drink and, no doubt, to discuss the meeting of the Board, among other matters. These occasions provided Burgess with information about the discussions of the Governors, both in relation to his own department and wider issues. Occasionally, Burgess would spend an evening with Nicolson, such as that when he met Nicolson and James Pope-Hennessy at the Travellers and then had a good dinner at Boulestin and went on "for a moment to the Boeuf."[13] One evening three months later, Burgess dined with Nicolson at the Reform Club and they discussed "B.B.C. affairs and whether in truth . . . the Governors are just there for eyewash."[14] Nonetheless, Nicolson took his duties as a Governor seriously.

On August 1, Burgess met Nicolson, Peter Pollock and Adam de Hegedus, a Hungarian journalist, at the Ritz Bar.[*] Burgess, who at this time was interested in Hungarians on behalf of Guy Liddell at M.I.5, had seconded Pollock to the work of keeping track of them. However, Pollock believed his job with M.I.5 was merely a ploy by Burgess to keep him in London.

> I lived in the Savoy and the Dorchester, for which M.I.5 or 6 – I couldn't tell the difference – paid. I knew White and Liddell from the Reform and Bentinck Street' . . . Pollock felt he couldn't be giving value for money: 'I had a list of people – all gay Hungarians, mostly nice people – I was supposed to keep my eye on. I didn't really know what I was supposed to do. I told Guy that when my unit was moved overseas I would go, and I did. To Algeria.[15]

---

[*] Nigel Nicolson published Hegedus's autobiography, *Don't Keep the Vanman Waiting,* in 1944.

Liddell was associated with the "double-cross" deception project, which used Enigma information to turn every German agent sent to Great Britain. He may have been assembling a census of Axis nationals resident in London. Hungary was at this time allied with Germany, which made Hungarians resident in London, gay or not, nice or not, persons of interest to the secret intelligence services. In any case, Burgess was working from time to time with Liddell, who was relaxing from time to time, as we have seen, at Burgess's Bentinck Street residence. Thus Burgess was in a position to be privy for most of the war to the activities and interests of M.I.5's counterespionage division.

In mid-September, 1941, George Barnes assigned Burgess to take over the flagship political Talks program of the Home Service: "The Week in Westminster" (TWW).[16] Broadcast every Saturday evening, it was a semi-official summary, usually by a member of the House of Commons, of the activities in Parliament. (Nearly three-quarters of a century later, a similar program remains on the B.B.C. schedule.) The program was closely supervised by the B.B.C. hierarchy, the Ministry of Information and the Foreign Office. At the end of the year Burgess was to describe it in this fashion:

The Week in Westminster was a peace time series describing the week's procedure in the House. It has been established over a number of years. The speakers are chosen on a rota from members of the parties in the House in order to preserve the balance of views. The series was revived in wartime after consultation with the Minister of Information . . . The first wartime talk was given on the 10th May 1941 by Mr. Kenneth Pickthorn. The series has continued when Parliament has been sitting ever since.[17]

All the political parties had an interest in the delicate process of deciding on the "rota" of presenters.

Bracken [then Minister of Information] had told the B.B.C. specifically in October 1942 that he wished it to be quite free to choose its own speakers in the well-established *The Week in Westminster* series and to decide for itself on the number in the

panel and the rotation in which the members would speak . . .
From September 1939 until May 1943 the order followed was
Conservative, Labour, Liberal, Conservative, Labour, National
Liberal, but in May 1943, after the Minister had said that he did
not think the B.B.C. need invite National Liberals as such, the
rota was simplified to read Conservative, Labour, Liberal . . .[18]

Burgess's role included the technical aspects of program
production itself, from timing scripts to editing them, as well as
nominating, preparing and evaluating the speakers. He was required
to become on familiar terms with many of the leading members of
Parliament, journalists and academic experts and with the details of
Parliamentary affairs, going to the House at least once or twice a
week and often much more frequently. In this way Burgess
gradually became the B.B.C.'s Parliamentary expert, the chief staff
liaison between the ordinary members of the Commons, in particular,
and the Corporation. According to Asa Briggs,

That good speakers were chosen [for *TWW*] and that some of
them established their reputation as a result was largely the work
of the B.B.C. The producers sometimes had to insist upon their
professional knowledge and experience even to the B.B.C.'s own
Board of Governors. Thus, George (later Sir George) Barnes
wrote bluntly in January 1942 that "the success of a series of
talks depends not upon the decision of a Board but on the
enthusiasm which the producer is able to impart to his
speaker."[19]

Almost immediately upon assuming responsibility for The Week
in Westminster, Burgess suggested a list of "Conservative speakers
with good broadcasting records," in effect nominating them for the
role of the voice of Parliament. But the following day Bracken
suggested a major change: that journalists, rather than M.P.s, should
be used on the program. Burgess set to work identifying likely
journalists: "Possible speakers:

1. Maurice Webb [chairman of the Parliamentary
correspondents; The Herald, Labour/TUC. If too left, then:]. 2.

H. Boardman of Manchester Guardian; John Carvel of the Star; Trevor Smith of the Australian News Service; William Barkley of *Daily Express*; J. E. Sewell, Telegraph.

The discussion went back and forth until it was decided to continue to use M.P.s, but with each member of the rota representing his or her party (not themselves) and speaking for a few weeks in succession, rather than changing each week.

At the end of 1941 the German army had been stopped at the Moscow suburbs and the combined German and Italian forces driven out of Egypt by those of the Empire.[20] On the other hand, Japan had destroyed much of the American Pacific Fleet at Pearl Harbor, taken the Philippines and was dominant throughout East and Southeast Asia, the Japanese Empire replacing those of France and Great Britain, although, having brought the United States into the war, these were to prove Pyrrhic victories.[*] On balance, the first three quarters of 1942 appeared to bring the Axis once more close to victory, in the East with the fall of Singapore, and in North Africa. In London, The Week in Westminster settled down to its rota of parliamentarians, increasingly chosen by Burgess himself for approval up the line through George Barnes to the Minister of Information. Jack Macnamara was mentioned, and a new M.P. from Scotland, Hector McNeil. The following is typical:

> In reply to your memo of today, the last rota was Moelwyn Hughes, Labour, Beverley Baxter, Conservative, and Captain Beechman, Liberal National. This rota will finish when Baxter does his last talk on the 18th July. The new rota consists of Megan Lloyd George, Opposition Liberal, George Strauss [Cripps' associate on *Tribune*], Labour, and G. S. Summers, Conservative. Megan [sic] has already started and broadcast last

---

[*] They also had disastrous consequences for Japanese Americans, 110,000 of whom, following on an Executive Order of February 19, 1942, were interned in detention camps. Many had their property confiscated or were forced to "sell" their farms and businesses to Caucasians. More than a few died from the harsh conditions and stress.

Saturday. Forthcoming dates that have been arranged are: G. R. Strauss, 25th July; Megan Lloyd George, 1st August; G.S. Summers, 8th August. At this point the House will probably rise for a number of weeks that cannot be stated definitely as yet, but after it resumes sitting the speakers will continue until they have done three or four times each . . . The proposed next Liberal National to replace Beechman is Geoffrey Shakespeare, which you are having approved. It will be seen that since it is agreed that each speaker will have several turns, we are fixed up for some time ahead with what I confidently hope will be a more satisfactory rota than some recent ones.[21]

The Talks Department continued to approve of Burgess's work, putting him in for a "salary Revision" on February 1, 1942: "Mr. Burgess is a very useful member of the Dept. He is fertile in ideas and . . . a tonic to the rest of us. He is a good critic of scripts but is inclined to be lenient with speakers. He is not a tidy office worker, but lately he has clearly tried to 'grow-up' and to improve that side of his work. He has earned his increment."[22]

Over fifty battalions of British troops were employed in 1942 suppressing an insurrection in India and Bengal was allowed to starve. Cripps spent the last week of March to the middle of April, 1942, in India in a last-ditch attempt to persuade Congress to support the Empire during the War in exchange for de facto independence status at its end. Undermined by the Viceroy and, perhaps, by Churchill himself, the Cripps Mission failed. By August, the Viceroy had thrown Nehru, Gandhi and much of the other leadership of Congress into prison. They would not emerge until the end of the war when they were released to negotiate the end of the Empire. Despite the failure of his mission, when Cripps returned to London he was widely seen as an alternative to Churchill as Prime Minister, with an approval rating in public opinion polls hovering around 70 per cent.[23] There was a feeling in the British political world all that summer that Cripps might, could, or should, unseat Churchill. Many, such as George Orwell, were beginning to see the war as a component of "the revolution," or visa versa, and the left-wing

Socialist Cripps was obviously a more plausible leader of a revolution than the right-wing Tory Churchill. On May 3rd Nicolson heard Cripps make "a speech which is uncompromisingly and radically Socialist. There will be no more rich, he says, and no more class distinctions."[24] Coincidentally or not, a "Twenty Year Pact" between Russia and Britain was signed on May 26, 1942.

Burgess was successful enough at the B.B.C. and becoming sufficiently well known that when in June, 1942, Cripps wished, somewhat optimistically, to begin planning for post-war reconstruction, he had Burgess and his colleagues Orwell and Empson and some others "come round after dinner . . . and discuss 'the place of the artist in society'."[25] Orwell wrote in his diary for June 7th: "Last Tuesday spent a long evening with Cripps (who had expressed a desire to meet some literary people) together with Empson, Jack Common, David Owen, Norman Cameron, Guy Burgess and another man (an official) whose name I didn't get.

About 2 ½ hours of it, with nothing to drink. The usual inconclusive discussion. Cripps, however, very human and willing to listen. The person who stood up to him most successfully was Jack Common. Cripps said several things that amazed and slightly horrified me. One was that many people whose opinion was worth considering believed that the war would be over by October - ie. that Germany would be flat out by that time. When I said that I should look on that as a disaster pure and simple (because if the war were won as easily as that there would have been no real upheaval here and the American millionaires would still be in situ) he appeared not to understand. He said that once the war was won the surviving great powers would in any case have to administer the world as a unit, and seemed not to feel that it made much difference whether the great powers were capitalist or socialist.* [Both David Owen and

---

* "Very interesting but perhaps rather hard on Cripps to report an impression like this from a private interview" [Orwell's handwritten footnote on typescript].

the man whose name I don't know supported him.] I saw that I was up against the official mind, which sees everything as a problem in administration and does not grasp that at a certain point, ie. when certain economic interest are menaced, public spirit ceases to function. [The basic assumption of such people is that everyone wants the world to function properly and will do his best to keep the wheels running. They don't realise that most of those who have the power don't care a damn about the world as a whole and are only intent on feathering their own nests.] I can't help feeling a strong impression that Cripps has already been got at. Not with money or anything of that kind of course, nor even by flattery and the sense of power, which in all probability he genuinely doesn't care about: but simply by responsibility, which automatically makes a man timid. Besides, as soon as you are in power your perspectives are foreshortened. Perhaps a bird's eye view is as distorted as a worm's eye view.[26]

(Orwell's image, as a Cold War patriarch, does not usually include his revolutionary socialist side, although that is clearly expressed in this passage. He was equally emphatic in "My Country Right or Left," written in autumn, 1940: "Only revolution can save England . . . I dare say the London gutters will run with blood. All right, let them, if it is necessary."[27]) It would appear that Cripps had invited a group that had both their work in common—B.B.C. Talks producers—and their ideology, which, if true, implies that Burgess's ideological sympathies were at this point generally known. Of course Cripps' own ideology was similar to that of his B.B.C. guests. According to Paul Anderson, in the mid-Thirties Cripps "had earned the enmity of the Labour right with his incendiary rhetoric for an all-or-nothing socialist programme, to be imposed by a Labour government that assumed dictatorial powers."[28]

By September, 1942, the rumors were that Cripps, stymied by Churchill, would resign. Burgess, rather extraordinarily, decided to intervene and convinced Nicolson to help. Nicolson's diary reads:

9th September, 1942

Guy Burgess has heard from his friends who are in close touch with Cripps that the latter is so discontented with the conduct of the war that he proposes to resign. That this project is both real and immediate is confirmed by the fact that Cripps has already sounded the *Times* and possibly Kemsley's papers as to whether they will give him press support. Guy had heard all this from Luker and E. H. Carr who are Cripps' advisors. Guy and I agreed that Cripps' attitude was probably wholly disinterested and sincere. That he really believed that Winston was incapable of dealing with the homefront and that his handling of the minor problems of production and strategy was fumbling and imprecise. We had agreed also that Cripps would find the atmosphere of Downing Street, with its late hours, casual talk, cigar smoke and endless whiskey, most impalatable. Whereas Winston never regards with affection a man of such inhuman austerity as Cripps, and cannot work with people easily unless his sentiment as well as his respect is aroused. We also agreed that Cripps (who in his way is a man of great innocence and a narrow vision) might be quite seriously unaware that his own resignation would gather all the elements of the opposition, and that in the end he would group around him an "alternative Government" and take Winston's place. We agreed that Cripps was actually too modest a man to realize what an immensely disturbing effect his resignation would produce, and too simple a man to see how it could be exploited by evil men to their advantage. At the same time we felt that there was a hope that if Winston would really show consideration for Cripps and give him a vital part in the direction of the war, then something might be done to avert that disaster.

Being in agreement with Burgess, Nicolson suggested they visit his fellow B.B.C. governor, Violet Bonham Carter, daughter of former Prime Minister Asquith, to ask her to intervene with Cripps to avoid a governmental crisis.

I suggested to Guy therefore that we should visit Violet and tell her the whole story. She is the only outside person I know who is on terms of intimate friendship with Winston and also in the confidence of Stafford and Lady Cripps. We told her the story. She said that she was in an awkward position as Lady Cripps had taken her into her confidence and told her much the same. She could not betray their confidence, much as she agreed with our point of view. We arranged therefore (a) that Violet should see Cripps or his wife and ask if she might say a word to Winston— a word of warning (b) that failing this I should go and see Bracken.[29]

If Cripps had resigned in early September he (or perhaps Beaverbrook, that "evil man") might well have been Prime Minister by the end of the month. And if he had been like Lloyd George, or Churchill, he might have done so. But he allowed himself to be persuaded by Churchill and Eden that the nobler path was to wait. Churchill then went to Moscow in August, 1942, solidifying the alliance between the Soviet Union and the British Empire. At the beginning of October, by which time the tide of war had begun to turn, Churchill was able to lever Cripps out of the War Cabinet, leaving him with many responsibilities but without the glamour of "a vital part in the direction of the war." In November, 1942, the British Empire's forces defeated the German and Italian armies at El Alamein, joint British and American forces invaded North Africa from the west and the Red Army defeated the Germans at Stalingrad. Churchill was secure for another two and half years.

George Orwell (as he signed himself on this occasion) had written to J. D. Bernal ("Dear Professor Bernal") in March, 1942, suggesting "a series of six half-hour talks . . . A sort of history of the rise of modern science from the end of the Middle Ages onwards, and then followed by a discussion of the future of science and the position of the scientific worker under Capitalism, Fascism and Socialism." The following month Burgess wrote to Bernal, using his nickname: "Dear Sage, What about meeting to have a talk sometime on the possibility of you giving a broadcast on science in the

USSR?" Bernal, who was close to Burgess, not least politically,[*] dropped the series of talks to India for Orwell, which was well-advanced, and did that for Burgess instead.[30] If hard feelings resulted, they were between Orwell and Bernal; the former and Burgess seem to have remained on good terms. For example, Burgess and Orwell collaborated in May, 1943, on parallel talks by Lord Winterton, who was Paymaster-General.[31] (Orwell had approached Winterton for his series "The Debate Continues.)

One of the attempts to assert (in this case, Labour) party control over The Week in Westminster took place in August of that year, as described in this memorandum to Barnes from Burgess:

1. Mr. William Whiteley, Parliamentary Secretary to the Treasury and Chief Labour Party Whip, rang me up on the 10th August and said that the Minister of Information had suggested to him that he should put before us a suggestion for a revision of the choice of speakers in "The Week in Westminster". He was anxious to do this in person.

2. After consultation with you, I saw him this morning. He told me that the Labour Party were anxious that more M.P.s should have a chance to take part in the series. I explained to him that it was our practice at the moment to allow a speaker three or four broadcasts in order to develop his broadcasting technique.

3. Mr. Whiteley asked how the speakers were at present chosen. I told him that names were submitted to the Ministry of Information for approval after consultation with the Whips.

4. He told me that the Whips office had never been consulted by the Minister and that he had raised this matter with the Minister who had promised that this should be done in the future. He accepted the fact that our standing in the matter was based on our

---

[*] "Only two members of the Royal Society belonged to the tiny Communist Party in Engalnd, and one of them was him." Canetti, Elias. Party in the Blitz. New York: New Directions, 2005, p. 126. The issue of Burgess's relationship with Bernal might reward exploration.

desire to get as good broadcasters as possible and that the political aspects, if any, were the proper concern of the Minister.

5. After discussion we agreed on the suggestion that in order to enlist as many speakers as possible in the series the number of contributions from individual Labour Party Members should be reduced to two. Mr. Whiteley promised to send me a list of about 20 members with the recommendation of the Whip's Office. I said we should like to feel free to make our selection from this list taking into account any technical broadcasting record we had of their previous performances and subject to a voice test where there was no record. He said that this was perfectly agreeable to him and that the Members who were put forward – after consultation with the junior Whips, would be informed of this.

I do not think that in fact we shall lose much by cutting down the contributions to two. The suggestion has, in fact, been made before and if we have – as we shall have – plenty to choose from we should be all right.

The mechanism by which the Labour Party Chief Whip – after personal consultation with the Minister of Information, gets in touch with me directly [he said?] seems a little curious. I hope, however, the situation was met adequately. I apologized for my juniority explaining that I had, in fact, been looking after the series for some time and was familiar with the arrangements. I think he accepted this.

I do not think there is any necessity to extend the principle of two broadcasts only to the Conservative Party unless they press for it and I should certainly like to keep Megan [Lloyd George] on as the almost permanent speaker for the Liberals (and this has been agreed).[32]

It would be interesting to know the actual words with which Burgess apologized for his "juniority."

The Week in Westminster was not Burgess's only B.B.C. responsibility. There was the very popular write-in program of Talks by John Hilton ("Forces Problems Answered"), meant to improve the morale of "other ranks," their wives and their families. Burgess tried to place Peter Pollock with Hilton (as he earlier had tried to place Pollock in M.I.5, or possibly M.I.6). Hilton responded on August 20, 1942:

> My dear Guy . . . I don't think I ever wrote you to say how much I like young Pollock. Whether he personally would be regarded as allocatable to the task of working with me in these matters I do not know, but he is just the type . . . I feel sure that if the talks are to open out in the way we have in mind, it must be in part by my having in parallel with me some young and junior officer of the Pollock type, who volunteered or was called up in the ordinary way for military service as a unit of the New Army, who did his turn as a private, went to an O.C.T.U., got his commission, and therefore is able to see the needs and problems of the great multitude of the Forces personnel from personal experience first-hand."[33]

The letter has a note at the bottom: P. W. Pollock, 6th Battalion Gordon Highlanders. On the 31st Burgess wrote to a Major Mackarness on the subject: JOHN HILTON: PROPOSAL OF JUNIOR OFFICER FOR ASSISTANCE.

> The name of Lieut. Pollock, 5th Battalion, Gordon Highlanders, has been suggested as the type wanted. He is known to Hilton, Major Sparrow of the Army Morale Committee, and myself. He has given unofficial but useful advice on the series. He has trained with the Army in this country for the last 2 ½ years. And it is understood that the Intelligence are interested in his transfer to or near London. (I believe they are in touch with the Adjutant-General's department over this proposal at the moment. Reference is Lt Col Speir, Room 055, War Office) . . .

John Sparrow of All Souls, "of the Army Morale Committee," was an interesting referent.[34] In any case, Pollock was not assigned to "Forces Problems Answered."

A year later the B.B.C. was concerned to find a successor to Hilton and to provide a support structure for whoever that might be. Concerning the latter, the program had heavy clerical demands, primarily having to do with handling correspondence, and a slot for a military assistant, another possible position for Pollock. On September 16th, 1943, Burgess wrote a memorandum to the Director of Talks on the subject of "Suggestions for creating a Bureau to support Hilton's successor".

Secretarial and administrative assistance . . . Stella Senior.

> Military assistant, "Lieutenant P. W. Pollock . . . was the officer thought most suitable by Hilton and myself, and also supported by Major Sparrow at the War Office who knows him . . . [35]

The B.B.C. first asked the War Office to release Wyn Griffiths (suggested by Burgess) to replace Hilton. This was refused. Burgess then suggested Jack Lawson, M.P. On the 8th of October, Barnes wrote Burgess, saying that he had asked George Blake to take the position as Hilton's successor, but he must have became uncertain as on the 12th Barnes wrote to the Controller of the Home Service, saying that Blake and Lawson were to be given a trial of six broadcasts each. On the 21st we find Burgess writing to B.B.C. Glasgow for assistance in setting up meetings: "I should like to take Blake round to see the various War Office and other officials involved." Hilton died at the beginning of November. Blake did not work out and in January, 1944, Burgess, who was persistent in such matters, was once again bringing Peter Pollock into the B.B.C. for a voice test.[36]

In September, 1942, the War Office's representative at the B.B.C. had become interested in Burgess. He wrote: "I was recently examining the lists of staff who were released for military service at the beginning of the year, and finding that Burgess was still with us although released for calling-up . . .

On 1st January 1942, I telephoned to him and asked him whether he had received a medical examination. He told me that he was examined more than a year ago when he was working with M.I. before he returned to the Corporation, and was placed in grade A1. He then said that he had no personal objection whatever to military service, but that he was at present "reserved" by the War Office and if I were now going to press the Ministry of Labour to call him up, he would like to inform the War Office first so that their "stop" action of this kind could be removed. I then discussed the matter with App.O. who telephoned the Director of Talks. The position is that Burgess still does work for the War Office in his spare time which does not interfere with his Corporation duties. He is extremely useful to Talks Department and they are anxious to keep him as long as possible. There is no replacement for him as yet and App.O. considered that we could leave matters to take their course. He had offered Burgess to the Ministry of Labour for military service and any special arrangements the War Office had made to reserve him were clearly not our affair. From the internal point of view, Burgess was not "double banked" and therefore no additional financial expense was involved.

Which can be taken to establish that during the War Burgess had some kind of official connection with M.I.5 "in his spare time." He told Driberg that, "from time to time," he reported to M.I.5 information about Germany received by him from a contact ("Orange"? see below). His expenses for this were paid for by M.I.5 in cash (as was M.I.5's custom), but, as noted by the War Office's B.B.C. representative, he was not on the M.I.5 payroll, not, in this sense, "double banked". It is reasonable to suppose that the information about Germany was also reported to Burgess's Soviet contacts, along with other information Burgess acquired, including, as usual, personnel and procedures of the B.B.C. and M.I.5.

During the winter of 1942/43 Burgess regularly socialized with a Bentinck Street group comprising Pollock, Hewit, Blunt and, often, still, with the others or alone, dining with Nicolson. For example, he had dinner at the Reform Club on October 8th with Nicolson and William Beveridge, whose eponymous report on the postwar welfare state was due for publication the following month.[37] A month later Burgess was at the Reform, once more, probably with Pollock, Hewit and Blunt, when Nicolson arrived to share his excitement about those turning points of the war: El Alemein and Torch, the Anglo-American invasion of North Africa. In the first three months of 1943 Burgess dined and went drinking with Nicolson several times, sometimes with Peter Pollock, sometimes with Robert Bernays, sometimes with Nicolson alone. Burgess was no doubt kept well-informed about behind the scenes discussions in Parliament, possibly also similar discussions in the Government.

The importance of the information that Burgess, Blunt and Maclean were able to provide to their Russian contacts is illustrated by an episode from the siege of Stalingrad. "On 26 December Beria told the GKO that the NKVD London 'resident' had passed on one of is agents' reports . . . that British intelligence received by the Foreign Office . . . had reliable information from Polish sources of a discussion between Hitler and Himmler.

> In the event of a significant worsening of the German situation, the German command would use poison gases and bacteria. Here it was underlined that Germany would in no instance consider itself defeated until all means at its disposal had been used. As a result of this meeting German industry, it is said, must be given authorization to produce large amounts of poison substances and apparatus for chemical and biological warfare.

> In the report the Polish agent doesn't indicate on which bit of the Front the Germans suggest using gas and bacteria first. Nevertheless, the British Foreign Office is taking this report seriously. Cadogan . . . personally told Eden about this. The British Foreign Office opinion is that Germany is not yet in quite such a tough position, that it will use such desperate measures.

This demonstrates that reports from Burgess, Blunt and Maclean were taken seriously, reached the highest levels in Moscow, and were both valuable and valued there.[38]

*　　*　　*

Around this time Burgess and the Administrative Assistant for the Talks section of the B.B.C. had another of the sort of exchange of memoranda over expenses that take place in many bureaucracies. Burgess was producing a series of talks on "Great Victorians" (in addition to his work on The Week in Westminster), which suited his fondness for the Victorian novelists. Burgess's side of the exchange gives us some detail about everyday (or every evening) life in the wartime B.B.C. On December 15, 1942, Burgess wrote, in explanation of a reimbursement claim, that he had been "On duty" for a "Great Victorian" reading, claiming two shillings for dinner and two shillings for a taxi home (as "transport [had] ceased"), then again two shillings for a taxi on the 27th ("Picking up Collin Brooks [journalist] and taking him to Bedford Square to discuss Lady Oxford's script") and again on the 29th ("Coming in evening to look after Great Victorian's reading. Dinner allowance"). Nearly all these were challenged by the Administrative Assistant. Burgess's response gives a flavor of his bureaucratic style as well as his business routines:

Thank you for your memo of January 7. I am sorry to have given you the trouble. I have added the information requested on the two dinner allowances involved (15/12 and 29/12). I have not put hours for Saturday since Saturday afternoons are outside Talks Department office hours. I have added the taxis home. What, in fact, happened was that in one case I walked some way with Brooks (15/12) and in the other I dropped him at his house (taxis being in short supply) (29/12). In the second case I have only charged a proportion of the taxi fare to the Corporation since I do not normally take taxis to Bentinck Street.

I do not think A.A. could have explained to you very clearly talks Producers' practice over office hours. I am not aware that my position differs fundamentally from that of any other producer. C(H) and D.T. laid it down long ago as a matter of general principle that Talks Producers should spend as much time as their work would allow making contacts outside the office.

I am sure you do not think – and neither you nor A.A. anywhere suggest in the correspondence—that I claim excessive allowances. I am, however, forwarding a note I wrote to Allowances Officer which is, I think, an indication that I do not.

I have been discussing with D.T. the question of entertainment of regular speakers such as Houghton and Hilton which I normally do but normally do not charge for, and D.T. has made it clear that he will support such exceptional claims from time to time. I add this as a warning for the future since these claims have been queried in the past.[39]

The Controller of the Home Service (C(H)) and the Director of Talks (D.T.) "laid it down long ago as a matter of general principle that Talks Producers should spend as much time as their work would allow making contacts outside the office." Burgess, we see, was in the habit of walking alone through the blacked-out London streets from his office to his home (however indirectly).

Sir Archibald Clark Kerr, the British Ambassador to the Soviet Union, was in London that winter, talking, according to his biographer, "with a broad range of individuals, pushing for a wider acceptance of the need to gain Stalin's trust by a commitment to the second front.

He met many of the young left, such as Richard Crossman and Ritchie Calder, and sought to make links between young English writers and their Soviet counterparts. He thus became friends with the young writer John Lehmann, who was also trying to establish literary links.[40]

As unlikely as it seems, the Ambassador was familiar with Lehmann's circle, having played host to Auden and Isherwood when the latter two were passing through Shanghai in 1938. Lehmann seems to have handed him on to Burgess. In any case, "Before returning to Moscow, Clark Kerr did get the chance to broadcast, on B.B.C. radio [7 February 1943], a speech which was widely reported."

His likely link here was Guy Burgess, who was involved at that time in commissioning politically acceptable material for the B.B.C.'s own propaganda effort. Clark Kerr spent a whole day rehearsing his 15-minute slot,* before recording his talk that evening in English, French and German. His theme was that the British people should ignore the attempts being made to paint the Soviet Union as ideological enemies. He ascribed to German propaganda this attempt to drive a wedge in the alliance by "rattling the so-called Bolshevist skeleton". Despite his own misgivings about attitudes in officialdom, Clark Kerr delivered a vigorous public tribute to the strength of the alliance. "We stand solidly together. We do not intend to be divided."[41]

Also at the beginning of 1943 Burgess added Captain Macnamara's Liberal colleague Wilfrid Roberts to the TWW rota:

All sources available (including your comments on him and contacts of mine in the House) would indicate that WILFRED ROBERTS is probably the best choice to succeed Megan Lloyd George as the Liberal speaker. His excellent broadcasting reputation goes back for some years but he has not I think spoken much lately.[42]

From time to time a problem arose of how to fill The Week in Westminster when Parliament was not in session. On March 9th, 1943, Burgess wrote to the Director of Talks:

After many discussions – which need not be put down here – it has been agreed that we should endeavour to keep the interests in Parliamentary institutions and the work of Members alive by occupying the "Week in Westminster" space with talks on Parliamentary matters when Parliament is not sitting . . . The

---

* Presumably with Burgess.

present idea is that we shall . . . endeavour to get a series of outstanding Members who for one reason or another will not be broadcasting in the "Week in Westminster" to do talks in the spaces available . . . Their subject would be a general reminiscent talk on Parliament and its work . . . Other Members will deal with such topics as: the drafting of Bills; work in constituencies . . . how committees such as the Beveridge, Scott, Uthwaite Committees are set up; how they work etc."[43]

In May it was decided to add an independent Member of Parliament to the rota. Burgess suggested William Gallacher, the House's pet Communist:

As instructed by D.T. I had a meeting with Sir Ian Fraser and Mr. Harold Nicolson to consult them about the choice of Independent speakers for "The Week in Westminster." . . . Points on these names were that Gallacher was an outstanding "Independent" and could be relied on to play the game. It was felt that the B.B.C. would be making a sensible and popular move by choosing him. Approval was expected from the Tory Party but the choice would probably lead to considerable opposition from the official Labour Party . . . If you agree, I propose to invite Gallacher first.[44]

As this indicates, Burgess and Nicolson worked closely together to select speakers. In June, Burgess wrote Nicolson: "You remember you mentioned to me that Sir George Arthur would like to give a talk on Lord Randolph Churchill.

I have now put it up to our people here. If you still think he's not too old, (and his broadcasting record is quite a good one up to fairly recently) and that a talk on Lord Randolph wouldn't lead to complications of any personal kind, we think it would be a good idea to do it. I would put it into one of the recess spaces for "The Week in Westminster."

Should I write to Sir George Arthur (who I do not know) directly or do you run into him in the natural course of events? I would, of course, go and see him anywhere at any time that he would suggest.

I'm going to be in the House on Thursday. I know its your meeting day here, but if the latter part of Questions is not enthralling could we possibly meet for a drink in the Stranger's Bar at about 11.45 a.m.?

GB[45]

This close, mutually beneficial, working relationship between Burgess and Nicolson was well-known at the B.B.C. For example, we have this note from the Assistant Director of Talks to one of the other producers:

It was agreed at the meeting that you would consult Harold Nicolson as to a speaker who might be invited to discuss the function and value of . . . Parliamentary Opposition. As you would naturally keep Burgess informed of your choice you might like to put up the enquiry to Nicolson through him. Alternatively, I could make the enquiry for you, or alternatively again, would you like to write a note to Nicolson asking leave to see him for me to endorse and forward to him?

[Annotated in ink:] "Burgess was dining with Harold Nicolson last night, agreed to discuss the question with him. I will report when I hear from him." Rowntree.[46]

In addition to working with Nicolson to fill TWW, Burgess also did some talent-spotting on his own. A memorandum from Burgess to the Director of Talks dated November 4th, concerning speaker arrangements for The Week in Westminster, again mentions Hector McNeil, Labour M.P., now Parliamentary Private Secretary in the Ministry of War Transport.

This man has never broadcast before, and is a choice of mine. I have, however, consulted the Labour Party who think very highly of him and he is also, if not popular, much respected by the Tories. I have great hopes that he may turn out a real winner, but this opinion as yet is only at the "hunch" stage."

202

The more general "insider" status of Burgess in the Westminster village can be seen from a September 3, 1943, letter to him from the Liberal "whip," Sir Percy Harris: "My dear Burgess,
You asked me, in confidence, if I could give you any indication when the "House" was likely to be sitting. My latest information is that it will be sitting for three days only on the 21st September. It will then adjourn for a fortnight. Then if we meet again on the 12th October, the present indication is to dispose of outstanding business; the number of days we sit depending on the work to be done.

I know you want to make your arrangements but please treat this information in the strictest confidence and it must not be communicated to anyone else.

To which Burgess responded on the 6th: "Many thanks for your letter of the 3rd September which I only got this morning.
I will treat the information you give me in the very strictest confidence. I would, however, like to say how very grateful I am to you for giving it to me.

I had a very agreeable dinner with Captain Grey and other Liberals the other night and we spoke much of you.

Another dispute with the finance section of the B.B.C. concerning Burgess's work-related expenses casts a light on his day to day activities in October and November of 1943, the means by which he maintained his "extensive connections in government, parliamentary and military circles." On October 5th he had dinner with Rosamond Lehmann, with whom he routinely produced programs (Paris forgiven), before she broadcast just before midnight, then drinks with her afterward. On October 9th Burgess had lunch with Eric Hooper of the Conservative Party's Political Research Centre. On the 14th he had lunch with Megan Lloyd George "to discuss very difficult coal debate" and on the 16th he claimed a weekly allowance for attendance at the House of Commons and had dinner with Megan Lloyd George after her broadcast in The Week in

Westminster.   On   the   20th   he   claimed   six   shillings   for
"entertainment" of the presenter of the talk "Can I Help You?"[47] If
this was his monthly average, his annual expenses (including a
weekly allowance of one pound for attendance at the House of
Commons for The Week in Westminster program) would have run to
over 200 pounds (6,700 pounds today), a considerable adjustment to
his salary.

Another exchange of comments with the fiscal administration
tells us something about Burgess's much-discussed personal
appearance: "on the occasion now under dispute [a funeral service
for John Hilton] I was representing the Corporation officially at an
official function.   (Incidentally, I was wearing my best clothes,
which matter for such an occasion . . .)".   Contrary to legend,
Burgess was not insistent on appearing poorly dressed.

Burgess wrote and then spoke to E. M. Forster in October, 1943,
in regard to commissioning Forster to give some talks on the Home
Service.   Forster declined, saying "that he is quite happy
broadcasting in the Indian Service [for Orwell] which, he says, gives
him more freedom to say what he wants than would the Home
Service."[48]   Forster was not inclined to reciprocate Burgess's
attempts to reach out to him. We have also a not overly friendly
glimpse of Burgess during this period from James Lees-Milne:

> I have been wanting to see Harold [Nicolson] since his return
> from Sweden.   He asked me to dine tonight.   To my
> disappointment he was not alone.   There were Godfrey
> Nicholson, [Tory] M.P., Guy Burgess and a Dr. Dietmar . . . Guy
> actually left us before dinner and rejoined us immediately after .
> . . Talk was about lying. Harold said he never lied except over
> sex matters.   Then he and Guy became engrossed in political
> shop which I found very tedious.   I am interested in politics *per
> se,* but long anecdotes on how Mr. Bevan snubbed Lady Astor,
> who got her own back by insulting Mr. Attlee strike me as
> childish and contemptible . . . Guy is obsessed with this aspect of
> the beastly business.[49]

And then a rather more appreciative observation from Nicolson himself at the very end of 1943:

I go round to the Reform where I dine with Guy Burgess. I have to make the 9.50 at Paddington and leave at 9.0. I say I must go to the lavatory and rush down there hurriedly. But I slip on the brass steps and fall with an immense crack. I pick myself up confusedly and in pain and say "All right Guy it is really all right." I then turn the hot water tap to the basin and the next I know is I am sitting on the floor of the lavatory with Guy's arm around me. "Have I fainted?" I ask. "Three times" he answers. He tells me that in the intervals of my three faints, I said to him "Do not worry Guy. I am not going to die in your club lavatory." I have no recollection of this.

Anyhow he is fussed and I have an enormous pain at the back of my skull. He takes me to Paddington by Tube and I find my sleeper. He says goodnight. And then he returns as I am undressing and gives me aspirin which he has managed to get out of a soldier in the train. And I used to think that Guy was a selfish man![50]

George Barnes filed an evaluation of Burgess's work on the last day of 1943: "He is full as ever of ideas, he shows signs, faint signs, of a growing sense of responsibility, though he still writes and speaks before he thinks. A bit of a sea-lawyer on matters of administration, but – yet – a valuable member of the Department." A grade increment was approved. Just after the New Year Burgess discussed with Goronwy Rees, who was in the Army at the time, and Nicolson, a suggestion from General Alexander (then in Italy) that the special Forces programming should be replaced with the schedule of programs used in Britain. Nicolson thought it a good idea in principal, but also thought there would be practical difficulties.[51] A few weeks later Burgess began planning some programs on European affairs, in anticipation of the Second Front.[52]

Burgess's work with the B.B.C. had settled into a routine. He was producer of the flagship Talks program, The Week in

Westminster, which he now ran more or less as he wished, and the producer from time to time of other programs. He knew many of the leading members of Parliament well and many had received favors from him as broadcasters on TWW. Burgess often worked a six-day week of twelve-hour days, ending with the Saturday evening broadcast of The Week in Westminster. As we have seen, the work entailed negotiating with his superiors in the Talks Department and those at more exalted levels in the Corporation, occasionally with officials in the Ministry of Information, the Foreign Office and the political parties. It included recruiting speakers and negotiating their contracts, then working with them to produce satisfactory scripts. It included occasional travel around England and many, if not most, evenings in the House and, after that was bombed, in "the Annex," meeting with his speakers and his other sources of information. There were lunches and dinners with politicians and journalists at the Reform, the RAC or the Travellers, at the Café Royal and other favored venues. From the summer of 1940, all this was complicated by the Blitz and the intermittent bombing that followed. He was also, according to Fitzroy Maclean, in some sense responsible for propaganda to occupied Europe and liaison with SIS and SOE (possibly as part of the M.I. connection mentioned above), which one would have thought a full-time job on its own.[53] This is substantiated by an entry under March 8, 1944, in the diary of Guy Liddell of M.I.5: "Kemball Johnston [of M.I.5] and Guy Burgess came to see me about Orange [an agent]. Burgess has ascertained that Orange got his information about [Polish General] Kukiel from the Swiss M.A. who got it from the Polish M.A. Burgess raised the question of Orange's future. He has the opportunity of becoming editor of the *Züricher Zeitung* [. . .][54] Burgess also maintained his connections with such as Blunt, Philby, Cairncross and, apparently, Rees.[*] These activities, also, no doubt took some time. There was the part-time work with M.I.5 and his other secret intelligence activities,

---

[*] There is a specific term in Russian for an agent who is the connection between various parts of a network: *svyaznika.*

including, quite possibly, reports to his Russian contacts concerning his British contacts. Burgess was very busy.

But workdays, even in wartime, eventually come to an end and Burgess would often then join those making their way through the dark streets of Soho to the Gargoyle Club. Opened in 1925 for the Bright Young Things of the time, the Gargoyle Club was founded and operated by David Tennant: handsome, rich, clever, alcoholic, heterosexual (even at Cambridge); son of Lord Glenconner, stepson of Viscount Grey of Fallodon, nephew of Margot Asquith, brother of the unique Stephen Tennant; Cambridge contemporary of Dadie Rylands and Steven Runciman. Each of the three floors of his Club was designed for a different effect: a ballroom the walls of which were mirrored mosaic; an interior dining room of "Tudor" design; a private apartment and vast wine cellars; and a rooftop dining area and garden for those occasions, which do occur, when the London weather was either appropriate or tolerable. All this connected by a very small elevator, finished in the art deco fashion of the day, groaning and occasionally stopping mid-passage with its passengers, who were then more or less expected to take advantage of the sudden intimacy. By opening night the Club members included such as "Somerset Maugham, Noel Coward, Gladys Cooper, Margaret Banerman, Michael Arlen, Leon Goossens, Lilian Braithwaite, Gordon Craig, George Grossmith, Virginia Woolf, Duncan Grant, Nancy Cunard, Adele Astaire, Edwina Mountbatten, Gilbert Frankau, Sibyl Colefax, an obligatory Guinness, Rothschild and Sitwell, a handful of MP's and the odd peer of the realm."[55] The Gargoyle roared through the Twenties and on through the Thirties, a place for cheap lunches for writers and artists and expensive, extensive, evenings for members of the Drones Club and such like decorative and often drug addicted creatures.

Tennant closed the Gargoyle during the first onslaught of the Blitz, then reopened it around the time that Germany invaded the Soviet Union at the end of June, 1941.

With the war, the cross-currents of social life multiplied exceedingly and a more hybrid membership, shaken to the surface in the time of emergency, was now thrust upon the Club's owner. The London based Free French were drawn to the Gargoyle; writers, poets, intellectuals and artists in flight from Europe found a form of refuge there. People from societies where the culture of the café was all important—Vienna, Poland, the Balkans—found in the Gargoyle a place where information and ideas could be exchanged in a way that they would be familiar with but one that was almost unknown elsewhere in this country.[56]

During the war it became the perfect setting for the inhabitants of London's ruling and chattering classes to meet one another and desired others: Mayfair and Bloomsbury; the Foreign Office and Fleet Street; secret agents and members of governments-in-exile; artists and musicians; whores of all sexes: "the one place where the Home Office, the Foreign Office, Bohemia, the sodden aristocracy, the odd Russian, the odd Hungarian could *all* go without it looking odd at all was the Gargoyle."[57] Peering at, or under, the tables, the curious visitor might find Dylan Thomas, Lucian Freud, Stephen Spender, Cyril Connolly, Peter Watson, Francis Bacon: an entire gazetteer of London in the Forties.

The Gargoyle makes its first appearance in Nicolson's diaries on April 30, 1942, as the context for one of his casual anti-Semitic observations: "Dine with Victor Cunard and go with him to his strange club where I meet Billy Smith and Brian Howard . . . I go away feeling that one can never be kind to a Jew [Howard] . . . Even their domestic affections are part of their acquisitiveness and senses of possession."[58] Guy Burgess, who was not even socially anti-Semitic, "would often fetch up there with Brian Howard* with whom he was very thick at this time and who was now a fully fledged member of M.I.5"[59] On July 15, Burgess and Peter Pollock dined at the Café Royal with Collin Brooks. They were met there by Nicolson and all went to the Gargoyle, where they joined Augustus

---

* "Brian [Howard] once said . . . '*I* am a has-been. That's something *you* can never be" (Luke, pp. 172-3).

John, Brian Howard and Mrs. Heber Percy and drank beer and other beverages until 1.30 in the morning.[60] (Mrs. Heber Percy was born Lady Dorothy Lygon and lives on as the younger sister of the beloved in *Brideshead Revisited*.) On the evening of September 7th, Burgess again dined with Nicolson and they again went on to see "poor Brian Howard at the Gargoyle." It seemed to be a regular event for Burgess that summer, dinner at the Café Royal, usually with Peter Pollock, occasionally with Nicolson, then on to the Gargoyle. It was at the Gargoyle one evening that Burgess asked the painter John Craxton if he would like to go home with him for some wine and recreation:

> "'Would you like to come back to my flat?' he offered. 'Would you like to be whipped—a wild thrashing? Wine thrown in?' Johnny said no, he didn't want to be whipped at all. 'I was terrified. I tell you who saved me. He was sitting opposite. Philip Toynbee.' That scene ended with a tussle between Guy and Philip rolling about on the floor amongst the dancers . . ."[61]

The "wine thrown in" remark rather undercuts the drama of the "wild thrashing." Many Gargoyle stories have Philip Toynbee rolling on the floor, not often, however, with Guy Burgess.

The evenings for Burgess and his fellow adventurers did not always end at the Gargoyle:

> There was the time . . . when having started their evening at the Gargoyle, Guy, Brian and Gerald Hamilton . . . departed in search of seamy adventure in a louche Soho basement club. While they were there the place was raided. When the police came up to their table, Brian, by this time very drunk indeed, replied to their polite request for his name and address by saying 'My name is Brian Howard, *I* live in Mayfair. No doubt *you* live in some dreary suburb.' Hamilton later remarked to Guy, who had behaved with typical assured nonchalance, that in his view this was a *most* tactless way of receiving the attentions of the civil arm.[62]

Burgess had given his Bentinck Street address, his job-title and employer's name: all grand enough. The civil arm, Special Branch, filed report after report about Hamilton without ever quite deciding whether he was an agent, and if so, for whom, or, on the other hand, simply a swindler. Or perhaps both. There are no Special Branch files, or, rather, none accessible to the historian, on Guy Burgess.

Burgess dined with Nicolson at the Café Royal on May 2, 1943, this time going on to Ritz, where they met Brian Howard, Hope-Nicolson, and John Rohdes and then the whole group went across the way to the Hotel Meurice.[63] (The diary precision of these dates and places is reassuring in a world that has been so thoroughly erased.) On Bastille day Burgess had dinner with Nicolson, who had lunched with Philip Toynbee and his wife[*] at the Gargoyle. James Lees-Milne was not at all fond of Burgess, but given the times and the place, could not avoid the occasional encounter. For Saturday, 16th October, 1943, Lees-Milne's diary recorded:

> When I got home for tea Jamesey [James Pope-Hennessy] telephoned proposing a night of adventure. I was thrilled and for once our enthusiasms coincided. We drank first at the Ritz, then the Gargoyle, dined at the White Tower and visited disreputable pubs in that area. The only person we met was Guy Burgess, drunk and truculent, and we soon shook him off . . ."[64]

This would have been after one of the Saturday night broadcasts of The Week in Westminster, and therefore quite late in the evening, or early in the Soho morning.

Lees-Milne was at the Ritz bar one Saturday in 1944 (the 25th of November), when, he writes, "Guy Burgess called to me. I dined with him and Charles Fletcher-Cooke[65] at the Gargoyle.

> Drank too much beer and gin mixed, and talked a great deal about politics and sex, disagreeing with Guy over both. He does and says the most dangerous and indiscreet things. However we laughed a lot. Mary Churchill who was there, joined us. I do not

---

[*] Anne Powell, mother of Polly Toynbee. She later married Richard Wolheim.

know her. She is prettier than her sister Diana and looks like her mother. She talked all the time about her father whom she adores unreservedly.[66]

Lees-Milne, with his reputation for *Country Life* refinement, apparently shared Burgess's (and Brian Howard's) taste for such late night expeditions in search of rough trade. James Pope-Hennessy, then Literary Editor of *The Spectator,* brought *his* to the Gargoyle. Robert Buhler remembered

Sitting one night at a table in the Gargoyle were Lucian Freud, Francis [Bacon] . . . Pope-Hennessy and a couple of his paratrooper 'rough-trade' boys, and myself . . . Evidently I had said something about his brother John which offended . . . I was immediately set upon by the two paratroopers. Now Lucian . . . was very brave. He jumped on the back of one of the bully boys while Francis kicked his shins.[67]

Perhaps it was at the Gargoyle that Pollock transferred his attentions from the sexually dominating Burgess to the masochistic Francis Bacon.

After leaving the Gargoyle, or as a substitute for it, there were less haughty Soho destinations: the Bag O'Nails, the Nest Club, the Shim-Sham Club and so forth.

The Bag O' Nails Club was in the basement of 9 Kingly Street and was a well known music hangout of the 1930's . . . It is to the history of British Swing music what Hampton court is to the history of England . . . The pianist was Harold Hood who later joined Nat Gonella's Georgians, a small jazz group which enjoyed considerable success between 1935 and 1939. Jazz players Buddy Featherstonhaugh and Teddy Joyce formed part of the house band of the Bag O' Nails . . . The Nest Club, The Bag O' Nails, Shim-Sham Club and The Cuba Club are names that occur over and over again in jazz history from this period . . . . Prominent players included Dave Wilkins, Leslie 'Jiver' Hutchinson, Frank Deniz, Yorke de Souza, Lauderic Caton, Carl

Barriteau and Bertie King. They remained after the war ended and some of them in the fledgling bop scene as bands.[68]

The Bag O' Nails conveniently also served as an air-raid shelter.

Other men in Burgess's circle managed their emotional and sexual needs in ways involving less risk. Harold Nicolson, to return to our exemplar of the lower upper class London political intelligentsia, had his two Jameses—Lees-Milne and Pope-Hennessy—who were more or less permanent fixtures at K.B.W., as well as amusements on holiday, especially before the war at Somerset Maugham's Villa Mauresque in the South of France, where the offerings included Louis Legrand, whom we have met before, "known as 'Loulou' . . . a ravishing sixteen-year-old male whore,

> slender, blond, tanned, with a soft mouth and a sweet smile; he wore gold bangles on both wrists and spent most of the day dressed only in a minute pair of faded swimming trunks . . . Loulou passed much of his time at the Mauresque, at the disposal not only of Haxton and Maugham . . . but of any male guest who desired his services, Gerald afterward discreetly settling the bill. Both Harolds, Nicolson and Acton, became appreciative customers (*"Mon cher Lulu,"* wrote Nicolson from Paris, *"merci pour la soirée délicieuse"*) . . . [69]

Nicolson "who took a pragmatic view of sex, was generally interested, at any given moment, in a variety of young male partners . . ." Concerning his relationship with the censorious architectural preservationist and diarist James Lees-Milne, Burgess's Lockers Park classmate, we are told:

> [A]lthough Harold [Nicolson] may only have been infatuated with [Lees-Milne] for a few months of 1933-4, he retained great affection for him thereafter, remaining a 'guide, philosopher and friend' to him for the next thirty years. And their sexual association also continued far beyond those initial months, possibly even up to Jim's marriage in 1951. Jim in effect joined a coterie of bright young literary men . . . who reveled in Harold's company and hospitality and looked to him as a father-

212

figure, an intellectual guru, a protector who might use his influence and connections on their behalf . . . In return, Harold . . . looked to his protégés to 'oblige' him in his rather perfunctory sexual desires, which most of them (including Jim) were quite happy to do . . .[70]

Burgess sexual desires were hardly perfunctory. And it amused him to exaggerate the frequency with which, and the unusual ways in which, he fulfilled them. These stories became part of his "cover," like James Angleton's bass fishing and orchids. Later, others obliged by repeating Burgess's tales, or adding their own to the cycle. Michael Burn contributed two or three:

Guy . . . asked me for a photograph of myself. When I gave him a pioneerish-looking open-shirted one, profiled against a pylon, he remarked, "I shall have to say it's one of my *Hitlerjügend* boyfriends" . . . He gave me a red hardback of the Minutes of the colossal Seventh Congress of the Comintern summoned in Moscow in the summer of 1935 to demand a worldwide united front against Fascism.

As far as I can tell, this exchange is unique in the annals of romance.

Burn went on to recall that Burgess made him "familiar with the name of John Cornford, the Cambridge Communist killed in Spain, and gave me the unforgettable love-poem Cornford wrote to Margot Heinemann just before his death . . .

I did not respond when Guy suggested that we should share a flat in London, remarking that it would help to pass the winters "and the summers could take care of themselves". Now and then I went to bed with him. But for some while I had felt myself to be falling under a dangerous spell which had only incidentally to do with politics and much to do with sex . . . Guy meanwhile continued cheerfully promiscuous, on one-night or Thousand-and-One-Night stands, and looked extremely well on it . . .[71]

Burn seemed to agree with Hewit, and differ with Pollock, about the attractions of Burgess's sexual practices. In any case, such "cheerful promiscuity," homosexual, heterosexual or, as with Joseph Ackerley, perhaps inter-species, was taken for granted along the axis between Broadcasting House and Westminster.

These vignettes place Burgess socially at a point typical of the Gargoyle crowd, the point where the B.B.C., Soho, Mayfair and Westminster met. Later, some suspected, or pretended to suspect, that the Club had functioned as a kind of secret intelligence postal exchange, among its other services. Bentinck Street, the Reform, the RAC, the Gargoyle and the more or less expensive Soho clubs and pubs did not exhaust Burgess's social life. At the end of March, 1943, the Administrative Assistant (Talks), who seems to have forgiven Burgess the various expense account disagreements, sent this curious short note to the Director of Talks and up the line to the Controller of the Home Service:

> Mr. Burgess has access to a private dining club, which meets once a fortnight on Thursday, made up of members of the Allied Governments, Foreign Office people, and diplomats generally. At the meeting this morning it was thought to be a useful ground for meeting future broadcasters.

It is possible that in the Spring of 1943, "members of the Allied Governments, Foreign Office people, and diplomats generally" had much to discuss of interest to Burgess and others, extending in this way, his extensive contacts remembered in Moscow even today. The Adminstrative Assistant continued his note as follows:

> Mr. Burgess is willing to take along any Producer who wishes to go, but points out that the cost per head is likely to be in the region of £2—that is, 10/- for food and 30/- for drink. May I please have sanction for passing claims up to £2. for any Producer attending this Club.

Barnes replied that there "would be no objection to a payment of 10/- for food plus a small payment for drink. The idea that drink should cost 20/- per person can only mean that wine is taken which is surely unnecessary, and I can hardly believe that members of the Allied Governments and the Foreign Office are willing to spend so much on drink at each of these dinners."[72] Perhaps Barnes was being ironic.

Early in March, 1944, Burgess, to his distress, heard that Peter Pollock had been reported missing in action in Italy and, coincidentally, that week Burgess submitted his second resignation from the B.B.C., this in order to move to the Foreign Office.[73] Burgess stated for the record at the end of the month: "Personally, it will be a real grief to leave the department and the division. I should like to emphasise this very strongly. Also to say that I should like to give any assistance that may be possible in the future to the department if this should be found useful."[74] The response to Burgess's resignation from Barnes was consternation, as can be found in a memorandum to Maconachie, then Controller of the Home Service: "The position as I see it is as follows:

1. I cannot spare Burgess for immediate transfer to the Foreign Office. I therefore recommend that we should insist on his giving three months' notice or, if the F.O.'s needs are to be considered paramount, on at least one month's notice.

2. I agree with you that it would be useless to keep Burgess against his will but his mind is by no means made up and I have told him that if he stays he would handle the proposed Foreign Affairs series. He has promised to let me know by 2.30 tomorrow whether he means to resign.[75]

On April 1st Maconachie wrote to the Director General of the B.B.C., through the Deputy Director:

Mr. Burgess submitted his resignation on 4th March in order to be free to take up work in the Foreign Office News Department. I discussed the matter with him, and he told me that, although he liked his present work in the B.B.C., he thought the chance of employment under the Foreign Office and of this leading to permanent appointment there, was one he should not miss. I found, however, that we had heard nothing from the Foreign Office as to their willingness to employ him and advised him not to take a risk, as he was ready to do, by resigning from the

B.B.C. without knowing that there was in fact anything to go to. He accordingly took back his resignation, but has now submitted it again.

D.T. and I think it quite useless to attempt to retain any Talks producer who really wants to leave. No producer, we think, can pull his weight in broadcasting, which demands wholehearted enthusiasm, if he is retained in it against his will - even if this were possible. I therefore recommend that Mr. Burgess' resignation should be accepted and that he should be released three months from the date of its submission, in accordance with his contract. It would, however, I think, be only fair to count the period of notice as beginning on 4th March, the date on which he first submitted his resignation, since he withdrew it at my suggestion. He would then be released on 4th June, but we could make him available to the Foreign Office from 1st May, for a maximum of two hours a day, to learn his work there.

Mr. Burgess is a very good producer and, although he has his failings, will be a serious loss to the Talks Department. That, however, I am afraid, cannot be helped.[76]

The resignation was accepted "with regret" on the 12th of April, as from the 4th of March, "this being the date on which you originally mentioned the matter," for purposes of the requisite three months notice and he was released part-time from the 1st of May to the Foreign Office.

On May 23rd Burgess filed a long memorandum of possible speakers for The Week in Westminster, over the next several months. This, leaving a neat set of guidelines for is successor, was his final contribution to the programme and to the B.B.C. On the 13th of June, we find that successor, Hilton Brown, a Talks producer specializing in broadcasts of purpose-written short stories, writing to Harold Nicolson:

As perhaps you know, I have recently taken over "The Week in Westminster" series in place of Guy Burgess. Guy had the great

advantage of knowing you personally. I haven't that, but would
like very much to make a start by making your acquaintance. I
wonder if you would come and have a drink with me in the
Strangers' Bar if you are in the House on Thursday between
twelve and one o'clock. I have to make it the Stranger's Bar
because that's one of the few places in the House which I am
allowed to enter. I feel I would greatly benefit if I could have a
talk with you about the series and get your views on it and your
advice.

Burgess's work at the B.B.C. was summed up by Barnes in a
Note for Staff File of 11th July, 1944:

Burgess has much to give the Corporation though my experience
of his work suggests that he is essentially a Producer and would
not succeed on the managerial side.

He is very clever, full of ideas, well informed, with a large circle
of acquaintances and is good at getting up a subject quickly. His
interests are wide, e.g. he has been equally successful in Foreign
Affairs, Parliament, History, and more unexpectedly the
interpretation of Government orders to the public, on which his
work with John Hilton and Douglas Houghton has been good
and his interest unflagging.

His office work is slipshod and he needs a good secretary to be
efficient. He is lazy and has not learnt to express himself exactly
when writing; he is not conscientious and takes a very liberal
view of his duties. He gets on well with speakers, is popular
with other producers as an 'enfant terrible' but easily gets across
other departments, e.g. Presentation and Administration, for his
manners are off-hand and he does not suffer fools.

In short, his real interest in broadcasting and his unusual gifts
should always make him eligible for a job on the programme
side, particularly as a Talks Producer.[77]

Notes to Chapter Five

1 January 15th, 1941. B.B.C. Written Archives Center, Caversham. Staff Records—Guy Burgess.

2 B.B.C. Written Archives Center, Caversham. Staff Records—Guy Burgess. This is the only indication found of Burgess having been actually employed by the Ministry of Information, unless his work with the J.B.C. could be described in that way.

3 B.B.C. Written Archives Center, Caversham. Burgess Talks, listing, no date, no author.

4 B.B.C. Written Archives Center, Caversham. R51/63/3 Talks Can I Help You? File 1C 1941. Letter for the Director of Talks. 6th March 1941.

5 B.B.C. Written Archives Center, Caversham. B.B.C. Memo. Subject: Projection of Europe to the Home Country. 7th June 1941.

6 Newsletter, September 25, 2000, Foreign Intelligence Service, Russian Federation, http://svr.gov.ru/smi/2004/bratishka20040125.htm.

7 Nicolson, Harold. Diaries in The Vita Sackville-West and Harold Nicolson manuscripts, letters and diaries [microform]: from Sissinghurst Castle, Kent, the Huntington Library, California, and other libraries, reel 14.

8 Nicolson, Harold. Diaries in The Vita Sackville-West and Harold Nicolson manuscripts, letters and diaries [microform], reel 14.

9 Houlbrook, Matt. Queer London: Perils and Pleasures in the Sexual Metropolis, 1918-1957, Chicago: University of Chicago Press, 2005, p. 83.

10 Briggs, Asa. The History of Broadcasting in the United Kingdom, Volume III: The War of Words. New York: Oxford University Press, 1995, p. 357.

11 The quibble about whether or not Blunt was a Communist has to do with his membership, or lack of it, in the Communist Party of Great Britain. There is no doubt about his beliefs. "Draft Suggestions for Talks on Russia," July 15, 1941, R51/520/1 B.B.C. Archive. See also West, W. J. Truth Betrayed. London: Duckworth, 1987, pp. 59-61.

12 Nicolson, Harold. Diaries in The Vita Sackville-West and Harold Nicolson manuscripts, letters and diaries [microform], reel 14, entry for January 2, 1942.

13 Nicolson, Harold. Diaries in The Vita Sackville-West and Harold Nicolson manuscripts, letters and diaries [microform], reel 14.

14 Nicolson, Harold. Diaries in The Vita Sackville-West and Harold Nicolson manuscripts, letters and diaries [microform], reel 14.

15 Carter, Miranda. Anthony Blunt: His Lives. London: Macmillan, 2001, p. 283.

16 B.B.C. Written Archives Center, Caversham. The Week in Westminster file. Memo. 14th September, 1941. From: Assistant Director of Talks. To: Burgess. Subject: The Week in Westminster. "Will you please definitely take over The Week in Westminster from Saturday, 4th October. Mr. Beechman has already been contracted for this date and I have passed you recent correspondence with him. I am attaching correspondence with Maxwell Fyfe who will be giving the talk on Saturday, 11th October. You will see that he has been contracted for this date . . .The file is worth reading and if it is not in Registry it is held by D.T."

17 Memo: The Week in Westminster. From: Guy Burgess. 31st December 1941.

18 Briggs, pp. 556-7.

19 Briggs, p. 35.

20 Gerhard Weinberg argues that this saved Britain from a planned German invasion in the fall of 1941. See: Weinberg, Gerhard L. A World at Arms: A Global History of World War II. Cambridge: Cambridge University Press, 1994, p. 268ff.

21 B.B.C. Written Archives Center, Caversham. The Week in Westminster file. Memo (Confidential). From: Mr. Burgess. Subject: TWW. To: D.T. 13th July 1942.

22 B.B.C. Written Archives Center, Caversham. The Week in Westminster file. From George Barnes, Director of Talks.

23 Clarke, Peter. The Crips Version: The Life of Sir Stafford Cripps 1889-1952. Allen Lane, The Penguin Press: London, 2002, p. 289; 330.

24 Nicolson, Harold. Diaries in The Vita Sackville-West and Harold Nicolson manuscripts, letters and diaries [microform], reel 14, entry for May 3, 1942.

25 Nicolson, Harold. Diaries in The Vita Sackville-West and Harold Nicolson manuscripts, letters and diaries [microform], reel 14, June 3, 1942. Orwell, Empson and Burgess also had in common, as B.B.C. producers, that each had commissioned talks in Basic English. West, W.D. Orwell: The Lost Writings. New York, Arbor House, 1985, p. 62.

26 Transcription from George Orwell: Diaries, courtesy of Gavin Freeguard.

27 Anderson, Paul. Introduction. Orwell in Tribune: 'As I Please' and
Other Writings, 1943-7. London: Politico, 2006, p. 21.
28 Anderson, p. 9.
29 Nicolson, Harold. Diaries in The Vita Sackville-West and Harold
Nicolson manuscripts, letters and diaries [microform], reel 14. Bonham-
Carter's diary entry reads simply: Harold brought a young man called
Burgess to see me – Very disturbed about Safford Cripps position with the
Government." Bodleian Library, Special Collections, MS Bonham Carter
20.
30 West, W.D. Orwell: The Lost Writings. New York, Arbor House, 1985,
pp. 28-30.
31 West, W.D. Orwell: The Lost Writings, pp. 250-1.
32 B.B.C. Written Archives Center, Caversham. The Week in Westminster
file. Memo. Subject: TWW. 11th August, 1942. From: Burgess.
33 B.B.C. Written Archives Center, Caversham. John Hilton file. Letter
from John Hilton to Guy Burgess, August 20th 1942.
34 See the biographical essay in Annan, Noel. The Dons. London:
HarperCollins, 2000, pp.193ff.
35 B.B.C. Written Archives Center, Caversham. John Hilton file.
Memorandum from Burgess to Director of Talks 16th September 1943.
36 Blake "gave a number of talks (c. November/December 1943) under the
general heading: 'Forces Problems Answered', i.e. 'Pay & Allowances'; 'Sick
Leave'; 'Army Trades'; 'Overseas Mail'; 'Leave'; and "G.B.'s Final talk"
(given on 21/12/43)." Private communication from Trish Hayes, Archives
Researcher, B.B.C. Written Archives Centre, Caversham Park, Reading.
37 Nicolson, Harold. Diaries in The Vita Sackville-West and Harold
Nicolson manuscripts, letters and diaries [microform], reel 14.
38 Bellamy, Chris. Absolute War: Sovie Russia in the Second World War:
A Modern History. London: Macmillan, 2007, p. 544. Bellamy credits the
report to Maclean, presumably because he was in the Foreign Office in
London at the time. It could as easily come from Burgess's contacts there
or in M.I.6. Bellamy's source is given as FSB Archives, Vol. III, Bk 2.
Doc. 1247, 'Soobshcheniye NKVD SSSR No 2134/B v GKO s
izlozhennym dannykh poluchenykh ot rezidenta NKVD v Londone, o
podgotovke Germanii k primeneniyu khimicheskikh I bakteriologicheskikh
sredstv vedeniya voyny', 26 December 1942, p. 565. This series may well

prove to be a rich source for information on what was provided to Moscow by the Burgess group.

[39] B.B.C. Written Archives Center, Caversham. Burgess file. Memorandum from Mr. Guy Burgess to A.O(H) thro' A.A.(Talks), 11th January, 1943.

[40] Gillies, Donald. Radical Diplomat: The Life of Archibald Clark Kerr, Lord Inverchapel, 1882-1951. I.B.Tauris: London, 1999, p. 140.

[41] Gillies, p. 140.

[42] B.B.C. Written Archives Center, Caversham. The Week in Westminster file. Memo. Subject: TWW From: Mr. Guy Burgess 5th February, 1943. To: D.T.

[43] B.B.C. Written Archives Center, Caversham. The Week in Westminster file. Memo. Subject: TWW From: Mr. Guy Burgess 9th March, 1943. To: D.T. Thro' Miss Rowntree.

[44] B.B.C. Written Archives Center, Caversham. The Week in Westminster file. Memorandum Subject: WEEK IN WESTMINSTER 11th May, 1943. From: Guy Burgess. To: DT. See also Nicolson, Harold. Diaries in The Vita Sackville-West and Harold Nicolson manuscripts, letters and diaries [microform]: from Sissinghurst Castle, Kent, the Huntington Library, California, and other libraries, reel 14, under May 6, 1943.

[45] B.B.C. Written Archives Center, Caversham. The Week in Westminster file. Reference: Home Talks [q.v.]/GB 23rd June, 1943 To Hon. Harold Nicolson, M.P.

[46] B.B.C. Written Archives Center, Caversham. The Week in Westminster file. From: Assistant Director of Talks Subject: "WEEK IN WESTMINSTER": RECESS TALK, SEPTEMBER 4th To: Miss Rowntree 19th August 1943.

[47]   5 October
     Late rehearsal of Miss Lehmann & coming in to attend transmission at 11.55 p.m. Dinner allowance. 2 shillings.
     Entertaining Miss Lehmann made necessary by mid-night broadcast and late rehearsal. 6 Shillings
     9 October
         Lunch Mr. Eric Hooper sanctioned by D.T. 18 shillings and 6 pence*
     16 October
         Weekly allowance for attendance at H. of C. Sanctioned by D.T.

---

1 pound

Coming in to attend transmission Miss Lloyd George - waiting on until after 8 p.m. Dinner allowance. 2 shillings

14 October

Lunch Miss Lloyd George sanctioned in advance by A.A. (Talks) to discuss very difficult coal debate at only time available to Miss Lloyd George

17 shillings

20 October

Entertainment Houghton "Can I Help You?" (first time I have claimed "Can I Help You?" entertainment for some time - occasional expenditure has been sanctioned)

6 shillings

23 October

Weekly expenditure for attendance at H. of C.

1 pound

Taxi back from H. of C. to keep appointment at B.H.

2 shillings and 9 pence

29 October

Taxi back from appointment summoned by D.T.

1 shilling and 9 pence

30 October Expenditure to cover week at H. of C.

1 pound

28 October Taxi to H. of C. from meeting to keep an appointment

2 shillings and 9 pence

30 October First class return fare to Cambridge. 18 shillings

Less 5% owing to failure to get travelling voucher 11 pence Total:

17 shillings and 1 pence

[Expenses =] 6 pounds 15 shillings and 10 pence

Brought forward 6 pounds 15 shillings and 10 pence

30 Oct Lunch allowance

2 shillings

Dinner allowance

5 shillings

Taxi to Liverpool Street Station out of office hours

3 shillings and 6 pence

Taxi back from Liverpool Street station out of office hours
    3 shillings and 6 pence
Taxis in Cambridge to and from station at 2 shillings each: (see note on back)
    4 shillings
Total expenses = 17 pounds 13 shillings and 10 pence
B.B.C. Written Archives Center, Caversham.

[48] West, W.D. Orwell: The Lost Writings, p. 275, quoting Burgess's note to the file of October 19, 1943.

[49] Lees-Milne, James. Diaries 1942-1945. Ancestral Voices & Prophesying Peace. London: John Murray, 1977, P. 249. (Wednesday, 1st December, 1943. Not mentioned in published Nicolson diaries.)

[50] Nicolson, Harold. Diaries in The Vita Sackville-West and Harold Nicolson manuscripts, letters and diaries [microform], reel 14, Thursday, December 27, 1943.

[51] "Wednesday, January 5, 1944. Dine with Guy Burgess and Goronwy Rees. Guy is worried about a proposal which Halay has put forward after discussing things with Alexander in Italy. It is that it would be good for morale all around if the programmes which reach the armies are identical with those at home. It is suggested therefore that we should scrap the Forces programme and use the Overseas for home and battle front. In principle this is a splendid proposal. In practice it raises all sorts of difficulties." Nicolson, Harold. Diaries in The Vita Sackville-West and Harold Nicolson manuscripts, letters and diaries [microform], reel 14.

[52] Nicolson, Harold. Diaries in The Vita Sackville-West and Harold Nicolson manuscripts, letters and diaries [microform], reel 14, Thursday, January 20, 1944.

[53] Maclean, Fitzroy. Take Nine Spies. Atheneum: New York, 1978, p. 230.

[54] Liddell, Guy. Diary, 1944, David Irving transcription, www.fpp.co.uk/History/Liddell/diary_1944.pdf

[55] Luke, Michael. David Tennant and the Gargoyle Years. Weidenfeld and Nicolson. London, 1991, p. 32.

[56] Luke, p. 144.

[57] Luke, p. 194.

[58] Nicolson, Harold. Diaries in The Vita Sackville-West and Harold Nicolson manuscripts, letters and diaries [microform], reel 14.

[59] Luke, pp. 148-9. It is very difficult to think of what an American parallel to Brian Howard in M.I.5 might have been—Truman Capote in the F.B.I.?
[60] Nicolson, Harold. Diaries in The Vita Sackville-West and Harold Nicolson manuscripts, letters and diaries [microform], reel 14.
[61] Luke, p. 177.
[62] Luke, p. 150.
[63] Nicolson, Harold. Diaries in The Vita Sackville-West and Harold Nicolson manuscripts, letters and diaries [microform], reel 14. Hedley Hope-Nicolson was the subject of a couplet by John Betjeman: "H is for Hedley, who lives in a Place./What he makes on his bottom, he spends on his face" for make up. His daughter was Brian Howard's biographer.
[64] Lees-Milne, James. Diaries 1942-1945. Ancestral Voices & Prophesying Peace. London: John Murray, 1977, p. 231.
[65] "Charles Fletcher Fletcher-Cooke was . . . in 1936 he was president of the Cambridge Union and editor of The Granta. Having taken a First in his Finals, and then a First in the Bar exams, he was called by Lincoln's Inn in 1938 and joined the chambers of Sir William Jowitt, who would become Lord Chancellor in 1945. During the Second World War he served in Naval Intelligence, reaching the rank of Lieutenant-Commander in the RNVR . . . In 1943 he was posted to America to liaise with US Naval Intelligence and on his return worked in the Cabinet Office as the Admiralty's representative on the Joint Intelligence Staff . . . He began his life in politics on the Left, and stood without success for Labour at East Dorset in the general election of 1945. Before becoming an MP, Fletcher-Cooke had acted for the Attlee administration in the matter of the seizure of British property after the war by the Communist governments of Romania and Yugoslavia. He had also served as legal adviser to the British delegation at the Danube Conference in Belgrade in 1948." Daily Telegraph, Published: 12:00AM GMT 28 Feb 2001
[66] Lees-Milne, p. 384.
[67] Luke, p. 183.
[68] www.bagonailssoho.co.uk, accessed November 30, 2010. The website has an interesting soundtrack.
[69] Hastings, Selina. The Secret Lives of Somerset Maugham: A Biography. New York: Random House, 2010, p. 419.
[70] Bloch, Michael. James Lees-Milne: The Life. London: John Murray, 2009, p. 60; p. 62.

71 Burn, Michael. Guy Burgess: The spy who loved me and the traitor I almost unmasked

The Times (London) May 9, 2003
www.timesonline.co.uk/tol/life_and_style/article882580.ece?token=null&of fset=12&page=2, accessed 20 August 2010.

72 B.B.C. Written Archives Center, Caversham. Burgess file. 28th March 1944.

73 Nicolson, Harold. Diaries in The Vita Sackville-West and Harold Nicolson manuscripts, letters and diaries [microform], reel 14, Thursday, March 2, 1944.

74 B.B.C. Written Archives Center, Caversham. Burgess file. 31th March 1944.

75 B.B.C. Written Archives Center, Caversham. Burgess file, 29th March, 1944.

76 B.B.C. Written Archives Center, Caversham. Burgess file.

77 B.B.C. Written Archives Center, Caversham. Burgess file. 11th July 1944.

Chapter Six

The Foreign Office

Foreign Office,
S.W. I.

27th March, 1944

Dear Foot,

I am writing to ask if you would be good enough to consider the release from employment in your Corporation of Mr. Guy Burgess, for service in our News Department . . . I understand that Mr. Burgess of your Talks Department is interested in this vacancy, and from our point of view he would appear to be well qualified to fill it. I fully appreciate that he is doing most valuable work with the British Broadcasting Corporation and I fear that his release may inconvenience you. But as I have said, our own need is great, and we should therefore be most grateful if you could see your way to facilitate his transfer to us.

Yours Sincerely,

Alexander Cadogan[1]

Thus the Permanent Undersecretary for Foreign Affairs to Robert William Foot, Director-General of the B.B.C.

It is useful to understand the responsibilities and operations of the Foreign Office's News Department and the other sections of the Foreign Office in which Burgess worked and his overt roles while working in them. It is equally useful to understand what might be meant by—and found in—the minutes of meetings of the Cabinet, the Defence Committee and the Joint Chiefs of Staff (properly, the Chiefs of the Imperial General Staff [CIGS]) and what information Burgess could have learned about the positions of Western countries on the postwar settlement in Europe, Britain's military strategy and NATO. We will begin with the News Department.

The Foreign Office's News Department was directed by William Ridsdale and his deputy, Norman Nash. Nash "was white-haired, kindly and avuncular," Ridsdale "Waspish," according to Alan Maclean, Donald Maclean's younger, more alcoholic, brother, who joined the News Department a couple of years after Burgess. The Department's job was to put over the Government's view on the current issues and crises of the day. The Department's "customers" were the foreign editors and diplomatic correspondents of the British press and the London correspondents of foreign newspapers. The staff, aside from Ridsdale and Nash, all worked "in an enormous room, the arena in which the daily Press Conference was held at 12.30." The room, Alan Maclean recalled, "contained three long tables, lots of chairs and most of our telephones.

> There was also a small room leading out of the arena which boasted a couple of desks and telephones, a Reuters ticker-tape machine which chattered out hot news and round-ups from all over the world, and a safe for the daily batch of incoming telegrams. One of us came in early to read through them and mark up the interesting bits. There was hardly room enough for us all to be in the room at the same time but we had no need of desks of our own and no paperwork. All our work was done on the telephone or face-to-face and we travelled very light."[2]

Ridsdale "had three regular sessions every day. At noon the diplomatic correspondents of the *Manchester Guardian,* Reuters, the *Daily Herald,* the B.B.C. and the *News Chronicle* would gather in a privileged huddle in his room for a briefing on whatever subjects they chose; at 3 p.m. he had us all in for half an hour to tell us what was happening at the deep end and to check on what we'd been up to that morning; and at 4 p.m. precisely the stately figure of *The Times* diplomatic correspondent hove into view for a private talk."[3] For the rest of the staff,

> The Twelve Thirty was the central point of our day. A short list of 'topics' was made up first thing in the morning after someone had done an early trawl through all the morning newspapers. We could make an educated guess at what would be the main stories on which we might be asked for a reaction. If the Department concerned authorized a formal statement which could be attributed to a Foreign Office spokesman, we all had a copy to keep handy. But the Twelve Thirty was a free for all and everything said by the man in the chair was on the record. In my time it was nearly always Peter Matthews but he could call on any of us to take a particular question so we all had to be ready to speak up if needed.

Which meant that everyone on staff, Burgess included, had spent the morning on the telephone or in face-to-face meetings with Whitehall experts on the expected news of the day or reading the message traffic flowing into and out from the Foreign Office.

Matthews was nearly blind as a result of a childhood accident and had chronic asthma, but he was, nonetheless, "a brilliant performer."

> The Twelve Thirty attracted 30 or 40 regular customers representing many nationalities and most shades of political persuasion and there was a sense of wary camaraderie among them our most interesting and even useful task was to provide off-the-record guidance on any subject to any well-disposed journalist who cared to ask for it. We hoped that he would incorporate it in whatever he was writing that day. If he needed to quote a source for off-the-record material the convention was to use 'diplomatic circles', 'usually reliable sources' or 'informed quarters'. We had to get to know all our regular

customers, British and foreign, and, much harder, to judge how indiscreet we could dare to be in each case.[4]

The News Department put out to the newspapers statements from the Foreign Office, some emanating from there in the first instance, some as reactions to events or press inquiries.

The process went like this: A newsworthy event would occur; News Department staff would inquire as to the Foreign Office's opinion of it in the proper quarter; a statement would be agreed upon and released to the press. The statement would of course be as innocuous as possible. Except that it was not to be expected that Burgess's official statements, any more than his private statements, would be innocuous. A "long, unfriendly piece by Freddy Kuh [of the *Chicago Sun-Times*] . . . began: 'A Foreign Office spokesman gazed dreamily out of the window across the Horse Guards' Parade and murmured, "Of course one of the troubles with America is that it has no government . . .'" This naturally caused a first-class rumpus and its onlie begetter, Guy Burgess . . . was delighted to receive an official raspberry from on high, adding new luster to his reputation as *enfant terrible*."[5] There was a statement in regard to Bulgaria on August 23, 1944, the unusual tone of which might indicate that Burgess was the source of this as well: "Authoritative British sources termed Foreign Minister Parvan Draganoff's peace speech yesterday, in which he insisted his country's declaration of war had been a mistake, as a rather silly show."[6]

Peregrine Fellowes, who served in the News Department with Burgess, said that "Some of the stuff he and Burgess had to decode and analyse was Top Secret and they used to have to do it in a locked room, where no one could interrupt them.

> There, Burgess used to sit on top of a kind of safe - or security cupboard - and read out the frequently hilarious messages in a variety of comic voices, making [Peregrine Fellowes] howl with laughter . . . He was constantly praising Communism and Russia and the way that the government in Moscow managed things, which was interpreted . . . as Guy being deliberately provocative, and contrary for effect.[7]

Peregrine Fellowes's amusing story, like others told and re-told by and about Burgess, distracts us by pointing away from the magician's quiet work on one side, behind his back or with a camera late at night, toward what we expect to notice: jokes, outrageous behavior, dirty fingernails. But if we ignore the amusing distractions, the patter and the costumes, we can note that Burgess's access to Foreign Service cables, according to Fellowes, was at one of the points where they flowed into Whitehall for decoding and analysis. No need to linger after hours to examine out baskets and safes left carelessly open. Burgess, from his arrival at the News Department, saw "telegraphic" communications to and from the Foreign Office and its embassies in both their encoded and decoded forms, as well as a succession of "keys" for decryption. This would have made Top Secret British diplomatic messages readable to those with whom he shared these materials and, by means of messages referred to in that traffic, would have provided an entry into American codes as well.[8]

If we require a reminder as to Burgess's motivations, there is from this period as clear a summary as is likely to be recovered. According to Yuri Modin, it was in June, 1944, shortly after Burgess joined the News Department, that "In recognition of their excellent services, the heads of the KGB decided to assign life pensions to our five principal agents in Britain, to be paid to them discreetly every month, every three months or every year by our London residence . . .

> They did not respond immediately, but eventually each agent wrote his own letter to the KGB containing his answer. First of all they thanked us for the gesture, which they appreciated; then they set out the motives for their involvement with the Soviet Union in fighting Fascism and promoting world revolution. In conclusion, they declared to a man that it had never entered their heads to carry out this work for money and that there could be no question of degrading their commitment by accepting the smallest payment . . . One of them, signed by a certain Guy Burgess, contained a passage which I have never forgotten: "I

cannot see how any self-respecting individual could live in my country and not work for the Party."[9]

There is an understandable fascination with the "housekeeping" aspect of secret intelligence activities. Although it is not something that Burgess talked about with Driberg or anyone else (other than, presumably, Blunt), Philby, perhaps Cairncross and Rees, others (many others) have described it.[10] Here is a recent description of how a spy (James MacGibbon) operated in wartime London: "A first rendezvous was arranged with James's courier, Natasha . . . [on] a street corner in the Ladbroke Grove area,

> where I would be standing looking up and down as if to find my direction. She would pass near me whispering a code word as she passed and at a discreet distance I would follow. When we came to a corner (it was a deeply dark night imposed by the blackout) and we were assured that we were not being followed, I would utter a code word and hand over my first note of information, then we would arrange the first cache.

> And so it went on. We never used the same 'drop' point more than once. When I left the matchbox in a new cache I gave details of the next; initially I left an empty box which she would mark with a cros to confirm she had found the right place before I left the next instalment of intelligence. This became a regular routine once or twice a month, with occasional meetings, always taking care that we were not being watched as we walked along talking about this and that—we became friends . . .[11]

It will be recalled that Burgess habitually walked home from the B.B.C. He probably also did so from the Foreign Office, walking untraceably through those blacked-out streets, although it is unlikely that he did so with any Natasha.

*   *   *

As Cadogan had explained to Foot, Burgess arrived in a Department in great need of reinforcements. There were discussions about neutrals and quasi-neutrals wishing to move toward the British; continuing points of difference with the French (various French); difficulties with Argentina: sympathetic with Nazi Germany to—and beyond—the end. The News Department was, it might be said, inundated with news. As a result it was now Burgess who was providing inside information to Harold Nicolson, rather than visa versa. For example, at the end of June Burgess reported to Nicolson that he had been "lunching with a man who lunched yesterday with [Field Marshall] Montgomery, who told him:

> We have been fighting a stiff battle the last three days S.W. of Caen and around the Odon. It seems a little thing by Russian standards. But apparently Montgomery regards it as a vital battle since if he can get his armour down on the open country south of Caen he can make a wide sweep. There is at H.Q. in Normandy an atmosphere of suppressed excitement which precedes a great victory. People are even talking of Paris. All this is based on the idea that the Germans have not in fact got the vast strategic reserves of which they speak. [12]

After Burgess told Nicolson this story, they went on to Pratt's club, near the Ritz, where they met, as often, Robert Bernays, M.P., and this evening met also Lord William Mabane, M.P., Parliamentary Secretary, Home Department; Basil, Fourth Marquess of Dufferin and Ava, Director of the Empire Division, Ministry of Information, and Lord Sherwood, Under-Secretary for Air, and all these exchanged with Burgess information and views of mutual interest.* Pratt's was the center of a certain London, a very small, innermost circle of what later would be called the Establishment. Charles Ritchie, the Canadian diplomat and society figure, wrote about a visit to Pratt's in 1940:

> I always enjoy Pratt's, the atmosphere of open fires and easy unbuttoned chat, the equality where cabinet ministers sit around

---

* Bernays was killed in a plane crash in January, Dufferin in action in Burma in March, 1945. Jack Macnamara had been killed in action in Italy in December, 1944.

the table and argue with subalterns—the decor of red curtains and the stuffed salmon caught by His Royal Highness the Duke of Edinburgh in 1886. The other night a rather tight, junior lieutenant back from the Middle East was dining there. Anthony Eden began holding forth at length on the Mediterranean situation. This youth, after listening for some time, turned to a friend and said, "I do not know who that man is but he is talking awful balls." Immense satisfaction of all members.[13]

Pratt's was a place where drunken dukes presided over dinners and Ministers spoke to one another in tones audible to all about matters that in their offices were discussed only in whispers. And why not? No one who could not be trusted would be found at Pratt's.

In October, 1944, Prime Minister Churchill and Foreign Minister Eden, perhaps to scupper Cripps, went to Moscow for bilateral meetings. The responsibilities for the press were handled from Moscow by Ambassador Clark Kerr's press officer, Thomas Barman, while the News Department in London informed the press representatives there, for example, that "Mr. Churchill and Mr. Eden . . . went to Moscow with the aim of convincing Premier Stalin that his best hope for security lay in some sort of world organization for peace rather than in strategic frontiers." Sometimes a press officer is a person who lies at home for his country. This was the meeting at which Churchill produced his "naughty document," dividing the Balkans into spheres of British and Soviet influence: Soviet 90% in Rumania, 75% in Bulgaria, 50% in Yugoslavia and Hungary, 10% in Greece. Stalin raised his share to 90% in Bulgaria and agreed.[14] With this, the British Government was asserting its right to bring Greece into the informal Empire, part of Churchill's projected chain of puppet kingdoms from Iraq to, perhaps, Spain. This Churchillian initiative ratified, in advance, as it were, the principle of a post-war division of Europe into Soviet and, initially, British, spheres of influence, defining the southern portion of what Churchill would later call an Iron Curtain. He had naming rights: it was a curtain that during his trip to Moscow he had helped fit and hang. The cost to Rumania, Bulgaria and Hungary of Churchill's demarcation of spheres of influence in the region is well-known. Less well-known was the cost to Greece in deaths, lives wasted in concentration camps, the absence of viable democratic—or even governmental— institutions for generations.[15]

Poland had not been listed on Churchill's "naughty document." The Red Army was already in residence and the Lublin Provisional Government, made up of Poles who had spent the war in Moscow, not in London, was gradually becoming simply the Government of Poland. There was at first some resistance from the British Government. *The New York Times* of January 1, 1945, printed a report from London that "A British Foreign Office commentator [that is, someone in the News Department] said today that Britain did not intend to recognize the Lublin Provisional Government at this time and expressed hope that the question would be threshed out at a "Big Three" conference . . . The Foreign Office commentator clearly implied hope that Russia would not recognize the Lublin group without consulting Great Britain and the United States." We know that Burgess was involved in the News Department's briefings about the Polish problem, because when he dined with Nicolson on February 26th, 1945, he showed him "the telegrams exchanged with Moscow." According to Nicolson,

> It is clear that the Ambassador's Commission (consisting of Molotov, Clark Kerr and the American Ambassador, and empowered to settle the composition of the new Provisional Polish Government) is not to be a farce in the least. They insist on Mikolajazyk [from London] being included in the Provisional Government. Archie [Clark Kerr] seems to be handling the thing well."[16]

From this we can see that Burgess had access to the Foreign Office cables between London and the Moscow Embassy; that he was able to remove them from the Foreign Office premises, taking them with him to dinner at one of Nicolson's clubs, where he showed them to Nicolson, who at this point had no governmental responsibilities. It is interesting that neither Nicolson nor Burgess saw anything unusual in this. In this case, if Burgess had sent these along, they might have given Molotov a certain confidence in his negotiations with Clark Kerr.

In the spring of 1945 Churchill, concerned with, among other matters, the situation in Poland, commissioned a study codenamed *Operation Unthinkable.* The goal of the exercise would be to "impose the will" of the British Empire on the Soviet Union, in the first instance, as it happened, in regard to Poland. The Chiefs of Staff produced a report for General Ismay on May 22 that set out a plan for war between the British Empire and the Soviet Union, using, inter alia, certain German military forces, re-equipped by the British.* The original "Unthinkable" report, with its projection of a July 1, 1945 attack on the Soviet Union by joint British, American and German forces, was transmitted to Moscow by Burgess, Cairncross or Philby: Burgess was best positioned to obtain it.

It is a truism that military staffs have plans for many eventualities. The U.S. military had in the 1930s rather elaborate plans for the conquest of Canada and actually conducted some military exercises along those lines. On the other hand, given Churchill's well-known personal history in regard to the Soviet Union—his sponsorship of British intervention in the Russian Civil War on the side of the "White," monarchist, forces; his advocacy of an attack on the Soviet Union's oil fields at the beginning of the Second World War—the "Unthinkable" planning document had a significance out of the ordinary. In Moscow they would have seen it in the context of Churchill's wartime grand strategy—refusing to send British forces to the Eastern Front, concentrating those forces in the Middle East, delaying as long as possible the opening of the Second Front. It seemed a declaration that as far as Churchill was concerned the wartime alliance was over and relations between the British Empire and the Soviet Union would shortly return to the

---

* Some months later, the Soviets were to repeatedly protest against the British Army having left captured German units intact, the soldiers in uniform and under the command of their own officers.

236

status quo pro ante. If Britain could hold India—and it was well-known that Churchill was determined to do so, whatever the cost to India; he had, after all, attempted to crush the movement for Indian Independence by imprisoning the leaders of Congress and had used mass starvation in Bengal *pour encourager les autres*—and the United States were to reinforce the Empire, the future looked dim both for a revolution in Britain and quite possibly for the survival of the Soviet Union, which was, for better or worse, the single existing socialist polity.

For the generation of John Cornford, Burgess and Kim Philby, choices of ways forward, toward a British revolution, were narrowing. Hobsbawm's path, that of the Marxist scholar, remained, but the path of building an indigenous revolutionary party seemed to be approaching a dead end as the British secret intelligence services again focused their full strength on the Communist Party. (Philby, as head of the anti-Soviet section of M.I.6, had special access to these efforts.) Burgess and Philby, Maclean, Cairncross and Blunt decided they had good reasons to remain on the path that had been pointed out by Arnold Deutsch, to work for a revolution at home by working to strengthen the international anti-imperialist and anti-capitalist forces, which is what he believed the Soviet Union to embody, no matter how odd that might look in retrospect.

On the other hand, the Chiefs of Staff concluded from the *Project Unthinkable* exercise that any conflict between the British Empire and the Soviet Union would almost immediately become "total war," and that there was little chance that the Empire would be successful in such a conflict. Ismay transmitted this conclusion to Churchill on June 8, 1945. On June 10 the Prime Minister commissioned a second study, with the same codename, which was to report on whether Great Britain could be successfully defended from a Soviet invasion. This report concluded, interestingly, that the question was moot as there would be little chance in the near future of the Soviet Union being able to mount a successful invasion. This conclusion remained a particularly closely held secret of the early years of the Cold War, rationalized, as it was in the West, on the public position that there was a threat of a Soviet conquest of Western Europe. The memorandum "Security of the British Empire," prepared by the Chiefs of the Imperial General Staff (which Kim Philby sent Moscow a copy of on November 6, 1945), declared the Soviet Union a major threat to the Empire (although not necessarily to Britain itself) and recommended the establishment of a special relationship with the United States that would commit the Americans to the defense of Western Europe, the establishment of military-political blocs, and military bases in Europe and other regions of the world.[17] This was a continuation of Churchill's foreign policy and was at odds with that of Attlee in the first year of his Government.

The following year the British military mission in Washington reported a conversation with the American Chiefs of Staff concerning strategy to be followed if the contemporary friction in the Venezia Giulia (Trieste) area led to a conflict between Soviet and Anglo-American forces. Once again it was concluded that any conflict would not remain localized. Eisenhower was quoted as saying that in the event of hostilities it would be necessary to withdraw Anglo-American forces from Italy, France and Germany to the Low Countries. The circulation of this report was highly restricted, limited to the Prime Minister, the ministers in charge of the Army and Navy, and the military chiefs.[18] These discussions may have influenced postwar planning in London and Washington: "what if," becoming "how might." At the time that they were created, the consideration at the highest levels of the British and American governments of scenarios for war between the British Empire, with or without the United States, and the Soviet Union, while the three were still allies, would have been, of course, of the greatest interest in Moscow. The documents recording these discussions were transmitted between London and Washington through the British embassy in Washington, where Donald Maclean saw everything.

*   *   *

The American Ninth Army captured the German prisoner of war camp Oflag 79 on April 12, 1945, freeing, among others, Peter Pollock.[19] By June Pollock was back in London, dining at the Kenneth Clark's with the Spenders, Nicolson and Edward Sackville-West and resuming his place in the Burgess ménage.[20]   Blunt, demobilized from the Army and M.I.5, became Surveyor of the King's Pictures, also in April, 1945, moving to a room at the Courtauld.   This was the first time in many years that Blunt and Burgess had not lived together. James Pope-Hennessy took Blunt's place as Burgess's housemate.

These household arrangements involved deeper emotional matters.   Although the rhetoric of homophobia framed homosexual relationships as exclusively shallow and promiscuous, even such a figure as Brian Howard had by 1945 begun to see things differently. After Peter Pollock made the first of several attempts to break with Burgess, Howard wrote to him that "We all of us – all five [Burgess, Blunt, Howard, Pollock and Eric Kessler]—share a certain emotional point of view about life that makes it not twice, but ten times more difficult for us to lead a happy and fruitful existence.

> We are haunted, day and night, whether we realize it or not, and not only by immaterial fears and enemies.   There are certain sensitive, prudent and strong-minded people of this kind – like K[essler] and B[lunt] – who come to find their position finally impossible.   They forget that their life is only, say, ten times more difficult to arrange than other people's.   They decide that it cannot be arranged at all.   So what do they do?   They take to their careers exactly as fugitives take to the hills, and if thence forward they consider themselves on a higher level, that level can be very barren, and very sad.[21]

Burgess was to write to Pollock in similar terms after their relationship finally ended two years later: "We tried to do what in our world is one of the hardest things there is to do . . . look, Pete – how few have succeeded. Why shld. I ever have thought we shld. succeed when Eric and Ian failed, where Dadie never began to succeed, where Anthony has never really managed or attempted anything beyond Jackie (which is different anyhow, they won't 'live together')?"[22] Pollock went on to trying to "succeed" with Francis Bacon and then, perhaps did so with Paul Danquah, after the world had changed.

*   *   *

In the Spring of 1945, as the war was coming to an end, the British political parties prepared for the first general election since 1935. The Labour Party's manifesto, "Let Us Face the Future," called for state action to ensure full employment, "the nationalization of several key industries, an urgent housing programme, the creation of a new national health service and . . . 'social provision against rainy days'."[23] In a word, Socialism. There were implications for the Foreign Office. "During the 1945 electoral campaign, Labour candidate then-Major Denis Healey (and still then a socialist) said that 'the crucial principle of our own foreign policy should be to protect, assist, encourage and aid in every way the Socialist revolution wherever it appears.'"[24] It was widely thought, especially by the Tories, that Labour under its anti-charismatic leader, Clement Attlee, would not have a chance against the Conservatives fighting under the banner of their Savior of the Empire. There were, however, some facts on the ground. The Labour Party had been the de facto domestic government for most of the war and was widely considered to have demonstrated its competence in that. And there was the sheer demographic fact that 75% of the British people were working-class and had learned from wartime socialism that the socialism was better, for them, than the alternative.[25] Finally, the Forces had gradually been converted to Socialism, not least by the programming of such as J. P. Priestley on the B.B.C., and by the experience of life in uniform. But the landslide that ensued in July was unexpected even by the Labour Party leadership itself. Immediately "most people realized that a rather amazing thing had happened, in effect marking off 'pre-1945' politically from 'post-1945'.

240

"My man," called out a blazered, straw-hated 14-year-old public schoolboy, John Rae, as he stood on Bishop's Stortford station with his trunk that late July. "No," came the porter's quiet but firm reply, "that sort of thing is all over now."[26]

The new Parliamentary session opened with a spirited rendition by the Labour majority of "The Red Flag."[27] Attlee took office, in fact, if certainly not in image, as if he were leading a revolution. Morrison, Dalton and Cripps at once set about taxing away the financial basis of the old ruling class and nationalizing the country's major industries, as promised. Ellen Wilkinson revolutionized the education system. Aneurin Bevan, perhaps with Cripps among the most radical of major British politicians ever to hold office, brought in the National Health Service. Never again would working class people bear the marks of the class system on their bodies: their children would be as tall as those of the wealthy, their elderly would not die of slow starvation and neglect.

The results of the election were announced in the middle of the Potsdam Conference. The new Prime Minister, Clement Attlee had been persuaded by King George VI to make the right-wing union leader, Ernest Bevin, Foreign Minister. It was said that the King was concerned that Dalton (Attlee's initial candidate for the office) might continue the Anglo-Soviet alliance. Attlee and Bevin then returned to Potsdam in the places of Churchill and Eden, joining the new American President, Harry Truman and his Secretary of State, Byrnes, and Stalin (who was unfamiliar with contested elections) and his Foreign Minister, Molotov: tripartite masters of the world. From a British and American point of view the Conference had one great success: Stalin promised to enter the war with Japan on August 15, two and a half months before the anticipated invasion of the Japanese home islands, which the Americans feared would cost the lives of a million American soldiers, marines and sailors. Truman at Potsdam told Stalin about the successful testing of the atomic bomb. Stalin showed no surprise and little interest. He quite possibly knew much more about it than did Truman. For the Russians, the end of the Great Patriotic War had brought with it the fulfillment of a certain

241

idea of national destiny going back to the time of Peter the Great. Russia was now, in the guise of the Soviet Union, the predominant European power. It was, however, about to be limited—the word would become "contained"—by a non-European power: the United States. According to Bevin's biographer, Alan Bullock,

> How far and in what direction Stalin would be able to press his advantage beyond the control of Eastern Europe, neither he nor anyone else could foresee in that summer of 1945. He was well aware that . . . the USA had become the most powerful state in the world, too powerful for the USSR, which had suffered immense losses in the war, to consider challenging in direct confrontation.[28]

The change in the White House had an unexpected, nearly catastrophic, effect on Britain. When, during the preparations for the Potsdam Conference, Truman had realized that while he and Byrnes were in Germany, the Secretary of the Treasury, Henry Morgenthau, was the senior Administration official in Washington and next in line to the Presidency if anything happened to them, Truman, finding the idea of a Jewish President intolerable, had demanded Morgenthau's resignation. Morgenthau's forced resignation, in turn, was linked to the repudiation of Keynes's agreement with Morgenthau and Roosevelt (Quebec II) to continue Lend-Lease aid to Britain for some time after the end of the European war. Truman instead terminated it on September 2, 1945. Lend-Lease to the Soviet Union ended on September 20, 1945.

> Lease-Lend [sic] had been offered for the duration of the war, and the war was over. But no-one had imagined that it would be withdrawn so abruptly. It was a devastating blow, leaving Britain in what the Chancellor, Hugh Dalton, called "an almost desperate plight." Without Lease-Lend Britain could not feed its population or pay its debts. It would eventually starve.[29]

While Dalton and Cripps patched together what came to be called "austerity," it would be Bevin's job to try to persuade the

American government that starvation in Britain—and Europe—was not in the interest of the United States.

The King proved to know what he had been about. Bevin was to be the Conservative Party's favorite Labour minister. His staff, many of whom had never before worked with someone of his background, "adored" him. The memoirs of members of the Foreign Office in his time are filled with praise for his strength and wisdom—and condescending amusement at his working class habits, speech patterns and vocabulary.[30] His policies were those of his Conservative predecessor and successor, Anthony Eden. That they were not those of the Prime Minister did not seem to trouble the Foreign Office, or Bevin. Bevin's policies—anti-Communist from the beginning, increasingly anti-Soviet and pro-American—were, perhaps, the necessary protection for the domestic policies, building the New Jerusalem of the welfare state, that were the central concern of the rest of the Government. Or, perhaps, they prevented the full implementation of those policies, sacrificing Socialism on the altar of the Atlantic Alliance. Be that as it may, they were the favored policies of a Foreign Office staffed with the protégées of his predecessors and, perhaps, ventriloquized through a very ill, vain, lonely old man, given to after hours tales of battles no one around him cared about or remembered.[31]

At the Labour Party Conference in May, 1945, "Bevin's famous 'Left understands Left' remark had been widely taken to mean that Labour would be sympathetic to revolutionary developments throughout the world: above all to the Soviet Union. For a time after the Labour Party came to power, some in the party, such as Healey, argued for a "socialist foreign policy," including a tighter Anglo-Soviet alliance, re-establishment of the Spanish Republic, decolonization. For many in the Labour movement, a socialist foreign policy and sympathy for the Soviet Union also implied distrust of the United States and its attempt to create what the *New Statesman* called a capitalist "economic empire."[32] But on August 20, 1945, "Bevin, making his first speech as Britain's new Foreign Secretary, solidly and completely lined the Labor Government up with the former Churchill Coalition Government on questions of foreign policy." Bevin was to be persuaded by his staff, the military chiefs, and their American counterparts, if persuasion was needed, that an apocalyptic struggle was at hand, requiring a militarized Atlantic Alliance, British control over the wider Middle East (from India to Tripoli) and a British atomic bomb (based in the Middle East). The Prime Minister, on the other hand, favored a decisive break with Churchill's policies and, perhaps, those of the Americans. He believed that conflict with the Soviet Union was avoidable. [33] Attlee's alternative, as had been Roosevelt's, was a strong United Nations Organization. But Attlee deferred to Bevin, needing Bevin (if only to stave off the periodic attempted palace coups) and apparently judging that socialism of a sort at home was worth the price, the price being American economic dominance.

Relations between Britain and Spain exemplified the divergences within the Foreign Office between those wishing to follow "a Socialist foreign policy" and those who wished to continue the policies of the Churchill Government (or to anticipate those of the American government). Comparatively early in Burgess's time in the News Department, it announced that Lord Templewood, the British Ambassador to Spain, had resigned.[*] Templewood was the Conservative politician, Samuel Hoare, who had spent the war in semi-exile in an ultimately successful effort to keep Franco from becoming an active German ally. Three weeks after Templewood's resignation, the Churchill Government refused to allow Dr. Juan Negrin, Prime Minister of the Spanish Republic in Exile, from broadcasting from London to a rally in New York. On January 2, 1945 it was reported that a "British observer," that is, a News Department spokesman, perhaps, given the tone, Burgess, "acknowledged tonight that the fundamental reason for the refusal of these facilities was that the British Government simply is not interested in Dr. Negrin—nor presumably in his ambitions to restore republican government, which was overthrown in Spain with the aid

---

[*] On December 17, 1944.

of Britain's present enemies." On February 10th there was a balancing move: Churchill rejected a proposal from Franco that the British Empire join Germany in an anti-Soviet alliance. A journalist commented that "Prime Minister Churchill's rebuke to Generalissimo Francisco Franco's confidential proposal for a western anti-Soviet alliance developed tonight into one of the war's most mysterious 'leak' stories. Foreign Office representatives declared there had been no official announcement of the contents of either Franco's letter to Mr. Churchill or the latter's answer. But it was plain that the contents could have been obtained here only through an official leak or through a plant." Franco's proposal may have been part of Himmler's effort to effect a reversal of alliances, which was an effort viewed not entirely unfavorably by elements in both the British and American governments and their respective militaries and secret intelligence agencies. It would be embodied, to some extent, in the *Operation Unthinkable* planning.

On February 27, 1946, with Churchill out of office, the now at least nominally Socialist Foreign Office briefed journalists that "The British Government is prepared to join with the United States and France in a strong three-power anti-Franco declaration, as proposed in the American note to London and Paris, but only on condition that there be no actual intervention in Spain's internal affairs." A week later the British Government agreed to an American proposal for an anti-Franco declaration issued jointly by the United States, Great Britain and France. Matters heated up again at the end of the year, when on December 21, the British ambassador to Spain was recalled. "It was reported [in London], without confirmation, earlier this week that the British Government was secretly planning to attempt the ouster of Generalissimo Franco as head of the Spanish state. At the same time, Morgan Phillips, secretary of the Labour party, boasted openly that the Labor Government was 'working continuously both inside and outside Spain' for the overthrow of the Franco regime." As late as April, 1947, Hugh McNeil, by then Minister of State, advocated some form of US/UK intervention in Spain to pressure Franco to leave that country.³⁴ Franco, however, with support from the American government and military, survived, although many tens of thousands of his Republican prisoners did not.

During his time in the Foreign Office, Burgess served a Government that was unsure whether an alliance with the United States was a good thing for Socialist Britain (or for the British Empire). It was, however, a Government that was quite sure that the United States, in all its complexity, was not a reliable partner for peace. Bevin feared that it would once more withdraw into isolationism. Most of the rest of the Government feared that it would not. The United States, even before the defeat of Japan, was pushed by corporate interests, eager to capture markets controlled by Great Britain, and pushed by the right wing of the Republican Party, rabidly anti-Communist, to accept Churchill's interpretation of the international situation in all matters except his conception of an equal partnership between the British Empire and the United States. One of the war aims of President Roosevelt had been the dismantling of the British Empire,[35] an enterprise taken over by his domestic opponents and made more pressing, and satisfying, as the great purge of Communists, Jews and homosexuals took hold in the America of the late 1940s, by the fact that Great Britain had a Government that "promoted too damned much Socialism at home and too much damned Imperialism abroad," in the artful phrase of one member of Congress. According to Alan Bullock,

> American business, without waiting for the end of the war, was already seeking to take advantage of Britain's economic weakness to capture her prewar markets (for example in Latin America) and such sources of supply as the Middle East oilfields where a vigorous fight for post-war concessions, with no holds barred, was already being waged between American and British oil interests.[36]

Under these circumstances, as odd as it seemed to Americans then (and now), many, if not most, Britains, Socialists and Tories both, who took an interest in international affairs were not convinced that the government of the United States had Britain's best interests at heart.

246

Among the political class, on both right and left, [anti-American] feelings were intensified by first the abrupt end of Lend-Lease and then the harsh terms, almost certainly reflecting distaste for the Labour government's nationalization programme, of the proposed $3.7 billion American Loan . . . James Callaghan . . . condemned "economic aggression by the United States" . . . "It is clear," complained the *New Statesman* in November 1946, "that on the matters that most affect Britain today, the United States is nearly as hostile to the aspirations of Socialist Britain as to the Soviet Union."[37]

The Labour rank and file were not pleased with the philosophical split in the foreign policy of the Government. On April 5, 1946, the Government "was subjected to bitter criticism from within its own ranks . . . when eighteen resolutions calling for a purge of Tories and reactionaries in the diplomatic service and the recasting of policy toward 'a true Socialist policy' were tabled for the annual party conference in June.

Some of the resolutions criticize Foreign Secretary Ernest Bevin by name and others by implication. Many indicate that it is hard to distinguish between Socialist Mr. Bevin and Conservative Anthony Eden . . . Two of Britain's most powerful unions, the National Union of Mine Workers and the Amalgamated Engineering Union, two smaller unions and two Labor constituencies have tabled resolutions calling for affiliation [with the Communist Party], and it is widely recognized that dissatisfaction with Mr. Bevin's foreign policy is one of the leading, if not the principal reason behind these demands for Communist affiliation.[38]

Matters were not made easier for Socialist Great Britain by the actions and activities of the new American government. As we have seen, Lend-Lease was cancelled on the dot of the letter of the agreement, perhaps not coincidentally as soon as the Socialists took office, and the loan from the United States this made essential was offered grudgingly, minimally, and at interest. Bevin's biographer commented that " A grant in aid was clearly out of the question; even a loan would have to bear interest and would only be made on conditions.

To a convinced multilateralist like Will Clayton, Vice-Chairman of the American negotiating team, the British request for aid was a Heaven-sent opportunity to commit the UK to Bretton Woods and the multilateral policies for international trade which he believed to be in Britain's and the world's best interest. He undertook to load the loan negotiations "with all the conditions the traffic would bear". To others, more concerned with their own interests, it was a chance to force the British to give up the sterling area, abandon imperial preference and eliminate quotas and exchange controls, all of which were seen as obstacles to American trade. As the Chairman of Sears, Roebuck wrote to Clayton, "If you succeed in doing away with the Empire preference and opening up the Empire to United States commerce, it may well be that we can afford to pay a couple of billion dollars for the privilege".[39]

However, even some congressmen realized that it might be importunate to push the British Government too far: "By July [1946] . . . the decisive argument in carrying the loan through the House was the value to the USA of keeping Britain independent and not driving her into the arms of Russia.

Minority leader Jesse Wolcott concluded that Congress' decision would determine for years to come "whether there shall be a coalition between the British sphere and the American sphere, or whether there shall be a coalition between the British sphere and the Soviet sphere".[40]

This was not as unlikely as it might seem today. In August a British trade delegation had gone to Moscow, carrying with it as an inducement an offer of twenty Rolls-Royce jet engines.[41]

The wartime alliance maintained a certain pro forma existence in such places as the Council of Foreign Ministers during its sessions in London and Paris from January to July, 1946, which prepared draft peace treaties with Italy, Romania, Hungary, Bulgaria and Finland (but not Germany or Austria, which had no independent governing authorities). These were then reviewed at the Paris Conference itself, which took place from July 29 to October 15 under conditions of some political complexity, as France had a three-party government and every Minister had a three-party Cabinet, including Communist Party representatives in both cases.[42] In other words, from the point of view of much of the American congress, France had a Communist government, or something as close to one as to make no difference. Nicholas Henderson, one of Bevin's assistants, provided a vivid sketch of the atmosphere in the meeting rooms of the Paris Conference:

> The British delegation was housed in the Hotel George V. Paris was still short of food, and much of what we ate had to be brought from England . . . Members of the party would slip out furtively from time to time to go to a black market restaurant . . After the [morning staff] meeting we all rushed off to the Palais du Luxembourg for the conference. . . each Foreign Minister has five advisers, sitting either side of him at the conference table, and looking as though butter would not melt in their mouths. Behind this front line are throngs of officials balancing papers on their knees. Every word spoken has to be translated into two other languages. There are many statements read out from previously prepared documents and then translated laboriously. There is the debate and the unrehearsed arguments. Nobody smiles, everyone mumbles. There is much inscrutable glancing at the ceiling. The atmosphere is smoky.[43]

The News Department of the Foreign Office was overwhelmed by the task of working from both Paris and London. By the end of July Ridsdale was frantically petitioning for permission to increase the Department's establishment:

> The News Department as at present staffed cannot cope with the demands made upon it . . . During the last three months, Mr. Richard Scott and I have spent over seven weeks in Paris and we are about to leave again for the "Peace Conference" which is likely to hold us there for another five weeks or so . . . when the

Peace Conference ends it will probably be necessary for me to proceed to America for the [United Nations General] Assembly . . . One of the most serious effects of the shortage of staff has been the enforced abandonment of the custom, maintained during the war and after, of night duty whereby members of the staff of the Department were always available at any hour of the 24 any day of the year. It has been necessary to curtail duty to 10 p.m. as it is not possible to maintain a roster covering all-night duty. This diminishes seriously our use and influence, in particular in so far as the American press is concerned . . . I submit that in such a critical period of international affairs when the adequate presentation of the British point of view is a matter of first-rate importance, we should not be hampered in our work and in our efficiency by such a state of affairs as I have outlined.

In the course of his appeal, Ridsdale gave a brief account of the pressure of his work:

So far as I personally am concerned, it is necessary and desirable that I should attend the numerous meetings with the Secretary of State when policy is being formulated. It has not been possible, without completely letting down the normal work, to attend many of the conferences where our presence is required and at which in fact it would be most useful to be present – international conferences abroad, conferences called in London by other Government offices and inter-departmental conferences

Ridsdale's plea was accepted by the Foreign Office. There are some interesting handwritten comments in the file:

I gather from Mr. Ridsdale that Mr. Wilson, aged 70, is not <u>very</u> much use & that Mr Matthews . . . is nearly blind. Owing to calls for News Dept staff at the Peace Conference etc, which mean the almost continuous absence of Mr Ridsdale and Mr Burgess, the remaining London staff under Mr Nash (aged 61) are in desperate straits. Messieurs Ridsdale & Burgess, too, in Paris, have a <u>very</u> rackety career, meals at all hours, hectic press conferences, etc.[44]

This would place Burgess in Paris during the summer of 1946, at the right hand of Ridsdale, the latter, at least, and quite possibly Burgess as well, attending "the numerous meetings with the Secretary of State when policy is being formulated." Perhaps the phrase about the "very rackety career" he was sharing with Ridsdale may be allowed to pass unexamined. (As a matter of interest, the Foreign Intelligence Service of the Russian Federation now judges that the information Burgess "extracted" about the positions of Western countries on the postwar settlement in Europe" was of particular value.)

According to Tom Driberg, Burgess's time in the News Department "was perhaps the happiest period of his career in England.

> When we were talking about it, he said: "I was tremendously patriotic about the News Department as a department, and I still am." His political conflicts and tensions were eased: this was the period of genuine Anglo-Soviet–American cooperation [sic]. (The only serious shock was the destruction of the Greek revolution at the end of 1944.) . . . Also, his original ambition to enter the public service, in the full sense of the term, had never left him. The News Department was a useful back-door to the Foreign Office itself.[45]

As it had been at the B.B.C., in the News Department Burgess's work was highly rated. Accompanying Ridsdale to the Paris Conference was a demonstration of the esteem in which he was held within the organization, the valuable work he did for the News Department and others. The "others," we now know from the later diaries of Guy Liddell, included M.I.5. Liddell noted, under November 2, 1945, that he "had a talk with Anthony, Mitchell and Guy Burgess about the future of ORANGE. It has been decided that Mitchell shall run him in future in conjunction with Burgess, since a good deal of his information relates to Fascist activities abroad, and Mitchell is the kind of person who is likely to get on with Burgess." The phrasing of this implies that Burgess, like Graham Mitchell, was an M.I.5. officer. As this was later denied, it may be that he had a less formal relationship with the organization, which, nonetheless, involved running agents.

That Fall, the most secret decision of the Attlee Government was arrived at by a few senior ministers, including Bevin, who arrived late, after "having lunched well," as the euphemism for drunkenness put it, worried about being bullied by the United States:

> Told of the cost of developing an atomic bomb, Hugh Dalton, Chancellor of the Exchequer and Sir Stafford Cripps, President of the Board of Trade, opposed: "it was urged that we must consider seriously whether we could afford to divert from civilian consumption and the restoration of our balance of payments the economic resources required for a project on this scale." Bevin responded: "No, Prime Minister, that won't do at all. We've *got* to have this . . . I don't mind for myself, but I don't want any other Foreign Secretary of this country to be talked at, or to, by the Secretary of State in the United States as I just have in my discussions with Mr Byrnes."[46]

So that future Secretaries of State of the United States would not speak rudely to future Foreign Secretaries, civilian consumption was reduced (e.g., post-war rationing was more severe than that in wartime) and the balance of payments was not restored. The decision was kept secret from Parliament, most of the Cabinet and, of course, from the British people. In mid-September, Field Marshal Montgomery, the Chief of the Imperial General Staff, "met with the American Joint Chiefs of Staff and reached agreement to begin talks as soon as possible on a coordinated strategy in case of war": nuclear war. [47]

The split within the Labour Party over foreign policy, during what was rapidly becoming the first phase of the Cold War, was illustrated in November, 1946, when a group of Labour MPs called for a "socialist alternative to an otherwise inevitable conflict between American capitalism and Soviet Communism." Attlee, sympathetic to this position, vetoed military exercises the Chiefs of Staff had proposed in the Middle East as he was sure that Stalin would realize that such exercises assumed war against the Soviet Union. The

Prime Minister also argued against Bevin's policy of maintaining British forces, and influence, in Greece and Turkey: "Of course it is difficult to tell how far Russian policy is dictated by expansion and how far by fear of attack by the US and ourselves. Fantastic as this is, it may very well be the real grounds of Russian policy. What we consider merely defence may seem to them preparations for an attack." Especially as they were, in the minds of the highest military authorities in the United States and Britain, preparations for an attack. In those years immediately following the end of the Second World War, Germany was a ruin, its citizens starving. The Communists won a clear lead over every other party in the French elections of November, 1946.[48] Italy teetered on the edge of civil war. Only Britain among the great Western European powers that had gone to war seven years earlier was able to maintain an army and navy and the conviction that it was perhaps still a great power. For the next four years, an analysis of the international situation as one in which peace was threatened primarily by American expansionism was common to the Socialist Prime Minister and that minor Foreign Office official, Guy Burgess.

Hector McNeil, who became Minister of State (then Number Two) in the Foreign Office in October, 1946, was as much a novelty in the Foreign Office as Bevin himself. McNeil, who was about the same age as Guy Burgess, was one of seven children of a Scottish shipwright who died when McNeil was nineteen. McNeil went to Glasgow University, excelling in debate, and after University became a journalist. He married in 1939, won a by-election in 1941, on his third try, and moved to London, supplementing his Parliamentary income with work on Beaverbrook's *Daily Express.* Burgess noticed him and, as we have seen, had him join the rota on *The Week in Westminster.* Susan Mary Patten, the brilliant young wife of a minor American diplomat in Paris, described McNeil to her friend Marietta Tree as follows: "Hector MacNeill [sic . . . is] Minister of State in England's present Labor government, and probably Foreign Minister should anything happen to Ernest Bevin . . .

MacNeill would interest you, if you don't know him already, and I do believe that he may be the most able man in the Labor Party, as people have told me he is. He has a strong Glasgow accent, is tremendously insistent on maintaining what he calls his simple working-class ways, "You'll pardon my paper collar, Mrs. Patten," but once he gets over pounding the table saying what a great thing nationalization is and talks about the subject in hand instead of in generalities he is mightily bright and impressive. We met him first through Fred Warner,* one of his two assistants; the other, whom we saw at the Hotel Georges V, is called Guy Burgess. They are very different types.[49]

Others besides Susan Mary Patten foresaw great things for McNeil.[50] He was close to Bevin, personally, and often deputized for him in Parliament and meetings. Bevin indeed imagined, or wished, that McNeil might be his successor as Foreign Minister. McNeil had made Burgess one of his two private secretaries in January, 1947, around the time that the British Government took the highly secret formal decision to build an atomic bomb.[51] It is with this appointment that Burgess gained that access to the minutes of meetings of the Cabinet, the Defence Committee and the Chiefs of the Imperial General Staff and the positions of Western countries on the postwar settlement in Europe, Britain's military strategy, and NATO that impressed Moscow.[52]

Ernest Bevin was the member of the Cabinet closest to the Prime Minister, whom, arguably, he could have replaced whenever he chose and whom, more certainly, he kept in place against Herbert Morrison's ambitions and the frustrations of those members of the Labour Party to Attlee's left, such as Cripps and Nye Bevan. In addition, Bevin was virtually deputy Prime Minister, lingering after Cabinet meetings to discuss with Attlee how to proceed.[53] He was chairman of the Overseas Reconstruction Committee, responsible for

---

* (Sir) Fred Warner, like Burgess, had been to Dartmouth, but had gone from there to Magdalen College, Oxford, rather than Trinity. While serving in the Private Office Warner lived "rather grandly in chambers in Albany."

dealing with Palestine and for the administration of the British occupation zones in Germany and Austria. As we have seen he was a member of the secret committee that made decisions on Britain's atomic programme and the manufacture of atomic weapons. Finally, "he took the lead in creating the Western European Union and Nato, the framework of Britain's post-war defense policy".[54] While Philby, then near the top of M.I.6, knew all there was to know about the British foreign intelligence effort, and Maclean, in Washington, had in his hands the flow of information about the relationship, including the atomic programs relationship, between the United States and Britain, Burgess, working in the Private Office in the much lower ranking position of private secretary to the Minister of State, had access to, was expected to have access to, anything of interest to his Minister and his Minister's Secretary of State, Bevin.

The Private Office is a feature of the British system of ministries led by serving members of the legislature (as compared to the American custom of Secretaries without seats in Congress). The Foreign Secretary has a private office, as do his Ministers of State. These operate similarly. According to Alan Bullock, "Bevin [and that would go for McNeil as well] could only cope with the demands made on him because he was able to rely on a Private Office whose staff were devoted to him."[55] According to Bullock,

> The work of the Private Office was at its most hectic in the middle of conferences abroad when all hours had to be worked and feats of improvisation performed behind the scenes by the PPS, one or other of his two assistants and the five secretaries . . . In more normal circumstances the PPS had still to organize an over-crowded day and see that the Secretary of State always had the papers he needed; learn to interpret his moods; translate his thoughts into English; smooth over unexpected problems; administer first aid when he was ill and generally ease his burdens.[56]

In addition to their official responsibilities, Bevin's staff took part in nominally out-of-working hours activities with the Foreign Secretary, who shared Churchill's tastes for monologue and whiskey.

Successive Private Secretaries . . . soon found . . .that if he had no engagements it was difficult to get Ernie Bevin to go home once he had finished work. On Saturdays in particular, although no engagements were arranged, he would come into the Foreign Office at his normal hour and it was often half-past two or half-past three before his Secretary could get away to a belated lunch, while the Foreign Minister, in the course of several whiskies, rumbled his way round a succession of topics which were on his mind.[57]

According to Nicholas Henderson's authoritative account, the Private Office was "the place where politics and diplomacy come together, Minister and machine interlock, home and abroad meet; a clearing-house for papers, a crossroads, a meeting-point, a bedlam."

It is the most exciting room in the whole Foreign Office. There is always something going on there and enough static in the air to produce shock at any time . . . A room which is always open to visitors and accustomed to awkward situations, the Private Office has acquired mementoes, pictures, statuary and incongruous gifts from all corners of the globe, that have piled up over the years like deposits in an archaeological site . . . [the] desks occupied by the Private Secretaries—desks laden with telephones and boxes, the hardware of officialdom . . . the mahogany table in the middle of the room . . . the red-bound Foreign Office lists . . . the high reading-desk covered with the day's newspapers . . . the ceaseless ebb and flow of boxes—some red, some black, some blue and some even yellow; rectangular boxes, flat boxes, long boxes and short boxes, the smallest, very squat and black, and bearing the portentous words Prime Minister . . . all of them borne into and out of the Private Office by a conveyor belt of office-keepers.[58]

This applies, appropriately reduced, to the Private Office of the Minister of State, where Warner and Burgess occupied a small, high-ceilinged room with windows overlooking Downing Street, between a larger anteroom for clerks and the room of the Minister himself.

This was Burgess's working environment for the two years that he served as the Minister of State's private secretary. During those two years it was, still, a nerve center of a world empire.

It is the duty of the private secretary to decide what part of the great stream of information flowing into the Foreign Office his minister should see. The documents coming into the Private Office included digests, over-views of events with the scope of a private edition of *The Times,* more detailed accounts of matters pertinent especially to the Foreign Office, and then the raw material of administration: cables from embassies[59] and foreign governments, reports from the various sections of the Foreign Office, Cabinet papers (annotated, perhaps, with the Prime Minister's terse comments in red ink: "I agree (or the opposite), C.R.A.".

As with Bevin's Private Secretaries, the role of Burgess and Warner was that of intermediaries between McNeil and the Foreign Office: to convey to the Minister the opinions of the various officials of the Foreign Office and to convey to them the orders and views of the Minister. All communications destined for the Minister of State came first to Burgess and Warner, who read them, determined whether they should be sent on to McNeil and if so whether they were ready to be seen or whether more information were needed. If the latter was the case, Warner or Burgess would send them back with a note, or, more likely, as maintaining friendly relations with the entire Westminster village was vital to their work, ring up the originator of the document and request the necessary additions. (Or, if they happened to wish to, they could ring up virtually anyone in Whitehall and ask for information about one thing or another, as they needed to keep one jump ahead of the Minister, or, perhaps, just out of curiosity.) When an item was in condition for the Minister to receive it, Warner or Burgess would likely summarize its contents, point out the important bits, and, perhaps, draft a response on the basis of their knowledge of the issue and the opinions of the official who had originated the item at hand, and their knowledge of McNeil, his goals, prejudices, opinions and relationship, at that moment, with the Secretary of State, Bevin.[60]

And then, it is said, from time to time, when Burgess and his Soviet contact met, "Burgess would bring gigantic files with him: these would be photographed, then quietly taken back to Hector McNeil's office. The most interesting items were telegraphed directly to Moscow."[61]

If the question of Burgess's access is easy to answer—it was virtually unlimited—that of his influence is more difficult to ascertain. Nicholas Henderson, the historian of the Private Office, observed that it "is sometimes difficult to determine the rationale for some foreign policy decision because notes by the Private Secretary, often attached to papers on submission to the Minister, perhaps in the overnight box, have been removed when the file is returned to the department . . ." This confidentionality "corresponds to the requirement of the Secretary of State to have the benefit of the views of the Private Secretary, given his personal knowledge of ministerial objectives, while safeguarding the needs of the Private Secretary for discretion and the avoidance of any impression that he is usurping the function of one or other political department."[62] In other words, it can be assumed, on the one hand, that the archives will be empty of notes from the Private Secretary to (at that date) his Minister, while it can also be assumed that there were such notes and that they were influential.

Burgess had moved from a position, in the News Department of the Foreign Office, where he had access to all that as a matter of routine passed in and out of the Ministry, to a position where everything of importance in foreign affairs passed over his desk and, in addition, a position from which he could influence—if not decisions, then the way matters to be decided were framed.[63] According to Burgess's Russian contact during this period, Yuri Modin, "When McNeil was asked to draw up a report or analyse a set of classified documents, the job was passed straight to Guy, who was only too happy to oblige. When everything was typed up and ready, all McNeil had to do was sign it and send it on to his colleagues in the government, or to the Prime Minister."[64]

Fred Warner, Burgess's fellow in McNeil's private office, said that Burgess "brimmed over with enthusiasm and bright ideas . . . he always arrived punctually at work.

> He seldom missed appointments . . . . His carelessness about dress and appearances constituted the only consistent black mark against him . . . Confidential papers were strewn over [his desk] like confetti, yet he could easily retrieve anything wanted urgently by burrowing like a squirrel beneath the daily newspapers and his drawing pad, on which he would sketch libelous caricatures of any subject that momentarily took his fancy . . .

One particular stream of information that Burgess had not been privy to in the News Department now was added to his copy-book. According to Stephen Dorrill "He had access to the yellow boxes in which M.I.6 sent their reports and also managed to make a copy of the key to the safe containing the secret reports to which only Bevin, McNeil and Orme Sargent had access."[65] Warner claimed, in regard to M.I.6's yellow boxes:

> I had the keys to the Minister's [McNeil] boxes, and Guy hadn't. It was a point of professional honour with me not to part with those keys to anyone. Except when I was sick or otherwise absent [!], the boxes were safe. Besides, Burgess never showed the least interest in the contents, though I now realize that this may have been bluff on his part . . .

("Of particular value" to Moscow, it is remembred, was information concerning "the activities of British and American Intelligence.") Warner then returned to his character sketch:

> I can't say that Guy automatically followed the Stalinist line. In fact, I doubt very much whether he cared a rap for the teachings of Marx or Lenin. In those days he sought to convey the impression of being a radical Social Democrat who believed firmly in Tawney.

(Warner seems to have been one of the very few people who worked with Burgess who did not receive the impression that he was a convinced Marxist, familiar with all the relevant texts.)

But the only writer he idolized personally was the novelist E. M. Forster, who still seemed to exert a powerful influence on him. That overworked maxim of Forster's about hoping he'd betray his country rather than his friend(s) was one Guy quoted ad nauseam. I'm quite convinced he meant it. Friendship mattered a lot to him.[66]

Warner, and perhaps Burgess, did not realize that Burgess's regard for Forster was unrequited. Burgess remained after the war as before something of an object of derision between Forster and Isherwood. For example, on March 1, 1947, Christopher Isherwood, visiting from California, had lunch with Jack Hewit, supper with Benjamin Britten and Peter Pears, stayed with Hewit on the 7th and on the 8th had supper with Guy Burgess[67] at the Reform Club. Joined by Pollock, they went to "several pubs and nightclubs." Isherwood got very drunk and fell down a flight of stairs in a nightclub, but was unhurt.[68] Isherwood told Forster that he thought he had been pushed by Burgess, but then in his memoir of the period, wrote that he had fallen on his own. Isherwood liked to play up to Forster's dislike of Burgess.[*]

In April, 1947, McNeil began the process of promoting Burgess to the Executive Class of the Foreign Service (Higher Executive Officer).[69] Burgess's application lists the Reform Club as his address; Anthony Frederick Blunt, Surveyor of Royal Pictures and Assistant Director of Courtauld Institute, and Sir Richard Maconachie of the B.B.C. (and retired Indian Civil Service), as references. Of course it was the former Talks Director Maconachie's word that would have counted and it is significant that Burgess felt he could count on Maconachie's word. The Medical Examiner's

---

[*] In London "I saw that [wisp?] in the distance, Guy Burgess. His meeting with you seems to have gone as I expected it would." Forster to Isherwood, 21-3-47 in Zeikowitz. Letters between Forster and Isherwood on Homosexuality and Literature. Palgrave Macmillan; annotated edition (August 5, 2008), p. 141.

Report was completed at the end of August, stating that Burgess was in good health, five foot eleven and a half inches tall, weight 12 stone (168 pounds), slightly near-sighted, but not in need of glasses. (Perhaps his eyesight had improved since childhood or the requirements of the Foreign Office were not as stringent as those of the Royal Navy.) The B.B.C. was asked to fill out a questionnaire, including "Whilst in your service was he honest, sober, and generally well conducted?" to which the answer was "Yes." "Are you aware of any circumstances tending to disqualify him for the situation which he now seeks?" "No." The B.B.C. administrative officer filling out the form noted that Burgess had been a Free-lance journalist and a temporary civil servant in the War Office (presumably a reference to Section D) and Foreign Office. A "Report on Service" of 20 September listed his conduct and efficiency to that date in the Foreign Office as "satisfactory."

An interesting meeting of cabinet ministers and officials, including Bevin, took place in the middle of this process, on June 16, 1947. "The committee 'Agreed that members of all subversive organizations of the Right or Left should continue to be subject to security scrutiny and should not be employed on work involving access to secret information, and that, in particular, Communists should not be employed in the public service on such work.'" Further "The private offices of ministers and senior civil servants would be no-go areas for communists."[70] Burgess's promotion was completed in September.

Burgess, as a student at Cambridge, had thought that the cause of Indian independence was the cause of the revolutionary movement in Britain itself. Events after the war largely ran in the other direction. Churchill had sabotaged Cripps's negotiations for Indian Dominion status in 1942.[71] The leadership of the Congress Party was then thrown into jail and held under harsh conditions for the duration of the war. The situation only worsened when Churchill refused to alleviate the Bengal famine during which at least three million people died, equivalent to the more famous Ukrainian famine of the 1930s. When Nehru and the other Congress Party leaders were released at the end of the war, the British government of India continued to play the Muslim League off against Congress, and the princely states against both, showing no inclination to leave. Nehru, and particularly Gandhi, had lost any trust in, and respect for, the British they had ever had.

Then, early in 1946 there were mutinies at several R.A.F. stations in India over demobilization and pay. On February 19th elements of the Royal Indian Navy mutinied and marched through the streets of Bombay, carrying the Indian national flag.

> Short-lived as were the mutinies of 1946, they finally convinced the British Government that the spring of the empire was broken. *Satyagraha* may have harried the British conscience, the Labour Government may have believed as an article of faith that the British should withdraw from India, but it was the non-political events of early 1946 that made clear that the end of the *raj* was near.[72]

The Indian Empire, in the final analysis, was held by force of arms. If those arms were no longer reliable, the Empire could not be held. On March 24th, 1946, Cripps returned to Delhi. It took him and his colleagues until the end of June to negotiate the terms of an interim government of India under the Viceroy. The Muslim League was intransigent; the plans negotiated by Cripps and his colleagues collapsed; there were communal riots in Calcutta. More plans were negotiated and an interim government, including representatives of both the Congress and the League was put in place in September. This was consumed by fighting, both figuratively and, in the streets and villages of India, literally. Attlee then convened a conference in London, which accomplished little. "Ernest Bevin seems to have realised the far-reaching implications and mourned them" writing to Attlee that "'You cannot read the telegrams from Egypt and the Middle East nowadays without realizing that not only is India going, but Malaya, Ceylon and the Middle East is going with it, with a tremendous repercussion on the African territories . . .'"[73] Attlee replied asking Bevin whether he was "really prepared to go back on the consistent [Labour Party] policy of 25 years, to govern by force if necessary and put in enough troops to hold the country down?"[74]   In February, 1947, Congress demanded that the League representatives should leave the interim government. Attlee reacted by announcing that the British would withdraw from India not later than June 1948, naming Mountbatten as Viceroy to accomplish this; which he did, with startling dispatch. Independence came in August, 1947. India had been the keystone and much of the substance of the Empire. It was gone.

Much of Bevin's time as Foreign Minister was taken up by the Palestine situation, which was triangular, if not pentagonal. It is perhaps not well known that this was closely related to his Cold War pre-occupations. The Zionist organizations, basing their claims on the one hand on the Balfour Declaration and on the other on the manifest impossibility for the remnant of the Holocaust to return to their former homes, were working toward a Jewish state. The Arabs, basing their claims on British promises dating back at least to the activities of T. E. Lawrence and St. John Philby, were working toward a Palestine free of Jews (as they had done during the war in collaboration with Nazi Germany), or, minimally, with only those Jews whose ancestors had lived in a subordinate position there for generations and were willing to continue to do so. It is crucial for an understanding of British policy in regard to Palestine that the Chiefs of the Imperial General Staff, in their turn, were working to develop in Palestine a vast military base for operations in what they believed was an inevitable war with the Soviet Union. Those plans included the basing of atomic weapons in the region.

Bevin and the Chiefs of Staff believed, as it was formulated as early as April, 1946, that, "with Russia as the only power with which Britain might become involved in war, it was essential to deny her the use of these areas and to retain bases in the Middle East from which alone it would be possible to attack Russian territory."[75] Prime Minister Attlee did not agree. On January 5th, 1947 (just as he was deciding to grant India nearly immediate independence) Attlee had sent Bevin an extraordinary Top Secret memorandum. The transmittal note reads: "I have set down for the purpose of clearing my own mind some considerations which have occurred to me on reading the papers on our policy in the Near East. I enclose a copy in order to inform you what is in my mind." The memorandum itself begins:

1. The broad conclusions of the Chiefs of Staff and of the Imperial Defence College are –
    a. That the U.K. which is the heart of the Commonwealth is extremely vulnerable to modern attack by long range weapons and that our present knowledge does not provide any effective method of passive defence.
    b. Therefore the only way to prevent such an attack is by a threat of counter attack so formidable that a potential enemy will be deterred through fear of his own losses.
    c. The only possible enemy is Russia.
    d. The only bases from which Russia could be attacked are situated in the Near East.
    e. Therefore the maintenance of British influence and consequently British forces in the Near East are essential to our safety.
    f. As a corollary we must secure our oil supplies in the Near East and endeavour to secure our communications through the Mediterranean if at all possible.
2. The consequence of this appreciation means heavy military commitments which must be considered in relation to our man power and our economic resources.

After outlining the extraordinary effort this would entail, Attlee concludes:

9. . . . I regard the strategy outlined above as a strategy of despair. I have the gravest doubts as to its efficacy. The deterrent does not seem to me to be sufficiently strong. I apprehend that the pursuit of this policy so far from preventing may precipitate hostilities.

10. Unless we are persuaded that the U.S.S.R. is irrevocably committed to a policy of world domination and that there is no possibility of her alteration, I think that before being committed

to this strategy we should seek to come to an agreement with the U.S.S.R. after consideration with Stalin of all our points of conflict.

Bevin's Conservative assistant, Pierson Dixon, responded with a point-by-point note of objections to Attlee's thoughts, ending with this "Summary":

(1) Effect of withdrawal from the Middle East would be disastrous to our position there, in the neighbouring countries and in Europe.

(2) It would lead the U.S. to despair of us and thus effectively divide the world into an American and a Russian bloc.

(3) This would heighten the probability of world war in which we would be massacred.

(4) Even if Russian world domination can be discounted bear will certainly not resist pushing a paw into soft places.

The note, rejecting the Prime Minister's position, was circulated for discussion at a meeting between Dixon, Sir Orme Sargent and Fred Warner, among others, Burgess not yet being in place.[76] It would be highly unlikely, however, that he did not learn about the exchange. His Russian career summary explicitly mentions his access to minutes of meetings of the Defence Committee and the Joint Chiefs of Staff (sic).

It would seem, as far as these highly emotional matters can be untangled more than half a century later, that for the British Government, the issue of Palestine was not about Jews, nor about Arabs, but about an anticipated Anglo-Soviet war.[77] And oil, of course. (Bevin was always incensed at charges of anti-semitism, which becomes more intelligible, in spite of his occasional anti-semitic remarks, if we realize that his attitude toward the Palestinian question was chiefly determined by what he saw as the military necessity for Imperial control of the area.) When the Palestinian Mandate ended and the State of Israel came into existence on May 15, 1948, it was immediately attacked by the neighboring states, including Jordan, the army of which, the Arab Legion, was a typical British colonial force, financed and officered by the British. In the final analysis, therefore, this was an intervention by the British Empire on the Arab side, be it on a rather small scale. There may have been a lingering hope among the CIGS that the great Middle Eastern base they desired could be constructed under Jordanian auspices somewhere between Amman and Gaza. The Israelis, however, took the Negev and that became impossible.[78]

Concerning another conflict, Burgess told Driberg that in retrospect he still mourned the British intervention that had stopped what he referred to as "the Greek revolution" of 1944, that is, the attempt by the Greek Communist Party to take power from the British-backed government of Royalists and former collaborators. In the winter 1946/47, matters in Greece had reached another crisis (one of a century-long series). On February 21st the British Government named April 1st as the date from which support for the Greek government would become the responsibility of the United States, if that country would accept it. (This was a feint: the last British troops, however, did not leave Greece until 1950.[79]) On the 24th of February the Foreign Office added Turkey to the responsibilities they wished to transfer to the United States. The reason for these announcements was to be found not in Greece, but in the City of London, where an economic crisis had arisen from the combination of the exigencies of the American loan, the ill-coordinated implementation of socialism among the basic industries, a coal shortage and a particularly harsh winter. Britain was no longer able to finance deficits with continental Europe and the United States with trade surpluses from Australia, West Africa, and above all with India, which instead of being a source of profit, had become a creditor.[80] According to C. C. S. Newton,

> Political as well as economic circumstances militated against downward adjustments of the balances. India, for example, held more than one-third of all sterling balances. Between 1945 and 1947 the Labour Government was conducting a series of extremely difficult negotiations with Indian political leaders, with the aim of giving the country its independence within a multi-racial Commonwealth. In 1946 and 1947 India was

plagued with food-supply problems, and lacked the foreign investment which neither the United States nor the International Bank appeared willing to provide but which was essential to any agricultural and industrial modernization programme. The British concern at that time was that the financial consequences feared by the Bank [of England] would be exacerbated by the political problems likely to develop in the Anglo-Indian relationship after independence, if excessive pressure was brought upon India to scale down sterling balances.[81]

As India moved closer to independence, its unfavorable balance of trade with Great Britain, for two centuries the foundation of the Empire, began to unwind. And as *its* industrial production and trade dropped that Spring, Britain had drawn down the US loan at a faster rate than planned.

The British declaration of its proposed withdrawal from Greece was met by observers in the State Department of the United States claiming, somewhat hysterically, that unless "urgent and immediate support is given to Greece, it seems probable that the Greek Government will be overthrown and a totalitarian regime of the extreme left will come to power . . . The capitulation of Greece to Soviet domination through lack of adequate support from the U.S. and Great Britain might eventually result in the loss of the whole Near and Middle East and northern Africa."[82] This early enunciation of the domino theory appears to envision an irresistible Soviet military force (perhaps the First Belorussian Front), sweeping from Tehran three thousand miles to Tangier, along the coast of a Mediterranean Sea controlled by the British and American fleets, just as the Red Army was demobilizing. Indeed, the secret diplomatic correspondence between London and Washington, passing through the office of the Foreign Secretary and the Minister of State, was as close to panic as such messages ever come. On February 26, 1947, Secretary of State Marshall recommended to President Truman that the United States assume responsibility for economic and military support to Greece and Turkey. Truman gave his approval that afternoon and promulgated the consequent "Truman Doctrine" in speech to a joint session of Congress on March 12, 1947.[83] (It had turned out, inter alia, that in as much as the "crisis" affected Turkey, it was based on false British intelligence assessments of non-existent Soviet troop movements.)

As an alternative possibility for the grand narrative of postwar history, in mid-January, Stalin had floated the idea of a renewal of the Anglo-Soviet Treaty and a UK/USSR military alliance.[84] This was discussed in Cabinet on February 3. The Cabinet noted that "The Soviet Government were no doubt apprehensive of United States economic penetration into Europe," which was, no doubt the case. The question was left open pending clarification of certain issues by Stalin.[85] The Treaty of Dunkirk, signed on March 4, 1947, still saw the danger to peace as coming not from the Soviet Union, but from Germany.[86] At the Moscow Council of Foreign Ministers Conference (10 March to 25 April, 1947) Bevin and Stalin agreed to begin negotiations on the renewal of the Anglo-Soviet treaty and "Bevin assur[ed] Stalin that he was anxious to work with Russia and avoid unfriendly feelings and Stalin responded[ed] in the same vein,"[87] each equally sincere. Stafford Cripps, then President of the Board of Trade, took the view that expanding trade with the Soviet Union (that is, exporting machine goods to it) was preferable to Britain's becoming economically dependent on aid from the United States.[88] The pamphlet *Keep Left,* by Richard Crossman and others, was published at the beginning of May, 1947 for the Labour Party Conference. This critique of Bevin's foreign policy argued for a "Third Force," European Socialist alliance based on Britain and France, as "working together, we are still strong enough to hold the balance of world power, to halt the division into a Western and Eastern bloc and so make the United Nations a reality."[89] It was opposed by another pamphlet, written by Denis Healey, *Cards on the Table,* supporting Bevin's pro-American policy. These dueling pamphlets defined the Labour Party's left and right wings until the advent of New Labour settled the debate.

The summer of 1947 brought the acute stage of the British financial crisis. The British Government had simply run out of dollars. Having been forced by the US to agree to free trade and the convertibility of the pound as a condition of the British loan, Britain was unable to protect its home market and was subjected to a drain of reserves by its European trading partners, which did not have similar restrictions: "some countries made not even a formal pretence of observing the gentlemen's agreements they had concluded with Britain".[90] The convertibility of the pound was suspended and rationing was extended. Again according to Newton:

> By insisting that discrimination and exchange controls were the central obstacles to a multilateral world, and by forcing the liberalization of sterling, in effect the Anglo-American Financial Agreement placed the burden of adjustment to the world disequilibrium on Britain, the world's greatest debtor. The traumatic events of 1947 convinced British Ministers and civil servants not that multilateralism was an unattainable goal, but that it could not be achieved in the absence of measures to correct the imbalance between the dollar and non-dollar areas of the world. The British view was that as the United States was the world's largest creditor Washington should take the initiative in correcting the disequilibrium.[91]

Britain, which in obedience to the terms of the American loan, had introduced sterling convertibility on July 15, suspended it on August 20, 1947 following a dramatic run on sterling. Sir Stafford Cripps was said to have remarked then: "We must be ready at any moment to switch over our friendship from the U.S. to Russia."[92] It was a sentiment that Burgess would have found sympathetic.

The Foreign Office informed the government of the United States in a series of secret and dramatic communications—passing through the offices of the Secretary and Minister of State—that not only was Great Britain itself on the verge of an economic collapse, but that as a result there was a "serious risk of losing most of Western Europe if the crisis here develops as it now seems almost certain to develop."[93] This background to what became the Marshall Plan contained, in addition to the proto-Cold War factors, American national economic concerns. It was feared that the Second World

War would be followed by a depression, as had the First World War, and that the chances of this happening would be greater if the European countries, including Great Britain, reverted to intra-European bilateral agreements, rather than "free trade" with the United States (with the latter maintaining its own tarrifs). One little-remembered aspect of the Marshall Plan was the concern in the United States that American international trade might be restricted by efforts of the European nations to maintain their economic independence. "The anxiety in Washington was that unless the flow of hard currency from the United States could be maintained, European nations would try increasingly to eliminate the dollar from intra-European trade by resorting to bilateralism, state trading, and exchange controls."[94] The American government argued that the problem was the inefficiency of the European economies, in particular, the newly socialistic economy of Great Britain. However, "British skepticism that the principal cause of the dollar shortage was merely "Europe's failure to produce" was borne out by events between 1947 and 1950. At the turn of 1949-50 western Europe's industrial output reached the highest point since the war, 122 per cent of the level achieved in 1938. Yet the dollar problem remained serious . . ."[95]

Nevertheless, it had appeared, early in the summer of 1947, "that Europe [aside from Britain] would not recover on its own. Britain was in no position to help and might well run into economic disaster herself. Stalin did not need to have 'a blue print for world revolution' or to think in terms of another war, which the Soviet Union was in no condition to wage. All the Russians had to do was wait, and the situation was bound to develop to their advantage."[96] These foreign policy events of the first half of the Attlee Government's time in office were observed by Guy Burgess from privileged positions in the News Department and the private office of the Minister of State. It is unlikely that much of possible interest to Moscow did not come to his attention and, having come to his attention (read aloud in comic voices, annotated with cartoons in the margin, brought along to dinner at the Reform Club), was not then

270

passed to his contacts.

The Marshall Plan is a fabled turning point in the Cold War. In part in order to prevent the reconstitution of pre-war Imperial Preference and similar continental policies potentially damaging to the prospects for the U.S. economy, in part to avoid the dominance of Europe by Soviet-supported Communist Parties, in part to implement American eonomic hegemony, Secretary of State Marshall announced on June 5, 1947 a plan to provide European countries with the dollars needed to finance trade with the United States, ensuring that dollars rather than pounds would be the primary vehicle for the world economy. McNeil was responsible for bilateral negotiations between the US and the UK for what was called the European Recovery Plan. In general, McNeil expressed the view that the American original draft was written from the point of view of US economic dominance, implying the duty of the UK and other countries to both submit to and reinforce that dominance. This was a view to which Burgess would have been sympathetic, and which he could have communicated to his contacts with other information concerning "the positions of Western countries on the postwar settlement in Europe." Indeed, Burgess and Maclean were crucial in conveying to the Soviets the various negotiation positions, and, perhaps, intentions involved in the development of the European Recovery Plan.

There is a description of Burgess in his role as a Soviet agent, as he appeared at the peak of his activity. Yuri Modin, on his first overseas assignment as an NKVD officer, had been sent to London to take over handling the Cambridge group whose "product" he had for some years been translating and analyzing at Moscow Center. He was very much an innocent abroad. He was nervous. M.I.5 had put in place during the 1930s (at the latest) a surveillance system along Continental lines. There were microphones concealed in the offices of the Communist Party and other places of interest; many telephones were tapped; people were followed, letters from abroad opened. One can follow in the files of M.I.5 virtually day by day the activities and conversations of persons of interest to the British secret police: Stafford Cripps, Ellen Wilkinson, James Klugmann. On the other hand, the protocol for physical surveillance had been developed in consultation with Anthony Blunt, who had shared that information with his Russian contacts. Forearmed then, but nervous, Modin set out to meet his agent:

> It was eight in the evening, at dusk. The venue was an outlying part of London, the weather was fine and you could see people clearly a long way off . . . [Burgess was] exactly on time . . . He carried himself well, a handsome man in fine clothes, startched shirt collar, gleaming shoes and well-cut overcoat. He was the image of a smooth British aristocrat, wth a free and easy manner and a firm step . . . I saw him a long way off, wandering tranquilly among the trees, a folded newspaper under his arm . . . he suggested we meet in one of his favorite pubs. This was out of the question and I explained how exposed I felt when going into a pub. He laughed aloud, the frank, ringing laugh I was later to know so well. Then he informed me that he was as allergic to the suburbs as I was to pubs . . .

They compromised on streets, parks or squares as meeting places.

> I went on to tackle the delicate question of what to do should we be stopped and questioned by the police or by MI5 . . . I suggested, a bit lamely, that we should say I was lost and was asking him the way . . . it might win us a few precious minutes to gather our wits . . . Again Burgess laughed his ringing laugh and looked me straight in the eye.
>
> "I've a better idea. You're a good-looking boy, and I'm a fiend known all over London for my insatiable appetite for good-looking boys. All we need say is we're lovers and looking for a bed."
>
> I was young enough to blush to the roots of my hair. Burgess chuckled with glee.
>
> "But, Guy," I said, "I'm a diplomat. It's not done . . . I'm a married man."

272

"You'd do anything for the cause, now, wouldn't you? And in the time it'll take them to check up on this, we'll be back in the saddle."

I changed the subject hastily.[97]

This story is interesting in a number of ways. One is that it shows how effortlessly Burgess established dominence over his "handler." This is quite contrary to standard practice. Intelligence professionals are instructed that their first priority is to control the relationship. That Burgess was controlling the relationship, and allowed to do so, reveals his extraordinary importance to the NKVD.

Modin's description of Burgess in his role as a secret agent is in marked contrast to the image projected by Burgess in other roles, and generally accepted in the specialist espionage literature.

> Burgess turned out to be an extremely conscientious worker. He answered my questions as best he could. He took no notes, because his memory was faultless: for example, he could remember word for word something you asked him three months earlier . . . When he passed me documents, he unfailingly told me which should be sent to the Centre without delay, and which could wait till later . . . He bore no resemblance to the ordinary types who followed people, played the informers and picked up bits of intelligence here and there. His task, he believed, as far finer and nobler. He wasn't working for the Soviet Union as such; he as in the vanguard of world revolution. His reasons for collaborating with us were truly ideological.

Which is a response, if not an answer to, the question often posed about Burgess and his friends: How could they work for a regime like that established by Stalin?

> Guy Burgess believed that world revolution was inevitable. Like his Cambridge friends, he saw Russia as the forward base of that revolution. There was no alternative, of course: he might have his reservations about Russia's domestic and foreign politics, and I often heard him berating our leaders, but in the end he saw the Soviet Union as the world's best hope. He and his friends

were sure that one day soon our country would provide itself with honest leaders more interested in questions of real importance to the world than in their own perks and privileges.[98]

There are many errors and misinterpretations in Modin's book, some trivial, some not, but these stories from his youth—from the high point of his life—ring true.

Bevin had jumped at the opportunity presented by Marshall's proposal, the opportunity, that is, to permanently involve the United States in European affairs. He quickly organized the European response to the Marshall Plan, beginning with a meeting on June 27 in Paris with Soviet Foreign Minister Molotov and their French counterpart Georges Bidault.[*] The public invitation extended by General Marshall was to all European governments, including that of the Soviet Union, but in Washington and London it was understood that the American government would be unhappy if the Soviet Union, or any country with a Communist or Communist influenced government, accepted. "On the evening of June 28 [American Ambassador Jefferson] Caffery saw Bevin and Duff Cooper and said: 'If the Communists get back into the government, France won't get a dollar from America'"[99] Molotov probably learned of this sentiment soon enough.

At one point in the negotiations Moscow learned that the British and American representatives were quarrelling over an aspect of the European contribution to the Marshall Plan. Lubyanka (KGB headquarters) ordered the London KGB "residence" to supply as much information about the matter as possible. Yuri Modin remembers turning to Burgess for help.

"Of course I can find the thing," he said. "But I have to tell you, you won't understand a word of it. We've tangled it up so badly with the Americans that even we don't understand it any more. And nobody's in any hurry to let in the light. If you insist, I'll

---

[*] In addition to Molotov, Soviet visitors to Paris included Yuri Modin and his family, in transit to London, where Modin was to take over as Burgess's contact.

bring you the paperwork, but I warn you there's a suitcaseful" . . .

"I'll take your suitcase . . . Bring me everything you can find."

"Righto, but you'll regret it."

In due course I received a bag full of papers. I leafed through them, understood nothing and like a dutiful agent sent the lot on to Moscow. Two weeks later they wired back: "We understand nothing. Ask Paul [Burgess] to tell us at least where it begins and where it ends!"

Burgess found this very droll. "I told you so. If you like, I'll distil it into a page or two."

And so he did. I typed the pages up and dispatched them by telegram.[100]

While American representatives ensured that it was understood, behind closed doors, that the Marshall Plan was an anti-Communist project, Soviet objections to the Marshall Plan were summarized by Molotov at the final meeting of the Paris Three Power Conference, July 2, 1947:

> When efforts are directed toward Europe helping herself in the first place and developing her economic potentialities as well as the exchange of goods between countries, such efforts are in conformity with the interests of the countries of Europe. When, however, it is stated . . . that the decisive hold on the rehabilitation of the economic life of European countries should belong to the United States and not to the European countries themselves, such a position stands in contradiction to the interests of European countries since it might lead to a denial of their economic independence, which denial is incompatible with national sovereignty. . .

> The Soviet Government, considering that the Anglo-French plan to set up a special organization for the coordination of the economies of European states would lead to interference in the

internal affairs of European countries, particularly those which have the greatest need for outside aid, and believing that this can only complicate relations between the countries of Europe and hamper their cooperation, rejects this plan as being altogether unsatisfactory and incapable of yielding any positive results.

On the other hand the Soviet Union favors the fullest development of economic collaboration between European and other countries on a healthy basis of equality and mutual respect for national interests and has itself constantly contributed and will contribute to this end by the expansion of trade with other countries . . .

What would the implementation of the Franco-British proposal concerning the setting up of a special organization or of a "Steering Committee" for the elaboration of a comprehensive European economic program lead to?

It would lead to no good results.

It would lead to Great Britain, France and that group of countries which follows them separating themselves from the other European states and thus dividing Europe into two groups of states and creating new difficulties in the relations between them.[101]

The Soviet Union, not wishing, inter alia, to become part of the dollar zone, withdrew from the preliminary talks, taking with it those nations within its sphere of influence. Bevin, as anticipated, then took the lead in organizing the western European structures needed to implement the US initiative.

The Paris conference responding to the proposals (the Committee for European Economic Cooperation) ended on September 22nd. In his speech welcoming the report of the Committee, Bevin stated, with diplomatic candor, that they "greatly regret the absence of those European countries who have not participated in this Conference" and that for "the future, as in the past, the door remains wide open."[102] The next day a group of nine

Communist parties, including the French and Italian, created the Communist Information Bureau (Cominform) to coordinate opposition to "American imperialism" and "the treacherous policy of the right-wing Socialists like . . . Attlee and Bevin."[103] Although in retrospect it appears that the Cold War was at this point well underway, at the time it seemed that matters had not yet quite jelled. While McNeil was in New York at the UN General Assembly meeting dueling with Vyshinsky, the young Secretary for Overseas Trade, Harold Wilson, signed an agreement in Moscow on December 27, 1947, providing for the exchange of Russian grain for British machinery and equipment.[104] Also at the end of 1947 even "Bevin could remark to Bidault that 'he doubted whether Russia was as great a danger as a resurgent Germany might become'."[105] Susan Mary Patten recorded that earlier in the year, "Bevin said sadly that it was a great pity that such a great people as the Americans do not understand socialism, and added, 'One forgets Marxism when one has piles of work on one's desk.'"[106]

Burgess was not confined to London during this period. We find, for example, that on November 21st he sent Isaiah Berlin a (typed) letter from the Foreign Office, which demonstrates, among other things, that the abortive Moscow expedition had not soured their friendship, that they were in regular contact, and that the two both delighted in gossip, high and low—as if that needed demonstration:

My dear Shya,

> After so many false alarms this is to warn you and confirm our arrangement that I am coming up to stay with you next week-end, i.e. Saturday, 29th. I hope this is still convenient since I am very much looking forward to it. Hector may dock during the week-end but fortunately his wife, I think, will go and meet him.

> I know all about Dalton, do you yet know that Goronwy is having twins? ("This is a situation that will last for the rest of our lives and one which it is impossible to refer to without a loud music-hall guffaw".) If they are both girls (and no-one yet

knows) Goronwy will spend the rest of his life, if you count it up, surrounded by a minimum of five women.

Would you let me know at the Reform whether it is still all right and what time you would like me to arrive.

/signed/ Luv, Guy Burgess[107]

Hugh Dalton had resigned as Chancellor of the Exchequer on November 13th after giving a journalist details of the budget before presenting them to the House. Isaiah Berlin was no longer—if ever he had been—a cloistered academic. As he could vie with Burgess as a possessor of inside information concerning the workings of the Whitehall policy machine, they had much information and gossip to share and discuss. Andrew Revai, Anthony Blunt's Hungarian journalist friend, also wished to discuss politics with Burgess, but Burgess would have none of it, denouncing him as a possible agent to Guy Liddell on January 31, 1948 and then again on February 20th.[108]

In addition to McNeil, Bevin had a second Minister of State, Christopher Mayhew, who had traveled to Russia with Anthony Blunt in 1935.[109] A dozen years later he was behind the formation of the Foreign Office's anti-Communist organization, the Information Research Department (IRD). (Sir) Ivone Kirkpatrick, who had been head of Chancery at the British Embassy in Berlin before the war and head of the German Section at the Foreign Officer from 1947 to 1949, was Mayhew's Assistant Under Secretary. IRD's first head, (Sir) Ralph Murray had worked at the B.B.C. in the 1930s, joining the Foreign Office in 1939 and was then assigned to the Political Warfare Executive, a career, to that point, paralleling that of Burgess. Murray and an assistant were appointed by late February 1948, and a budget approved. Many of the first recruits for IRD were inherited from the PWE/SOE. It was Kirkpatrick who "was responsible for recruiting 'contract' staff for the IRD, including writers with wartime experience in propaganda and East European émigrés. Eight permanent officials including . . . Guy Burgess and Robert Conquest . . . supervised the work."[110] This may have been another instance where Burgess's reputation as a propaganda expert, and his experience with PWE/SOE, had an effect. It was, perhaps, only a coincidence that the IRD worked closely with Section IX of M.I.6, the anti-Soviet part of that organization, which had been supervised by Kim Philby. After a few months familiarizing himself with IRD, Burgess was sent on a tour of British Embassies in the Middle East in order to establish liaison relationships between them and the newly established department. As he did frequently, Burgess took his mother with him, visiting, among others, Philby, who was now the M.I.6 chief of station in Istanbul.* At this time, according to Modin, Burgess was acting as Philby's connection with the KGB. Burgess was also at this time the connection between Maclean and the KGB, when Maclean happened to be visiting London during his tour of duty in Washington.

Burgess did not stay long with the IRD, it tiring of him or he with it. A thick smokescreen of the usual kind of stories has concealed the details from view. In any case, he soon returned to McNeil's office.

Two years after the end of the war, Bevin had come to agree with the CIGS and the American government that the existing Soviet Union was a greater threat than the once and possibly future Germany and had begun to support the creation of what eventually became the West German state. In spite of the complex, not overly friendly, negotiations in Washington all that winter concerning the development of atomic energy and weapons, on January 27, 1948 Bevin had the British Ambassador in Washington, Lord Inverchapel** propose to the American State Department a military alliance for the defense of Europe.[111] Two weeks later, in

---

* One of the stories about Burgess's diving skill has him on this occasion diving through a window of Philby's villa into the Bosporus. There is another describing the grace with which he went off the diving board at the RAC. These images bring to mind the diver at Paestum, eternally moving through the air to the water that is, at least metaphorically, the solution to the pathos of life.
** Archibald Clark Kerr.

Czechoslovakia, which had a majority-Communist government under a non-Communist president, the Communist ministers began a creeping coup. Some of the non-Communist ministers resigned on February 25th and on March 10th the Foreign Minister, Jan Masaryk, was found dead in the courtyard under the windows of his apartment in the ministry. On March 12, 1948, Secretary of State Marshall sent a Top Secret letter to Inverchapel: "Please inform Mr. Bevin that in accordance with your *aide-memoire* of 11 March, we are prepared to proceed at once in the joint discussions on the establishment of an Atlantic security system."[112] Bevin met with the French and BENELUX foreign ministers in Brussels from 7 March and signed the Treaty of Brussels on 17 March 1948.[113] The treaty set up the Western Union Defence Organization, which was to evolve into NATO. Burgess had been the chief note-taker for the McNeil-led British delegation for the meetings that led to the Brussels Pact.[114]

Burgess told Driberg that he thought the main object of the Brussels meetings was "to set up an international organization strong enough to deal with Communism *in Western Europe*—particularly, of course, in France and Italy, where the communists were so numerous . . . 'the great aim of British policy was to get G.I.s committed to Europe'."[115] A top secret memorandum of March 24, 1948, from Bevin to his colleagues in the Cabinet concerning his conversations with the Foreign Ministers of France, Belgium, the Netherlands and Luxemburg on a number of subjects arising from the treaty includes the following point, which appears to lend some support to Burgess's recollection:

> The second question was that of Communist infiltration. This had been considered by the British Cabinet just before Mr. Bevin left London and his colleagues attached the greatest importance to it. The Prime Minister's statement in the House of Commons on 15th March showed the dangers in the United Kingdom, where infiltration had taken place in some scientific and research institutions and even in the administration itself. He thought that their chief intelligence experts should concert together with a view to overhauling all security questions, including a study of

the methods to prevent the sudden disturbances in factories and workshops by Communist cells. He was convinced that they could learn a great deal from each other on how to proceed.

Information concerning the creation of NATO, which began at Brussels, is among that noted by the Foreign Intelligence Service of the Russian Federation as having been contributed to its predecessor services by Burgess.

The Berlin Crisis was the great Cold War event of 1948/1949. The British and American governments had decided the previous summer to begin the reconstruction of what became West Germany as the economic linch-pin of Western Europe. The London Conferences in the first quarter of 1948 on the future of Germany included Britain, France, the United States, Belgium and the Netherlands, but not the Soviet Union. Once again Burgess played a part in keeping Molotov informed about the cards held by his opponents. According to Modin,

Moscow had fired off several notes of protest and Molotov was ranting in his office. He clamoured for fresh information every day . . . At one point he became seriously overwrought when he spotted a provision in which the British and the Americans appeared to disagree over the future status of Berlin. He wished to know how they planned to get around this . . . Molotov, in his usual way, harassed the KGB for results.

"Do what you like," he said, "but I must know what they're saying to their chiefs. And I also need to know what London and Washington are telling them to do next. And I want this information by six o'clock tonight."

The situation hung fire for a while. The two governments were clearly failing to agree. Molotov's impatience grew by the minute.

Burgess called late that night and gave the agreed code. Korovin [Modin's colleague] met him. I don't know what the substance of the message was, but the fact is that Molotov received the information well before the British delegates, who had to wait until the convened the following day.[116]

The Soviets objected to their exclusion from the London meetings and walked out of the Allied Control Council, ending the post-war arrangements that in theory described a joint military government of all of Germany.

Planning for a new currency for the British, American and French occupation zones, the essential first step in the creation and economic revival of a separate West German state, took place in the first few months of 1948. When the currency was introduced, the Soviet Union objected to what it claimed was a violation of previous agreements and began a blockade of Berlin, which came into effect on the 25th of June. The blockade, and the great Anglo-American Airlift that frustrated it, would continue for nearly a year. The Berlin Airlift, from Bevin's point of view, had the additional virtue of bringing American Air Force back into Europe, extending the de facto borders of the U.S. to the Elbe. Soon the great squares of Berlin were filled with crowds cheering British and American politicians, generals, anti-Communist ex-Communists; crowds of Germans many, if not most of whom, had filled those squares a few years earlier to cheer their Nazi counterparts. Meanwhile, "the US drew up Plan Trojan, targeting 30 Soviet cities for nuclear attack; at the time the USSR had no means to reply."[117] Which may have been why Stalin allowed the Airlift to succeed.

The Berlin Crisis was the context for one of the often-told stories about Burgess's time at the Foreign Office. Bevin had gone to Sandbanks on holiday in the middle of June, 1948. "He had only been away a few days, however, when the Berlin crisis made it necessary for McNeil to call him back to London. A torpedo boat was sent across the Solent to fetch him,"[118] an event memorialized by Burgess, who drew a cartoon of Bevin, huge in the diminutive torpedo boat, crying: "'ector needs me!" McNeil added the proper initial "H" and showed it to Bevin, who was amused. It seems that this was not the only one of Burgess's cartoons passed around the Cabinet table.

The third meeting of the General Assembly of the United

Nations began in Paris on September 21, 1948, "with a series of set speeches from one after another of the leading delegates, with Vyshinsky renewing the two-year-old debate on disarmament. He proposed that each of the five permanent members of the Security Council should cut its armed forces by one-third; that the offensive use of atomic weapons should be banned by treaty," thus claiming the banner of peace, soon to be decorated with Picasso's dove, for the Soviet Union. In a rather curious speech for a Socialist minister, "Bevin . . . addressed the Assembly on 27 September . . . [he] rejected as false and misguided 'the idea that the possession of Colonies is bad in itself, and that colonial Powers cannot be trusted to guide backwards peoples',"[119] as in, for example, Kenya, where a few years later a hundred thousand people would be guided into concentration camps, thousands killed, raped, castrated. Burgess who was with the British delegation to the meeting, caught the attention of Brian Urquhart, who was to become a longtime United Nations official,

> The British team at the Assembly comprised a wide variety of personalities and sexual preferences. Among them the most flamboyant was Guy Burgess [accompanying McNeil], who had long been notorious . . . An evening meeting of the Balkan Subcommittee, which was trying to deal with the violent and chaotic situation on the northern borders of Greece, offered an excellent opportunity for Burgess's propensity to shock. The group consisted of the foreign ministers of Great Britain, Greece and of Greece's Balkan neighbors, the latter being eminently conventional, old-fashioned Communists, and Burgess's appearance one evening drunk and heavily painted and powdered for a night on the town, caused much outrage. When I mentioned this episode to Sir Alexander Cadogan, the head of the British Delegation, he replied icily that the Foreign Office traditionally tolerated innocent eccentricity.[120]

Cadogan, whose aristocratic family owned much of the area around Sloane Square, and who seems to have been the very model of the impeccable inside player in the corridors of Whitehall, had authorized Burgess's abortive attempt to get to Moscow in 1940 and pulled him from the B.B.C. into the Foreign Office in 1944. Perhaps he found Burgess amusing. Or perhaps he valued his work.

That work, for the Foreign Office, as Cadogan knew (or partly knew), had been extensive. Entering the News Department in the Spring of 1944, according to Peregrine Fellowes he had access to the most secret cables, including those concerning discussions about the opening of the Second Front, perhaps the negotiations with General Kesselring in Italy (Allan Dulles's "Operation Sunrise"), which had looked to Stalin so much like a potential reversal of alliances, the preparations for Potsdam, the post-war peace conferences and the founding meetings of the United Nations. The interlude at the IRD familiarized him with that early Cold War organization, its goals, plans, structure and personnel, as well as with the identities and personalities of members of M.I.6 in London and around the Mediterranean (among "the activites of British and American intelligence," information about which he is said to have communicated to Moscow). As McNeil's assistant, Burgess participated in or was familiar with the negotiations concerning the Brussels Treaty, the beginnings of NATO, of the OECD, plans for Germany (including the discussions about whether to send an armored column down the autobahn during the Berlin Crisis), perhaps both the Anglo-American and the Cabinet discussions of the development of atomic weapons. At least that much he knew and gave to his contacts.

Notes to Chapter Six

1 B.B.C. Written Archives Center, Caversham. Staff Records—Guy Burgess.
2 Maclean, Alan. No, I Tell a Lie, It was the Tuesday: A Trudge Round the Life and Times of Alan Maclean. London: Kyle Cathie, Ltd., 1997, p. 68-9.
3 Maclean, pp. 70-1.
4 Maclean, pp. 69-70.
5 Maclean, pp. 71-2. Of course America did have no Government in the British sense of a Cabinet taking collective decisions and assuming collective responsibility for them. John Maynard Keynes summed up his impression of the Government of the United States in this metaphor: "I liken them to bees who for weeks will fly round in all directions . . . providing both the menace of stings and the hope of honey; and at last, perhaps because the queen in the White Hive has emitted some faint, indistinguishable odour, suddenly swarm to a single spot." Skidelsky, Robert. John Maynard Keynes: Fighting for Britain: 1937-1946. London: Papermac, 2001, p. 367. Keynes had found that it was extraordinarily difficult to pinpoint authority in Washington, when (or whether) a decision had been made and who had made it.
6 This and other similar citations are from the *New York Times* of the date indicated.
7 "He was, as I have said and as you pointed out in your obituary, tremendously funny and would keep my father in stitches, making fun of all the people they were working with. There is no doubt that Pa rather loved him and of the three spies he turns out to have known well, Philby, Maclean and Burgess, Guy Burgess was the one whose defection saddened him the most. In fact, he could never bring himself to speak ill of him. When he used to go to Russia on Shell business, after he had left the Foreign Office and joined Shell in the early 1950s, he always dreaded running into Burgess. He was quite Willing to cut either Philby or Maclean dead, both of whom he despised, but he knew that if he saw Burgess, within minutes he would be laughing and it would be impossible to get away. Luckily for him, it never happened." Fellowes, Julian. Private communication via Elisa Segrave, 12 January 2011.
8 "During his work with Soviet Intelligence G. Burgess extracted and handed to us the telegraphic correspondence between the English Ministry of Foreign Affairs and its missions abroad." Foreign Intelligence Service, Russian Federation, http://svr.gov.ru/history/ber.htm

9 Modin, Yuri. With Jean-Chalrles Deniau and Aguieszka Ziarek. Translated by Anthony Roberts. My Five Cambridge Friends: Burges, Maclean, Philby, Blunt, and Cairncross by their KGB Controller. New York: Farrar Straus Gioux, 1994, pp. 44-5. This source should be used with great care. The usual strictures concerning materials from intelligence professionals apply. Many of Modin's statements about matters of which he does not have direct knowledge are demonstrably incorrect. That said, Modin's personal recollections ring true.
10 Donald Maclean was posted to the Washington Embassy in April, 1944. Kim Philby was working for M.I.6, Anthony Blunt for M.I.5, both in London. John Cairncross was at Bletchley Park, working on Enigma as a German language expert.
11 MacGibbon, Hamish. Diary. London Review of Books, 16 June 2011, p. 40.
12 Nicolson, Harold. Diaries in The Vita Sackville-West and Harold Nicolson manuscripts, letters and diaries [microform]: from Sissinghurst Castle, Kent, the Huntington Library, California, and other libraries, reel 14. Wednesday, June 28, 1944.
13 Ritchie, Charles. Undiplomatic Diaries: 1937-1971. Toronto: McClelland & Stewart, 2008, p. 90.
14 Gillies, Donald. Radical Diplomat: The Life of Archibald Clark Kerr, Lord Inverchapel, 1882-1951. I. B. Tauris: London, 1999, p. 161.
15 According to Anthony Eden, the naughty proposal was first raised with Stalin by Eden, not Churchill. Nicolson, Harold. Diaries in The Vita Sackville-West and Harold Nicolson manuscripts, letters and diaries [microform], reel 14, December 20, 1944. "Naughty" is a curious way to describe a *realpolitik* agreement of this magnitude.
16 Nicolson, Harold. Diaries and Letters: The War Years, 1939-1945. Edited by Nigel Nicolson. Atheneum: New York, 1967, p. 439.
17 "Returning to the 'Cambridge Five'—Triumph or Failure?" Newsletter, April 3, 2008, Foreign Intelligence Service, Russian Federation, http://svr.gov.ru/smi/2008/argned20080403.htm
18 National Archives, Kew, CAB 120/691.
19 Nicolson, Harold. Diaries in The Vita Sackville-West and Harold Nicolson manuscripts, letters and diaries [microform], reel 14, Monday, April 16, 1945.

[20] Nicolson, Harold. Diaries in The Vita Sackville-West and Harold Nicolson manuscripts, letters and diaries [microform], reel 14, Tuesday, June 5, 1945.

[21] October 21, 1945. Carter, Miranda. Anthony Blunt: His Lives. London: Macmillan, 2001, pp. 323-4.

[22] Carter, Miranda. Anthony Blunt: His Lives. London: Macmillan, 2001, p. 324.

[23] Kynaston, David. Austerity Britain: 1945-51. London: Bloomsbury, 2007, p. 21.

[24] Kynaston, p. 64.

[25] Kynaston, p. 39.

[26] Kynaston, p. 80.

[27] Beckett, Francis: Clem Attlee: A Biography. Politico's Publishing: London, 2000, p. 218.

[28] Bullock, Alan. Ernest Bevin: Foreign Secretary 1945-1951. London: W.W. Norton & Company, 1983, p. 11.

[29] Beckett, p. 221.

[30] See, for example, Henderson, Nicholas. The Private Office Revisited. London: Profile Books, 2001; Roberts, Frank. Dealing with Dictators: The Destruction and Revival of Europe 1930-70. London: Weidenfeld & Nicolson, 1991; Bullock, Alan. Ernest Bevin: Foreign Secretary 1945-1951. London: W.W. Norton & Company, 1983.

[31] In early September, 1945, Burgess had dinner with Pollock and Nicolson at the Greek Restaurant and then they went on to the Gargoyle, where they encountered the unusually sober Philip Toynbee and the as usual very drunk Dylan Thomas. Burgess told Nicolson
Bevin may regard his task as too easy believing as he does that Trades Union fraternity extends beyond all boundaries. He says that Bevin consults the F.O. staff consistently—and that he is very pleased with them. "Even in the Ministry of Labour I never had a staff equal to this". ...In regard to Greece he is 100% in favour of Anthony [Eden]'s policy.

[32] Peter Weiler, British Labour and the Cold War: The Foreign Policy of the Labour Governments, 1945-1951, The Journal of British Studies, Vol. 26, No. 1, England's Foreign Relations (Jan., 1987), pp. 54-82.

[33] Beckett, p. 219.

[34] FRUS, 1947, Volume III, p. 1073.

---

35 Weinberg, Gerhard L. Visions of Victory: The Hopes of Eight World War II Leaders. Cambridge: University Press, 2005, pp. 175ff.

36 Bullock, p. 15.

37 Kynaston, pp. 133-4.

38 New York Times, April 6, 1946.

39 Bullock, p. 122.

40 Bullock, p. 273.

41 Burgess, Simon. Stafford Cripps: A Political Life. London: Victor Gollancz, 1999, p. 219.

42 Bullock, p. 312.

43 Henderson, pp. 59-61.

44 National Archives, UK, FO 366/1739.

45 Driberg, Tom. Guy Burgess: A Portrait with Background. London: Weidenfeld and Nicolson, 1956, 62.

46 Hennessy, Peter. The Secret State: Preparing for the Worst, 1945-2010. Second Edition. London: Penguin Books, 2010, pp. 50-1.

47 Bullock, p. 315.

48 Bullock, p. 327.

49 Alsop, Susan Mary Patton. To Marietta from Paris: 1945-1960. Doubleday & Company: Garden City, New York, 1975, pp. 130-1. The original of this letter is missing from the archive at Harvard that, interestingly, contains all the others in the correspondence.

50 Matthews, Herbert L. Mr. McNeil of Downing Street. The New York Times, December, 29, 1946, p. 89.

51 Bullock, p. 246.

52 The authority here for this question of Burgess's access to materials is the Foreign Intelligence Service of the Russian Federation: http://svr.gov.ru/history/ber.htm

53 Beckett, p. 232.

54 Bullock, p. 57.

55 Henderson, p. 2.

56 Bullock, pp. 290-1.

57 Bullock, p. 291.

58 Henderson, pp. 10-11.

59 Noted specifically by the Russian Foreign Intelligence Service as having been made available to their predecessor organization by Burgess.

60 I am indebted to the kindness of Mr. Paul Heardman, private secretary to the Minister of State for Europe, for this information.

61 Modin, p. 130. Modin describes the process as follows: "Burgess, operating from his post as Hector McNeil's private secretary, was supplying regular consignments, giving us full access to the documents of a number of partilamentary committees and to the secrets of the Ministry of Defence . . . Going over all this required unfailing concentration. I wore gloves to avoid leaving fingerprints on the paper, and translated the texts with all the accuracy I could muster. I typed the transcripts up myself, stamped them and passed them on to the KGB resident for signature. There were then put into cipher and telegrammed to the Centre, while the borrowed document was returned to the safe or desk it had come from" p. 143.

62 Henderson, p. xvi.

63 For Burgess's view of the operations of the Private Office and the influence of Foreign Office officials on Bevin, see Driberg, p. 63-7.

64 Modin, p. 130.

65 Dorril. Stephen. M.I.6: 50 Years of Special Operations. London: Fourth Estate, 2000), p. 68. I owe this reference to Elaine Alahendra, Historians Team, FCO. It is difficult to understand how Dorril knew that Burgess had made a copy of the key. It seems more likely he was given one, as useful for his duties.

66 Sir Frederick Warner, quoted in Boyle, Andrew. The Fourth Man: The Fourth Man: The Definitive Account of Kim Philby, Guy Burgess, and Donald Maclean and Who Recruited Them to Spy for Russia. The Dial Press/James Wade, 1979, p. 279-83.

67 Isherwood, Christopher. Diaries, Volume One, 1939-1960. Edited and Introduced by Katherine Bucknell. Michael di Capua Books. HarperFlamingo, 1996, p. 391.

68 Isherwood, Christopher. Lost Years: A memoir. Edited and Introduced by Katherine Bucknell HarperCollins, 2000, p. 99-100.

69 National Archives, UK, CSC 11/38 Z 172650.

70 Hennessy, p. 93-4.

71 Burgess, Simon [no relation]. Stafford Cripps: A Political Life. London: Victor Gollancz, 1999, Chapter 12.

72 Gopal, Sarvepalli. Jawaharlal Nehru: A Biography. Volue I: 1889-1947. Cambridge, MA.: Harvard University Press, 1976, p. 312.

73 Beckett, pp. 240-1.

74 Bullock, p. 360.

---

75 Bullock, p. 243, citing COS Report, Strategic Position of the British Commonwealth, D.O. (46) 47 of 2 April 1946.

76 National Archives, UK, FO 800/476.

77 "Everyone here has been depressed by the failure of the London [Conference of Foreign Ministers]. While the Russian stubbornness worries us, my friend [Nicholas] Nabokov, who has been living in the Russian Zone, tells me that the Russian officers are terrified of an imperialist war by England and America against them and feel that they are on the defensive." Alsop, Susan Mary. Letters to Marietta, p. 51.

78 Perhaps the early Soviet support for the state of Israel was linked to the role Israel played in blocking plans for a great British base in Palestine.

79 Bullock, pp. 369-70.

80 Newton, C. C. S. The Sterling Crisis of 1947 and the British Response to the Marshall Plan. The Economic History Review, New Series, Vol. 37, No. 3. (Aug., 1984), p. 393.

81 Newton, p. 399.

82 FRUS, 1947, Volume V, p. 30.

83 Bullock, p. 378.

84 Bullock, p. 372.

85 CAB/128/9.

86 Bullock, p. 359.

87 Bullock, p. 381.

88 Burgess, Simon., p. 230.

89 Bullock, p. 396.

90 Newton, p. 400.

91 Newton, p. 401.

92 Bullock, p. 442.

93 Presumably a reference to the installation of Communist governments in France and Italy. FRUS, 1947, Volume II, p. 48.

94 Newton, p. 394.

95 "At the start of 1950 one-third of America's exports of $16 billion were being financed through foreign assistance; once this assistance was terminated the problems of 1947 would quickly reappear. . . In the end, it was the rearmament programme, started early in 1950 and given a powerful impetus by the Korean War, which reduced the dollar gap to a manageable level . . . for a decade the extravagance and relish with which the United

States played the role of world policeman after 1950 did much to stimulate international economic expansion." Newton, pp. 407-08.
[96] Bullock, p. 418.
[97] Modin, pp. 151-2.
[98] Modin, pp. 152-3.
[99] Morgan, Ted. A Covert Life: Jay Lovestone: Communist, Anti-Communist, and Spymaster. New York: Random House, 1999, p. 181.
[100] Modin, pp. 158-9. Modin's account has since been substantiated, at least in part:

> Early in the morning of June 30, Molotov received important information, which showed the Western powers' position in an extremely disadvantageous light, in a ciphered cable sent by Soviet Deputy Foreign Minister Andrei Vyshinsky. The information had been supplied through the channels of the Soviet intelligence service. The cable, alluding to London sources, informed Molotov that as a result of meetings between U.S. Under Secretary of State Clayton and British ministers, an agreement was reached on the following:
>
>> a) Britain and the USA agreed that the Marshall Plan should be regarded as a plan for the reconstruction of Europe, not as assistance to Europe, and that it should not be a continuation of UNRRA [United Nations Relief and Rehabilitation Administration).
>> b) Britain and the USA have agreed that the reconstruction of Europe may be achieved by setting up of a series of functional committees for coal, steel, transport, agriculture and food, under the leadership of one main committee.
>> c) Any organization set up for the realization of the Marshall Plan should operate outside the United Nations framework. That is explained by the fact that Germany is not a member of the United Nations Organization.
>> d) Britain and the USA believe that Germany is still the key to the European economy. Therefore it is, in fact, one of the bases of any plan for rehabilitation of the continent.
>> e) ...Britain and America will oppose payment of [German] reparations to the Soviet Union from the current production.

> Throughout this period the Soviet leadership had well-placed informants of a special nature in the British Foreign Office. Thus Moscow's privileged information from these espionage sources about the principal results of Clayton's London conversations was accurate.

Narinsky, Mikhail, "The Soviet Union and the Marshall Plan," in "New Evidence on the Soviet Rejection of the Marshall Plan, 1947: Two Reports," Cold War International History Project Working Paper Series, No. 9, Washington D.C., March 1994, p. 45.

[101] Department of State (Ed.). A Decade of American Foreign Policy, Basic Documents 1941-1949. Washington: Department of State Printing Office, 1985, pp. 807-809.

[102] Archives historiques des Communautés européennes, Florence, Villa Il Poggiolo. Dépôts, DEP. Organisation de coopération et de développement économiques, OECD. Committee for European Economic Co-operation, CEEC. CEEC 03, Address given by Ernest Bevin (Paris, 22 September 1947).

[103] Bullock, pp. 484-5.

[104] Bullock, p. 502.

[105] Bullock, p. 269.

[106] Alsop, p. 113.

[107] Isaiah Berlin Papers, Special Collections & Western MSS., Bodleian Library, Oxford University. It may or may not be significant that this is the only letter from this year in Berlin's files.

[108] Liddell, Diaries, National Archives, KV4/467ff, February 20, 1948.

[109] Carter, Miranda. Anthony Blunt: His Lives. London: Macmillan, 2001, p. 132.

[110] Lashmar, Paul and James Oliver. Britain's Secret Propaganda War. Sutton Publishing Limited, Phoenix Mill, Thrupp, Stroud, Gloucestershire, U.K., 1995, pp. 24-31; Aldrich, Richard James. British Intelligence, strategy, and the cold war, 1945-51. Routledge, London and New York, 1992, p. 94.

[111] Bullock, p. 522.

[112] Bullock, p. 530.

[113] Jebb, Gladwyn. The Memoirs of Lord Gladwyn. New York: Weybright and Talley, Inc., 1972, p. 213.

[114] Driberg, p. 78.

292

[115] Driberg, p. 78.
[116] Modin, pp. 155.
[117] Johnson, R. W. "Living on the Edge," London Review of Books, 28 April 2011, p. 32.
[118] Bullock, p. 575.
[119] Bullock, p. 605.
120 Urquhart, Brian, A Life in Peace and War. New York: Harper & Row, 1987, p. 117.

Chapter Seven

Foreign Service: Far East and Washington

McNeil, wishing to further his protégé's career in the Foreign Office, decided that Burgess should have experience beyond the Minister of State's private office. Therefore, on November 1, 1948, Burgess was assigned as a regular, established, Foreign Service Officer to the Far Eastern Department of the Foreign Office, under Peter Scarlett, who reported, in his turn, to Under-Secretary Sir Esler Denning. Instead of sitting at the right hand of a Minister of State, Burgess was now the junior member of a group of four Foreign Office staff specializing in China, minuting files containing correspondence from British officials in China and contributing to the drafting of replies. Burgess had no experience with Far Eastern matters; for that matter, neither had Peter Scarlett. But Burgess had an intense interest in the Chinese revolution and the Foreign Office's Far Eastern Department offered a privileged perspective on the culminating months of the civil war between the Kuomintang and the Communist Party.

Beginning as early as mid-January 1949, Burgess's annotations in the Foreign Office "jackets," folders containing the background to, and successive drafts of, documents, provide a running commentary on Chinese events and the statements of the Chinese Communist Party with reference to the Cominform and the various attitudes and histories of the Soviet and other Communist parties. Burgess's annotations in the files at the National Archives are often followed by Peter Scarlett's "I agree." According to Edwin Martin, whose work is the standard account of Anglo-American policy in regard to China, "Guy Burgess was the Far Eastern Department's resident expert on the Soviet Union and Sino-Soviet relations . . . Burgess's views on China appear to have been generally accepted at the time by his colleagues in the Far Eastern Department."[1]

At the end of January, inviting comment from the I.R.D., with which he seems to have been on good terms, Burgess mentioned the pre-occupation of the Soviet representative to the U.N., Vyshinsky, with the Chinese Communist Party and the progress of the civil war in China. *   In February, in regard to military action in Yunnan, in the far south, Burgess observed that: "The situation in Yunnan . . . is one of political tide turning before coat turning had begun . . . In fact it looks as though the effort of the CCP to organize and develop its strength in Yunnan that was advocated & outlined in the documents captured in Hong Kong is proceeding according to plan."[2]   The following month, we have a rather lengthy appreciation of the Soviet attitudes toward the Chinese Revolution as presented in a lecture by a certain Professor Gluschakov. Burgess commented:

> I think in view of the nakedness of the land that this public lecture on Chinese Affairs delivered in Moscow is worth reflective attention.
>
> We must assume that Comrade Professor Gluschakov' remarks were laid on . . . because even the Soviet intelligentsia is kicking at the relative silence of the Soviet press on Communist triumphs in the largest country in the world and the one which, after Germany, has attracted the most intensive Stalinist theoretical speculation in the past.
>
> That the lecture is so (deliberately) perfunctory and cautious could provide a small argument in favour of those who argue that the Kremlin was not quite ready for the CCP's triumph or quite certain of the loyalty of its organisers. This is supported by Chancery's letter (within) which points out as of "special

---

* As we have seen, many of Burgess's annotations indicating that documents received or created by the Far Eastern section should be copied to Paton at I.R.D. and in at least one instance, Paton minuted his thanks, which hardly supports the stories from Mayhew and others that Burgess had been thrown out of the I.R.D.

interest" that "good generals" are placed "before the party line in the explanation of the successes of the Liberation Army" . . . On the other hand this might well be explained quite naturally be the context of this placing – which is military. The lecture, however, is only reported from notes which do not appear to be very full ones. Other points of interest seem to be-

I.   that "the Chinese people under the leadership of the Communist Party" are stated to have "saved China from the Japanese." This is in contradiction to the usual Soviet line that it was the Red Army who, in a brilliant if short campaign, beat the Japanese. And also by its emphasis on the CCP rather than the army, let alone generals, to Chancery's argument . . .

II.   para starred X is the basic Stalinist theoretical line on China.

III.   the width of the popular front is stressed . . . It is in fact wider than any other popular front that has ever been attempted for revolutionary purposes.

IV.   the stressing of the validity of the Sino-Soviet Treaty . . . contradicts a recent (but unproved) CCP attack on it.

V.   It is not clear from this report whether the statement "perhaps China would go (to Communism) by its own path" was meant as an admission or as an analysis.[3]

The distribution list again included the I.R.D.

Commenting on a report of a meeting of the Communist Student Congress in Peking, Burgess observed:

The pattern and political aims of the all China Student Congress follows in general the line of Communist Youth movements the world over. The China Student movement is perhaps of particular importance:

1) Because the C.C.P. in a backward country must and is relying on recruitment of technical and administrative cadres, of which it is woefully short, from the student movement . . .

2) because of the role the student intelligentsia always played in the Chinese, as in the Russian, revolutionary movement. It is no accident that the C.C.P. was founded simultaneously in China and in Paris – the headquarters of the student movement from the

'20's onwards.

3) This and the scale is indicated by the statement that "during the anti-Japanese war more than 10000 students went to Yunnan from K.M.T. areas many of whom had emerged to be key political and administrative cadres before the civil war broke out in 1946".

4) The students have been a useful link with the villages in the past. Now that towns are for the first time being taken over they will have a new and more important role . . . already "mass student movement who have taken over cities" is being spoken of. In Peking 5000 students organized propaganda teams after the liberation to propel the new regime which has been able to recruit 480 of them to fill its administrative shortage.

There have been hints in other papers that the centralizing and organizing apparatus for the Asiatic functions of the world student movement hitherto being controlled from Paris and Prague is being passed to China. Thus China may become the centre for S.E. Asia, throughout which, I shld. Imagine, student movements are also of political importance.

When the North Atlantic Pact was signed on April 4, Burgess noted: "Peking, the seat of the CCP, was immediate in broadcasting the CCP's advance support for the USSR in the event of war with the Atlantic Powers." (In March, 1949, the U.S. Strategic Air Command's War Plan I-49 "envisaged B-29 and B-50 bombers dropping 133 nuclear bombs on 70 Soviet cities, killing three million civilians and injuring four million more."[4]) Unlike similar statements by Maurice Thorez and Palmiro Togliatti on behalf of the French and Italian Communist parties, Burgess pointed out, the Chinese statement was not hedged about with conditions.[5]

As the Korean crisis developed, Burgess as a matter of course saw reports about Korea from military intelligence and from the Supreme Command Allied Powers Tokyo, General MacArthur's headquarters in the Far East. For example, "On 5 April he commented on a secret report from the War Office which contained 'a summary of all information received concerning Russian assistance to the Chinese communist forces'."[6]   In some cases Burgess's notes refer to information he has received from the British Joint Intelligence Committee (JIC), the summit of the British intelligence organization. He "wrote a memo on 29 April in which he noted that the papers available to him 'contain the JIC . . . view[s] on the nature of Russian air assistance'"[7] to China.

Later that Spring, Burgess drafted a letter, for Scarlett's signature, to J. P. Coghill, British Embassy Representative in Canton, in response to one from the latter. Burgess's draft was sent off unchanged:

Dear Coghill,

Thank you for your letter of the 26th May and for the queries raised in it. As you say the questions being both speculative and theological (Communist) might be discussed at great length. Like you I will try to be brief. Taking your points in order-

(a) It is not only on the stand the Chinese Communists took on the side of the Cominform against Tito that we base our opinion that they speak with the voice of the Kremlin. You make the point that this is natural "where the Chinese Communists have no natural interest". This point was also made by Peter Fleming in his second China article. We believe it to be misguided. To take only the example alluded to in the INTEL 198. The Chinese Communists were early, if not the first, in the field in denouncing the Atlantic Pact. They broadcast about it on the very night of its signature. Now what more "vital interest" can a party struggling for power in the course of a prolonged civil war have than to promise a perspective at least of external peace, once internal victory has been secured. Or at any rate to avoid hinting at war. Not so the Chinese Communist leaders. They went further than even Togliatti and Thorez (who not being in power or immediate hope of it have after all less to lose) and told the Chinese people that in the event of war, for which the Atlantic Pact was a preparation, China would "march with the Soviet Union", in a quarrel, that is, in no sense Chinese but purely ideological, and in respect of a pact that does not, be it noted, touch the Far East.

(b) On this point I entirely agree with your criticism. This section of the intel. was, for your personal information, severely challenged here by Northern Department, and we also have criticised this theory elsewhere. There is some evidence for it (it has been advanced in Cominform circles) but we do not agree.

(c) The word "perhaps" was meant as an important qualification. The Chinese Communist Leaders have themselves stated publicly that they will be assisted by the Union of Soviet Socialist Republics and privately, as revealed by the Secret report of the plenary of the Chinese Communist Party Central Committee which we captured in Hong Kong, it looks as though they assumed the same thing.

As regard the second half of your paragraph though it is not my line of country, surely certain satellites have been assisted. For instance Poland was given quite a lot of rather expensive aid (even if this was only the price paid to keep her out of the Marshall plan) We also know from most secret (but not most reliable) reports that there is much fear in Prague that Soviet industrial exports to Czechoslovakia might be cut down in favour of Communist China's superior claims.

(d) The important word is eventual. That is, our speculation is about the ultimate intention – it may not be for a decade or so. Such would be orthodox Marxism. Even so this would not apply to trade, as apart from concessions etc., what was said in the intel. was not in fact meant to exclude the argument you advance, with which I agree.

What will happen in the future none of us know. At the moment we think the Chinese Communist Part is orthodox. In this opinion we are supported by the Bolshevik monthly, "October".[8]

There is much more of this in the National Archives at Kew: notes, comments, drafts—exactly the sort of thing that one would expect to find in the normal course of events from a junior, but respected, foreign service officer going to work each day in the Foreign Office, sitting at his desk, reading all the relevant cables from the Far East, from secret intelligence sources, from American diplomatic and military sources.

Burgess's expertise on Chinese affairs was utilized by the Foreign Office beyond his work in the Far East department. He was a lecturer at a Foreign Office summer school at Oxford in the summer of 1949, subsequent to the UK decision to recognize the People's Republic.[9] That Spring he had lectured M.I.5 and M.I.6 officers on China. Arthur Martin, a [then] recent recruit to M.I.5 recalled: "I heard him talk about China. Burgess was clearly a clever boy. But it was more than that. He had a magnetic personality."[10]

Burgess's quintessential "insider" status in a different London world was certified in June, 1949, when "an exceptionally large number of Apostles and 'Angels,'" twenty-five to thirty of this segment of Britain's elite, attended the annual dinner of the Apostles Society, with Burgess presiding, at his particular club, the RAC. The principal speaker was the Bloomsbury figure, Desmond MacCarthy. Eric Hobsbawm, who was there, remembered that Burgess made it clear on this occasion that he was a Marxist.[11] (But of course so were most of the Cabinet.) Given Burgess's public aspirations, hosting the Society's annual dinner was an apotheosis.

And then, in classical fashion: Nemesis. During an argument about Spain Fred Warner knocked Burgess down the staircase of "a West End club." The club was probably the RAC.* Burgess said that

---

* Goronwy Rees, in his series of articles in the newspaper *The People*, sets the accident in Le Boeuf sur let Toit, but that too neatly fits Rees's, or *The People's*, purpose. In any case, why would Fred Warner have been in a gay nightclub? On the other hand, Mrs. Bassett thought the staircase in question was in the Foreign Office. The RAC is a likely compromise.

his "head had been broken in three places," skull fractures, accompanied by a severe concussion. Recovery from an injury of this type takes a year or more and leaves lingering effects, including disinhibition, excitability, unusual sensitivity to alcohol and other personality issues. It took Burgess some years to recover, if he ever did. He never functioned well after that, was often in pain, was given drugs by his physicians and found others, drank more and became more susceptible to the effects of drinking. His friends, his mother and even his step-father became worried about him. His Russian contacts were worried as well. He knew so much. They were beginning to think their Cambridge network was winding down. Donald Maclean, now in Egypt, was having a nervous breakdown, drinking too much, causing scenes that could not be kept secret. According to Modin, Maclean at this time wrote a note to Moscow Center, asking to be taken with his family to Russia. He was ignored.

> At the same time, much the same thing was happening to Burgess . . . I saw him weakening psychologically and physically, before my eyes. We at the London residence became aware at an early stage that he had begun to drink seriously. He was frequently drunk in public, unshaven, ill-dressed and incoherent . . . He was supplying less and less information.[12]

Harold Nicolson, not knowing of, or perhaps not appreciating, the significance of Burgess's injuries, assumed its effects to be solely the result of alcoholism, as did (and have) many others.[13]

*   *   *

In spite of its Socialist Government, Britain in 1949 remained in many ways a country of strictly limited personal freedom. Attlee had approved a "purge" of Communists in the Civil Service; the press, publishing, and the theatre were tightly controlled and, of course, homosexuality was illegal. During a Brains Trust program on the B.B.C. on May 24th, 1949, Harold Nicolson had rather bravely answered the question "What existing legislation should be repealed?" by suggesting that covering sex offences.[14] The legal handicaps of people who engaged in homosexual activities were compounded by the prejudiced attitudes and actions of some people who did not, or did not admit, that they engaged in homosexual activities. This official homophobia, or the homophobia of some officials, combined with the behavioral consequences of Burgess's injuries to end his Foreign Office career.

On July 16th, 1949, Burgess telephoned Guy Liddell "to say that there had been a proposal to close down the China News Agency."

> He had said that he did not think there was any possibility of doing this unless it was inciting people to acts of violence. He wanted my confirmation. I said that that would be my view.

> He then apologised for having been responsible for the trouble about the Chinese documents from Hong Kong, which indicated that the Chinese might attempt to eliminate the currency of the Hong Kong Shanghai Bank in Southern China. He fully realised that the fault lay entirely with the Foreign Office representatives in Singapore, who had had a copy of the documents at the earliest possible moment.

> I explained to Burgess the difficulties which we were encountering in Hong Kong vis a vis the Police.[15]

In November, 1949, Burgess went on leave, traveling to Tangier and neighboring Gibraltar, traveling, as usual, with his mother. The memoirs of an M.I.6 officer, Desmond Bristow include the following description of a conflict with the frankly homophobic local M.I.6 representatives. Bristow recalled that Kenneth Mills, the M.I.6 representative in Gibraltar, had telephoned him in Madrid, where Bristow was chief of station. "'Desmond, do you know a chap called Guy Burgess?' he asked."

> "Yes, unfortunately I do know the little poof—not well, I might add. The little shit is a friend of Philby's and Tommy Harris's. God knows why they like him . . . Why do you ask?'

'He's here in Gib, claiming that he's a good friend of Philby, that he knows you and is personal assistant to Sir Hector McNeil, and has asked me to change money for him. When I said I would have to check with you first, he went on to explain that he was on very friendly terms with Guy Liddell [then deputy director of M.I.5], and did I know Dick White . . . Again I told him I would have to check with you. Well, he continued rattling on, then he started asking questions, persistently, and generally behaved like an insidious little bastard. What really rocked me was the way he slanged off the Americans, and expressed great admiration for Mao Tse Tung. Tell me, what do I do?'

In a very exasperated tone, I replied, "Fuck him! On second thoughts, no, he'd probably enjoy that. Just chuck him out; even though he is in the FO."

'Don't exchange any money or do anything . . . We must not get involved?' asked Ken.

'No bloody fear,' said I.

Bristow thought at the time, and nearly half a century later, that it was perfectly appropriate, in an official conversation, to refer to a fellow official as a "little poof" (Burgess was nearly six feet tall and more heavy than not, for whatever that is worth) and to make a joke about it, and to refuse him the perfectly reasonable request for check cashing privileges apparently simply on the basis of Burgess's sexual preferences and closer adherence to the foreign policy attitudes of the Government of the day than those in favour in his sector of M.I.6 And, of course, while trying to establish his bona fides with references to McNeil, Liddell and the others, Burgess had not exaggerated (although Bristow seems to have misremembered the tense of the reference to McNeil).

Bristow continued: "A week or two later, it must have been early January 1950, the telephone rang. It was Teddy Dunlop [another M.I.6 officer] calling from Tangier. 'Hello, Desmond, I have a problem in the name of Guy Burgess. He's rude, keeps pestering me for money and generally behaving in an appalling fashion.' He sounded very irritated."

'Well, for a start don't give him a penny and keep him out of the office.'

'But Desmond, he knows everyone! How can I just have him kicked out?

'I don't know,' I replied. 'Maybe he's an FO agent spying on us,' I added jokingly.

'Well, if that's the case he should not have gone around broadcasting the name of the Swiss diplomat who allowed the British to use the Swiss diplomatic bag to bring rare pieces of equipment and information out of Switzerland.' He continued with more horrifying news about Burgess. 'Also he should not have pinched Harry Dean's Arab bum boy. He has created one hell of a scandal and that alone has really fixed him in Tangier.' (Harry owned a famous bar in Tangier and was a roaring queer – but a very likeable chap, who was well known in the area and had a lot of powerful friends. Burgess had set the gays of Tangier alight, it seemed.)

Teddy was very concerned. The [homosexual] Tangier community was scandalized by the behaviour of this member of the British Foreign Service. I told Teddy to collaborate with Ken and send a report to head office. Ken sent his report to M.I.5, in which he boldly stated that Burgess should not be in the employ of the Foreign Office let alone be a personal assistant for a minister of the Crown. Teddy sent a report to me and I sent my report to head office (M.I.6) with a covering report to the Foreign Office . . . In February 1950 Ken had to go to England on personal business; on arrival he was called to a meeting with Guy Liddell and Bernard Hill, M.I.5's legal adviser.

Liddell did not wish to transmit the report to the Foreign Office, but Hill insisted.[1]* The Foreign Office reprimanded Burgess.[16]

In March, 1950, Bristow met with David Footman, his supervisor at SIS, whose assistant told Bristow that he had not forwarded Bristow's report on Spanish Communism to the Foreign Office. Footman said: "'I was just preparing a note asking you to explain why Pat Todd should be kept on; he seems very pro-Franco to me . . . Oh, by the way, I do not think you or your colleagues should write reports about other colleagues.'" Bristow recalled replying: "'Listen, Footman; one, Burgess is no colleague of mine or of any of us in SIS for that matter and therefore should be no colleague of yours.' . . . 'All I am trying to say, is that we must not act as if we are Gestapo!'"[17] Given that SIS *is* administratively part of the Foreign Office, Footman was correct, and Bristow wrong, about their being colleagues. And one can only imagine what the literally pro-Fascist, homophobic, Bristow would have thought if he had known that Footman and Burgess had been on friendly terms for more than a decade, not to mention Liddell, that frequenter of Bentinck Street. Nonetheless, Burgess's mental and physical condition was deteriorating and he had made powerful enemies in the British secret intelligence services.

The rotations of Foreign Office personnel in the summer of 1950 sent Donald Maclean, who had been on leave in England after his breakdown in Cairo, to be head of the American Department in London, frequently a perch from which ambassadors were plucked.[18] Burgess, to his consternation, learned on May 9th that he had been appointed to the British embassy in Washington and on May 17th he

---

* There is a story that Burgess, Mills and Dunlop, while drinking together in Gibraltar, had gotten into an argument about Spain, which Dunlop and Mills supported. It should be noted that it was not, at the time, the policy of Attlee's Socialist Government to favor fascist Spain. In other words, Burgess was supporting the policy of his Government, while the SIS men were publicly opposing it. In the course of the argument, Burgess publicly referred to Mills and Dunlop as British secret intelligence officers, a serious violation and, perhaps, an example of the disinhibition consequent on his injuries. Or he was too drunk to care. Or both.

was officially notified that the enquiry conducted into SIS's complaint about the Gibraltar affair had been terminated.[19] As if to underline the defeat of the efforts of Desmond Bristow and his friends in this matter, David Footman and Guy Liddell attended Burgess's going-away party, which also included Burgess's former roommates Patricia Parry (Mrs. Richard Llewellyn-Davies), Teresa Mayer (Mrs. Victor Rothschild), Anthony Blunt and Jack Hewit; Countess Rohan (a society hostess popular with the mothers of Burgess and Maclean); Hector McNeil, now the Secretary of State for Scotland; James Pope-Hennessy and others, including Goronwy Rees: a Cabinet minister, a Rothschild, a future Baroness, the Surveyor of the King's Pictures, a society hostess, a well-known author or two or three, the group "placed" Burgess, if not at the center, only slightly off-center, in the London society of the day.[20]

It is not clear why the Foreign Office sent Burgess to Washington, rather than, say, Peking or Tokyo, which would seem to have been the obvious postings. It was well known in Whitehall that Burgess made no effort, and would make no effort, to conceal his homosexuality, his Marxism or his objections to American foreign policy and domestic politics. And many of his colleagues, particularly those involved with personnel decisions, would have been aware that he was not well. Under similar circumstances they had recently granted Donald Maclean an extensive period of leave. Perhaps it was simply a bureaucratic, functional decision. Britain was about to recognize the new Chinese government; the American government would be interested in the rationale for this; Burgess was the Foreign Office's expert on Chinese Communism. His friends did what they could to protect him: Philby, now as M.I.6's representative in Washington, a First Secretary in the Embassy, put him up in his house in Washington and, as we shall see, Donald Maclean's younger brother Alan gave him hospitality in his New York apartment when Burgess visited that city.

The American monopoly of atomic weapons, jealously kept from the British, in spite of the Quebec agreements, had ended in September, 1949, when the Soviet Union tested an atomic bomb.

The Korean War began on June 25, 1950, following the failure of efforts to hold reunification elections on the peninsula and increasing hostilities between the two governments claiming it. Two days later Gladwyn Jebb, who had tried to send Isaiah Berlin and Burgess to Moscow in 1940, arrived in New York as British Permanent Representative on the Security Council of the United Nations. Jebb found the atmosphere in the United States that summer "dangerous and quite explosive . . . the majority of the American people were convinced that they would be before long at war with the USSR."[21] It was a psychological atmosphere similar in kind, if not in degree, to that in Berlin in 1933, Leningrad in 1937. The United States to which Burgess had been sent was in the grip of the early stages of a two-decade-long "Great Fear": persecutions intended to drive from public life everyone who, in Great Britain, would have been members of the Socialist Government and, of course, those to their left. At his going-away party, Hector McNeil had tried to warn Burgess of what lay ahead for him: "There are three basic don'ts, Guy, to bear particularly in mind when you're dealing with Americans.

> The first is Communism, the second is homosexuality, and the third is the colour bar. Do please memorize them, won't you?" Burgess smiled his seraphic smile and at once quipped back: "I've got it, Hector, so there, don't worry. What you're trying to say in your nice, long-winded way is − 'Guy, for God's sake don't make a pass at Paul Robeson.'"[22]

Phrased as a joke, this did sum up, in terms of the hatred of men like Senator Eastland for the great Black singer, actor and athlete, who was the frequent spokesperson for the Popular Front and Communist Party, the accelerating purge of dissidents and marginalized groups in the United States. The Republican majority in Congress (and its Dixiecrat allies) were determined to reverse the New Deal and to drive its supporters from public life, out of the country or into prison. The purges, which did not discriminate among Communists, minorities and homosexuals, focused in particular on Jews, still subjected to restrictions on where they could live, where they could go to college, which occupations they could pursue and in which hotels they could stay, and, of course, on African-Americans: throughout the South disenfranchised, held in debt peonage, which has been called slavery by another name; in the North restricted to living in ghettos and working, for the most part, as manual laborers and servants. Homosexuals, of any race or religion, were equated with Communists, hounded from government employment and harassed by the police.

Thanks to the assiduousness of the Federal Bureau of Investigation, for Burgess's time in Washington we have what occasionally seems to be a day-by-day record of his travels and encounters with individuals in the United States.

Kim Philby was then a First Secretary at the Washington Embassy, duties unspecified in the Foreign Office list (indicating to all who knew how to read such documents that those duties were as M.I.6 station chief). He lived at 4100 Nebraska Avenue, near American University: then and now a good neighborhood. It was a large house, necessarily, containing Kim and Aileen, their four children, one a baby, a Scotch nanny and Philby's secretary, who lived in an attic room. A room was created in the basement for Burgess.[23] Given Burgess's physical condition (it must have been about this time or a few months earlier that he was diagnosed with diabetes), his habits and the protection afforded by Philby's status, it was a sensible arrangement to which Burgess accommodated himself as best he could. "The Philby children . . . remember 'Uncle Guy' as a generous but slightly alarming figure smelling strongly of alcohol and tobacco.

> His thick fingers with heavily bitten nails were yellow with nicotine and constantly employed in making repairs to John Philby's 'O' gauge electric train set which occupied a place of honour, covering most of Burgess's room in the basement. Burgess, who was always bringing presents home for the children, including a large wig-wam, was fascinated by the trains and spent hours playing with them.[24]

On arrival at the embassy in the first week of August, Burgess had found an invitation to spend the following weekend at Highlands, the eighteenth-century estate, famous for its gardens, of Nicholas and Emily Sinkler Roosevelt, in Montgomery County, Pennsylvania, near Philadelphia. Nicholas Roosevelt, a retired investment banker, was a cousin of Franklin Roosevelt.   Mrs. Roosevelt, whose family was from South Carolina, had met Burgess's step-father almost thirty years earlier, in Egypt. The Roosevelts and Bassetts having stayed in touch with one another, Colonel Bassett had notified the Roosevelts of Burgess's Washington posting, hence the invitation.   Nicholas Roosevelt later told the FBI that on this visit "he talked with Burgess regarding international affairs, including the British China policy." Roosevelt thought "that Burgess was well versed on this question and skillfully presented the British Government's thesis that it was wiser to recognize Communist China and foster relations between China and Great Britain than to refuse to recognize her and force China into a closer rapprochement with the USSR . . . [Roosevelt] recalled that Burgess impressed him as a staunch defender of British Socialism and that . . . Burgess told him he was a member of the Labor Party in Great Britain."[25] The Roosevelts said that "Burgess appeared to be emotionally unstable, being gay and exhilarated at times, quarrelsome, worried, and distracted at others," symptoms of uncontrolled diabetes, among other things. Burgess wrote to Mrs. Roosevelt on August 15th:

> I have just finished writing my mother a letter (which she will of course show to Jack) telling her about my visit to [Highlands]. It wld. be much easier if private correspondence cld. adopt the technique of official correspondence – because then you wld. have a copy of my letter to her & wld. see for yourself how very much I enjoyed it & how very grateful I am. As it is I shall have to try & convince you - & I can't write skillfully enough to express what an impressive place in the sense of expressing in detail a way of life I found the [Highlands] to be, quite apart from the sheer loveliness of the sticks and stones, the box & the vistas – they being only the material out of which you and your

husband seem to me to have the other & bigger thing. I really did enjoy it and also meeting your friends & members of your family – who of course also fitted in & helped to make it . . .

I gave your love to [redacted] with whom incidentally I am going to a party this evening & he told me how kind you had been to him in S. Carolina. I told him I knew this from my experiences in Pennsylvania & I do hope very much to see you both again.

With all thanks

Affectionately

/s/ GUY B.[26]

After this first visit, the Roosevelts gave Burgess letters of introduction to various of their friends and relatives, including the Alsop brothers, Joseph and Stewart, once-famous newspaper columnists.[27] Burgess had met Joseph Alsop during his brief visit to Washington in 1940. They had not taken to one another then, nor did they in 1950. (Ten years later, the notoriously difficult Joseph Alsop married the then-widowed and famously charming Susan Mary Patten, following a pattern of such in England as Tom Driberg and James Lees-Milne. Susan Mary Patten Alsop, who had been a fixture of the Paris diplomatic scene in the late-1940s, would manage Joseph Alsop's social life in Kennedy-era Washington.) The meeting between Stewart Alsop and Burgess seems to have been cordial. Burgess's second "bread and butter letter," thanking Mrs. Roosevelt for her hospitality, was sent on 22 September:

I trust you received my telegram. The reasons you did not receive the earlier letter that I shld. have written are too numerous to trouble you with, so I hope you will take as sufficient about half or less of my apologies. The reasons included:

(1) I had deferred writing to you until I had met your cousin

[Stewart Alsop] . . . It was, in fact, well worth waiting to meet yr. cousin since I thought he was even nicer than you had told me. And his wife, who I met separately, is certainly as beautiful and attractive as I had heard from you that she was.

(2) I now have a motorcar & I wanted to tell you what I thought of the weekend tour I made with the [Counsel General?] here (who is one of my oldest London friends) of your Jefferson architecture & Virginia. It is easy to do since I thought quite simply that Monticello was one of the most civilized & beautiful houses I had ever seen & the most c[ivilized] & b[eautiful] anyone had ever built for himself. About the University of Virginia it is hard to speak unless one falls back on merely saying it is a triumph. Or, more important, worthy of the man that one hour in Monticello had made me love. [Jefferson's] capacity was only, it seemed to me, exceeded by his taste. It particularly struck me (as a detail only) that he achieved regularity without repetition. (The symmetry of the 2 main sides of the campus.)

If you wld. like me to come & see you & yr. husband I wld. v. much like to & I now have a good car. So it only needs me being told where. And, I suppose, when. I find yr. countrymen v. nice to mine, & to me.

Yrs very sincerely [ ] Guy Burgess

P.S. . . . While writing the above yr. niece rang me up & we have arranged to meet in her house at what seems a good time next Sunday. That is 1/2 an hour before whatever time it is that the Symphony Concert begins. Guy.[28]

The weekend having gone well, in October the Roosevelts again invited Burgess to visit for a few days. The following summer, the Roosevelts summed up their impression of Burgess for the FBI by saying that "Burgess appeared to drink rather heavily during his visits, but he never lost control of himself or became intoxicated." They thought that he "had a brilliant mind, talked knowledgeably on many subjects and impressed them as a keen, young British diplomat who was interesting and stimulating."

Burgess's working accommodations were in the British Embassy's Chancery on Massachusetts Avenue, where his office was near those of Philby, Geoffrey Patterson (Philby's opposite number, representing M.I.5), and Wilfrid Mann, who worked on atomic energy intelligence matters with the U. S. Atomic Energy Commission and with the CIA.[29] Bureaucracies tend to group office spaces by function, for obvious reasons. The location of Burgess's office in the Chancery, in the absence of other evidence, would indicate that his work had something in common with that of Philby, Patterson and Mann. In other words, that it had to do with secret intelligence matters, communications concerning which were handled by Philby's staff. According to Mann, at this time Burgess "was always more or less the worse for wear owing to the combined effects of alcohol and diabetes. He was, however, invariably at his work . . . before I arrived. As the door of his office was slightly nearer to the front entrance he would also almost always call out good morning and button-hole me for five or ten minutes . . ."[30] Mann, who as a scientist might have been more aware of these matters that other observers, writes elsewhere that Burgess's diabetes lowered his alcohol tolerance. Burgess's health issues were also noticed by another embassy official, whom Burgess told that he had severe sinus problems "caused by a blow to his head, when a colleague (Sir) Fred Warner had 'deliberately' pushed him down the stairs of a London night club."[31] The pressure from the sinus condition pushing on Burgess's fractured skull was acutely painful. The Soviet doctors he consulted a few years later were fascinated, he said, by the damage to his skull shown on x-rays.

When Burgess first arrived in Washington he had continued his work as a specialist in Far Eastern affairs, assigned by the Counselor, Hubert Graves, Donald Maclean's successor in that post, to Denis Greenhill, head of the Middle Eastern Section, who was involved in Korean matters. Burgess's work in Far Eastern affairs is attested to by the fact that he was on the distribution list for a secret cable concerning Chinese troop movements that Graves sent to only three others: the Ambassador, the military attaché, and Greenhill.[32] There remains in the thoroughly "weeded" file of the Embassy's papers from this period a document written by Burgess soon after his arrival. This secret memorandum of August 29, 1950, was addressed to Greenhill and then Graves.[*] It is a report of a conversation with an unidentified acting head of Mission in Washington, who had relayed to Burgess a conversation he had had with the Nationalist Chinese military attaché. "The Chinese was, source said, cock a hoop" because of "the state of affairs in S. China, where . . . organized resistance controlled by the nationalists was powerfully increasing." The memorandum lists three reasons for the military attaché's optimism, concluding:

> In spite of State Department announcements to the contrary, the actual course of events in Formosa indicated a real change in U.S. policy in the direction of increased military support being in fact available from MacArthur in spheres other than that of the 7th Fleet. Recent Taiwan telegrams . . . appear to go some way towards confirming this last point.

Greenhill commented on this last statement:

> . . . we have the recent State Dept. memo on aid to Chiang which indicates the "real change" is in fact only a modification to help Formosa in self defence. Very strong representations by the military survey group might, of course, with local political pressure lead to some very substantial aid being sent over and above self defence.[33]

Greenhill may have been misled by the State Department's memorandum, in part because, as Burgess had observed some years

---

[*] Typically, Greenhill's memoirs give the impression that Burgess, although assigned to his section, did no work for it. See: Greenhill, Denis. More by Accident. Wilton: Bishop Wilton, York., 1992, p. 73. Greenhill's memoir seems more sympathetic to Burgess than most of its kind.

earlier, America did not have a Government in the British sense. Decisions took place by means of an on-going debate among the various departments of the Executive branch, each with allies (and enemies) in Congress, with frequent interventions from lobbyists, business interests, and others. The State Department may have wished to limit US assistance to the Nationalist government, but the Department of Defense, not to mention MacArthur, may have had other intentions. The British found the process opaque.

By the date of Burgess's memorandum, North Korean forces had pushed the South Korean and American armies into a small area at the extreme southern end of the peninsula, the Pusan Perimeter. President Truman ordered the Seventh Fleet to position itself between Taiwan and the mainland both in order to protect the Nationalist government on the island and to keep it from mounting operations against the mainland. This was, in effect, a late intervention in the Chinese civil war. According to David Halberstam, the American intervention was taken as a major affront by the Chinese Communist leaders. "It kept them from making their country whole. The United States had, in effect, stepped between them and the completion of their revolution, at the very moment when the Americans were cutting off all conceivable channels of communications to them."[34] The State department may have wished only to "help Formosa in self defence," but the representatives of the China Lobby in the Senate had more aggressive aims ("unleashing Chiang") and General MacArthur was already referring to Taiwan as "an unsinkable aircraft carrier and submarine tender ideally located to accomplish offensive strategy and at the same time checkmate defensive or counter-offensive operations by friendly forces based on Okinawa and the Philippines."[35] Another set of reasons for the military attaché to be "cock a hoop."

From August 7 to November 27, 1950, Burgess, as Greenhill's assistant, was an alternate member of the United Kingdom's delegation to the Far Eastern Commission. The Far Eastern Commission was composed of representatives of eleven nations (including the Soviet Union until its delegates walked out in protest

315

of the exclusion of delegates from the People's Republic). It formulated "the policies, principles and standards in conformity with which the fulfillment by Japan of its obligations under the terms of surrender may be accomplished" and reviewed "on the request of any member any directive issued to the Supreme Commander for the Allied Powers or any action taken by the Supreme Commander involving policy discussions within the jurisdiction of the Commission." Burgess was on the Steering and Reparations committees, and the "Strengthening of Democratic Tendencies", "War Criminals", "Aliens in Japan", "Occupation Costs", and "Financial and Monetary Problems" subcommittees."[36] A State Department official who served as legal representative on the "Aliens in Japan" subcommittee "recalled that prior to the time that Burgess became associated with the committee, the United States had attempted to get approval of a paper giving civil and criminal jurisdiction of United Nations nationals located in Japan to the Japanese Government.

> She said that most members of the Commission, including the British, were rather reluctant to agree with the United States on this proposal. She said, however, that after Burgess came on the committee, he was much more co-operative with the United States in connection with this proposal than had been the prior British representative. She said that he had a good attitude with respect to the work of the committee, and that he seemed to believe firmly in cooperation between the British and Americans . . .[37]

The FBI also interviewed someone who was "at three or four parties during the period between August 1950 and May 1951 at which Burgess was also present." He said that at this time,

> Burgess was an extremely difficult individual to talk to and that he usually sat in a corner and said nothing . . . Burgess sat and drew caricatures of various individuals at the party. In addition to the caricatures of persons attending the party he drew one of Stalin . . . an extremely well drawn caricature indicating that he had either copied it from some publication or had practiced

drawing it considerably . . .[38]

The FBI was told that Burgess talked about cars, rather than, say, politics, on social occasions, which sounds as if Burgess, in McCarthyite Washington, was being uncharacteristically careful. On the other hand, that August he had bought a 1941 Lincoln Continental convertible and had doubled his investment in the next few weeks with extra bits of equipment and repairs for the car. He may have simply wanted to talk about his car.

When Sir Gladwyn Jebb arrived in New York as the British Permanent Representative to the United Nations Security Council immediately after the opening of the Korean War, he moved into the Wave Hill mansion, in Riverdale, overlooking the Hudson, in preference to the Oyster Bay mansion which had been purchased by his predecessor, Sir Alexander Cadogan.[39] Jebb's debates with the Soviet representative, Malik, were televised, making Jebb a rather unlikely media personality. Although Jebb became something of a spokesman for the American position in regard to Korea, on August 29th he supported Malik, against the United States, in inviting representatives of the People's Republic to appear at the Security Council. In mid-September the Inchon Landing led to a change in the war, relieving the forces trapped within the Pusan Perimeter and eventually reconstituting the 38th parallel as the de facto border. The General Assembly, meeting at the end of September, brought Foreign Minister Bevin and Minister of State Hector McNeil to New York. Bevin's health was fast declining and he spent just a week in New York, saying he had come "to bask in Jebb's renown." One of the people the FBI interviewed in July, 1951, said that he had met Burgess in early September, 1950, at Alan Maclean's apartment on East 55th Street. Burgess was staying at the apartment for several days, saying that he was working with Jebb at the United Nations.[40] Burgess told Driberg that during this period he would go to New York for the weekends "and Gladwyn and I used to cry on each other's shoulders about the American attitude to the Far East,"[41] something that Jebb did not mention in his memoirs. When not working, Burgess found other things to do. He told Norman Luker

317

that the Everard Turkish Baths on 28th Street was a place where "you can get anything you desire." He also played racquets at the Racquet and Tennis Club, 370 Park Avenue, with Robert Grant III (whom *Time* magazine called "the king of U.S. racquets players"), a stockbroker who had been at Eton with Burgess, and visited the Meadowbrook Club, on Long Island, probably for golf.[42]

Some accounts of Burgess's time as a Foreign Office official in Washington give the impression that he did little but write polite letters to Americans thanking them for addressing inquiries to the Ambassador. But the United States was at war in Korea and Britain played the role there that it would later play in Iraq and Afghanistan: supplying smaller, but significant, forces; demonstrating that the war in question was not solely an American effort. William Manchester, in his biography of General MacArthur, asserts that Burgess (and Philby) "sat on the top-secret Inter-Allied Board"[43] responsible for policy decisions about the conduct of the war, and that therefore they, with Maclean as head of the American department in London from November 1, were in a position to learn, and transmit, crucial military intelligence matters. In the words of Dean Rusk: "It can be assumed that (1) anything we in our government knew about Korea would have been known at the British Embassy and (2) that officers in the Embassy of the rank of [Philby and Burgess] would have known what the British Embassy knew."[44] And anything known to Philby and Burgess would have soon been known in Moscow.

At the beginning of November Burgess was assigned as escort to Anthony Eden, the once and future Foreign Secretary, when Eden represented the former War Cabinet at the unveiling of a statue in Arlington National Cemetery of Sir John Dill, the British head of the Combined Chiefs of Staff during World War II. Truman was staying in Blair House, across the way from the White House, as the latter was being renovated. Just as Truman was about to meet Eden at the White House for the drive to Arlington Cemetery, Puerto Rican revolutionaries attempted to assassinate the President, dying in the effort, but hardly delaying the phlegmatic Truman's itinerary for the day. The motorcade, its security heavily reinforced, traveled across the Potomac to Arlington; the statue was unveiled; speeches were made. It is probable that Burgess is indiscernibly in the background of the official pictures, in the foreground of which folded chairs are occupied by Truman, Eden, Marshall and others of that rank.

Eden met with Ambassador Franks, Secretary Acheson, the President, probably the Joint Chiefs of Staff (or one or two), etc. As Eden was undoubtedly about to become Foreign Secretary, his American hosts would probably have thoroughly briefed him about their plans in the Far East. Was Burgess, as the Eden's escort, present at these meetings? It would be unusual for an official in his situation to be left out in the hallway. He must have seemed harmless enough, losing his car keys, according to Eden, at crucial moments as he drove Eden around town. (Although that was rather odd for Burgess, with his interest in cars.) Eden, probably knowing Burgess was the Embassy's (and the Foreign Office's) expert on Chinese Communism, might have chatted to him about his meetings whether or not Burgess was included in those meetings. In addition, "Burgess's hostility to German rearmament, outlined on frequent journeys together round the American capital, had seemed to Eden more sensible than Churchill's [attitude]. Burgess had also been instrumental in effecting a reunion between Eden and the ageing Cordell Hull."[45] The fellow in the next office at the Chancery, H. A. R. Philby, Jr., had access to secure communications, if Eden had wished to cable London (or visa versa).

Eden wrote the usual note of thanks to his escort on November 8:

My dear Burgess—

Thank you so much for all your kindnesses. I was so well looked after that I am still in robust health, after quite a stormy flight to New York and many engagements since. Truly I enjoyed every moment of my stay in Washington, and you will know how much you helped to make this possible. Renewed greetings and gratitude. Yours sincerely,

Anthony Eden

China entered the war at the end of November. In response to a November 30 press conference comment by Truman implying that he might authorize the use of atomic weapons against the Chinese forces, Attlee flew immediately to the United States, to remind the American government that it was obliged to consult Britain about decisions involving the use of nuclear weapons. During Attlee's stop-over in New York, Jebb apparently emphasized to Attlee his (Jebb's) disagreement with the American intention to charge the Chinese with aggression (he saw their intervention as defensive) and his conviction that the British recognition of the People's Republic was a better course than American non-recognition. Prime Minister Attlee arrived in Washington on December 4th. Six meetings between Truman and Attlee were held on December 5th, 6th, 7th and 8th. According to the joint statement issued on December 8th:

> We have reviewed together the outstanding problems facing our two countries in international affairs . . . We considered two questions regarding China which are already before the United Nations . . . On the question of the Chinese seat in the United Nations, the two governments differ. The United Kingdom has recognized the Central People's Government and considers that its representatives should occupy China's seat in the United Nations. The United States has opposed and continues to oppose the seating of the Chinese communist representatives in the United Nations. We have discussed our difference of view on this point and are determined to prevent it from interfering with our united effort in support of our common objectives . . . The President stated that it was his hope that world conditions would never call for the use of the atomic bomb. The President told the Prime Minister that it was also his desire to keep the Prime Minister at all times informed of developments which might bring about a change in the situation.^{46}

In the normal course of events, the British embassy in Washington would have provided support to the Attlee party: expertise in regard to Chinese Communism and its relationship with the Soviet Union, expertise on atomic matters as handled in the US, and also the embassy's secure communications systems for the deluge of top secret messages flowing between the Attlee party and Whitehall—Messrs Burgess, Mann and Philby, respectively. The messages themselves went to, inter alios, the head of the Foreign Office's American department, Donald Maclean.[47] Maclean, according to Verne Newton, "Could tell Stalin exactly how far the United Nations allies were prepared to go, which threats most unnerved Washington and London, which rifts divided MacArthur from the British and American chiefs of staff, and what current of dissent ran between Anglo-American statesmen."[48] Relations between the US and Great Britain deteriorated that winter as the war situation worsened, Jebb "only just" avoiding a public break with the Americans over a resolution condemning Chinese "aggression" in Korea. Alan Maclean, as Jebb's private secretary, would have been privy to these conversations as well as those with Bevin and McNeil two months earlier.

As Burgess's work with the Far Eastern Commission came to an end, he began to make more frequent visits to New York, spending nearly two weeks in mid-November at the Sutton Hotel, another few days there in early December, six days in February and three in March. (The Sutton Hotel was a semi-residential hotel on East 56th Street, around the corner from Alan Maclean's apartment, with a swimming pool and some literary renown as it had been when first opened managed by Nathanael West.)[49] When not at the Sutton Hotel, Burgess slept at the apartments of friends, often that of Alan Maclean, which at this period Maclean shared with an artist, James Farmer. This happened frequently enough that Jebb had the impression that Burgess shared Maclean's New York apartment.[50] Perhaps Burgess, who had done the sort of work for McNeil that Maclean was doing for Jebb, was helpful to Maclean—or Jebb— during this very busy period. It is also possible that there were two distinct reasons for Burgess's visits to New York, those symbolized by his hotel stays, paid for by the Embassy, and those marked by his nights at Maclean's flat. It is reasonable to assume that, like Donald

Maclean a few years earlier, he might have found the anonymity of New York City useful for meetings with Soviet contacts.

One of the more interesting, and longest, interviews conducted by the FBI after Burgess and Maclean disappeared from London, was with an American journalist (name redacted in the transcripts), who told the FBI that "he had first met Guy Burgess around January, 1951, when he received a telephone call from him at the former office of the Foreign Policy Association in the National Press Building, Washington, D.C., at which time Burgess stated that he was interested in questions concerning the Far East.

Burgess later came to his office in the Press building and told him that his, Burgess', job at the British Embassy was to analyze the motivations and tendencies of the American attitude toward the Far East, not only in regard to the official government opinion, but also in regard to the opinion of the general American public . . . Burgess wanted him to obtain various published materials which would adequately reflect the precise public opinion in the United States with regard to China.

Burgess visited the journalist four or five times between January and early March to discuss "the China question . . . on all but one of these occasions he took Burgess to the Press Club bar where they would drink and talk.

He later met with Burgess and discussed with him the course of official American policy toward China and tried to analyze for him the tendencies, impulses and concepts of the present Administration together with the problems of the Administration in attempting to follow these concepts with so many Republican critics holding different views. [He] told Burgess he thought that as time went on, the critics of the Administration would become more influential, but that the over-riding question was the war in Korea, and that political policy depended on battle reports from the Korean front. [He] told Burgess that it was his opinion that if the Korean War were prolonged, the United States would become thoroughly pro-Chiang Kai Shek.

The journalist told the FBI "that Burgess had later written a report to the British Foreign Office built on the concept that American public opinion with regard to China and the Far East depended upon battle reports from Korea. "Concerning Burgess' personal opinion with regard to China, "he seemed to be in agreement with the official British attitude, which was that the rise of Communism in China was a Chinese matter which had been accelerated by the Chiang Kai Shek Administration because of the latter's inefficient and dishonest methods. [He] stated that it was of great importance to Burgess, as a student of China, that the Chinese situation be allowed to follow through in its own right to a natural conclusion, and that it bothered Burgess to think that the United States might try to control the Chinese situation." The unnamed American journalist "said that Burgess had talked a great deal about H. A. R. Philby of the British Embassy.

> He stated that Burgess not only stayed with the Philbys but also ate his evening meal there. In this connection, [the journalist] stated he did not believe Burgess to be as irresponsible as newspaper accounts of him indicated. He pointed out in this regard that Burgess was very meticulous about being on time in the Philby home for dinner . . . Burgess talked about Philby a great deal, telling him what a nice fellow Philby was, and that Burgess seemed to like Philby very much.

In one discussion the journalist had with Burgess, "the latter had made known his general dislike for the United States Congress, in particular the attitude of some members of Congress toward homosexuals in the State Department." The journalist explained to the FBI "that at about this time Senator McCarthy had been making accusations concerning pro-Communists in the State Department, and that information concerning homosexualism in the State Department was at that time linked to some extent in Congress with the pro-Communist investigations. [He] stated that Burgess seemed to consider the fact that investigation of homosexuals was being made by Congress as a personal affront." The last time this journalist saw Burgess was in early March of 1951, when Burgess took him to lunch to reciprocate for all of the drinks that he had been furnished at the Press Club. He told the FBI "that at that time Burgess was ill, but that he was not aware of the nature of this illness."[51]

The Philbys, as is expected of diplomats, did much official entertaining. Mann mentions a Thanksgiving Day dinner party in 1950[*] (which Burgess might have attended, as he would have returned from his mid-November New York visit by that time) and a famous dinner party on Friday, January 19, 1951. The guests at dinner that unseasonably warm night included CIA official James Angleton and his wife Cicely; William Harvey, the ex-FBI agent who was then responsible for counter-intelligence at the CIA, and his wife; Robert Lamphere (the FBI liaison to the CIA) and his wife; Robert Mackenzie, the embassy's regional security officer, and Geraldine Dack, one of Philby's secretaries, and Dr. Wilfrid and Miriam Mann. (Both Mann and Lamphere were intimately involved in the Fuchs affair.[**]) Mann's account is the least dramatized version of an often-told story: "It began, as would any normal dinner, with *aperitifs* [pitchers of Martinis].

> It proceeded pleasantly and without any untoward incident and after dessert we adjourned to the living-room for coffee. It was at that point that Burgess entered. Neither Miriam nor I can recall that [he was] "obviously intoxicated" . . . Nor was it "very late" . . . because coffee was just about to be served, the time was probably not later than 9.30 pm.

The phrases in quotation marks refer to accounts in the popular espionage literature.

> Guy [sic] was however in his usual aggressive mood and, almost immediately after being introduced, he commented to [Mrs. Harvey] that it was strange to see the face he had been doodling all his life suddenly appear before him. She immediately

---

[*] According to Verne W. Newton, citing Wilfrid Mann, this party was at the Angletons' (Newton, p. 292).
[**] Dr. Klaus Fuchs, an Anglo-German physicist, was sentenced to fourteen years in prison for passing nuclear research secrets to the Soviet Union.

responded by asking him to draw her. She was a pleasant woman but her jaw was a little prominent; Guy caricatured her face . . . so that it looked like the prow of a dreadnaught with its underwater battering ram.*** She immediately rose, took her husband by the arm, saying "I've never been so insulted in all my life, take me home", and they immediately left . . . After a few minutes' embarrassment everything became very calm and I recollect sitting for twenty or thirty minutes with [Angleton] on the low wall between the front garden and the sidewalk on Nebraska Avenue enjoying the cool of the evening while our wives conversed with the remaining guests inside.**** When we returned Kim Philby was in his shirt-sleeves, in bright red braces, and in tears . . . and Aileen had disappeared . . .

Philby had good reason to cry; Burgess had made him a powerful enemy.

Guy took me into the kitchen and poured nearly half of a tumbler of scotch into two glasses on the kitchen counter and proposed some health or another . . . after about three such mutual toasts I wandered back into the living room to find that Miriam had left with many of the other guests . . .

In an interesting aside, Mann commented at this point in his story that the "ubiquitous Washington cocktail parties were useful sources of background information, especially when someone after a few drinks would become very confidential and perhaps make a few injudicious remarks about the [sic] organization . . ."

. . . when the time came to depart I was still sober enough to realize that after the kitchen session with Guy it would be better not to drive my car. The ambassador, Sir Oliver Franks, had a reputation for being tough on traffic offences . . . *Just a few months later, Kim Philby himself used this well-known trait of*

*** Mann insisted that the caricature was only of the face, contrary to secondary accounts, including my own.
**** For what it is worth, there is no wall there today.

the ambassador to trick him into sending Guy Burgess home in disgrace . . . (Emphasis added.)

Mann thought he could consume six martinis on an empty stomach ("rather more if they were combined with something to eat, and still feel confident that I was in control of my head and my tongue"), which makes it significant that he had someone else drive him home that night. The next morning he returned to the Philby's house to pick up his car. He went in, spoke briefly to Aileen, who then said: "The boys are upstairs in bed. Why don't you go up to see them?"

> The sound of voices led me to the right door. As I entered it, I can still see Philby and Burgess in the double bed that was facing me. They were propped up on pillows, wearing pajamas; one, or even both of them, may have been wearing a dressing gown as well. They were drinking champagne together, and asked me to have a glass too as a pick-me-up . . . I got the impression that both Philby and Burgess were enjoying the situation immensely . . . The situation made me feel puzzled and uncomfortable rather than alarmed. Aileen had treated the whole matter lightly and almost flippantly. I did *not* get the impression that the situation was homosexual in the sense that the two of them had spent the night together (indeed I gathered that one or both of them had already paid an early morning visit to the Embassy before my arrival).[52]

The next day Alger Hiss was convicted of perjury and three days after that Klaus Fuchs confessed to atomic espionage.

Perhaps Philby chose, of all possible occasions and locations, to have sex with Burgess in the middle of the day in his own bed, with Aileen, cheery enough, nearby, waving chance visitors into the marital bedroom. Or perhaps this may be what we are meant to believe, to look at, so that we do not notice something else. Robert Maxwell's Pergamon Press, the publisher of Mann's book, was known to be used from time to time by the CIA and Mann's memoir bears some signs of CIA production (such as the absence of

326

Angleton's name in the account of the dinner party). It is interesting that it is Mann, the atomic energy expert, who tells the story of Philby, Burgess, the bed, and the bottle of champagne; Mann, who had thought he had had too much to drink the night before to drive home. Had he had enough to drink to talk to Burgess about his atomic energy work during dinner? Perhaps that morning Philby and Burgess were celebrating the *success* of the dinner party. Gathered at the Philbys' were those responsible for U.S. foreign intelligence collection, for liaison between CIA and the FBI, for liaison between the British and the U.S. intelligence services for, inter alia, the VENONA code-breaking project, and for liaison between the British and the American atomic programs.[53] What was spoken about at dinner and after, between rounds of drinks? We are not told. This was not the only party that year at the Philbys' house, not the only party they, and Burgess, attended, perhaps at the Angletons', perhaps at the Manns', certainly at the Greenhills' and at the embassy residence. These stories (the Philby party, other tales about Burgess in Washington and New York) are told as if the normative point of view were that of the alcoholic, obese, ill-educated, racist employee of the secret police and his equally civilized spouse. But that is not necessarily the only way to look at things.[54]

The VENONA project began in February 1943, when the American military intelligence services began collecting encrypted Soviet messages. This was—and no doubt is—standard practice. Even if the messages cannot be read, there is much to be learned from "traffic analysis," and always the hope of at some future time being able to decipher the messages. The VENONA encrypting system began with a code book in which letters, words, and phrases were equated to numbers. A code clerk would take a plain text message and encode the message using numbers from the codebook. The messages were further modified, in other words double-encrypted, by use of a one-time pad. The use of a one-time pad effectively randomizes the code and renders it unreadable.[55] But the Soviet code clerks had made a crucial error: they had used the same one-time pad more than one time. This allowed the American and

English experts assigned to the project, with enormous effort, to read some of the messages. (The key American liaison official was Robert Lamphere of the FBI, one of the guests at the party at the Philbys.) From the time that Kim Philby arrived in Washington in 1949 he occasionally visited Arlington Hall for discussions about VENONA and received copies of summaries of VENONA translations. "In January 1949 that Meredith Gardner broke a number of messages from the KGB station at the Soviet consulate-general in New York to Moscow Centre referring to an agent with the cover name Homer.

> This spy had been in Washington in mid-1945 and gained access to the secret messages between Truman and Churchill on the fate of the leaders of the Polish Home Army. In April 1951, the Venona decoders found the vital clue in one of the messages. For part of 1944, Homer had had regular contacts with his Soviet control in New York, using his pregnant wife as an excuse. The names had been narrowed down to just one - Donald Maclean.[56]

It took the VENONA decoders until April, 1951 to realize that Homer was Donald Maclean. On April 11, 1951, Guy Liddell made the following diary entry:

> Dick told me about the case of a Soviet agent that we had been looking for, who leaked from the British Embassy in 1944 or 1945 . . . Recent ACORN material served to narrow the field; this material has been in the possession of the Americans for a long time, but for some unknown reason has only just reached us. There are two people who might possibly fill the bill; one, Donald Maclean and the other, John Russell. Maclean is now head of the American Department in the Foreign Office and is the brother of Nancy Maclean who was formerly in this office.

Philby would have realized it long before and made appropriate plans.

The Citadel, a military preparatory school in Charleston, South Carolina was host to a three-day Southeastern Regional International Relations Club's annual meeting, opening March 1, 1951. In response to a request from the school's president for a speaker, the

British embassy sent Burgess. It was the practice of the Washington Embassy, as with most embassies, to send diplomats on tours around the country, to give speeches about policy objectives and to report on what they were able to observe about the characteristics and mood of the local inhabitants. Burgess drove from Washington to Charleston, bringing with him or picking up on the way a certain James Turck. Turck was driving Burgess's Lincoln, near Richmond, Virginia, when they were stopped for going eighty miles an hour in a sixty mile an hour zone. Turck was issued a citation and when Burgess, citing diplomatic immunity, protested, they were taken to a local justice of the peace, who levied a fine. While Burgess was cashing a check to pay Turck's fine, the justice of the peace called a friend of his, a judge, to find out if diplomatic immunity covered a diplomat's driver. The judge thought not, but he was not sure, so that he called his friend, John Battle, the Governor of Virginia, who did not clarify the law, but supported the justice of the peace. Burgess came back, paid the fine, and he and Turck continued on their way, not knowing about the telephone calls.

The keynote speaker at The Citadel conference was the Deputy Director of the Office of West European Affairs at the State Department, Dr. Francis Williamson, who spoke on "The Problems of Europe in American Foreign Policy. Williamson said that "Complete utilization of [America's] resources and the continued confidence of the North Atlantic Pact Nations are essential if world domination by the Soviet Union is to be prevented." He was followed that afternoon by Albert Fequant, Second Secretary of the French Embassy, speaking on "Indo-China and Problems of Asia" and Professor Paul Clyde of Duke University whose topic was "China and the Problems of Asia." Professor Clyde spoke on the theme that "We, not the communists, have been the chief perpetrators of the Chinese revolution" by failing to support the development of Chinese democracy. Guy Burgess opened the evening's session with a speech on "Britain: Partner for Peace," which sounds like a standard Embassy theme. According to an account in the local newspaper, he "characterized the British

Government's colonial policy in India as that country's 'greatest "classical mistake' . . . 'We offered them justice, peace, incorrupt government, but not social equality . . . By leaving the social structure frozen, the country was left vulnerable for communist proselytizing' . . . Burgess defended his country's recognition of Communist China by declaring that recognition of a government does not mean approval or disapproval of its political ideologies . . . 'My country's recognition of the Chinese Communist government has nothing to do with "weakness" or "appeasement,"' he declared. 'We feel that by continuing relations at least one Western foot can be kept in the Chinese door. We are not sufficiently mobilized to run the risk of breaking with China and possibly precipitating World War III. We are fighting a delaying action.'"[57] All of which was consistent with Prime Minister Attlee's position during the December meetings with President Truman; the speech may well have been a standard document for general use by embassy personnel. In 1951, in South Carolina, however, it was, no doubt, controversial. Burgess did not make himself popular in Charleston. The speech was not well received and, according to one of the other speakers (probably Albert Fequant) who "knew Guy Burgess very well and went around with him in Washington, D.C. a good deal . . . Burgess seemed to be drunk during entire conference." Drinking with Fequant, as it happened. He was sober enough at a cocktail party for the crème de la crème of Charleston one evening to be charming to the assembled Pinckneys, Roosevelt relatives and such, but suffered at least one blackout from drinking or diabetes or, most likely, a combination of the two.[58]

Governor Battle, for some reason, waited until March 14, and then wrote a letter to the State Department's chief of protocol (including a statement from Turck about earlier traffic incidents on the journey to Charleston), complaining about the speeding incident and abuse of diplomatic immunity by Burgess and other diplomats. The letter reached the British embassy on March 30. Meanwhile, in mid-March, Burgess again went to New York, where he saw W. H. Auden on the 17th.[59] A few months later, Auden, when interviewed by the *Sunday Express,* said that "Burgess was an open Communist in the late 1930's . . . We met several times while he was at the Embassy in Washington. Burgess was still pro-Communist. We met last in March of this year. We talked about [the atomic spies] Fuchs and <u>Nunn-May</u>"[60] Auden later told the Italian police that in March Burgess had said he planned to go to Italy the following summer and that Auden had invited him to stay with him in Ischia.[61]

Burgess seems to have enjoyed the Charleston area and when his mother visited him in April, he wrote to Emily Roosevelt to ask if they could stay with her at her house in Charleston during a motoring trip through the South. They did so for a few days at the beginning of the month, then moved to a hotel, as they waited for Burgess's car to be repaired. While visiting the Roosevelt's, "Burgess appeared to be deeply mortified because of his misconduct at the time of his previous visit to Charleston and, because of this or possibly the presence of his mother, he was exceedingly judicious in his drinking" while at Gippy Plantation, the Roosevelt's Charleston estate.

> In this connection, [Mrs. Roosevelt] stated that Mrs. Bassett told her Guy had suffered concussion of the brain when he fell down the stairs at the Foreign Office [sic] in London about three years ago, and for this reason, Mrs. Bassett said that Guy should never drink potent beverages . . . [Mrs. Roosevelt] said that on the occasion of Burgess' visit . . . he appeared to be calm and serene, was cheerful, looked well, and exhibited no signs of tension. He told her that he had applied to the Foreign Office for release from his present assignment because, as he put it, he felt he could be of greater value in the Foreign Office at London.[62]

Someone (or possibly two) people in Charleston who met Burgess at this time later gave their impressions to the FBI: One "described Burgess as a bright minded and well informed man who appeared younger than his years." He "stated that Burgess revealed during their conversation that he was captivated by 'a fine assortment of crackpot economic ideas, such as those advanced by

the late British economist, Professor Keynes, holding that a country
can spend itself to prosperity by unlimited borrowing.'"

> In this connection [he said] that Burgess expressed considerable
> enthusiasm over a biography of Professor Keynes recently
> published in London by a friend of Burgess [Roy Harrod] . . .
> Burgess lent him this book but [he] sent it back to Burgess at the
> British Embassy with the comment that it was too deep for him .
> . .

This gentleman or another, possibly an English teacher at The
Citadel, from the context, told the FBI "that he met Burgess and his
mother on April 5, 1951,

> He considered Burgess intelligent but something of a smart
> aleck" or "know-it-all" . . . he noticed, however, that Burgess
> was making every effort to be pleasant . . . he found Burgess to
> be far above average as a conversationalist. He said that Burgess
> talked learnedly about literature and was well up on the current
> developments in the search for the Boswell papers.[63]

Various people told the FBI that Burgess had seemed lonely in
the United States, repeatedly asking for introductions to people who
might be interesting to talk with.

President Truman dismissed General MacArthur on April 11.
According to Greenhill, the British embassy was flooded with
"outraged letters attributing [his] fall to British influence.

> The Ambassador rightly said that those that were rational and
> temperately worded should be answered in similar vein. Burgess
> was deputed to do the job. He sat for weeks in a haze of
> cigarette smoke in a small office, reading and re-reading the
> growing pile of letters. . . . He told me he wanted to write a
> personal letter to Donald Maclean [then head of the American
> section of the FO], and in the end showed me a messy draft. . .
> .My recollection is that it was unexpectedly favourable to
> Truman's policy.[64]

Early in the week of April 15th, Ambassador Franks, after
considering the Virginia traffic violation/diplomatic immunity affair,

and consulting with the Foreign Office, called Burgess in and told him to return to London. According to Dr. Mann, Franks had decided to do this because of his rule against abuse of diplomatic immunity. According to others—Philby, Modin—Burgess and Philby had planned the Virginia incident as a way to get Burgess to London to help Maclean with the conscequencs of the VENONA decryption. Perhaps both.

Burgess traveled to New York for a day or two in the third week of April, then again on the 27th and stayed there, at the apartment of Norman Luker (formerly Stafford Cripps' speech writer, then of the B.B.C.) until his ship left for England five days later. Burgess left his car in Washington, much to the interest of the FBI a few weeks later:

> Mayflower Motors informed that an automobile belonging to Guy F. de M. Burgess was presently parked in their lot . . . This car examined and found to contain a large number of graphs purporting to compare defense expenditures as a percentage of national income and defense manpower, i.e., men in armed forces as a percentage of all men aged eighteen dash forty four years. Both graphs showed comparison between the U.S. and U.K. for year 1943 to 1950 relative to above. This car also contained road maps of the Carolinas, Delaware, Maryland, Virginia and West Virginia; book entitled "The Works of Jane Austen"; Bantam book entitled "Up at the Villa" by Somerset Maugham; book entitled "The Future of Nations" by E. H. Carr and a five by seven photograph of a small boy and a girl.[65]

Burgess went to parties in New York, including a diplomatic affair attended by many British diplomats. A farewell party was given for Burgess on the night of the 30th, with music provided by Luker and his roommate, who seem to have been professional musicians or gifted amateurs. There was sound-recording equipment in their apartment, which was used that night to record some songs. Burgess also used it to record his memories of his meeting with Churchill. In addition to the recording, Burgess left his memento of that occasion, the inscribed collection of Churchill's speeches, behind. It was confiscated by the FBI when they searched Alan Maclean's apartment after he, too, was recalled to London.[66] Luker told the FBI:

> On that evening, the greater part of which was spent in making music for our guests, present day politics were not discussed— except that long after midnight—one significant remark was made to me by Burgess. It was that the memory of such an evening of music making among friends would never be forgotten. He felt that war was imminent and that it probably would take place within ten days. As he was slightly under the influence of drink—his remark made no impression on me—but in view of his disappearance, he obviously felt that there was significance in the remark which he repeated in the sober light of the following morning . . ."[67]

Burgess telephoned Emily Roosevelt the day before he sailed "to say goodbye . . . Burgess sounded as though he were in good spirits and promised to write her a long letter as soon as he arrived in London . . . Eve Bassett returned to England by air." Burgess did write, actually just after this conversation, again expressing thanks for the hospitality in Charleston, ending with: "As I told you on the phone I'm so pressed with packing etc. plus my mother that I wld. prefer to write you a proper letter of thanks later. I'll put some politics in too. I'm v. depressed . . . Much love."

By May 1, Guy Liddell's Watchers were attempting to keep Maclean under surveillance. By May 18th it had been decided to move toward interrogating him. Aside from which, according to Liddell, "The only interesting development has been a visit by Maclean to the V. & A. Museum, where he met Peter Flood [sic], who is a known member of the underground Berger Group. Whether he was seeing Flood about something in his own particular field at the Museum is not known, but apparently Maclean knew him very well. Maclean is evidently drinking fairly heavily."[68]

Burgess landed in England on May 7 and soon thereafter he visited Goronwy Rees, bringing presents, as he usually did, for Rees's family. Burgess seemed happy to be back in England. He told Rees that Michael Berry, his Eton classmate, had offered him a job on *The Daily Telegraph* (which Berry owned), but he was not sure that he would take it.[69]   Pamela Berry, as a matter of fact, arranged a party for the 29th to discuss Burgess's future.   It went ahead without him, including in addition to the Berrys, Blunt, Rab and Sydney Butler, John Betjeman, Lady Elizabeth Cavendish, and Isaiah Berlin.[70]   Not a list of people with jobs available, except the Berrys, who might have wanted the others to take a look at Burgess to advise as to whether he was still employable.   (Legend has it that Betjeman and the young Lady Cavendish fell in love that night.)

The events from Burgess's arrival in England to his arrival in Moscow have received much attention.   There are—various—nearly hour-by-hour accounts, not all similar.   The following is based on publicly accessible sources.

Burgess had picked up an American on the Queen Mary, Bernard Miller, who was on his way to register at the University of Geneva Medical School.   Miller stayed in Switzerland for a week and then made his way back to London, arriving about May 21st. Burgess took him out to dinner and drinks at the Reform Club and the Gargoyle, introducing him to David Tennant, Jack Hewit and other friends.   Miller told the FBI that at that point Burgess seemed unhappy.   Colonel Bassett wrote Mrs. Roosevelt on May 23, telling her that Burgess had arrived and that "he has been out of London most of the time since . . . His future is undecided at present.   It seems he can't bear to serve anywhere but London but how far the Foreign Office is likely to come into line with his views remains to be seen.   Most of their men, I gather, are tumbling over each other to get overseas, so perhaps he will get what he wants!"[71]   Around this time Burgess gave Maclean lunch at the R.A.C.   According to Burgess, he had written a memorandum on American policy in the Far East that, as a matter of course, had "gone through the machine," from the Washington Embassy to Maclean in his role as head of the American Department, and he had gone to the Foreign Office to talk about it with Maclean.   Maclean suggested lunch; the Reform Club dining room was full; they walked a few yards to the R.A.C., where

Maclean at once said that he was being followed "by the dicks." After that day they lunched twice more. Burgess told Driberg that it was at the third lunch that Maclean said that he wanted to go to Moscow and asked Burgess to help him.[72] Some time that week, according to Anthony Blunt, Burgess held a series of discussions with "his Russian contact."

> At the first meetings between Guy and his Russian contact the discussions were entirely about Donald's escape and no mention was made of Guy's going with him, but at a later stage I remember Guy coming to see me at Portman Square and saying that "they"—i.e. those in control of his contact—had decided that he should go with Donald, on the grounds that Donald was not in a fit state to carry out the complicated arrangements which had been made. I accepted what he said at its face value, and it was only much later that Kim told me . . . that his last words to Guy in America were: "Don't you go too". In fact I have no doubt that the suggestion was made by Guy himself. He realized that his career in the Foreign Office was ruined, and although he had hopes of getting a job on the Daily Telegraph from his friend Michael Berry, I doubt whether he was really counting on this. In fact he knew he was finished and decided to get out, not taking into account the consequences that this action might have for his friends. . . On the Friday afternoon he came to see me at Portman Square to say good-bye. It was the last time I saw him.[73]

The morning of Friday, May 25th the Foreign Secretary, Bevin's successor Herbert Morrison, decided, on the basis of VENONA, to have Maclean interrogated.[74] On the afternoon of the 25th Miller met Burgess at the Reform Club. Burgess gave him "detailed written instructions" for making contacts that would help him get into an English medical school and told him that he was having dinner that evening with "a friend who was having marital difficulties." He said he was going away for the weekend with the friend in order to "help this friend help himself." Then the conversation turned to the Korean War. The next day Miller received a telephone call from

Hewit, who told him that Burgess had not come home that night and wanted to know if Miller knew where Burgess had gone. The following day there were more conversations with Hewit and others, who were disturbed at Burgess's absence, as he never went away without telling his mother, which he had not done. They told Miller that Burgess had been "going down hill, mentally, for a long time." They said he used cocaine for relief from severe headaches, resulting from his fall, and mentioned his diabetes.[75] They were worried about him.

The evening of the 25th Burgess had driven to Maclean's country home and then the two of them drove to Southampton, where they boarded a ship for France.

Notes to Chapter Seven

[1] Martin, Edwin W. Divided Counsel: The Anglo-American Response to Communist Victory in China. Lexington: The University Press of Kentucky, 1986, p. 239.

[2] National Archives (UK), Kew, FO 371/75742.

[3] National Archives (UK), Kew, FO 371/75745.

[4] Johnson, R. W. "Living on the Edge," London Review of Books, 28 Aril 2011, p. 32.

[5] Martin, Edwin W. Divided Counsel: The Anglo-American Response to Communist Victory in China. Lexington: The University Press of Kentucky, 1986, pp. 15-16, citing FO371/75747. See also FO371/75759.

[6] The Times, 2 February 1981, quoted in Penrose, Barrie and Freeman, Simon. Conspiracy of Silence: The Secret Life of Anthony Blunt. New York, Farrar Straus Giroux, 1987, p. 324.

[7] The Times, 2 February 1981, quoted in Penrose, Barrie and Freeman, Simon, p. 324.

[8] National Archives (UK), Kew, FO 371/75759.

[9] Rees, Goronwy. A Chapter of Accidents, p. 184-5, quoted in Boyle, Andrew. The Fourth Man: The Definitive Account of Kim Philby, Guy Burgess, and Donald Maclean and Who Recruited Them to Spy for Russia. The Dial Press/James Wade, 1979, p. 334.

[10] In Penrose, Barrie and Freeman, Simon, p. 324.

[11] Deacon, Richard. The Cambridge Apostles: A History of Cambridge University's Elite Intellectual Secret Society. Farrar, Straus & Giroux, New York, 1985, p. 149-150; Hobsbawm, private communication.

[12] Modin, Yuri. With Jean-Chalrles Deniau and Aguieszka Ziarek. Translated by Anthony Roberts. My Five Cambridge Friends: Burges, Maclean, Philby, Blunt, and Cairncross by their KGB Controller. New York: Farrar Straus Gioux, 1994, pp. 165. Modin dates this to the summer of 1948, but it is clear from Cecil's account of Maclean's breakdown that it was the summer of 1949.

[13] On January 25th, 1950, Nicolson wrote to Vita Sackville-West that he had "dined with Guy Burgess. Oh my dear, what a sad, sad thing this constant drinking is! Guy used to be one of the most rapid and acute minds I knew. Now he is just an imitation (and a pretty bad one) of what he once ws. Not that he was actually drunk yesterday. He was just soaked and silly. I felt angy about it."Nicolson, Harold. Harold Nicolson's Diaries and

Letters 1945-62. Edited by Nigel Nicolson. London: William Collins Sons & Col Ltd., 1968, p. 184.

[14] Nicolson, Harold. Harold Nicolson's Diaries and Letters 1945-62. Edited by Nigel Nicolson. London: William Collins Sons & Col Ltd., 1968, p. 170.

[15] Liddell, Guy. Diaries, National Archives, KV4/467ff.

[16] Bristow, Desmond. A Game of Moles. The Deceptions of an M.I.6 Officer. With Bill Bristow. London, Little, Brown and Company, 1993, pp. 210-213. Guy Liddell give this account in his diary under January 23, 1950: "Carey Foster came to see me about Guy Burgess. He is speaking to Ashley-Clarke, who is now head of the Personnel Dept., having succeeded Harold Caccia (the latter has gone as Minister in Vienna). He wanted to know my views. Hill had told him that a prosecution under the Official Secrets Act would lie against Guy Burgess, but that for various reasons it would be undersirable to proceed. I said that he could be quite sure that Hill would be right on his facts; it would be undersirable to proceed, for two reasons. Firstly, that one would not wish any further publicity in regard to S.I.S.'s affairs, and secondly, that Counsel for the Defence would be able to say, for example, [one and a half lines blanked out] Although a technical offence was committed, we never liked to prosecute in cases of this kind. My own view was that Guy Burgess was not the sort of person who would deliberately pass confidential information to unauthorized parties he was, however, extremely keen and enthusiastic in matters which interested him and would be easily induced by a man like Freddie Kuh to say more than he ought to. So far as his drinking was concerned, I had gained the impression that owing to a severe warning from a doctor, he had more or less gone on the wagon. I did not think that he often got wholly out of control but there was no doubt that drink loosened his tongue. Personally I should have thought that a severe reprimand from somebody he respected might be the answer to the present situation."

[17] Bristow, p. 215-7. Guy Liddell's record of the story, which he got from Mills, is less colorful, limited to a drunken argument between Burgess and the Princess de Rohan in the latter's room. See Liddell Diaries, February 17, 1950.

[18] Cecil, Robert. A Divided Life: A Biography of Donald Maclean. The Bodley Head, London, 1988, pp. 89; 94; 118.

[19] West, Nigel and Oleg Tsarev. The Crown Jewels: The British Secrets at the Heart of the KGB Archives. Yale University Press, New Haven and London, 1999, p. 183.

[20] Penrose, Barrie and Freeman, Simon, p. 327.

[21] Jebb, Gladwyn. The Memoirs of Lord Gladwyn. New York: Weybright and Talley, Inc., 1972, p. 229-31.

[22] Boyle, p 352-3. The anecdote was said by Boyle to have been told to him by David Footman.

[23] Newton, Verne W. The Cambridge Spies: The Untold Story of Maclean, Philby, and Burgess in America. Lanham, Maryland: Madison Books, 1991, p. 271. Newton's is an unsually well-documented book for the genre. Burgess's Foreign Office rank is variously given. US governmet records confirm that it was as a Second Secretary, a middling, but not inconsiderable, rank: "Burgess's British passport No. 1674591, issued July 20, 1950, valid to July 20, 1951; Admitted to the US at NYC on August 4, 1950, visa no. V-1016533 (Second Secretary)." Federal Bureau of Investigations. FOIA Electronic Reading Room, Philby 9a, p. 78.

[24] Page, Bruce. Leitch, David. Knightley, Phillip. Philby: The Spy Who Betrayed a Generation. Andre Deutsch, Limited, London, 1968, p. 210.

[25] Federal Bureau of Investigations. FOIA Electronic Reading Room, Philby 1b, p. 84.

[26] Federal Bureau of Investigations. FOIA Electronic Reading Room, Philby 1b, pp. 85-6.

[27] Newton, p. 275ff.

[28] Federal Bureau of Investigations. FOIA Electronic Reading Room, Philby 1b, pp. 86-8.

[29] See: National Archives, UK, FO 115/4524 letter of February 2, 1951 to C.E. Steel, British Embassy, Washington from Roger Makins, F.O. Mann's story is complicated. James Angleton told Ted Szulc, according to Szulc, that Mann had been in some sense a Soviet asset and having been "turned" by Angleton, had been moved to a non-sensitive Washington job, where he was stored until Angleton needed him to assist in the development of the Israeli atomic bomb.

[30] Mann, Wilfrid Basil. Was There a Fifth Man? Quintessential Recollections. Oxford: Pergamon Press, 1982, pp. 78-9.

[31] Greenhill, Denis. More by Accident. Wilton: Bishop Wilton, York., 1992, p. 73.

32 Newton, p. 274.

33 National Archives, Kew, FO 115/4483.

34 Halberstam, David. The Coldest Winter: America and the Korean War. New York: Hyperion, 2007, p. 318.

35 MacArthur, Douglas. Report on the Current Estimate of Korean Operations: July 20, 1950. In Imparato, Edward T. General MacArthur: Speeches and Reports: 1908-1964. New York: Turner Publishing Company, 2000, p. 158.

36 Federal Bureau of Investigations. FOIA Electronic Reading Room, Philby 2a, pp. 103-4. See: Blakeslee, Goerge. The Far Eastern Commission: a study in international cooperation: 1945 to 1952.

37 Federal Bureau of Investigations. FOIA Electronic Reading Room, Philby 2a, p. 105.

38 Federal Bureau of Investigations. FOIA Electronic Reading Room, Philby 2a, pp. 94-5.

39 Jebb, p. 228ff. See: www.wavehill.org/about/history.html and Jebb, p. 245.

40 Federal Bureau of Investigations. FOIA Electronic Reading Room, Philby 2a, p. 85.

41 Driberg, Tom. Guy Burgess: A Portrait with Background. London: Weidenfeld and Nicolson, 1956, p. 84.

42 Federal Bureau of Investigations. FOIA Electronic Reading Room, Philby 8 c, p. 25.

43 Manchester, William. American Caesar: Douglas MacArthur 1880-1964. New York: Dell, 1983, p. 711.

44 Manchester, William. American Caesar: Douglas MacArthur 1880-1964. New York: Dell, 1983, p. 712 fn.

45 Thorpe, D. R. Eden: The Life and Times of Anthony Eden, First Earl of Avon, 1897-1977. London, Chatto & Windus, 2003, p. 362.

46 "Among those who participated as advisors to the President were the Secretary of State Dean Acheson, the Secretary of the Treasury John W. Snyder, the Secretary of Defense General George C. Marshall, the Secretary of the Interior Oscar L. Chapman, the Secretary of Commerce Charles Sawyer, the Chairman of the Joint Chiefs of Staff General of the Army Omar N. Bradley, Mr. W. Averill Harriman, the Chairman of the National Security Resources Board W. Stuart Symington, and Ambassador-designate Walter S. Gifford. Mr. Attlee's advisors included the British Ambassador,

Sir Oliver S. Franks, Field Marshal Sir William Slim, Chief of the Imperial General Staff, Marshal of the Royal Air Force Lord Tedder, Sir Roger Makins [Deputy Under-Secretary and advisor on atomic affairs] and Mr. R. H. Scott of the Foreign Office, and Sir Edwin Plowden, Chief of the Economic Planning Staff."
trumanlibrary.org/publicpapers/viewpapers.php?pid=991, accessed May 2, 2011.

[47] National Archives, UK, FO 371/84105, cited in Newton, Verne W. The Cambridge Spies: The Untold Story of Maclean, Philby, and Burgess in America. Lanham, Maryland: Madison Books, 1991, p.297.

[48] Newton, p. 300.

[49] Federal Bureau of Investigations. FOIA Electronic Reading Room, Philby 2a, p. 82.

[50] Newton, p. 281.

[51] Federal Bureau of Investigations. FOIA Electronic Reading Room, Philby 1c, pp. 24-7.

52 Mann, pp. 81-5.

[53] It is perhaps of interest in this regard that years later, in Moscow, "Donald Maclean . . . was more open about his part in the passing of secrets on the atomic bomb," according to George Blake. RED FILES: Secret Victories of the KGB - George Blake Interview, PBS, www.pbs.org/redfiles/kgb/deep/interv/k_int_george_blake.htm.

[54] It is also possible that the story of Philby and Burgess in bed together is a red herring, meant to distract attention from the question of what Philby and Burgess knew. Mann was the only witness and his account is distinctly odd. Saturday mornings were workdays at the British embassy and Mann does briefly refer to indications that Philby or Burgess had already been to work. The most obvious indication would have been that one or the other or both were wearing business attire, perhaps having removed their suit coats and put on dressing gowns—a common enough practice for men of their background. We then have quite a different story. (Of course that leaves the issue of he pajamas.)

[55] Adapted from: "Remembrances of Venona" by Mr. William P. Crowell www.nsa.gov/public_info/declass/venona/remembrances.shtml

[56] Meredith Gardner. The Telegraph (UK) 08/20/2002.

57 The News and Courier, Charleston, South Carolina, March 1, 1951. Mr. Jeremy Reynolds was kind enough to find this for me in the library of The Citadel.

58 Newton, pp. 313-17.

59 Newton, p. 320.

60 Federal Bureau of Investigations. FOIA Electronic Reading Room, Philby 1b, p. 84. See: www.nationalarchives.gov.uk/releases/2007/march/atom.htm?foi=rss

61 National Archives, UK, KV 2/2588.

62 Federal Bureau of Investigations. FOIA Electronic Reading Room, Philby 1b, pp. 89-90.

63 Federal Bureau of Investigations. FOIA Electronic Reading Room, Philby 1b, p. 93.

64 Greenhill, Lord. The Times, 7 September 1977, and Greenhll, Denis. More by Accident. Wilton: Bishop Wilton, York., 1992, p. 75.

65 Federal Bureau of Investigations. FOIA Electronic Reading Room, Philby 1a, FBI Washington Field Office to Director June 7, 1951.

66 Newton, pp. 323-4.

67 Federal Bureau of Investigations. FOIA Electronic Reading Room, Philby 6c, p. 36ff.

68 Peter Floud was head of the Department of Circulation at the Museum and an expert on the work of William Morris. He had worked for the Ministry of Home Security during the war and at the United Nations Relief and Rehibilitation Adminstration in the immediate post-war period.

69 Rees, Jenny. Looking for Mr. Nobody: The Secret Life of Goronwy Rees. London: Weidenfield & Nicolson, 1994, p. 159.

70 Carter, Miranda. Anthony Blunt: His Lives. London: Macmillan, 2001, p. 346.

71 Federal Bureau of Investigations. FOIA Electronic Reading Room, Philby 1b, pp. 115-6; 92.

72 Driberg, pp. 92-4.

73 Blunt Memoir, British Library, ADD Ms. 88902/1, p. 76.

74 Cecil, p. 135. This is an interesting, and interested, essay, not to be accepted without corroborating evidence, but, in this case, the date is widely accepted.

75 Federal Bureau of Investigations. FOIA Electronic Reading Room, Philby 1b, pp. 25-28.

Chapter Eight

Moscow

> Donald Maclean and Guy Burgess, have
> absconded . . . Benzie . . . is very worried
> about Guy, partly because of Anthony, and
> partly because Philip Toynbee was a great
> friend of Maclean. I fear this all means a
> witch hunt. *Harold Nicolson's Diary,*
> *Thursday, June 7, 1951*

The story of the missing diplomats sold many newspapers that summer. Burgess's step-father was quoted in one of them on June 11th: "He suggested that one or both men might be aboard a small ship in the Mediterranean unaware of the search.

He said his stepson was "a sick man . . . He was treated by doctors in America for very severe sinus trouble and suspected diabetes . . . His blackouts were very bad. He was not so impetuous but his mother and I believe he is now on a tramp steamer or some small ship on the Mediterranean that is not connected with the shore by radio" . . . He said it was "Ridiculous" to believe that his stepson had gone to Moscow . . .
1

So Mrs. Bassett no doubt wished to believe.

Burgess's blackouts in Charleston had caused some consternation, people having what they took to be interesting and friendly conversations with him one day only to find the next that Burgess had no memory of them. The tramp steamer story

345

reinforced one sown by Burgess himself, via Spender, whom he seemed to believe was a reliable conduit to the British secret police. Burgess gave Spender the impression that he had gone to Ischia, near Naples, to visit W. H. Auden.   Auden was soon visited by representatives of the Italian and British authorities and his telephone was tapped by the former. A secret telegram from A. S. Martin of the SIS commented:

> Our object is to get a detailed chronological account of AUDEN's association with BURGESS, a list of their mutual friends as they fit into the story, and, of course, AUDEN's views on whether any aspect of their association could, in retrospect, seem significant to his disappearance . . . The value of the interview may well lie as much in what AUDEN fails to say as in what he volunteers.[2]

Auden wrote to Spender from Ischia on June 14:

> Stephen, dear,
>
> Hell! The combination of that phone call and some lady who thought she saw La B [Burgess] in the train on his way to Ischia, has turned this place into a mad-house. The house watched night and day by plain-clothes men, etc. etc. The climax has been the interview with me published in the Daily Express which I dare say you've seen. Needless to say, the rather nice young reporter who came suffers from that form of deafness characteristic of reporters which hears what it wants to hear instead of what is actually said. Reuter's came to-day and I've tried to straighten the story out but the whole business makes me feel sick to my stomach. I still believe Guy to be a victim, but the horrible thing about our age is that one cannot be certain.
>
> How is everyone. If you can get one of the servants to pack up my camera and post it, I should be grateful.
>
> Much love to all
>
> Wystan

And then again on the 20th:

> Dearest Stephen,
>
> Many thanks for your letter of June 18th. I feel exactly as you
> do about the B-M [Burgess-Maclean] business. Whatever the
> real factors are, they are unintelligible; even the word betrayal
> has become meaningless. I still have to say, however, one can
> trust no-one; one may not know who they are, but I believe
> passionately they do exist somewhere at this moment.
>
> If G[enopeo's] story is true—and it is the only plausible
> explanation of their extraordinary rout—that they were already
> under suspicion by MI.5, then why did the Foreign Office a) do
> nothing for days after they were missing b) insist on a totally
> preposterous story about the love that does not tell its name? . . .[3]

Some years later Auden wrote a letter to the *Sunday Times* to
correct a story that he had snubbed Burgess: "It was true, Auden
said, that he had been out when Burgess called, but that was all. 'It
would be dishonourable of me to deny a friendship because the party
in queston has become publicly notorious.'"[4]

John Lehmann is mentioned from time to time in the Security
Service's Auden file, usually as one of a list of Burgess's friends (for
example, second on a list provided by Jack Hewit to W. J. Skardon:
between Spender and Rees), men, also including Isherwood, Auden,
Tom Wylie and Brian Howard, who "used to foregather at Chester
Square for long and earnest discussions on political affairs,"
discussions which Hewit stated elsewhere that he found boring.
Skardon had interrogated Klaus Fuchs and would spend much of the
rest of his career interrogating (or "interviewing") Philby, Blunt,
Cairncross and those who knew them. There were, however, some
crossed wires at M.I.5. Despite the collapse of their love affair at the
end of the War, Peter Pollock had seen Burgess just two days before
his disappearance and had left his Rolls-Royce behind Burgess's flat.
Pollock told Miranda Carter that in the weeks after Burgess and

Maclean disappeared "The papers were full of Burgess and the mystery Rolls-Royce.

> Anthony [!] had been sent by M.I.5 to find out what I knew about Guy. He told me later that M.I.5 searched my bank accounts. Anthony seemed very anxious. The best thing, he said, was to be quiet as quiet, not to make any statement. I thought he was telling me this out of kindness but it was really because poor old Jackie Hewit was talking to anyone who'd listen. He was saying, "You keep me out of it and I'll keep you out of it." He kept his side of the bargain.[5]

Nicolson was not alone in connecting Toynbee to Maclean. A tap was placed on Toynbee's telephone, but, for the most part, the listeners heard only Cyril Connolly and his friends:

> 14.6.51: Connolly "had seen them both separately just before they went off but he could not give any explanation. It had been he who had told BURGESS [May 9] that AUDEN was in London and to ring up Stephen in order to see him . . . CYRIL had known GUY very well before the war but not much since. He had always disliked him intensely . . .."

> 14.6.51: [John] Lehmann tells Connolly that Rosamond was sure that Burgess was a Communist and that "someone in America had found out about 'them' and that the thing was going to explode."

When Connolly's article, "The Missing Diplomats," was published by *The Sunday Times,* on September 21, 1952, M.I.5 did not believe much of what Connolly had to say, especially about Burgess, and judged Connolly's views to be "venomous."[6]

By June 20th the United States had broken off the atomic energy intelligence liaison relationship with Britain.[7] Coming after Fuchs and Nunn May, Maclean and Burgess was too much to justify to Congress. All that summer the FBI interviewed everyone who had had contact with Burgess and Maclean. The reports of these interviews run to hundreds of pages. The British secret intelligence services were similarly occupied. The tapping of Toynbee's telephone was probably not unique. Almost as soon as Burgess and Maclean disappeared M.I.5 realized that there was a connection between Litzi Philby and Edith Tudor-Hart and that the Leicas in the latter's studio were significant: the illegal Henri Pieck had used one to photograph documents given him by the Foreign Office code clerk John H. King.[8] M.I.5 knew that visits to the Soviet embassy were not necessarily the only way to deliver large amounts of communications to and from British embassies, minutes of Cabinet meetings and the like.

Burgess and Maclean had been—the term of art is "exfiltrated"—to Moscow via Paris, Berne and Prague* "just as the Slansky purges were getting underway in the latter place".[9] Neither was Moscow tranquil in the summer of 1951. When Burgess and Maclean appeared in Moscow, "'Nobody,' said Maclean, 'knew why we were there.'

> This can be translated to mean that, until Stalin had been told, nobody knew how the defectors should be treated. So long as they were in the small circle of NKVD men, who had been handling their case, all was well. They were taken to a hotel overlooking the Kremlin and, as it was a fine June evening, they all had dinner on the balcony and remained there until 3 a.m., consuming immense quantities of vodka. Twelve years later Maclean told Nigel Burgess, who had come to Moscow for his brother's funeral, 'People were running about all over the place looking for us and there we were on the balcony boozing.' Within a few days the party was definitely over; they were put under Beria's surveillance and dispatched for debriefing to Kuibyshev.[10]

Beria, as head of the secret police, had long been at the top of the Soviet hierarchy that had received information from Burgess,

---

* It is possible that it was when they reached Prague that Burgess's contacts decided that he was too ill—and too alcoholic—to be allowed to return to London and the curiosity of M.I.5.

Maclean, Blunt, Cairncross and other members of the Comintern generation of agents. There may have been a concern in the group handling Burgess and Maclean that M.I.6 (or the CIA) would attempt to assassinate them if they were seen in Moscow. And there were internal disagreements as to their bona fides. In any case, after that celebratory drink on a balcony overlooking the Kremlin, Maclean and Burgess were sent, for protection and debriefing, to Kuybyshev, the city to the east of Moscow, where the diplomatic corps had spent much of the Second World War.[*]

By 1952, "Stalin was losing his grip, not only physically but also mentally, and the slightest mistake could arouse his distrust.

By all accounts he was consumed with thoughts about plots against him. He suspected Molotov, Mikoian, and Voroshilov, for example, of being agents of Western governments . . . In December 1952 he dismissed his loyal private secretary of many years, A. N. Poskrebyshev, for "passing secret documents" and had his longtime bodyguard, N. S. Vlasik arrested . . .[11]

Stalin was about to launch his final purge, the so-called "Doctors Plot," which was to be the beginning of an anti-Semitic purge, for which he was preparing the ground by using Khrushchev to limit the power of the secret police chief, Beria, who, although not Jewish, was often described in terms implying that he was. The Soviet press announced the discovery of the "Doctor's Plot," on January 13, 1953. Stalin died a few weeks later and the plot, with its projected pogrom, evaporated. A struggle for power began between Beria and Khrushchev, with Beria initially in the stronger position. Beria, astonishingly, immediately set out on a reform effort, including conducting "a wholesale purge of the foreign intelligence directorate, dismissing its chief, S. R. Savchenko, and recalling at least two hundred foreign agents to Moscow."[12] He began to open the gates of the GULAG, repudiated the Doctors' Plot and attempted to ease

---

[*] Burgess told Driberg it was six months. He said that Kuybyshev "was permanently like Glasgow on a Saturday night in the nineteenth century" (Driberg, p. 100).

tensions in Korea.[13]   By June, however, the other members of Stalin's inner circle, led by Khrushchev, arrested and, most likely, shot him immediately, although his execution was not announced for some months.

The British authorities did not learn that Burgess and Maclean were alive and in the Soviet Union until Vladimir Mikhailovitch Petrov, the Canberra MGB controller for Australia and an adherent of Beria, defected on the 3rd of April, 1954, perhaps fearing that the fall of Beria had endangered him.   He immediately told his Australian interrogators that Soviet secret intelligence, possibly the N.K.V.D. had recruited Burgess and Maclean "as students and targeted them into Foreign Office . . . Moscow valued them highly and when Burgess and Maclean considered Security Service were on their track M.G.B. ordered their withdrawal . . . escape arrangements handled by [Filipp Vasilievich] Kislitsyn now M.G.B. officer under Petrov in Canberra. These included planning trip over Czech border . . . Burgess and Maclean brought out valuable Foreign Office information and are now living in Kuibyshev."[14] The telegram from Canberra to London conveying this information is annotated in ink: "What did they know?"[15]

It took until September of the following year for the Petrov revelations to reach the British newspapers.   Under enormous pressure, on September 23, 1955, the British Government issued a White Paper about Burgess and Maclean, summarizing their background, the circumstances of their move to Moscow and also that of Mrs. Maclean, which had followed, and some other details. After describing Burgess's academic career ("brilliant") and his employment by the B.B.C., "one of the war propaganda organizations" and the Foreign Office, the White Paper noted that "Early in 1950 the security authorities informed the Foreign Office that in late 1949 while on holiday abroad Burgess had been guilty of indiscreet talk about secret matters of which he had official knowledge."   This would have been the matters described by Desmond Bristow.

For this he was severely reprimanded. Apart from this lapse his service in the Foreign Office up to the time of his appointment to Washington was satisfactory and there seemed good reason to hope that he would make a useful career . . . In Washington, however, his work and behaviour gave rise to complaint. The Ambassador reported that his work had been unsatisfactory in that he lacked thoroughness and balance in routine matters, that he had come to the unfavourable notice of the Department of State because of his reckless driving and that he had had to be reprimanded for carelessness in leaving confidential papers unattended. The Ambassador requested that Burgess be removed from Washington and this was approved. He was recalled to London in early May 1951 and was asked to resign from the Foreign Service. Consideration was being given to the steps that should be taken in the event of his refusing to do so. It was at this point that he disappeared.

According to the Government, then, Burgess had a good career up until 1949, after which he had become erratic. (Burgess agreed, attributing his erratic behavior to his injuries and illnesses and the alcohol with which he self-medicated.) The White Paper went on to observe that "Investigations into Burgess' past have since shown that he, like Maclean, went through a period of Communist leanings while at Cambridge and that he too on leaving the university outwardly renounced his views.

No trace can be found in his subsequent career of direct participation in the activities of left-wing organizations; indeed he was known after leaving Cambridge to have had some contact with organisations such as the Anglo-German Club.[16]

The *Daily Express,* managed to get an interview with Colonel and Mrs. Bassett a few weeks later. Colonel Bassett told the reporter:

If the Foreign Office say what they have, it is no good flying in the face of what they think. I don't believe, myself, what they think. We don't want to say anything in mitigation. Just let the thing run its own course. The word "spy" is not a nice word. It is not the word at all that I would apply to this case in any sense. If the Foreign Office like to think they were definitely doing some dirty work they must think it. The Foreign Office statement is very vague. They just believe this and that. In view of what has transpired in all these years they have come to the conclusion that they were actually in contact with the wrong people. They might be in contact with people. These contacts are very often foisted on to you. A lot of fellows at that age think they can change world politics and perhaps make the world a better place to live in. These ideological ideas are at the root of the whole thing. Mind you, I never had the slightest suspicion from Guy that there was anything going on at all. But I do think that a lot of fellows of that sort consider things should be put right somehow and I think probably that was at the back of their minds, and I would not say they have not been doing a bit of good. We see a certain change in attitude lately. The whole thing is ridiculous. Neither of these fellows was in any sort of position to have access to top-secret documents. They are not things that you can bandy about from room to room, carry about and take in a taxicab to the Russian Embassy. We have no statement, official or unofficial. We are absolutely in the dark except for what appears in the Press. [17]

A most interesting statement from Colonel Bassett. One wonders what the men at his club made of it.

Burgess and Maclean were moved from Kuibyshev to Moscow, Maclean's wife and children joining them in September, 1953. They were given what were considered good apartments in the center of the city and small dachas outside the city. Maclean, who was learning Russian, began a career as a foreign policy consultant to the Soviet Ministry of Foreign Affairs.[18] In February, 1956, during preparations for a state visit to London by Khrushchev and Bulganin, the Moscow correspondents of the *Sunday Times,* Reuters, *Tass* and *Pravda* were called to the National Hotel. There they found Burgess and Maclean, dressed as if for a day's desk work at the Foreign

Office (in Burgess's case, probably rather better dressed than would have been his habit). Burgess and Maclean read a prepared statement and left without taking questions. The statement began: "It seems to us doubts and speculation as to our present whereabouts and our former activity may represent a small but significant factor which has hitherto been used by opponents of Anglo-Soviet understanding. In view of these considerations we thought it better to publish this statement." The statement itself claimed as the rationale for their residence in the Soviet Union that:

> We arrived in the Soviet Union in order to make our contribution to a policy aimed at achieving greater mutual understanding between the Soviet Union and the West . . . When we were in Cambridge we were both Communists. We ceased our political activities not because we were to any extent not in agreement with Marxist analysis of the situation which we still observe at the present moment, but because as has now become clear to us, we wrongly presumed that being in the service of the state we could more than anywhere else put into practice our ideals . . . We neither of us have ever been Soviet agents.

After sketching a version of Maclean's career and reasons for leaving Britain, the statement went on:

> As regards Burgess, having decided to leave Cambridge, he joined the B.B.C.. Later, he was offered other posts. Having agreed to this, he worked at first in one of the departments of the British Secret Service and later in the Foreign Office. During all this time he sympathized with Soviet policy . . . At the same time, he was increasingly alarmed by the postwar character of Anglo-American policy. The greatest anxiety was caused by the fact that at first no modus vivendi was reached between East and West and later on no attempts were made to reach it . . . Neither when he was working in the B.B.C., when he was a Foreign Office official, nor when he was connected with the Secret Service or counter espionage—M.I.5—did he make a secret with his friends or colleagues of his views or of the fact that he had been a Communist.

The statement claims, after this, that because Burgess's Communist views were known, he could not have been a Soviet agent. It then goes on to describe "the circumstances which arose a week or so after his return to London from Washington in 1951":

He visited Maclean at the American department of the Foreign Office. During this meeting they discovered that their knowledge and appreciation of the political situation and the danger of war were identical . . . Burgess, who already a few months previously had started looking for other work, intending to leave the diplomatic service, was faced with the fact that the Foreign Office, somewhat later and independently of Burgess' decision, had decided not to employ him any longer in the diplomatic service. There can be no doubt that no agent would have left the Foreign Office on his own initiative. However, at the decisive moment Burgess had doubts as to whether he wished or could do work for which he was striving without acting against his own conscience. For this reason, when Maclean told Burgess that he himself had decided no longer to work for the Foreign Office and its policy, and also proposed that both of them should go to the USSR, it was not difficult for Burgess to agree to this.

The statement concluded: "Our life in the Soviet Union has convinced us that we took at that time the correct decision."[19]

One of the journalistic accounts of Burgess's life in the Soviet Union includes a story that after the news conference Burgess's mother "flew to Moscow and holidayed with Guy at the Black Sea resort of Sochi . . ." On her return to London "She joked to [Tom] Driberg: 'You know . . . I think that Soviet discipline is *good* for Guy.'"[20]

The British papers became very active. First off the mark was the *Sunday Express,* which asked Burgess for an article. His response was published on February 19th. It reiterated the Moscow press conference's statement's assertions about the actions he and Maclean had taken as an effort toward peace and Anglo-Soviet understanding. It then elaborated on the latter theme along two lines:

355

the danger of rearming Germany and the incorrectness of American policy in the Far East.

> Speaking for myself, what I object to is not Anglo-American friendship but Anglo-American policy. It always has seemed, and it does still seem, to me that to give unlimited backing to, and to rearm, precisely the same expansionist social forces in Germany which have created two wars in this century is a wild and dangerous gamble. I have told my friends here that I knew many in the West who also had the gravest doubts as to the safety of this policy. The Hitlers of the future, like the Hitlers of the past, can be easily dealt with if there is Anglo-Soviet collaboration. Surely it would be better for England to achieve that collaboration now and not wait till it is force on her by circumstances.

This is a position that had been more or less orthodox in the British Foreign Office in the first year or two of the Attlee administration.

> Similarly, as regards the Far East and the American occupation of Formosa, when I was in the Far Eastern department of the Foreign Office the danger that could spring from this and from not recognising the Chinese Government were fully understood. I myself well remember writing a speech for my chief in the Foreign Office on this subject. Part of it ran roughly as follows:- - "The Chinese People's Government is a Government of the Chinese people by the Chinese people and for the Chinese people. That is why we have recognised it and this is why it is surprising that the U.S. has not got around to doing so."

The Burgess's op-ed piece closed with a historical reference and an appeal: "In the year 1906 Sir Arthur Nicolson came to St. Petersburg and in the course of careful negotiations managed to reach a settlement with the Russian Government . . . Is it too naïve to hope that a similar settlement can be reached in 1956?" On the one hand this article fit in with Khrushchev's policy in that year that culminated in his secret speech repudiating Stalin, the Hungarian revolt and Suez. On the other, most of the article does seem to have been written by Burgess, especially the parts about Germany and Far Eastern policy, which simply repeated the sort of thing he had said during much of the previous decade.

On March 11th, *The People,* a mass market sensationalist newspaper, began publication of a five-part series with the title "Guy Burgess Stripped Bare! His Closest Friend Speaks at Last." It was a very effective operation. Most of the stories about Burgess that "everyone knows," everyone, that is, who has heard of Burgess, come from this series if not from the earlier articles by Cyril Connolly. Up until this point, Burgess was simply one of the missing diplomats, part of the duo of Burgess and Maclean. Those with knowledge of Foreign Office organization and procedures could deduce from Macmillan's statement something of what Burgess and Maclean would have known and been able to do over the course of their careers. It was important to the Foreign Office, to the U.S. government, to the secret intelligence agencies in both countries, to minimize this. The colorful stories retailed in *The People* articles, of parties at Bentinck Street, the details about the state of Burgess's clothing and fingernails, the sensationalistic presentation of his sexual preferences, were all effective in this regard. How could a disheveled homosexual drunkard with dirty fingernails have done serious harm to the British Empire? On the 29th of March, *The Daily Telegraph,* a more respectable newspaper (owned by Burgess's friend Michael Berry), named Goronwy Rees as the author of the Burgess articles. Or, perhaps, the word "author" should be kept in quotation marks. Isaiah Berlin said: "Of course, Rees did not write them as they were published, they were written by somebody on the newspaper."[21] Be that as it may, the consequences for Rees were catastrophic. The University College of Wales, Aberystwyth, where Rees was Principal, could not tolerate a man with friends like Burgess, even ex-friends like Burgess. "Many members of the College were profoundly disturbed by the course of events and believed strongly that the affair should not be ignored.

It looked at one time as if the matter would be quickly resolved by Rees's resignation, but this did not come about . . . However .

. . two prominent members of the Council, had tendered their resignations, and several others signified their intention to do so unless a committee of enquiry were appointed . . . Rees announced his intention to resign . . . The Committee was chaired by the Rt Hon. Henry Willink, Master of Magdalene College, Cambridge. J. W. F. Hill, President of the Council of Nottingham University and W. J. Worboys, Chairman of the Council of Industrial Design, were the other members. G. H. Baxter, recently retired from the post of Assistant Under-Secretary of State for Commonwealth Relations, was appointed Secretary . . . The Report was 'received' by the Council at its meeting on 15 March 1957, together with a statement from the Principal indicating that he had been unable to accept the Committee's findings. His resignation, which had already been tendered on 11 February, was accepted by the Council.[22]

The participation of Willink, Hill, Worboys and Baxter, members of the national assemblage of "the great and the good," was particularly significant.

What came about this time to be called the Establishment, no more than Aberystwyth, could not tolerate a man who betrayed a friend, even—or especially—if he believed that friend had betrayed his country. Victor Rothschild, who was named in the articles, was furious. Harold Nicolson's anger was at least equal to Rothschild's. Rees was isolated. Why had he done it? For the money, in part: Rees always lived beyond his means. To divert suspicion from himself, as he must have realized that he was high on the list of those of interest to M.I.5, given his long association with Burgess. Perhaps, perversely enough, for the renown. After that, only Stephen Spender and Melvin Lasky, of the CIA-funded magazine *Encounter,* would give him work.[23]

Meanwhile, Tom Driberg, who as a Member of Parliament had known Burgess well, not least by having appeared on *The Week in Westminster,* now a free-lance journalist and an M.P., wrote first a sympathetic article in the left-wing *Reynolds's Newspaper* and then a letter to Burgess, in care of the National Hotel in Moscow, suggesting a visit to Moscow and an interview. In reply he received a telegram dated March 15th, 1956, agreeing to the plan and then a letter of the same date. The letter stated, in part: "I don't want to go here into a long screed about not having been an agent. There is no evidence that I was: in fact I wasn't, and that's that . . ."[24] In both the telegram and letter Burgess made it clear that he would have to secure agreement from his hosts before inviting Driberg to Moscow. Some weeks later Driberg received a telephone call from Burgess, beginning the planning for Driberg's trip to Moscow. Approval had been granted. On July 27th he booked a first class return air ticket on Air France to Moscow and a fourteen day "luxe-class" Intourist set of vouchers, totaling just under £300. Driberg reached Moscow on August 10th. Burgess, tanned from a vacation with his mother in Sochi, on the Black Sea, was living in a suite in the Moskva Hotel. (Burgess spent much of the last years of his life not in Moscow, but in various sanatoria in Sochi and Tiflis.) Driberg published a series of articles based on his interviews with Burgess, then a book. Burgess and his mother, it seems, spoke with one another on the telephone quite regularly.[25] In October, Driberg, planning another visit to Moscow, was asked by Mrs. Bassett to take with him a pair of Burgess's shoes and some socks, as a mother would. Driberg did as he was asked and returned with some photographs of Burgess for his mother.

Driberg and Burgess continued to correspond for the next few years, their relationship mutually beneficial: Driberg received considerable royalties for his book, at least 5,000 pounds, and he helped Burgess furnish his new apartment (Bolshaya Peregobskaia, Dom 33/55, Flat 68) in Moscow with a suite of furniture shipped from London and helped with the considerable task of keeping Burgess supplied with books (often from Heywood Hill's bookstore in Mayfair).[*] (A Moscow visitor in Fall, 1958—Mary Adams, an old

---

[*] Maclean also had furniture and books shipped out to him from London. (Cecil, p. 170).

B.B.C. colleague—described a visit she and Hugh Gibb[**] had with Burgess: "Naturally I was staggered to see his flat with all the furniture from England. He seems to be very comfortable but lonely and longing to set foot in England again. Very anxious to know what all his old acquaintances thought about him." A couple of years later—January, 1961—Burgess wrote to Driberg, saying "I am v. well & happy & <u>doing</u> quite well. I now can't imagine living in the world of expense accounts & hate" and suggesting that *Reynolds's* make him their Moscow correspondent. He also passed on news about his companion Tolya, a sort of Russian Jack Hewit, who "has got a good new job—organising & playing in concerts in a big factory . . . I continue to be v. happy with him. I don't know what saint in yr. calendar to thank. Perhaps only Greek Church, or Armenian, has such a saint."[26]

Burgess had other correspondents, some well documented, some not. Beginning in June, 1958, Burgess and Harold Nicolson "wrote regularly to each other until Burgess's death in 1963 . . .

> [Nicolson] gave Burgess a running commentary on the changing London landscape, detailing the demolition of Guy's favourite landmarks and the construction of characterless skyscrapers. There was social news, too, about the Reform Club and friends including Blunt, Fred Warner and James Pope-Hennessy. Burgess's letters were . . . always affectionate and open. He said that he had given up promiscuity and that he was, more or less, faithful to his live-in lover, Tolya. Yes, he missed some things about England – his mother, the streets of London, the Reform, the countryside – but he maintained that he really was happy.[27]

One of the first of these letters, a passage from which was quoted at the beginning of this book, is typical: "My dear Harold,

> Yr. letter, the second letter, from the "shameless port" of Famagusta reached me here in one of <u>my</u> favorite shameless places – Tiflis – to you & me & many Russians – but more officially what it always was . . .Tbilisi. I think the Georgian

---

[**] Perhaps the documentary film-maker.

word just more expressive of this lovely, romantic, gay, open hearted, sly, secret-living, friendly (to foreigners—less to Russians), place, with I should think the highest standard of living and eating, of clean thick cream daily silk tunics, belted round waists which seem immune to the expansive effect of litres of wine, anywhere in the Soviet Union – higher indeed than many West European towns we both know . . . I am writing in the late morning. The early morning was spent lying in hot mineral water . . .

My dear Harold, what a nice letter yours was, and so full of information. I was very touched and grateful. Gossip is, apart from the Reform Club & the streets of London & occasionally the English countryside, the only thing I really miss. The English Colony here, tho' dears, are apt to gossip about rather different things, and Russian gossip, even in English, though penetrating, indiscreet and amusing, is not about one's own parish and I moved rather late for it . . . Oddly enough as you say about yourself, I haven't quite tumbled into compulsive drink (tho' Washington life compelled me to it for a time all right— those stories are true), not even here. The difficulty here is that Russians, particularly officials, do some of them drink every day, or in small amounts, but only on occasions, but then in quantities that make Western eyes goggle & Western stomachs turn . . . So the only thing to do is to avoid occasions . . . Particularly in my case since I've never absolutely recovered in all ways from having had my skull cracked in three places by Fred Warner – that also contributed to Washington . . . About Goronwy, whom you mention. I was very proud that Rosamond Lehmann wrote to my mother saying she had told him that the one person who might not be too angry with him was Guy. I was proud because it was indeed the case that I _had_ already answered some of those who wrote to me in sympathy & protest some defense of him. I am sure there must be some explanation, perhaps some pressure even, that we don't know about. Even if he was desperately short of money, or in a fit of drunken hysteria, I said, it is forgivable for the Goronwy we know & like. Perhaps in such a fit, he was trapped by some clever Fleet Street horror & outmaneuvered and then too late to go back. I don't know. Out of sheer curiosity I would like to hear whats happened to him. I was very fond also of his wife & children & do hope he's not really ruined and they too. There's very little money in the background, none on his, & not much on hers . . .

P.S. Do show this letter to any friend, James or <u>Anthony</u> etc. Would James write? Please [show it] to him.[28]

Nicolson responded on June 20, 1958 with two single-spaced typed pages:

"My dear Guy . . .
I was glad indeed to get your letter from Tiflis. I remember an old Byzantine bath at Broussa which I attended in the company of a very religious man who is now a Catholic priest and who twisted his dry lips in disgust at what he called "this dirty hole". After being banged and rubbed and tossed with violence such as I have never experienced we retired to the cooling room and lay on divans looking out upon the Bythinian Olympus and drinking coffee . . .

You say you enjoy gossip- but it is difficult when one knows one's letters will be opened and analised [sic] for hidden meanings to convey gossip without giving away one's friends . . .

Fred [Warner] is back from Rangoon looking well and happy . . . Anthony Blunt whom I see occasionally is calm . . . Your friend Geronway [sic] has disappeared . . James is, as I think I told you . . . completing his life of Queen Mary . . . Bless you, my dear Guy and all my affection . . .

362

Moscow

Burgess himself wrote very long letters.

BOLSHAYA PIROGOVSKAYA STREET
NUMBER 53/55, APARTMENT 68

My dear Harold,

You will see that I am coming out of Purdah over my address. I think I'm no longer news & won't be besieged any more by journalists. Nor do I expect "C." to assassinate me. Allan Dulles & his bands of criminal LATS, LITS & ESTHONIANS & others paid for on an open vote of Congress are of course a different matter. (Not quite so silly as it sounds in my case – the Dulles Brothers, to whom we all owe so much if only as inspiration for some of Osbert Lancaster's cracks, did take rather an interest in me & my whereabouts earlier this year but by getting drunk with one of their chief & far from merry men I think I convinced them I'm a man of no importance, which of course is true.)

Dear Harold, thank you so much for your letter of June 20th. It is very kind indeed of you to have opened & to be willing to carry on a correspondence which I will not abuse by writing too often, hope you not bored & regretting it . . .

I am just off for the second time this year to the land of Colchis . . . beautiful tho' the Caucasian Riviera is, I have never enjoyed bathing so much as while staying in a Turkish house in Vannekoy on the edge of the Bosphorus & diving in from my bedroom window on the first floor & nearly breaking my neck by hitting a Dolphin . . .

I agree about the difficulty of writing gossip – but was delighted with what you squeezed out in yr. two letters . . .
Burgess then related what he thought of as an amusing story:

All Soviet offices have annual "control" inspections from the Party Authorities, to hear complaints, to see everything is in order in staff conditions etc. A year or two ago the commission [?] came to the Lenin Library, here in Moscow. One of the librarians they interviewed was a very old lady in charge of English, or I think perhaps a French section. They checked her language. She spoke perfectly – too perfectly. And there was something faintly aristocratic also about her manner and air as well as her style & vocabulary. They asked her about her background & relations – had she aristocratic friends abroad— important émigrés perhaps? Very few left she said, though there was a girl in England. Who? They said. My great niece or 2nd removed cousin she said, Elizabeth, the Queen. How long they said have you, with such relatives abroad, been working in the Lenin Library? Since 1918 she said. How they said did you worm yourself into this job? At that date, how could you get such a position?

"Oh" she said "Vladimir Ilyich (Lenin) gave it me. As you know he was very kind." And a check revealed it was true . . .

I'm so bad about answering letters – which I think is an unforgiveable as you do that the double hurdles are ever in my mind – that my various correspondences are in danger of petering out. Its very remarkable that they still exist . . .

Is Gaitskell destroying what is still our party or only himself? I fear both. I like him but the provincial effects of Winchester seem over riding.

I've just read Stephen Spender's autobiography. I haven't laughed so much since I last read Rousseau's . . . *

---

* Burgess has more to say about Spender in a later letter: "I was of the generation hit by the pistol shot in the Thirties. I notice that the intellectuals of the '60's, the young at Aldermaston, have again been hit by the continuing fusillade. I notice this with the pleasure one greets others getting into the same boat; and with sorrow that they don't know how rough the crossing is. I don't like those of my generation who, like Stephen Spender, got out and are now in the pay of the enemy . . . I have just compared with amusement the completely contradictory accounts Stephen gives in his fascinating autobiography, nothing so similar <u>quite</u> since Rousseau, of his activities as a Communist "agent" – his denial of the same activities in the God that Failed. American policy

My v. dear Harold.
Yr. grateful Guy.

Another letter to Nicholson casts an interesting light on the relationship between Burgess and his mother:

Thank you so very much for suggesting that you would go & see my mother. It is very kind & I was as touched as I could be. And so is she. I wrote to her to ask her if she is well enough and have now had her reply. As I thought, she would like it very much . . .

Anthony is very kind as one wld. know about going to see her & so are some other friends. It would give her real joy I know. One thing may shock you – she knows all about my private life & has long absorbed the facts, which of course, unless she has got too old, she would not I imagine mention to someone nearly of her generation.

Burgess's health continued to deteriorate, adding to his diabetes his father's heart ailment.

I have been condemned to some months inactivity because (this private & not for general circulation) of angina pectoris which first showed itself in the land of Colchis. Not of course either fatal or even dangerous but painful & a bore.

He was staying at the Council of Ministers Sanatorium, Sochi, now the ultra deluxe Grand Hotel and Spa Rodina.

In 1959 Burgess "made an approach" to Prime Minister Macmillan, who was in Moscow for talks on expanding Anglo-Soviet trade and cultural ties, asking whether he would be allowed to return to England for a month to visit his mother and be free to return to Moscow. David Ormsby-Gore, Minister of State in the Foreign Office (Hector MacNeil's successor, many times removed), reported

---

may – perhaps is changing. However I do not think they will cease to finance Stephen & he is quite capable of changing tune in time & play the better one now perhaps heard winding from Kennedy."

to the Cabinet on February 25th that the evidence against Burgess "is quite insufficient to sustain a prosecution under Section I of the Official Secrets Act . . . We cannot hope to obtain legal proof that Burgess has committed any treasonable act while in the Soviet Union or any seditious act" in England. "Indeed if he knew how little evidence we had, he would be more likely to be encouraged than deterred." The Minister of State therefore recommended that he should be told that no guarantee against prosecution could be given and that the Security Service should hint that there might be one.[29]

In 1962, when his mother was dying, Burgess made inquiries about whether he would be allowed to visit London. The British Government went into a panic and warrants were issued under the Official Secrets Act for the arrest of Maclean and Burgess by Scotland Yard in case they travel to London. (In Burgess's case for comments in his interviews with Driberg that had been removed before publication.) John Mossman visited Burgess at this time describing him in this way in the London *Daily Mail* of April 19, 1962:

> Guy Burgess, ailing and overweight, tortured by ulcers and drinking heavily, is still in full control of a brilliant mind. He still has a great sense of humour, daringly enough used as frequently against the Russian political bosses as against Western politicians . . . He has been living in a three-roomed bachelor apartment overlooking the golden domes of the Novo Deivichy monastery. . . He has been seriously ill twice during the past year and has had at least one operation on his stomach . . . He has always insisted vehemently that it was Maclean who talked him into going to the Soviet Union . . . of late he has been doing most of his work at home, reading his books, listening to the latest jazz and classical records sent from London, and dreaming of the past.

Burgess took up, or was taken up by, Jeremy Wolfenden, a young correspondent—son of the eponymous report author—alcoholic, homosexual, Etonian.

In his own disreputable way Guy Burgess is very amusing, but he has to be taken in small quantities . . . apart from anything else, to spend 48 hours with him would involve being drunk for at least 47. He has a totally bizarre, and often completely perverse [idea] of the way in which the outside world works, but he makes up for this with a whole range of very funny, though libelous and patently untrue, stories about Isaiah Berlin, Maurice Bowra and Wystan Auden.[30]

Burgess died on August 30, 1963. He was then, finally, allowed to return to England, his brother Nigel bringing his ashes from Russia and burying them in the churchyard at West Meon, near what had been his family's country house.[31] Perhaps, under the precept about not speaking ill of the dead, it might be permitted to leave the last words to Burgess's friend, Sir Roy Harrod and his Russian contact, Yuri Modin. In 1972, Harrod wrote to Rees about his book, *A Chapter of Accidents,* which had just appeared:

Guy was such a charming, cultivated, civilized and loveable person. I cannot bear to think of that memory of him being sullied. Your account presents him as half drunk, half sex debauchee. Could anything be further from the truth? It is really too bad of you.[32]

Twenty years later, Modin wrote: "Looking back on his life, I have always found it hard to understand how this remarkable student could have sacrificed a future as a high official, a man of the world and diplomat to join our side in what was after all a doubtful, dangerous, thankless endeavour, offering no personal reward other than that of advancing the cause of revolution in the world."[33]

Notes to Chapter Eight

[1] FBI, FOIA, Philby 2d, p. 12. Washington City News Service.
[2] National Archives, UK, KV 2/2588.
[3] New York Public Library, Berg Collection.
[4] Quoted in Wood, Michael. "I really mean like," a review of The Complete Works of W. H. Auden: Prose Vol. IV, 1950-62, in London Review of Books, 2 June 2011, p. 6.
[5] Carter, Miranda. Anthony Blunt: His Lives. London: Macmillan, 2001, pp, 350-1.
[6] National Archives, UK, KV2/3436: Cyril Connolly.
[7] See, inter alia, National Archives, UK, letter to Sir Roger Makins of June 20th, from F. W. Marten at the British Embassy, Washington, FO 115/4524.
[8] National Archives, UK, KV2/1014.
[9] Miles, Jonathan. The Dangerous Otto Katz: The Many Lives of a Soviet Spy. New York: Bloomsbury, 2010, p. 281.
[10] Cecil, Robert. A Divided Life: A Biography of Donald Maclean. The Bodley Head, London, 1988, p. 164.
[11] Knight, Amy. Beria: Stalin's First Lieutenant. Princeton: Princeton University Press, 1993, p. 166; 170.
[12] Knight p. 184.
[13] Andrei Sakharov wrote to a friend at the time of Stalin's death: "I am under the influence of a great man's death. I am thinking of his humanity." He expanded on this in his Memoirs: "I still believed that the Soviet state represented a breakthrough into the future, a prottype (though not as yet a fully realized one) for all other countries to imitate . . . On March 27, 1953, a far-reaching amnesty was proclaimed . . . One important result of the amnesty was a sharp reduction in the forced labor available for a system based on slavery. On the negative side, the release of common criminals led to a temporary increase in crime. But the amnesty's most serous failing was that it did not apply to political prisoners . . . It took several more years for the survivors to regain their freedom." Sakharov, Andrei. Memoirs. Trans. Richard Lourie. New York: Alfred A. Knopf, 1990, pp. 164-5.
[14] National Archives, U.K., PF 137694/V2.
[15] KV2/3440 Vladimir Petrov file.
[16] FBI, FOIA, Philby 7a.

17 FBI, FOIA, FBI Philby 3a, p. 74.

18 Cherkasov, Pyotr. Second Life "HOMER." Newsletter, May 21, 2003, Foreign Intelligence Service, Russian Federation, http://svr.gov.ru/smi/2003/izvestija-ru20030521.htm

19 Published in all major newspapers, February 11 and 12, 1956.

20 Penrose, Barrie and Freeman, Simon. Conspiracy of Silence: The Secret Life of Anthony Blunt. New York, Farrar Straus Giroux, 1987, p. 387.

21 Rees, Jenny. Looking for Mr. Nobody: The Secret Life of Goronwy Rees. London: Phoenix, 1997, p. 187.

22 www.archiveswales.org.uk/anw/get_collection.php?inst_id=1&coll_id=204 38&expand=, accessed May 0, 2011.

23 Sutherland, John, Stephen Spender: a literary life, Oxford University, 2005, Press, p. 403.

24 Driberg, Tom. Guy Burgess: A Portrait with Background. London: Weidenfeld and Nicolson, 1956, p. 4.

25 Christ Church Archives, Oxford, Driberg Papers.

26 Christ Church Archives, Oxford, Driberg Papers.

27 Penrose, Barrie and Freeman, Simon, p. 391.

28 Harold Nicolson Papers, Box 2, folder 2, Department of Rare Books and Special Collections, Princeton University Library.

29 National Archives, UK, CAB/129/96.

30 Faulks, Sebastian. The Fatal Englishman: Three Short Lives. New York: Vintage Books, 1996, p. 254-5.

31 Cecil, p. 174-5.

32 British Library, Add 71192 f. 3

33 Modin, Yuri. With Jean-Chalrles Deniau and Aguieszka Ziarek. Translated by Anthony Roberts. My Five Cambridge Friends: Burges, Maclean, Philby, Blunt, and Cairncross by their KGB Controller. New York: Farrar Straus Gioux, 1994, pp. 68-9.

The Summing Up

> Stendhal's "The pistol shot in the theatre", the thrust of political exaction & ideology into personal circum-stance, as the author writes, have always been at and for me. You were born too early to be hit by this at the age at which one acts, & the intelligentsia of the 40's & 50's were born too late. I was of the generation hit by the pistol shot in the thirties. I notice that the intellectuals of the '60's, the young at Aldermaston, have again been hit by the continuing fusillade. I notice this with the pleasure one greets others getting into the same boat; and with sorrow that they don't know how rough the crossing is. *Guy Burgess to Harold Nicolson, 1962.*

Guy Burgess made no secret that he was, indeed, defined himself as, both a homosexual and a Marxist. He was one of the few Englishmen of his time to live, more or less successfully, as if homosexuality were nothing unusual. Given that homosexuality was illegal and that the social customs of the day made it, at best, an object of ridicule, this was a courageous decision. From an early twenty-first century perspective he enriched that aspiration by wishing to lead, with that modification, the customary intimate life of someone of his class: shared, that is, with another person of his education, interests and background. But his lifelong friendship with Anthony Blunt, which counted for much, was not a sexual relationship and his domestic arrangements with Jack Hewit were of another, more traditional, type. In this—the wish for simultaneous emotional, intellectual and sexual companionship—for all his efforts

371

with Peter Pollock (and perhaps others like Michael Burn), he failed.[1]

He was interested in work (*faber,* as contrasted with *laborans,* in Arendt's taxonomy): the work of a historian, a producer, a diplomat, and did his best to succeed in that series of more or less related occupations. He had a commitment to institutions as such, perhaps acquired from all those military and naval officers, Justices of the Peace and bankers in his family background. He tried, and succeeded, to make a contribution to the B.B.C. and the Foreign Office, both of which he took quite seriously (as compared, for example, to Philby's contempt for his Secret Intelligence Service). And then, of course, there was his social life in the customary usage of the phrase: the Reform, RAC and Gargoyle clubs; the Apostles; the dinners and drinks, and drinks, everywhere from the Strangers Bar in the House of Commons to the Ritz and the back bar of the Café Royal to places the names of which no visitor could remember the next morning.

Finally, and, in the end, the determinate aspect of his life, there was the political. Burgess was a revolutionary. As Eric Hobsbawm has observed, "he never ceased from start to finish to regard himself as a Communist." There were more Communists, *communists,* and revolutionaries in his generation than the standard account would have us believe, and more ways to play these roles, the least active of which, after the end of the Spanish Civil War, might have been that of a public member of the Communist Party of Great Britain itself. (Although John Cornford, if he had lived, might have animated the CPGB.) They thought that the society in which they had come of age was deeply unjust and that its Empire spread injustice throughout the world. Later, after the war, they saw in capitalist America the Empire's successor as the guarantor of inequality and then as the main threat to peace in the world. People like George Orwell volunteered for training in the Home Army, hoping to use their weapons expertise in the coming revolution. He and many other writers (William Empson, say, and J. B. Priestley and Eric Hobsbawm himself), used their pens with the same intention. Others like Ellen Wilkinson, Nye Bevan and Stafford Cripps used politics at the highest levels to partially transform the class-ridden structures at the center of the British Empire. Burgess with Blunt, Maclean, Philby, Cairncross, Rees (for a time), Michael Straight (for a time), possibly Phillip Toynbee and others, went underground to work, as they saw it, for the revolution and peace. Or, in John Cornford's phrase, for Communism and for liberty.

Burgess's political commitment was determinate for his life. In the end it cost him everything else he valued: the possibility of fulfilling intimate relationships; the social life that revolved around the B.B.C., Fleet Street and Whitehall; a respected institutional role, even the chance to be with his mother as she lay dying.

The agents of successful revolutions are celebrated. Those working toward revolutions that fail, or do not take place, are forgotten, or remembered with that condescension history's victors reserve for those they have vanguished. Burgess's name is almost always preceded by one of two Homeric epithets: "The spy Guy Burgess" or "The traitor Guy Burgess." The second of these, in a technical sense, is simply untrue. As Noel Annan, the score keeper for his generation, observed, Burgess "never committed treason as the Soviet Union was never at war with Britain . . ."[2]

> To him Britain's imperial past and the Royal Navy were being betrayed by feeble aristocrats like Halifax, and the ruling class behaving with all the folly born of the contradictions in capitalism as Marx had predicted. He was a true Stalinist in hating liberals more than imperialists . . . Burgess in a dotty, quixotic way retained a romantic notion of his country. He simply believed that Britain's future lay with Russia not America.[3]

This leaves the question of the first epithet: How effective was he as a spy?

On one level, the technical, as it were, he was extraordinarily effective: no one knew, no one suspected, that he was a spy. During the debate in the House of Commons on November 7th, 1955, one member said: "Of Burgess, what is it that the security people were able to say? Nothing at all. Indeed, but for the fact that he left this country, Burgess might easily be working at the B.B.C. today."[4] Christopher Isherwood told the FBI "that he knew of no possible Comintern connections which Burgess might have had and stated that it was inconceivable to him that the Soviets would ever choose a person such as Burgess to work as an espionage agent . . . he cannot imagine Burgess' engaging in any clandestine activity for any prolonged period of time without wanting to let someone know of his activities."[5]   Dick White, sometime head of both M.I.5 and M.I.6, agreed: "It really was very challenging to anyone's sanity to suppose that a man of Burgess's type could be a secret agent of anybody's . . ."[6]

While M.I.5 was attending rallies addressed by Stafford Cripps, following Ellen Wilkinson to hotel rooms she shared with Otto Katz, watching, with great interest, the comings and goings of Peter Lorre, it is quite possible that it did not open a file on Burgess until after he crossed the channel with Donald Maclean.

And then there is the matter of how much information he was able to obtain, its importance, and the implications of his having conveyed it to the Soviet Union. There is an FBI memorandum concerning the "national security implications resulting from "defection" of Burgess and Maclean.

US/UK/Canada planning on atomic energy and postwar Europe undoubtedly reached Soviets . . . All UK and possibly some US diplomatic codes [are] in Soviet possession . . . It certainly must be assumed that any data known to Maclean and Burgess has been compromised.

We now have an opinion from a more authoritative source. According to the publication of the Foreign Intelligence Service of the Russian Federation which has already been referred to:

During his work with the Soviet intelligence G. Burgess extracted and handed to us a large number of valuable documentary materials. Among them were the telegraphic communications between the Foreign Office and its diplomatic missions; minutes of meetings of the Cabinet, the Defence

Committee and the Chiefs of the Imperial General Staff and the secret operations of the Foreign Office in various countries . . . Of particular value was the information G. Burgess obtained about the positions of Western countries on the postwar settlement in Europe, Britain's military strategy, NATO, the activities of British and American intelligence agencies . . . G. Burgess, having extensive connections in government, parliamentary and military circles, actively contributed to the career development of other agents working with the London residency, and also served as an agent connecting others to Moscow.[7]

In so far as secrecy is important in the conduct of foreign affairs, Burgess and Maclean ensured that hardly anything important done by the British Foreign Office in the 1940s was not known to the Soviet foreign intelligence services. Given the Anglo-American relationship at that time, this was most likely also the case in regard to the activities of the American State Department.

Burgess not only obtained, and passed on, information on his own, he maintained the network initiated by Arnold Deutsch. The work of Blunt, Cairncross, and Philby, perhaps for a time that of Rees and others, was facilitated and encouraged by Burgess. In addition to the Foreign Office information gathered by Burgess and Maclean, Burgess, Blunt and Philby made British secret intelligence operations transparent to the Soviets (and Philby opened a window onto those of the American services). Cairncross worked at Bletchley Park and in the Treasury, Rees in military intelligence. And then there were years of conversations in Parliament, at the B.B.C., in the clubs and at the high tables of Oxbridge. It is unlikely that much known to Harold Nicolson, for example, that might have been of interest to Burgess's contacts, was not known by them. Nicolson, Macnamara, Llewellyn-Davies, Megan Lloyd George, Liddell and Footman, Michael Straight, Isaiah Berlin, John Strachey, Fred Warner, Gladwyn Jebb, Hector MacNeil: a generation or two of M.P.s, dons, intelligence service executives, Foreign Office officials and cabinet ministers talking, as they did, in the privacy of their clubs to one of their own; in the years after Burgess went to Moscow, startled awake in the middle of the night by the memory of a conversation at Pratt's, a confidence lightly exchanged in the Strangers Bar.

In Moscow, Burgess repeatedly and explicitly denied that he had been an agent. Well, he would, won't he? He wanted to go home. It didn't matter.   The British Government would not let him into England and the Soviets would not let him leave the Soviet Union. The latter did what they could to make him comfortable—the apartment in central Moscow; the dacha; the boyfriend; the excursions to the Black Sea; permission to work the embassy circuit, meeting old friends, old enemies, when they visited Moscow; finally, increasingly, medical care. And yet he never stopped wanting to return to England: to the Reform Club and Le Boeuf sur le Toit, to fast cars on country lanes, to Anthony Blunt and his mother, to brilliant conversations and disreputable pick-ups. But he could not return to England: he knew too much and too much about too many people. He died, then, in his simulacrum of a Mayfair flat, famous as "the spy, Guy Burgess."

Notes to The Summing Up

[1] Unfortunately, "One of the most damaging outcomes of the case was that it helped to fuel an upsurge of Puritanism and homophobia in Britain far harsher than anything seem in the previous thirty years. Burgess became a symbol of the evils of homosexuality –predatoriness, blackmail, betrayal, mistrust—and conveniently tied them up with the other great evil of the day, Communism . . . After 1951, prosecutions for homosexual activities grew sharply in Britain." Carter, Miranda. Anthony Blunt: His Lives. London: Macmillan, 2001, p. 355.

[2] Noel Annan, Foreword in Cecil, Robert. A Divided Life: A Biography of Donald Maclean. The Bodley Head, London, 1988, p. xvi.

[3] Annan, Noel. Our Age: English Intellectuals Between the World Wars: A Group Portrait. New York: Random House, 1990, p. 225-6.

[4] Alfred Robens, Hansard, 7 November 1955, 1602, p. 26.

[5] FBI FOIA, Philby Files, pp. 73-4.

[6] Carter, Miranda. Anthony Blunt: His Lives. London: Macmillan, 2001, p. 345, citing Bower, Perfect English Spy, p. 113.

[7] Foreign Intelligence Service, Russian Federation. http://svr.gov.ru/history/ber.htm

Appendix

B.B.C. Programs Produced by Burgess, 1937-38

Erin O'Neill, then Archivist at Caversham, found this typewritten listing in Spring, 2010. It had no identifying marks as to when it was produced, by whom, or for what purpose.

Date	Programme Title
1.1.1937	Miscellaneous talks and readings
April – June, 1937	Series on Food and Exercise (4 talks)
5.6.1937	Old Vienna: Count A. von Hessenstein
12.4.1937 19.4.1937 26.4.1937	Franz Joseph – The Stricken Emperor: Count A. von Hessenstein Finding a House: by a retired Colonial Wild Life in the New Forest: C.R. Acton
3.4.1937	When George IV was Crowned: Roger Fulford
17.4.1937	Your Handwriting and Your Character: Robert James
1.5.1937	Tramping through the White Sea: H.S. Marchant
8.5.1937	"At First Hand": Igor Vinogradoff (a series of six talks on Great Historical Events)
10.5.1937	Loose Box
13.5.1937	Science: Sir William Bragg

15.5.1937	Loose Box
19.7.1937	Adventures in Afghanistan: Audrey Harris
26.7.1937	Building the Telegraph Line to Lhasa: W. H. King
2.8.1937	Albania, a Fish and a Motor Car: David Footman
16.8.1937	A Schoolmaster in Russia: J.E. Whittaker
4.9.1937	Cinema Talk (a Debate)
October 1937	"Spending and Saving": (No date) "Thrift": (No date)
14.10.1937	At Home Today ('Mother and Doctor': a Conversation on Ante-Natal Care)
18.11.1937	At Home Today ('Mother and Doctor': Feeding the Baby)
11.1.1938	"How I began": Debroy Somers
21.1.1938	(No title recorded)
24.2.1938	Book Talks: Desmond MacCarthy (Monthly)
10.3.1938	(No title recorded)
22.4.1938	Eastern Europe (11 Talks)
10.5.1938	My Best Story (8 Talks)
7.4.1938	Forgotten Anniversaries (6 Talks) (Fortnightly)

9.4.1938	Sport
15.6.1938	"Motor Cars and Motor Bikes"
4.7.1938	How I Look at Painting [Anthony Blunt]
8.8.1938	How I Look at Painting [Anthony Blunt]
4.7.1938	The Past Week – Harold Nicolson
18.8.1938	The Past Week – Harold Nicolson
October (No date or time)	Great Occasions in Parliament (Monthly
11, 18, 25.10.1938	It Occurs to Me: Lord Elton
3.11.1938	China in Wartime: Christopher Isherwood (National Programme)
1, 8, 15.11.1938	The Mediterranean (Also for discussion groups)
October (no date or time) November (not date or time)	Great Occasions in Parliament
27.12.1938	Great Occasions in Parliament

The Mediterranean Talks: Series of 11 talks given weekly on Thursday in National Programme. 8.30pm. – 9.00pm. from 6 October 1938 to 15 December 1938. Burgess producer or co-producer of whole series (reprinted in 'The Listener'.)[*]

---

[*] B.B.C. Written Archives Center, Caversham.

Appendix

Bibliography

Archives

Berg Collection, New York Public Library, New York, U.S.A.

B.B.C. Written Archives Centre, Caversham, U.K.

Bodleian Libraries (Special Collections & Western Manuscripts), Oxford, U.K.
British Library, London, U.K.

Churchill Archives Centre, Churchill College, Cambridge, U.K.

Eton College Archive, Windsor, U.K.

King's College Archive Centre, Cambridge, U.K.

Library of Congress, Washington, D.C., U.S.A.

National Archives, U.K.

Parliamentary Archives, House of Lords, Westminster, London, U.K.

Princeton University Library (Department of Rare Books and Special Collections), Princeton, U.S.A.

General Bibliography

Aldrich, Richard James. British Intelligence, strategy, and the cold war, 1945-51. Routledge, London and New York, 1992.
Alsop, Susan Mary. Letters to Marietta from Paris: 1945-1960. New York: Doubleday, 1975.
Anderson, Paul. Introduction. Orwell in Tribune: 'As I Please' and Other Writings, 1943-7. London: Politico, 2006.
Annan, Noel. New York Review of Books, 22 October 1987.
Annan, Noel. The Dons: Mentors, Eccentrics and Geniuses. London: HarperCollins, 2000, pp.170ff.
Archives historiques des Communautés européennes, Florence, Villa Il Poggiolo. Dépôts, DEP. Organisation de coopération et de

développement économiques, OECD. Committee for European
Economic Co-operation, CEEC. CEEC 03, Address given by
Ernest Bevin (Paris, 22 September 1947).

Barden, Ruth J.D. A History of Lockers Park: Lockers Park School,
Hemel Hempstead, 1874 – 1999. Sacombe Press, Ltd., n.d.

Beckett, Francis: Clem Attlee: A Biography. Politico's Publishing:
London, 2000.

Bell, Julian. New Statesman & Nation, February 16, 1935.

Berlin, Isaiah. Letters: 1928-1946. Edited by Henry Hardy.
Cambridge University Press, 2004.

Bloch, Michael. James Lees-Milne: The Life. London: John
Murray, 2009.

Blunt, Anthony. Unpublished memoir. British Library, ADD Ms.
88902/1.

Branson, Noreen and Margot Heinemann. Britain in the 1930's.
New York, Praeger Publishers, 1971.

Breitman, Richard, Goda, Norman J., Naftali, Timothy, Wolfe,
Robert. U.S. Intelligence and the Nazis. Washington, D.C.:
National Archives, 2004.

Briggs, Asa. The History of Broadcasting in the United Kingdom,
Volume III: The War of Words. New York: Oxford University
Press, 1995.

Bullock, Alan. Ernest Bevin: Foreign Secretary 1945-1951.
London: W.W. Norton & Company, 1983.

Burgess, Simon [no relation]. Stafford Cripps: A Political Life.
London: Victor Gollancz, 1999.

Burn, Michael. Guy Burgess: The spy who loved me and the traitor I
almost unmasked. The Times (London), May 9, 2003.

Cairncross, John. The Enigma Spy: The Story of the Man who
Changed the Course of World War II. London: Century, 1997.

Canetti, Elias. Party in the Blitz. New York: New Directions, 2005.

Cannadine, David. G. M. Trevelyan: A Life in History. London:
Penguin Books, 1992.

Card, Tim. Eton Renewed: A History from 1860 to the Present Day. London: John Murray, 1994.

Carter, Miranda. Anthony Blunt: His Lives. London: Macmillan, 2001.

Cecil, Robert. A Divided Life: A Biography of Donald Maclean. London: The Bodley Head, 1988.

Channon, Sir Henry. "Chips": The Diaries of Sir Henry Channon. Edited by Robert Rhodes James. London: A Phoenix Giant Paperback, 1993.

Cherkasov, Pyotr. Second Life "HOMER." Newsletter, May 21, 2003, Foreign Intelligence Service, Russian Federation, http://svr.gov.ru/smi/2003/izvestija-ru20030521.htm

Christ Church Archives, Oxford, Driberg Papers.

Clarke, Peter. The Cripps Version: The Life of Sir Stafford Cripps. London: Allen Lane, The Penguin Press, 2002.

Collini, Stefan. "On the Lower Slopes," review of Shades of Greene: One Generation of an English Family by Jeremy Lewis. London Review of Books, 5 August 2010.

Conant, Jennet. The Irregulars: Roald Dahl and the British Spy Ring in Wartime Washington. New York: Simon & Schuster, 2008.

Cooke, Alistair. "'Neville Chamberlain's Private Army'," in Cooke, Alistair, ed., Tory Policy-Making: The Conservative Research Department, 1929-2009. London: Manor Creative, n.d.

Cornford, John. "The Struggle for Power in Western Europe," in Sloan, Pat. editor. John Cornford: A Memoir. Fife: Borderline Press, 1978 reprint of 1938 Jonathan Cape.

Cripps, Stafford. The Struggle for Peace. London: Victor Gollancz Ltd, 1936.

Deacon, Richard. The Cambridge Apostles: A history of Cambridge University's elite intellectual secret society. New York: Farrar, Straus & Giroux, 1985.

Dennis Proctor Lewes. London Review of Books, Letters, Vol. 2 No. 18 · 18 September 1980.

Department of State (Ed.). A Decade of American Foreign Policy, Basic Documents 1941-1949. Washington: Department of State Printing Office, 1985.

Dilks, David (ed.). The Diaries of Sir Alexander Cadogan, O.M.: 1938-1945. G. P. Putnam's Sons: New York,1972.

Dobbs, Michael. Winston's War: A Novel of Conspiracy. London: HarperCollins, 2002.

Driberg, Tom. Guy Burgess: A Portrait with Background. London: Weidenfeld and Nicolson, 1956.

Eton College Chronicle, Thursday, October 6, 1927, No. 2026.

Eton Vikings Club, The Eaton Boating Book, Third Edition, Eton: Spottiswoode, Ballantyne & Co. Ltd., 1933.

Faulks, Sebastian. The Fatal Englishman: Three Short Lives. New York: Vintage Books, 1996.

Federal Bureau of Investigations. FOIA Electronic Reading Room, Philby.

Foot, M.R.D. SOE: An outline history of the Special Operations Executive 1940-46. University Publications of America, 1986.

Foreign Relations of the United States, 1947, Volume III, p. 1073.

Foreign Relations of the United States, 1947, Volume V, p. 30.

Gilbert, Martin. Winston S. Churchill. Volume V: 1922-1939. London: Heinemann, 1976.

Gillies, Donald. Radical Diplomat: The Life of Archibald Clark Kerr, Lord Inverchapel, 1882-1951. I.B.Tauris: London, 1999.

Gopal, Sarvepalli. Jawaharlal Nehru: A Biography. Volume I: 1889-1947. Cambridge, MA.: Harvard University Press, 1976.

Gorodetsky, Gabriel. Stafford Cripps in Moscow, 1940-1942: Diaries and Papers. Edgware, Middlesex, Great Britain: Vallentine Mitchell, 2007.

Grant Duff, Sheila. The Parting of the Ways: A Personal Account of the Thirties. Peter Owen: London, 1982.

Greenhill, Denis. More by Accident. Wilton: Bishop Wilton, York, 1992.

Halberstam, David. The Coldest Winter: America and the Korean War. New York: Hyperion, 2007.

Hansard, February 13, 1946.

Harold Nicolson Papers, Box 2, folder 2, Department of Rare Books and Special Collections, Princeton University Library.

Hart, Lieutenant General H. G. (edited by his son). The New Annual Army List, Militia List and Yeomanry Cavalry List, for 1896. London: John Murray, Albemarle Street, 1896.

Hastings, Selina. Rosamond Lehmann. London: Vintage, 2003.

Henderson, Nicholas. The Private Office Revisited. London: Profile Books, 2001.

Hennessy, Peter. The Secret State: Whitehall and the Cold War. London: Penguin, 2003.

Henri, Ernst. Hitler Over Europe? London: Dent, 1939.

Hewison, Robert. Under Siege: Literary Life in London, 1939-45. London: Weidenfeld and Nicolson, 1977.

Hinsley, F. H. British Intelligence in the Second World War. Abridged Edition. London: HMSO, 1993.

Hoare, Philip. Serious Pleaasures: The Life of Stephen Tennant. London: Hamish Haliton, 1990.

Hobsbawm, Eric. Interesting Times: A Twentieth Century Life. London: Allen Lane/Penguin, 2002.

Holzman, Michael. James Jesus Angleton, The CIA, & the Craft of Counterintelligence. Amherst: The University of Massachusetts Press, 2008.

Houlbrook, Matt. Queer London: Perils and Pleasures in the Sexual Metropolis, 1918-1957, Chicago: University of Chicago Press, 2005.

Ignatieff, Michael. Isaiah Berlin: A Life. London: Chatto & Windus, 1998.

Isherwood, Christopher. Diaries, Volume One, 1939-1960. Edited and Introduced by Katherine Bucknell. Michael di Capua Books. HarperFlamingo, 1996.

Isherwood, Christopher. Lost Years: A memoir. Edited and Introduced by Katherine Bucknell HarperCollins, 2000.

Jebb, Gladwyn. The Memoirs of Lord Gladwyn. New York:
  Weybright and Talley, Inc., 1972.
Johnson, R. W. "Living on the Edge," London Review of Books, 28
  April 2011, p. 32.
Kershaw, Ian. Making Friends with Hitler: Lord Londonderry, the
  Nazis and the Road to War. New York: Penguin Press, 2004.
Kiernan, V. G. V.G. Kiernan on Treason, London Review of Books,
  vol. 9 No.12, 25 June 1987.
Kiernan, V. G., letter quoted in Carter, Miranda. Anthony Blunt:
  His Lives. London: Macmillan, 2001, p. 113.
Kiernan, Victor. "Recollections," in Sloan, Pat. editor. John
  Cornford: A Memoir. Fife: Borderline Press, 1978 reprint of
  1938 Jonathan Cape.
Kings College Archive.
Knight, Amy. Beria: Stalin's First Lieutenant. Princeton:
  Princeton University Press, 1993.
Kynaston, David. Austerity Britain: 1945-51. London: Bloomsbury,
  2007.
Lancaster, Marie-Jaqueline. Brian Howard: Portrait of a Failure.
  San Francisco, Greencandy Press, 2007.
Lashmar, Paul and James Oliver. Britain's Secret Propaganda War.
  Sutton Publishing Limited, Phoenix Mill, Thrupp, Stroud,
  Gloucestershire, U.K., 1995.
Laybourn, Keith. The General Strike of 1926. Manchester:
  Manchester University Press, 1993.
Lean, E. Tangye. The Napoleonists: A Study in Political
  Disaffection 1760/1960. London: Oxford University Press,
  1970.
Lees-Milne, James. Diaries 1942-1945. Ancestral Voices &
  Prophesying Peace. London: John Murray, 1977.
Liddell, Guy. Diary, 1944,
  www.fpp.co.uk/History/Liddell/diary_1944.pdf; 1945-1953,
  National Archives, KV4/467ff.

Luke, Michael. David Tennant and the Gargoyle Years. Weidenfeld and Nicolson. London, 1991.

MacArthur, Douglas. Report on the Current Estimate of Korean Operations: July 20, 1950 in Imparato, Edward T. General MacArthur: Speeches and Reports: 1908-1964. New York: Turner Publishing Company, 2000.

Maclean, Alan. No, I Tell a Lie, It was the Tuesday: A Trudge Round the Life and Times of Alan Maclean. London: Kyle Cathie, Ltd., 1997.

MacNeice, Louis. The Strings are False. An Unfinished Autobiography. London: Faber and Faber, 1965.

MacNiece, Louis to Anthony Blunt, 7 May 1936, King's College Library, MacNeice Letters, quoted in Carter, Miranda. Anthony Blunt: His Lives. London: Macmillan, 2001, p. 96.

McLynn, Frank. Fitzroy Maclean. London: John Murray, 1992.

Manchester, William. American Caesar: Douglas MacArthur 1880-1964. New York: Dell, 1983.

Martin, Edwin W. Divided Counsel: The Anglo-American Response to Communist Victory in China. Lexington: The University Press of Kentucky, 1986.

Marx, Karl. Communist Manifesto, quoted in Cornford, John. "Left?", in Sloan, Pat. editor. John Cornford: A Memoir. Fife: Borderline Press, 1978 reprint of 1938 Jonathan Cape.

Matthews, Herbert L. Mr. McNeil of Downing Street. The New York Times, December, 29, 1946.

Meredith Gardner. The Telegraph (UK) 08/20/2002.

Mitford, Jessica. Hons and Rebels. London: Indigo, 2000/

More, Thomas. Utopia. Book I "Pasturage Destroying Husbandry," in Craik, Henry, ed. English Prose. Vol. I. New York: The Macmillan Company, 1916.

Morgan, Ted. A Covert Life: Jay Lovestone: Communist, Anti-Communist, and Spymaster. New York: Random House, 1999.

National Archive, Kew.

New York Public Library, Berg Collection.

Newton, C. C. S. The Sterling Crisis of 1947 and the British Response to the Marshall Plan. The Economic History Review, New Series, Vol. 37, No. 3. (Aug., 1984).

Nicholson, Harold. Diaries and Letters, v. 2, The War Years 1939 – 1945 (New York, 1967), p. 96;

Nicolson, Harold. Diaries and Letters, 1930-1939. Edited by Nigel Nicolson. New York: Atheneum, 1966, pp. 351-2.

Nicolson, Harold. Diaries in The Vita Sackville-West and Harold Nicolson manuscripts, letters and diaries [microform]: from Sissinghurst Castle, Kent, the Huntington Library, California, and other libraries.

Nicolson, Harold. Harold Nicolson's Diaries and Letters 1945-62. Edited by Nigel Nicolson. London: William Collins Sons & Col Ltd., 1968.

Nicolson, Nigel. Long Life: Memoirs, London: Phoenix, 1997.

Nussbaum, Martha C. From Disgust to Humanity: Sexual Orientation & Constitutional Law. Oxford University Press, 2010.

Orwell, George. Orwell in Tribune: "As I Please" and other writings 1943-7. Paul Anderson, ed. London: Politico, 2006.

Orwell, George. The Lost Writings. West, W. J., ed. New York: Arbor House, 1985.

Orwell, George. The War Commentaries. West, W. J., ed. New York: Random House, 1985.

Rees, Goronwy. A Chapter of Accidents. New York: Library Press, 1972.

Rees, Jenny. Looking for Mr Nobody: The Secret Life of Goronwy Rees. London: Phoenix, 1997.

Reith, J. C. W. Into the Wind. London: Hodder & Stoughton, 1949.

Ritchie, Charles. The Siren Years: A Canadian Diplomat Abroad, 1937-1945. Toronto: McClelland & Stewart Ltd, 1974.

Ritchie, Charles. Undiplomatic Diaries: 1937-1971. Toronto: McClelland & Stewart, 2008.

Roberts, Frank. Dealing with Dictators: The Destruction and Revival of Europe 1930-70. London: Weidenfeld & Nicolson, 1991.

Rogers, Ben. A. J. Ayer: A Life. New York: Grove Press, 1999.

Rothschild, Nathaniel Mayer Victor, Lord. Random Variables. London: Collins, 1984.

Sakharov, Andrei. Memoirs. Trans. Richard Lourie. New York: Alfred A. Knopf, 1990.

Skidelsky, Robert. John Maynard Keynes: Hopes Betrayed 1883-1920, New York: Penguin Books, 1983.

Sloan, Pat. editor. John Cornford: A Memoir. Fife: Borderline Press, 1978 reprint of 1938 Jonathan Cape.

Smith, Bradley F. Sharing Secrets with Stalin: How the Allies Traded Intelligence, 1941-1945. Lawrence, Kansas: University of Kansas Press, 1996.

Spender, Stephen. World Wining World. London: Faber and Faber, 1951.

Stafford, David. Churchill and Secret Service. Woodstock, New York: Overlook Press, 1998.

Stansky, Peter and William Abrahams. Journey to the Frontier: Two Roads to the Spanish Civil War. Little, Brown and Company. An Atlantic Monthly Press Book. Boston, 1966.

Stansky, Peter. The First Day of the Blitz. New Haven: Yale University Press, 2007.

Strachan, Alan. Secrets Dreams: A Biography of Michael Redgrave. London, Orion, 2004.

Straight, Michael. After Long Silence. W. W. Norton & Company, Inc.: New York, 1983.

Sutherland, John, Stephen Spender: a literary life, Oxford University Press, 2005.

Taylor, A. J. P. English History: 1914-1945. Oxford University Press, New York, 1965.

The Eton Calendar for the Lent School-Time, 192.

The News and Courier, Charleston, South Carolina, March 1, 1951.

The Papers of George Humphrey Wolferstan Rylands,
   GBR/0272/PP/GHWR/3/73,

The Sir Winston Churchill Archive, CHAR 2/350/23.

Thomas, Hugh. John Strachey. New York: Harper & Row, 1973.

Thorpe, D. R. Eden: The Life and Times of Anthony Eden, First
   Earl of Avon, 1897-1977. London, Chatto & Windus, 2003.

Tracey, Herbert (ed.). The British Labour Party: Its History,
   Growth, Policy and Leaders. London: Casxton, 1948.

Trevor-Roper, Hugh. Letters from Oxford: Hugh Trevor-Roper to
   Bernard Berenson, Davenport-Hines, Richard, ed. London:
   Weidenfeld & Nicholson, 2006.

Truman Presidential Library.
   trumanlibrary.org/publicpapers/viewpapers.php?pid=991,
   accessed May 2, 2011.

Tunstall, Jeremy. The Westminster Lobby Correspondents: A
   Sociological Study of National Political Journalism. London:
   Routledge & Kegan Paul, 1970.

Urquhart, Brian, A Life in Peace and War. New York: Harper &
   Row, 1987.

Victoria and Albert Theatre Collections Centre, Michael Redgrave
   Archive.

Weiler, Peter. British Labour and the Cold War: The Foreign Policy
   of the Labour Governments, 1945-1951, The Journal of British
   Studies, Vol. 26, No. 1, England's Foreign Relations (Jan.,
   1987).

Weinberg, Gerhard L. A World at Arms: A Global History of
   World War II. Cambridge: Cambridge University Press, 1994.

Weinberg, Gerhard L. Visions of Victory: The Hopes of Eight
   World War II Leaders. Cambridge: University Press, 2005.

Archives. Yale University Press, New Haven and London, 1999.

West, W. J. Truth Betrayed. London: Duckworth, 1987.

Wright, Adrian. John Lehmann: A Pagan Adventure. London:
   Duckworth, 1998.

Zeikowitz. Letters between Forster and Isherwood on
Homosexuality and Literature. Palgrave Macmillan; annotated
edition (August 5, 2008).

Websites

Foreign Intelligence Service of the Russian Federation: Biographies
and Newsletter, 2000 – present: http://svr.gov.ru
Federal Bureau of Investigation; FBI Records: The Vault--
http://vault.fbi.gov
This is a new designation. Materials referenced are under the
previous designation of FOIA Electronic Reading room.
www.archiveswales.org.uk/anw/get_collection.php?inst_id=1&coll_i
d=20438&expand=, accessed May 0, 2011.
www.bagonailssoho.co.uk, accessed November 30, 2010. The
website has an interesting soundtrack.
www.geocities.com/layedwyer/gillman.htm accessed 24 July 2010.
www.memorials.inportsmouth.co.uk/churches/cathedral/gillman.htm
www.spanishrefugees-basquechildren.org/C5-Stoneham_Camp.htm
www.timesonline.co.uk/tol/life_and_style/article882580.ece?token=
null&offset=12&page=2, accessed 20 August 2010.
www.timesonline.co.uk/tol/life_and_style/article882580.ece?token=
null&offset=12&page=2, accessed 20 August 2010.

Espionage Literature

Andrew, Christopher. The Defence of the Realm: The Authorized
History of MI5. London: Allen Lane, 2009.
Andrew, Christopher and Mitrokhin, Vasili. The Mitrokhin Archive
and the Secret History of the KGB. New York: Basic Books,
1999.
Andrew, Christopher and Gordievsky, Oleg. KGB: The Inside
Story. London: Hodder & Stoughton, 1990.

Bickham Sweet-Escott. Baker Street Irregular. London, Methuen, 1965.

Blake, George. RED FILES: Secret Victories of the KGB - George Blake Interview, PBS, www.pbs.org/redfiles/kgb/deep/interv/k_int_george_blake.htm.

Bower, Tom. The Perfect English Spy: Sir Dick White and the Secret War 1935-90. London: Heinemann, 1995.

Boyle, Andrew. The Fourth Man: The Fourth Man: The Definitive Account of Kim Philby, Guy Burgess, and Donald Maclean and Who Recruited Them to Spy for Russia. The Dial Press/James Wade, 1979.

Boyle, Andrew. The Climate of Treason. London: Coronet Books, 1980.

Bristow, Desmond. A Game of Moles. The Deceptions of an M.I.6 Officer. With Bill Bristow. London, Little, Brown and Company, 1993.

Borovik, Genrikh. The Philby Files: The Secret Life of the Master Spy – KGB Archives Revealed. Edited and with an Introduction by Phillip Knightley. London: Warner Books, 1995.

Costello, John. Mask of Treachery. New York, William Morrow and Company, 1988.

Crowell. William P. "Remembrances of Venona." www.nsa.gov/public_info/declass/venona/remembrances.shtml

Dorril. Stephen. M.I.6: 50 Years of Special Operations. London: Fourth Estate, 2000), p. 68.

Duff, William E. A Time for Spies: Theodore Stehanovich Mally and the Era of the Great Illegals. Vanderbilt University Press, 1999.

Jeffery, Keith. The Secret History of M.I.6: 1909-1949. The Penguin Press: New York, 2010.

Knightley, Phillip. The Master Spy. New York: Knopf, 1999.

Koch, Stephen. Double Lives: Stalin, Willi Muenzenberg and the Seduction of the Intellectuals. New York: Enigma Books, 2004.

Maclean, Fitzroy. Take Nine Spies. Atheneum: New York, 1978.

Mann, Wilfrid Basil. Was There a Fifth Man? Quintessential Recollections. Oxford: Pergamon Press, 1982.

Miles, Jonathan. The Dangerous Otto Katz: The Many Lives of a Soviet Spy. New York: Bloomsbury, 2010.

Modin, Yuri and Deniau, Jean-Charles; Ziarek Aguieszka. Roberts, Anthony, trans. My Five Cambridge Friends: Burgess, Maclean, Philby, Blunt, and Cairncross by their KB Controller. New York: Farrar Strauss Giroux, 1994.

Newton, Verne W. The Cambridge Spies: The Untold Story of Maclean, Philby, and Burgess in America. Madison Books, Lanham, Maryland, 1991.

Page, Bruce. Leitch, David. Knightley, Phillip. Philby: The Spy Who Betrayed a Generation. Andre Deutsch, Limited, London, 1968.

Penrose, Barrie and Freeman, Simon. Conspiracy of Silence: The Secret Life of Anthony Blunt. New York, Farrar Straus Giroux, 1987.

Perry, Roland. The Fifth Man. London: Pan Macmillan, 1994.

Philby, Kim. My Silent War: The Soviet Master Agent Tells His Own Story. New York: Grove Press, 1968.

Pincher, Chapman. Too Secret Too Long: The Great Betrayal of Britain's Crucial Secrets and the Cover-up. London: Sidgwick & Jackson, 1984.

Pincher, Chapman. Treachery: Betrayals, Blunders, and Cover-ups: Six Decades of Espionage Against America and Great Britain. New York: Random House, 2009.

Seaman, David. (Research) Mather, John S. (editor). The Great Spy Scandal. London: A Daily Express Publication, 1955.

West, Nigel. MI5: The Circus: MI5 Operations 1945-1972. Briarcliff Manor, New York: Stein and Day, 1983.

West, Nigel. MI5: The True Story of the Most Secret Counterespionage Organization in the World. Briarcliff Manor, New York: Stein and Day, 1982.

West, Nigel and Oleg Tsarev. The Crown Jewels: The British Secrets at the Heart of the KGB Archives. New Haven: Yale University Press, 1999.

West, Rebecca. The Meaning of Treason. London: Virago Press, 1982.

Wright, Peter. Spy Catcher: The Candid Autobiography of a Senior Intelligence Officer. New York: Viking, 1987.

Index

219, 232, 237, 239, 260, 272,
278, 286, 287, 292, 307, 335,
336, 338, 343, 347, 350, 360,
362, 365, 368, 369, 371, 373,
375, 376, 377, 381, 385, 386,
389, 390, 396
Boardman, H., 186
Bombay, 262
Bonham Carter, Violet, 190
Boothby, Robert, 86, 116
Bowra, Maurice, 56, 57, 367
Bracken, 185, 191
Bracken, Brendan, 184
Braithwaite, Lilian, 207
Branson, Noreen, 15, 35, 67, 68, 385
Bretton Woods, 248
Brewer, Charles, 100
Brickendonbury Hall, 159
Brideshead Revisited, 209
Briggs, Asa, 142, 167, 168, 171,
174, 181, 185, 218, 219, 385
Bristow, Desmond, 303, 304, 306,
307, 339, 351, 395
British Empire, 9, 10, 11, 15, 17,
20, 26, 27, 34, 37, 115, 140,
146, 158, 160, 179, 181, 187,
191, 233, 234, 236, 237, 238,
240, 245, 246, 248, 262, 266,
267, 357, 372
Britten, Benjamin, 119, 120, 260
Broadcasting House, 93, 167, 179,
214
Brooks, Collin, 198, 208
Browne, Thomas, 54
Brownell, Sonia, 144
Bulgaria, 230, 234, 248
Bullock, Alan, 242, 246, 255, 287,
288, 289, 290, 291, 292, 293,
385
Burgess, Malcolm, 17
Burgess, Nigel, 367

Burn, Michael, 45, 69, 102, 213,
225, 372, 385
Byrnes, James, 241, 242, 252

C

Cadogan, Alexander, 109, 111, 148,
150, 151, 170, 197, 227, 232,
283, 284, 317, 387
Café Royal, 86, 110, 118, 119, 206,
208, 210, 372
Cairncross, John, 61, 126, 128, 162,
169, 206, 232, 236, 237, 286,
338, 347, 350, 369, 373, 375,
385, 396
Cambridge, viii, 17, 24, 27, 28, 29,
30, 32, 33, 35, 36, 37, 41, 43, 44,
45, 46, 47, 48, 49, 50, 51, 52, 54,
56, 57, 59, 61, 62, 65, 66, 67, 69,
70, 74, 75, 76, 77, 81, 83, 84, 89,
98, 108, 115, 119, 120, 122,
124, 126, 127, 130, 132, 168,
169, 171, 172, 207, 213, 219,
222, 223, 224, 261, 271, 273,
286, 288, 289, 302, 338, 340,
342, 352, 354, 358, 369, 384,
385, 386, 387, 393, 396
Cambridge Platonists, 54
Cameron, Norman, 188
Canada, 10, 166, 236, 374
Canetti, Elias, 163, 173, 192, 385
Cannes, 101
Capitalism, 52, 55, 252, 373
Cards on the Table, 268
Carr, E. H., 116
Carter, Miranda, viii, 2, 5, 66, 68,
69, 70, 72, 124, 127, 128, 130,
132, 162, 164, 173, 219, 220,
287, 292, 343, 347, 368, 377,
386, 389, 390
Cartland, Ronald, 142
Carvel, John, 186

Printed in Great Britain
by Amazon.co.uk, Ltd.,
Marston Gate.